Sentencing
Guidelines

SENTENCING
GUIDELINES

Lessons from Pennsylvania

John H. Kramer
Jeffery T. Ulmer

LYNNE
RIENNER
PUBLISHERS

BOULDER
LONDON

Published in the United States of America in 2009 by
Lynne Rienner Publishers, Inc.
1800 30th Street, Boulder, Colorado 80301
www.rienner.com

and in the United Kingdom by
Lynne Rienner Publishers, Inc.
3 Henrietta Street, Covent Garden, London WC2E 8LU

Library of Congress Cataloging-in-Publication Data
Kramer, John H., 1943–
Sentencing guidelines : lessons from Pennsylvania / John H. Kramer,
Jeffery T. Ulmer.
    p. cm.
  Includes bibliographical references and index.
  ISBN-13: 978-1-58826-599-9 (hardcover : alk. paper)
    1. Sentences (Criminal procedure)—Pennsylvania.   2. Prison
sentences—Pennsylvania. 3. Sentences (Criminal procedure)—Social
aspects—Pennsylvania. 4. Pennsylvania Commission on Sentencing—History.
I. Ulmer, Jeffery T., 1966–   II. Title.
KFP583.2.K73 2008
345.748'0772—dc22

                                                        2008012826

British Cataloguing in Publication Data
A Cataloguing in Publication record for this book
is available from the British Library.

Printed and bound in the United States of America

⊛   Printed on 30% postconsumer recycled paper

∞   The paper used in this publication meets the requirements
        of the American National Standard for Permanence of
        Paper for Printed Library Materials Z39.48-1992.

     5   4   3   2   1

Contents

Tables and Figures

Tables

Figures

Preface

ONE SUMMER DAY in 2007, Jeff's young son Jacob was in Jeff's office. Jacob saw a stream of numbers and odd-looking symbols on the computer screen, and asked Jeff what they meant. Jeff explained that we were trying to see whether criminals got punished only for what they did or for other reasons, such as being black, or Hispanic, or a woman. He explained that there were rules about how people should be punished for crimes, and that we were curious whether the courts followed these rules. Then, Jeff explained that we were looking at whether the kind of punishment people got depended on *where* they were being punished. When Jacob asked what our answers were to these questions, Jeff said that courts did not always follow the rules and that location definitely affected punishment. Jacob thought for long moment, and then said with a sincerity only a nine-year-old can muster, "Dad, you've got to tell people about this!"

Max Weber said that social scientists must strive to be value-neutral in their research, that science cannot decide moral questions for society, and that one of the jobs of social science was to objectively point out the consequences of our political and social choices. In other words, social research should not be an exercise in seeing what one wants to see; one must rigorously and fairly test ideas, be willing to see them falsified, and endeavor to keep ideology out of the analysis. But Weber also said (and this is sometimes forgotten) that value neutrality always exists within the boundaries of *value relevance*. Most of the interesting things we study have some implications for social values, and a great deal of what we study is contested moral terrain. The very choice to study one thing over another is a value choice, an assessment of one research problem's importance over the other. The earliest origins of sociology, not to mention criminology and criminal justice studies, were ameliorative. Founding sociological figures such as Weber, Emile Durkheim, W. E. B. DuBois, Robert Park, Herbert Blumer, and criminology pioneer Edwin Sutherland exhorted their successors to explain the causes and consequences of vexing social problems, so the public could better understand those problems.

ix

It is this tradition of value relevance that has kept us engaged in courts and sentencing research throughout our careers. We agree that the quality of justice that the courts dispense, and the fairness with which they dispense it, are fundamental to the legitimacy of a society's rule of law (Tyler and Huo 2002). Our research is primarily motivated by the hope that it will be useful for improving the quality of justice and its fairness. In short, we think the study of sentencing matters, and we spend much of this book explaining why.

We are also fascinated by how courts—indeed all criminal justice organizations (Walker 1993)—function as arenas for fundamental sociological issues and dilemmas. It is here that the perennial dialectics between discretion and its constraint, uniformity vs. individualization, and what Weber called formal and substantive rationality play out (Savelsberg 1992). Courts and sentencing decisions also exist within larger social and political contexts, often reflecting and contributing to prevailing patterns of social stratification (hence, the potential for disparity based on social statuses such as race, ethnicity, age, and gender). Sentencing guidelines theselves are the product of complex political forces and bear the imprint of social movements and interest groups concerned with causes such as just deserts, crime control, victim advocacy, and civil rights. Finally, sentencing guidelines present an ongoing experiment in policy implementation and transformation (Estes and Edmonds 1981; Hall and McGinty 1997)—a continuous opportunity to observe what happens when the goals and consequences of policies, set by higher and more centralized authorities, depend on the actions of local, decentralized actors, who have their own constraints and incentive structures embedded in local organizational and community culture.

This book is an attempt to present in a systematic and integrated way the "focal concerns perspective" that has evolved from our earlier work and with the contributions of several colleagues. Our theoretical framework combines two distinct but highly interrelated conceptual directions. First is the notion of courts as communities (Eisenstein et al. 1988) and court communities as social worlds (Ulmer 1997). From this body of work comes our emphasis on the locality of justice, or what our colleague James Eisenstein calls the local "contours of justice." Since 2001, we have been meshing this emphasis on courts as distinctive communities, or social worlds, with the focal concerns model of sentencing that we developed with Darrell Steffensmeier during the 1990s. This perspective keys off Steffensmeier's early work on the attribution of character based on social status characteristics, as well as Celesta Albonetti's causal attribution and uncertainty reduction perspective on judicial discretion. The framework grew out of our own inductive observations based on qualitative interviews with dozens of judges, prosecutors, defense attorneys, and probation officers as they described what motivated sentencing decisions (we describe this research in Ulmer and Kramer 1996, 1998; Ulmer 1997; and Steffensmeier, Ulmer, and Kramer 1998). In Chapter 1, we state this integrated court communities and focal concerns perspective in propositional form, and subsequent chapters explore its empirical implications vis-à-vis sentencing under guidelines.

Given that this book is the culmination of a long research journey, some of the empirical chapters of this book extend previously published studies. Chapter 4 is a modified version of an article in *Criminology* (Kramer and Ulmer 2002). The core of Chapter 6 builds on Ulmer and Johnson (2004) with a refined sample of cases, different methodological choices, and new analyses (see the Research Methods Appendix). Similarly, in Chapter 7 we add new data and analyses to an earlier article (Ulmer and Bradley 2006). Chapter 8 is a modified version of an article in *Journal of Research in Crime and Delinquency* (Ulmer, Kurlychek, and Kramer 2007). Finally, Chapters 1–3, 5, and 9–10 are completely new contributions.

We want to acknowledge the many people who have helped us. We thank Cassia Spohn and an anonymous reviewer for their extremely valuable comments that improved the book's overall quality. We thank editor Leanne Anderson for her early enthusiasm and advocacy; her many suggestions have made our book more interesting and useful than it would have been otherwise.

We also express our indebtedness to our Penn State colleagues whose ideas and suggestions have sharpened our thinking: Darrell Steffensmeier, James Eisenstein, Brian Johnson, Steve Demuth, Megan Kurlychek, Mindy Bradley, Carrie Williamson, and Ben Feldmeyer. We thank Craig Wiernik, Katie Hamilton, and Martha Gault for their research assistance.

We actually had some difficulty deciding the order of authorship for this book, because we each contributed to it equally—and in the end we produced a book that is much stronger than what either of us could have done individually. We eventually agreed that John should be first, to represent his legacy of work with the Pennsylvania Commission on Sentencing and his fostering of the scholarly agenda that has driven two decades of research on sentencing in Pennsylvania. Without his work, neither this book nor the research agenda that preceded it would have been possible. In the remainder of this preface, we offer individual acknowledgments.

From Jeffery Ulmer

For me, this book is the capstone to a twenty-year research journey. During my visit to Penn State University as a prospective sociology graduate student, I talked with John Kramer for over two hours, mostly about sentencing and guidelines. From that point forward, I more or less owe the trajectory of my career to the opportunities afforded me by John and my early career experiences with the Pennsylvania Commission on Sentencing. My graduate research on sentencing, case processing, and court organizational relations in Pennsylvania became my first book, and my back-and-forth collaboration with John and Darrell Steffensmeier on a series of articles in the 1990s helped me earn tenure at Purdue University. Since my return to Penn State in 2000, I've continued to pursue interesting developments in both Pennsylvania and federal sentencing with various colleagues, old and new.

One of my personal and intellectual mentors, David Maines, once told me to hang out with people smarter than I was, so that their smartness would rub off. I have always taken that advice to heart. I am very fortunate to have a smart and exciting network of fellow travelers in the courts and sentencing research world, such as Rod Engen, Randy Gainey, Sara Steen, Cassia Spohn, Celesta Albonetti, Kevin Blackwell, Paula Kautt, Kate Auerhahn, David Holleran, and Shawn Bushway. Discussions and exchanges with these people have made me sharpen my ideas and have constantly pushed me to raise my game.

From John Kramer

This book represents a combination of my work as executive director of the Pennsylvania Commission on Sentencing (1979–1998) and my position as Penn State University professor (1973–present). I am extremely fortunate to have been given the chance to combine the two jobs, which at times required balancing a policy-driven role as executive director with my research-driven role as a faculty member.

The most unforgettable part of this endeavor has been the wonderful colleagues that I cherish as friends and respect as professionals. This list of individuals is too long to thank each and every one, but some are just too important not to identify.

I must start with the members of the original Pennsylvania Commission on Sentencing. During the nineteen years I served as executive director, I worked with almost fifty different commissioners, each of whom brought their own views and leadership to the process. And while the commission was created out of controversy and conflict between the legislature and the judiciary, never did I see that conflict in the dialogue among commissioners themselves—drawn from both the legislature and the bench—as they completed the arduous task of determining the shape, scope, and prescriptions of the sentencing guidelines.

The heart and soul of the commission was Judge Richard P. Conaboy. As documented in Chapter 2, Judge Conaboy was instrumental not only in creating the commission, but also the first set of guidelines. Also vital as an originator, member, and eventually chair of the commission, Anthony J. Scirica (now Chief Judge of the US Third Circuit Court) brokered the guidelines along with Representative Norm Berson through the General Assembly and provided wise counsel and leadership throughout the early years. Over the life of the commission, many other judges made tremendous contributions; among the most visible were John O'Brien, Melvin Levy, Robert Dauer, and Curtis Carson.

Pennsylvania's commission was one of the few that included legislators, and this might have been viewed as politicizing the commission. Certainly, at times the political environment put pressure on the commission, but I would argue—and the record demonstrates—the legislative members never backed down, choosing instead to focus on the writing and implementation of the best guidelines possible. During my appearances before the Democratic and Republican caucuses in the House and Senate, each legislative member of the commission had to grant me access to the caucuses while I was challenged by them. An illustration of the support offered by each legislative member of the commission came from Senator George Gekas. As we stood in his office preparing to walk into the Senate Republican caucus, Senator Gekas looked at me and said, "John, I think I am ruining my political career supporting you in this." With that he opened the door, we went into the caucus, and he never backed off from his support. Similar comments could be made about Senator James Kelley, Representative Terry McVerry, and Representative Norm Berson on that first commission. Their replacements over the years were similar in their ability to put aside politics and focus on the guidelines.

The commission had three gubernatorial appointments: a district attorney, a defense attorney, and a law professor or criminologist. Again, I cannot list them all by name, but I will say that while each appointed attorney was an advocate for their fellow DAs and defense attorneys, they made their points and justifications and then listened as the countering points of view were expressed. The high quality of the commissioners is perhaps illustrated best by the 1982 appointment and seventeen-year tenure of Al Blumstein. One of the foremost criminologists in the world, Al's contributions to the commission were less visible than his many publications and presentations, but no less valuable.

The early work of the commission was strongly supported by a superb staff. My associate director, Rob Lubitz, worked with me for ten years before moving on to become executive director of the North Carolina sentencing commission. John McCloskey also worked with us for ten years before pursuing his desire to become a Roman Catholic priest. Cynthia Kempinen joined the commission staff upon completing her PhD at Penn State; she still serves as the associate director of research. The intelligence, hard work, and dedication of these individuals were incredible. Working with them was one of the consistently great parts of the commission. Never satisfied, but always positive, they were driven to seek improvements in the guidelines, in supporting legislation, or in the monitoring and evaluation process. Later staff such as Jody Hobbs and Mark Bergstrom, my replacement as executive director, continued this tradition.

In my alter-ego as professor at Penn State, I appreciated the support of many wonderful colleagues. In particular, Darrell Steffensmeier kept me grounded and reminded me of my academic obligations when the policy world tended to draw me away. Other colleagues such as Tom Bernard and John Mc-Carthy also kept my feet in the academic world.

Separate attention and thanks must go to the many graduate students who have assisted the commission and led my research efforts over the years. Two stand out for particular note. Brian Johnson, emerging as one of the leading US sentencing scholars, "cut his teeth" working with commission data. My co-author, Jeff Ulmer, started out by working with the commission before he completed his PhD and took his first academic position at Purdue University. But we enticed him back to Penn State as a faculty colleague, and this book represents tremendous work on his part. A wonderful scholar, Jeff worked diligently on updating analyses, reworking chapters, and making sure we completed the book.

My last recognition and thanks go to Marcia, my wife of forty years, and to my kids, Kim and Chad—friends like no others. They wondered when I would be home, when I would relax, and tolerated my travels around the state—but always encouraged my efforts. I have been so lucky to have them as my last leg of support.

When I look back on the past three decades and the relationships that were affected or developed as a consequence of my work with the commission, I am extremely grateful. The only thing I have not noted is what the guidelines themselves did to Pennsylvania's justice system. I hope they have improved justice, but what I know is that the system of justice is built on a strong foundation of judges, district attorneys, defense attorneys, probation officers, legislators, and others. I have had the good fortune to work with and see the efforts of these people, and while we did not always see justice in the same way, they broadened my perspective and earned my respect.

1

Understanding Sentencing

THE 1970S WERE a time when a wide range of committees, judges, and commentators challenged the system of sentencing in the United States. Sentencing guidelines, along with mandatory minimum sentencing laws, emerged from these challenges and their aftermath. Now, over fifteen states, as well as the federal criminal justice system, have adopted sentencing guidelines, and nearly every state has enacted mandatory minimum sentencing laws in one form or another. This book details the experience of Pennsylvania as the second state to adopt sentencing guidelines, and examines the impact of these guidelines over time. It also describes how mandatory minimums arose as an alternative, somewhat competing sentencing structure in Pennsylvania, and briefly examines how Pennsylvania's prosecutors have used their discretion to apply mandatory minimums.

The earliest states to reform their sentencing statutes were Maine, California, Illinois, and Indiana. The reforms these states adopted are generally referred to as "determinate sentencing statutes," in that they abolished indeterminate sentences and replaced them with fixed periods of confinement set by the judge, with the date of release reduced by good time. The changes in these four states may have been the first formal legislative attempts to adopt determinate sentencing, but they did not inspire similar reforms in other states. In fact, rather than adopting these first innovations, later reforms focused on creating sentencing commissions mandated to establish sentencing guidelines.

In some respects, case studies of sentencing commissions are studies of social change and organizations' ability to produce it. To this end, Pennsylvania's guideline system is a case study of one small agency that was created and caught in what David Garland calls "late twentieth-century modernity's" criminal justice climate, a period that Garland dates from 1970. He observes: "What is remarkable about the 1970s assault upon correctionalism is that far from being the culmination of existing reform programmes it was a sudden turning of progressive opinion against them." He captures the time of this transition during the 1960s, when "televised images of urban race riots, violent civil rights struggles, anti-war demonstrations, political assassinations, and worsening street crime reshaped the attitudes of the middle-American public" (Garland 2001, pp. 53, 97). It was during this time that the sentencing reform movement took shape, merging the liberal view that reliance on incarceration was biased and excessive, with a strengthening conservative view that criminal penalties were too lenient.

In many ways, state legislatures and criminal justice systems are the engine of innovation in criminal justice policy. They are a crucible for testing the possibilities and limitations of criminal justice developments like sentencing reforms. This book adds to the literature by supplying the first relatively detailed history and empirical analysis of a sentencing commission and the development of its guidelines, based on our participant observation as well as on archival material and interviews. One of us, John Kramer, served as the original executive director of the Pennsylvania Commission on Sentencing (PCS) from 1979 until 1998 (and also served as staff director of the US Sentencing Commission from 1996 to 1998). The other, Jeffery Ulmer, worked for the PCS from 1988 to 1994 as a graduate assistant and then as a postdoctoral research associate. Since then, he has published a book (Ulmer 1997) and many articles on sentencing in Pennsylvania. Our chief challenge is to objectively study something that we (especially Kramer) were closely involved in creating and sustaining. On the other hand, the advantage of being a participant observer of the process is rarely available to social scientists, and gives the scientist access to valuable insider information. Our goal here is to be as dispassionate and objective as possible in our reporting, so that others can better understand the evolution of an agency and its decisions, and the empirical consequences of those decisions. We see this book as making at least two contributions.

First, it contributes to the empirical research literature on courts and their sentencing practices. We investigate various forms of extralegal sentencing disparity under Pennsylvania's guidelines: disparity associated with race, ethnicity, and gender, "trial penalties" (sentencing differences between those convicted by trial and those who plead guilty), and the effect of county contexts on between-county sentencing differences. We also examine the factors that affect how Pennsylvania prosecutors use their discretion to apply or not apply mandatory minimum sentences, and analyze the impact of changes in Pennsylvania's guidelines on courts' sentencing practices over time.

Second, the book provides lessons on the possibilities and pitfalls of criminal justice reforms, as well as on the complexity of criminal justice discretion and the delicacy of attempting to structure it. As a detailed case study of one state's ongoing experiences in sentencing reform, this book contributes to our understanding of broader criminal justice issues as well. These include generic issues such as the "success" or "failure" of reforms (and the many things these terms can mean), the control and use of decisionmaking discretion in criminal justice organizations, and the relationship between such organizations and their social, organizational, and political environments.

While writing this book, several developments made our efforts all the more timely. In 2005, the US Supreme Court issued opinions in *Blakely v. Washington* (124 S. Ct. 2531 [2004]) and *United States v. Booker/Fanfan* (125 S. Ct. 738 [2005]), which have had major impact on the federal sentencing guidelines as well as on many state guideline systems (we address this in Chapters 3 and 10). Following on the logic in *Blakely* and *Booker,* at the end of 2007 the US Supreme Court issued *Kimbrough v. United States* (06-6330) and *Gall v. United States* (06-7949), which gave federal judges considerably more discretion to deviate from the US Sentencing Guidelines when deemed unreasonable for particular offenders involved in crack cocaine and ecstacy offense cases.

The US Sentencing Guidelines are thus now advisory and, we would argue, are coming to resemble Pennsylvania's guidelines in their legal status. That is, both sets of guidelines advise courts, and courts must consider them. Now, however, federal courts have more of the kind of leeway to deviate from guidelines that Pennsylvania courts have had since that state's guidelines were implemented (though it remains to be seen how much leeway federal courts will eventually have under advisory federal guidelines). This means that the potential for variation in sentencing between local courts, and disparity between individual defendants, now looms larger in the federal court system, which operates under the most visible, and arguably the most consequential, set of guidelines in the United States: the US Sentencing Guidelines. In this book, we identify the social processes that produce local court variation in sentencing, and those that can lead to individual sentencing disparity, all of which now seem to be quite relevant for federal sentencing. There will be a need for federal sentencing policy strategies to structure sentencing discretion without removing it, as well as a need for creative ways to address sentencing disparity, and we hope our discussion of these matters will help stimulate the search for such strategies.

The Social Environment of Guidelines: Court Communities and Focal Concerns

Of course, sentencing guidelines are not implemented in a vacuum. Some sociologists refer to policy formation and implementation as "the transformation of intentions" (Estes and Edmonds 1981; Hall 1997; Hall and McGinty 1997). Local communities and organizations are fully capable of transforming the formal intentions of externally imposed policies such as sentencing guidelines. Peter Hall captures the problem of policymakers versus policy implementers when he notes that, on the one hand, "policy actors dependent upon those who follow them to complete their intentions, set the terms that both limit and facilitate later actions," but on the other hand that "later actors may reinforce, clarify, subvert, or amend initial intentions and content" (1997, p. 401). Below, we briefly review two theoretical perspectives or heuristic lenses through which to view sentencing under guidelines: court communities and focal concerns. We use these perspectives to articulate six guiding propositions that frame our analysis of sentencing under guidelines.

Local variation in the implementation of broad criminal sentencing policies, such as sentencing guidelines, is a persistent theme in research on state criminal courts (Flemming, Nardulli, and Eisenstein 1992; Myers and Talarico 1987; Nardulli, Eisenstein, and Flemming 1988; Ulmer 1997). Since political, economic, social, and cultural differences exist between counties and their courts, it is reasonable that differences could emerge between local courts in the way they interpret and use sentencing guidelines, or in the ways in which local culture, relations, and practices mesh with guidelines (or not). Furthermore, the potential complexity of interpreting and applying guidelines and the ability to depart from them in certain situations provide ample opportunity for between-court variation in guideline implementation and sentencing practices.

The *court community perspective* views courts as communities or social worlds based on participants' shared workplace and interdependent working relations between key sponsoring agencies, such as the prosecutor's office, judges' bench, and defense bar (Eisenstein, Flemming, and Nardulli 1988; Flemming, Nardulli, and Eisenstein 1992; Ulmer 1997). These court communities develop distinctive social orders that produce distinctive local organizational cultures. These local social arrangements and the cultures they encompass shape formal and informal case-processing and sentencing norms (see Eisenstein, Flemming, and Nardulli 1988; Ulmer and Kramer 1998; Ulmer 1997). These court communities are said to foster their own locally varying substantive legal rationalities, which influence sentencing outcomes and processes as least as much as do formal policies and legal structures (Engen et al. 2003; Savelsberg 1992; Ulmer and Kramer 1996). Therefore, court communities are apt to have distinctive organizational cultures and distinctive relationships to external organizations and externally imposed policies.

For example, court communities typically have locally distinctive, informal, and ever-evolving case-processing and sentencing norms, or "going rates" as a key dimension of their processual order (Eisenstein, Flemming, and Nardulli 1988; Ulmer 1997; see also Sudnow 1965). These going rates often provide members of courtroom workgroups with "templates" for case-processing strategies, typical plea-bargaining terms, and sentences, and are continually open to modification based on actors' solutions to problematic situations.

Into this mix of local court communities and their social orders come sentencing guidelines, as an attempt to manage a variety of dilemmas: between flexible discretion and rule-bound control, between uniformity and individualization, and between centralization and decentralized localism. In sociological terms, guidelines represent an attempt to impose a regime of formal rationality (approximating what sociologist Max Weber called a "gapless system of rules" that are to be applied universally and uniformly, with a minimum of decisionmaker discretion—see Savelsberg 1992; Ewing 1987) onto a traditionally "substantively rational" process.

Substantive rationality in legal decisionmaking refers to criteria that are guided by, or in service of, ideological factors and goals external to the law. Substantive rationality in criminal sentencing is thus a type of rationality that is oriented toward flexible and individualized decisionmaking in service of a potentially wide variety of extralegal goals (for helpful theoretical reviews, see Savelsberg 1992; Marsh 2000; Mears and Field 2000). For example, some substantive goals could center around the welfare of either the offender, the victim, or the community (Levin 1977). Other substantive goals could center around crime control or crime suppression (Packer 1968). Still others could center around organizational goals such as efficiency, accountability, or power. On the other hand, the flexibility inherent in substantive rationality also permits the possibility of bias, discrimination, and unwarranted disparity.

In the "real world" of sentencing, then, locally interpreted substantive rationality coexists with and may even subvert such formally rational policies (Ulmer and Kramer 1998; see also Kautt 2002). Clearly, sentencing is a complex, localized, interpretive process, and formally rational sentencing policies like guidelines cannot, and do not seek to, eliminate all discretion (Savelsberg 1992; Ulmer 1997). In fact, sentencing guidelines, by definition, do not represent *pure* formal, bureaucratic rationality, since they allow downward or upward departures for offenders and offenses seen as atypical. Guidelines have "windows of discretion" (Cirillo 1986) that allow for response to atypical situations. Therefore, all guidelines intentionally present opportunity for the exercise of various substantively rational criteria in sentencing (a purely formally rational sentencing system would look like an all-encompassing set of mandatory sentences, with no departures possible). This leads to our first general guiding proposition:

> *Proposition 1: Sentencing severity and decision criteria (even guideline-based), use of guidelines, and compliance and departure from guidelines are all likely to vary between local court communities.*

If the court community perspective orients us toward the importance of the contours of local courts and their environments in the implementation of guidelines, the *focal concerns perspective* orients us to the subjective interests and goals of individuals within the "courtroom workgroup" (a term coined by James Eisenstein and Herbert Jacob [1977]): prosecutors, judges, and defense attorneys. This perspective partly evolved out of and incorporated prior research and theorizing (Steffensmeier 1980; Wheeler, Weisburd, and Bode 1982; Albonetti 1986, 1991; Steffensmeier, Kramer, and Streifel 1993), but also it was in large part developed inductively, out of a qualitative research project involving scores of interviews with judges, prosecutors, and defense attorneys (see Steffensmeier, Ulmer, and Kramer 1998; Ulmer and Kramer 1996; Ulmer 1997). When we asked interviewees about the criteria that drove sentencing decisions, they strongly emphasized three focal concerns, and typically spoke at length about the factors that influenced their own and others' subjective assessments of the focal concerns.

The focal concerns perspective emphasizes particular kinds of substantively rational criteria at work in sentencing decisions, which are in turn embedded in the culture and organization of court communities. In addition, the focal concerns perspective integrates key insights from other important theories of criminal justice decisionmaking. This perspective argues that three interpretively defined focal concerns of punishment—blameworthiness, protection of the community, and practical constraints—determine punishment decisions. Thus:

> *Proposition 2: Sentencing decisions are joint acts (often reflecting the influence of prosecutors and defense attorneys as well as judges) made on the basis of decisionmakers' definitions of blameworthiness, community protection needs, and practical constraints and consequences.*

There is actually general agreement in the sentencing literature that legally prescribed factors, such as offense type and severity or prior record, are typically the strongest predictors of punishment outcomes (Spohn 2000; Zatz 2000). The question is whether these are the only meaningful influences, as law and policy intend. The focal concerns perspective (and the theories that are consistent with it) is not compatible with this strict normative/legalistic view.

The focal concerns perspective describes a punishment decisionmaking process in which such a strictly legalistic decisionmaking process is implausible. The decisionmaking process described by focal concerns is one in which both legal and extralegal considerations affect the interpretation and prioritization of focal concerns through local substantive rationality (Savelsberg 1992; Kramer and Ulmer 2002). For example, this perspective envisions court community actors making situational attributions about a defendant's character based on his or her social status as well as practical contingencies (among other factors). Moreover, punishment decisionmaking processes and interpretations of focal concerns may be locally variable because they are embedded in local court communities' organizational cultures and influences.

In sum, the focal concerns and normative/legalistic perspectives differ in the kinds of decisionmaking processes they predict. Evidence of extralegal influences on punishment *in addition to* legally prescribed influences, as well as interactions between extralegal factors themselves, would be compatible with the focal concerns perspective but not the normative/legalistic perspective (see Steffensmeier, Ulmer, and Kramer 1998; Spohn and Holleran 2000). Key questions then arise regarding sentencing disparity, such as: How much do court actors rely on sentencing guidelines' codifications of definitions of blameworthiness and dangerousness, versus extra-guideline factors? Which extra-guideline factors influence sentencing (including decisions to depart from guidelines) in addition to guideline-related factors, and how do they do so? Thus:

> *Proposition 3: Definitions of blameworthiness and dangerousness are mostly determined by formal legal and policy structures such as guidelines, but are also potentially determined by local decisionmakers' substantively rational interests such as attitudes, stereotypes, and biases.*

Several theories of extralegal influences on sentencing exist, each emphasizing ways in which extralegal considerations may affect punishment decisions: uncertainty avoidance and causal attribution theory, racial/ethnic threat theory, and the organizational efficiency hypothesis. We discuss these further in later chapters. We do not pit the focal concerns and court community perspectives in competition against these other theories. Rather, we use them as a heuristic framework to integrate and organize the propositions from various other theories that are compatible in principle with focal concerns, but that we view as incomplete explanations of punishment decisionmaking on their own.

According to Celesta Albonetti (1991), sentencing suffers from operating in a context of bounded rationality (March and Simon 1958). In this bounded context, court actors make highly consequential decisions with insufficient information, which produces uncertainty. Sometimes, their decisions rest on little information regarding the background and moral character of the defendant (though this lack of information is often alleviated by pre-sentence reports or information brought out at trial), and almost always the decisions have little information on outcomes such as recidivism risk of offenders. Beyond that, even when more extensive information is available, the risk and seriousness of recidivism are never fully predictable for a particular defendant, a defendant's moral character is never fully knowable, and human decisionmaking processes have built-in limitations to the amount and complexity of information that can be considered. In this context, judges and other court community actors make situational imputations about the character and expected future behavior of defendants (Steffensmeier 1980), and assess the implications of these imputed characteristics in terms of the three focal concerns: defendant blameworthiness, defendant dangerousness and community protection, and practical constraints and consequences connected to the punishment decision. Most likely, court actors make these character imputations based on legally relevant factors (like sentencing guidelines), but they may also make them on the basis of stereotypes based on the social status of defendants, including race, ethnicity, gender, age, and social class. In fact, as we explain in Chapters 5 and 8, defendant social status characteristics are likely to influence sentencing in combination; that is, they are likely to be mutually conditional (Steffensmeier, Ulmer, and Kramer 1998; Spohn and Holleran 2000). In other words, the influence of defendant race or ethnicity on sentencing may depend on defendant gender and age. For example, racial or ethnic stereotypes of dangerousness or blameworthiness might be gender- and age-specific. As a case in point, judges or prosecutors might view the dangerousness of a young Hispanic female differently than the dangerousness of a young Hispanic male. Thus:

> *Proposition 4: The influence of defendant social status characteristics (race, ethnicity, gender, age, class, etc.) on sentencing outcomes is likely to be conditional. The influence of status characteristics on sentencing likely depends on a defendant's specific combination of status characteristics.*

Furthermore, organizational or case-processing factors, such as caseloads or a defendant's decision to plead guilty or go to trial, can influence assessments of practical constraints and consequences. In addition, a defendant's choice to plead guilty or not also may have ramifications for how court actors define his or her blameworthiness. We return to these themes in Chapter 7.

We argue that the use of and reliance on these focal concerns tend to characterize all courts generally, but their meaning, relative emphasis and priority, and situational interpretation are embedded in the local court community's legal and organizational culture. For example, definitions of what kinds of offenses and offenders are especially blameworthy or dangerous are likely to vary according to a local court community's culture and politics. Furthermore, practical constraints and consequences are highly likely to be produced by local court community conditions. Thus:

> *Proposition 5: The interpretation and prioritization of the focal concerns is influenced by the local culture, politics, organization, and resources of court communities, aside from the influence of guidelines. This is especially true of practical constraints and consequences.*

In fact, we see sentencing guidelines as attempts by sentencing commissions and legislatures to codify and structure judgments about blameworthiness and dangerousness, in order to achieve "just deserts" punishment and to protect the community. Guidelines that are descriptive (i.e., based on past local practices) are more likely to have a "good fit" with local views of blameworthiness and dangerousness. However, descriptive guidelines may merely codify existing disparate practices, and may not achieve the larger sentencing policy goals of sentencing commissions or legislatures. On the other hand, guidelines that are prescriptive (i.e., based on sentencing commissions' and legislatures' definitions of appropriate punishments as matters of policy) are more likely to be discrepant from local court community definitions, resulting in higher departures (Kramer and Scirica 1986).

Our theoretical perspective thus emphasizes that sentencing guidelines meet the messy world of politics and policy processes in their development and evolution, and that guidelines are implemented in local courts within their particular organizational and social environments. Guidelines are interpreted and used (or departed from) by individuals who are part of a court community, and these individuals have their own subjective interests, goals, ideologies, and biases. Figure 1.1 summarizes the focal concerns model, and the many potential, and potentially competing, influences on definitions of blameworthiness, community protection, and practical constraints.

The figure displays the lines of influence from guidelines to the focal concerns, and also shows lines of influence from the state level to the guidelines. The other lines of influence in the figure reflect the embeddedness of the focal concerns in local court communities and their larger environments. However, the consequences of sentencing decisions can later modify court community participants' definitions of defendants and consequently the focal concerns.

The focal concerns are directly informed by the sentencing guidelines. In fact, guidelines can be seen as the state's codification and structuring of judgments about blameworthiness and community protection and practical constraints (some guideline systems, such as Minnesota's and Washington's, require consideration of prison resources). The influences on focal concerns do not stop there, however. Court community culture as well as individual decisionmaker attitudes or ideologies are quite likely to shape perceptions of what defendants and crimes are seen as more or less blameworthy and what kinds of crimes and offenders present threats to the community. Furthermore, the practical constraints and consequences entailed in any sentencing decision are directly shaped by the court's caseload characteristics, size, and resources, and also by local and state correctional resources. The salience and perceived importance of practical constraints connected to sentencing decisions are also shaped by individual views and court community culture. For example, the degree to which a court community's culture emphasizes efficiency as a goal would affect the salience of the need to move cases quickly by eliciting guilty pleas (see Chapter 7). The degree to which a judge or prosecutor's punishment decisions are influenced by the fact that a woman defendant is single and has a child will depend on that judge or prosecutor's beliefs or ideologies about gender, motherhood, and children (see Chapters 4 and 5, for example). Features of the court community are in turn reciprocally related to the sociocultural and political features of the surrounding community, which in turn are potentially related to larger state and societal patterns. In fact, Figure 1.1 is an oversimplification of the potential lines of influence on decisionmakers' definitions of focal

Figure 1.1   Factors Influencing Sentencing Decisions

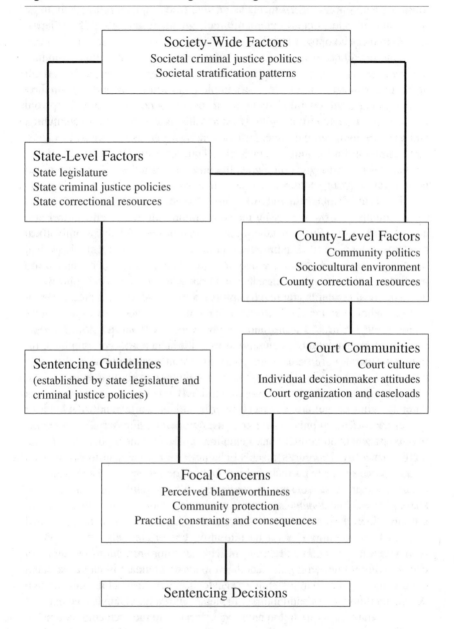

concerns, and on court communities, but it does illustrate the competition that sentencing guidelines face.

Importantly, the restrictiveness or presumptiveness of guideline systems conditions the degree to which extra-guideline factors can influence sentencing. For example, more disparity (at least at the sentencing stage) is possible in Pennsylvania, whose guidelines are less restrictive and allow more discretion at the sentencing stage, than in Minnesota or in the federal system, whose guidelines are more restrictive of sentencing-stage discretion. Thus:

> *Proposition 6: The less that a guideline system restricts sentencing-stage discretion, the more that local interpretations of focal concerns can influence sentencing, and the greater the potential for disparity.*

It would seem that, from a disparity viewpoint (as well as for achieving desired larger policy goals), more restrictive guidelines would be preferable to less restrictive guidelines. However, as we discuss later, the restrictiveness of guidelines also invokes a dilemma between formal rationality and uniformity, on the one hand, and substantive rationality, flexibility, individualized sentencing, and localized discretion on the other (see Walker 1993; Ulmer and Kramer 1996). Also, sharply restricting discretion at the sentencing stage risks displacing it to earlier criminal justice stages, such as the charging and guilty plea processes. Observers have been concerned about these issues since the earliest beginnings of sentencing guidelines (see Savelsberg 1992). We return to this theme in several places later in the book, especially in the concluding chapter. For now, we note that our theoretical framework leads us to *expect* important extra-guideline influences on sentencing to exist in Pennsylvania's sentencing system. The empirical questions, then, become what kind, and how much? At the same time, we are interested in the guidelines' capacity for structuring local actors' interpretations of blameworthiness and community protection.

Pennsylvania presents a particularly instructive context in which to study guideline sentencing—and sentencing in general—for two reasons. First, its local courts are extremely diverse in terms of size, political contexts, sociocultural features, and crime concerns. Second, as we explain below, unique features of its sentencing guidelines and their history present a situation that throws into bold relief the universal dilemma of sentencing: the dilemma between the goal of uniformity and logically formal-rational rules, on the one hand, and the goal of individualized justice, which necessitates local discretion and substantively rational considerations, on the other (see Savelsberg 1992; Ulmer and Kramer 1996). However, we would argue that the Pennsylvania context is advantageous theoretically in that the tensions and negotiations between logically formal rationality and substantive rationality in sentencing are particularly pronounced. Therefore, the Pennsylvania context is instructive as an opportunity to see how these tensions and negotiations play out empirically, and thus advance our understanding of the interrelationship of formal and substantive rationality in sentencing.

Overview

In this book we examine in depth the history, development, and impact of sentencing guidelines in Pennsylvania. Chapters 2 and 3 review the context for Pennsylvania's sentencing reform, and present a historical overview of the development and continuing evolution of the guidelines. Next we present a variety of research examining the impact of the guidelines on sentencing patterns and disparity. Chapter 4 investigates the guidelines' impact by examining local court "corrections" to the guidelines, in the form of departures, for serious violent offenders. Chapter 5 focuses on a crucial issue for guidelines: unwarranted disparity based on race, ethnicity, and gender. Chapter 6 presents a detailed analysis of between-court variation in Pennsylvania sentencing, and how county and court characteristics affect sentencing severity. Chapter 7 discusses the nature, prevalence, and predictors of the so-called trial penalty under Pennsylvania's guidelines. Chapter 8 discusses how mandatory minimums represent a somewhat competing sentencing structure vis-à-vis the guidelines, one that is largely controlled by prosecutors. The chapter then analyzes the predictors of prosecutors' decisions to apply mandatory minimums among a sample of mandatory-eligible offenders. Chapter 9 investigates the impact of the guidelines in terms of revisions in 1994 and 1997 that changed statewide sentencing practices.

Our discussion of the history and evolution of the Pennsylvania guidelines, as well as their impact on sentencing practices, can be read as a case study illustrating the notion of policy as the transformation of intentions. Throughout the empirical chapters, we return again and again to our theme: the embeddedness of the Pennsylvania guidelines in local court communities and the focal concerns of their participants. We conclude the book with important lessons to be learned from the Pennsylvania experience with sentencing reform.

2

Constructing Pennsylvania's Sentencing Guidelines

IN THIS CHAPTER we briefly review the context of Pennsylvania's sentencing reform in terms of the sentencing reform movement, dating from the early 1970s, and the academic, political, and ethical debates that framed so much of that movement. From this contextual basis we then review sentencing reform in Pennsylvania and the development of Pennsylvania's sentencing guidelines. Our review is brief, so readers interested in more detail on the sentencing reform movement are encouraged to read the original foundations of the movement as detailed in Marvin Frankel's book *Criminal Sentences* (1972), and good reviews of the movement in Michael Tonry's book *Sentencing Matters* (1996) and Cassia Spohn's book *How Do Judges Decide?* (2002).

The Sentencing Reform Movement

The century leading to 1970 could be viewed as the rehabilitation century. Rehabilitation of offenders replaced punishment as the guiding philosophy. Importantly, rehabilitation shifted the focus away from the seriousness of the offender's crime to the nature of the offender's problem. Consequently, it was deemed that treatment and punishment should fit the rehabilitation needs of the offender, which had major consequences for sentencing. Under this rubric, judges were not prepared for, nor in a position to determine, the offender's treatment needs. Rather, treatment specialists in offender rehabilitation were needed to implement sentences that would ensure reform of the offender. The resulting sentencing implementation model was the "indeterminate sentence," along with a growth of probation and parole supervision to provide community treatment. By the early 1900s the indeterminate sentencing movement, initiated in the late nineteenth century, had been adopted in almost all states.[1] There were two important products of the rehabilitation movement. First, the focus on the offender rather than the crime meant that the form and length of "treatment" might have little to do with the severity of the offense. Second, the judge was given great latitude to determine who was incarcerated, although relatively little control over the length of confinement, as release power was shifted to a paroling authority who could determine when the offender was ready for reintegration into society. Both of these aspects of indeterminate sentencing were considerably criticized, and by the mid-1970s state legislatures began to reject indeterminate sentencing in favor of determinate models.

Attacks on Rehabilitation

The 1960s and early 1970s saw significant challenges to the fairness of indeterminate sentences (Allen 1964; American Friends Service Committee 1971) and the effectiveness of treatment in changing offenders (Bailey 1966; Martinson 1974; Robinson and Smith 1971). By the early 1970s, building on these challenges, detractors of indeterminate sentencing and the rehabilitative principles on which it rested began to attract attention. Perhaps the strongest statement in opposition to the indeterminate sentencing system was the American Friends Service Committee's 1971 report *Struggle for Justice*. This report was the first, and most strident, of several attacks on indeterminate sentencing and the treatment model on which it was built.

Struggle for Justice viewed the indeterminate sentencing system as racist, punitive, and ineffective. It indicted the rehabilitative, indeterminate system design, determining that "the individualized treatment model, the ideal toward which reformers have been urging us for at least a century, is theoretically faulty, systematically discriminatory in administration, and inconsistent with some of our most basic concepts of justice" (American Friends Service Committee 1971, p. 12).

This indictment of the system of laws and punishments set the stage for numerous proposals (von Hirsch 1976; Twentieth Century Fund 1976; Singer 1978), but the voice that resonated most with policy reformers was that of Judge Marvin Frankel (1972). Judge Frankel, in a series of lectures at the University of Cincinnati, indicted the extensive discretion given judges at sentencing, and the lack of accountability for these decisions. As a key remedy for these problems, he called for the establishment of a new unit of government called a "sentencing commission" to structure discretion and appellate review of sentences. These proposals became important ingredients of the sentencing reform movement, as ultimately expressed in Pennsylvania. But it was US senator Edward Kennedy who took the initiative to turn Judge Frankel's ideas into legislation.

The Kennedy Proposal

Senator Kennedy's legislation proposed the creation of a federal commission to write sentencing guidelines as espoused by Judge Frankel. Kennedy's legislation, submitted in 1975, was the subject of considerable revision before its final passage in 1984, but served as an important framework for states, particularly Minnesota and Pennsylvania, that began drafting sentencing legislation in the latter part of the 1970s.

The foundation for Senator Kennedy's proposal for sentencing reform rested on his view that

> sentencing in America today is a national scandal. Every day our system of sentencing breeds massive injustice. Judges are free to roam at will, dispensing ad hoc justice in ways that defy both reason and fairness. Different judges mete out widely differing sentences to similar offenders convicted of similar crimes. There are no guidelines to aid them in the exercise of their discretion, nor is there any mechanism for appellate review of sentences. (O'Donnell, Churgin, and Curtis 1977, p. 1)

Kennedy's focal concern was sentencing disparity, and he reasoned that the base of this problem was the indeterminate sentence and the rehabilitative purpose on which it rested. He went beyond Frankel, however, by introducing what would become known as "truth in sentencing," to address the important public concern of unserved sentences.

Pennsylvania's Sentencing Reform

Act 319 of 1978 created the Pennsylvania Commission on Sentencing, with the mandate of developing and promulgating sentencing guidelines. But to understand the role of the commission, its membership, and mandate, it is important to briefly review the context within which a few members of the Pennsylvania General Assembly advocated the adoption of sentencing commission legislation and the compromises necessary to gain passage.

It was not strong concern with sentencing disparity, nor a desire to be at the vanguard of the sentencing reform movement, that stimulated change in Pennsylvania. Rather, sentencing commission legislation in Pennsylvania resulted from an attempt to avoid mandatory minimum legislation that would severely restrict judicial discretion. In 1976, reflecting frustration with lenient sentences, legislation was introduced that would have required a mandatory minimum of one year for a second conviction for serious felonies, including burglary. Although a relatively minor piece of legislation in view of the mandatory minimums adopted since, the bill was projected to increase the state prison population by 3,100 inmates (McClea 1976). Two mandatory sentencing bills containing overlapping but conflicting provisions passed both the House and the Senate in 1976, but failed to achieve concurrence, although there was clear consensus for restricting judicial sentencing discretion. With the view that adoption of similar legislation in the next session of the General Assembly was likely, a group of legislators and concerned interest groups determined that sentencing reform needed careful assessment. Perhaps the key goal of many of the eventual authors of the sentencing commission legislation was to deflect the move to mandatory minimums and preserve judicial discretion. However, it was also clear that the General Assembly was determined to pass some form of legislation restricting sentencing discretion. In the spring of 1977 a small core group of legislators were seeking to stifle the move to mandatory minimums, and it was this core group who undertook an assessment of sentencing reform.

The Joint Council on Criminal Justice, funded by Law Enforcement Assistance Administration money in the 1970s, was created to serve as an independent criminal justice voice and played an important early role in Pennsylvania's sentencing reform. In 1977, this council, chaired by Judge Richard Conaboy, decided to study sentencing reform options with the goal of assisting key legislators in determining the best approach for Pennsylvania. To this end, in the spring of 1977, the council held a conference at which panels presented the pros and cons of mandatory minimums (coauthor John Kramer served on this panel), legislatively-set presumptive guidelines (such as had been recently passed in California), and sentencing commission–authored guidelines, as Senator Kennedy's federal legislation had proposed. Judge Conaboy and state representatives Anthony J. Scirica and Norman Berson came away from this conference focused on creating a sentencing commission to write sentencing guidelines. An important factor in the decision to focus on creating a sentencing commission was Judge Frankel's influence on Representative Scirica, who had attended a presentation by Frankel at Villanova University prior to this conference and was reportedly influenced by Frankel's attacks on judicial discretion. With the shadow of mandatory minimums looming, sentencing guidelines seemed like a good compromise: sentencing experts could develop guidelines for judges and avoid the severe judicial restraints inherent in mandatory minimums. Thus there were two key competing forces. The first comprised the General Assembly and those of its members who were concerned about excessive leniency for serious violent offenses in particular. The second force comprised supporters of judicial discretion who believed that sentencing legislation was inevitable and would likely come in the form of mandatory minimums. This latter group viewed sentencing guidelines as a viable alternative to mandatory minimums that would impose some constraints on judges, but still avoid the total constraints imposed by mandatory minimums. In was in this context that the 1977 session of the General Assembly began, and in which Representatives Scirica and Berson introduced legislation to create a sentencing commission to write sentencing guidelines.

This legislation faced several problems. First, although the final vote on establishing a sentencing commission and sentencing guidelines was unanimous, this vote did not reflect coalescence behind sentencing reform. Many members of the General Assembly took little interest, and those who did express interest tended to be concerned about leniency, with a special target being the perceived leniency of the Philadelphia judiciary.[2] Although there was no research documenting this belief, this perception of leniency was widely espoused.

Pennsylvania diverged from Kennedy's proposed legislation (and from similar legislation passed in Minnesota), which directed sentencing commissions to take into account prison capacity in developing guidelines. This issue was not raised in floor debates, nor was it mentioned during deliberations. Consequently, Act 319 provided no such directive. Further, during the development of the guidelines, when the impact on prison populations became a concern, commissioners quickly expressed the view that the legislature did not want to base the guidelines on current prison capacity, and the issue was dropped.

The lack of a central role for corrections in the decisions made by the sentencing commission was reinforced during the commission's membership discussions. When the Joint Council on Criminal Justice recommended incorporating five appointments by the governor, including representatives of the Department of Correction and the Board of Probation and Parole, the motion was rejected because it would have created an ineffectively large commission, and because it was determined that input from these bodies could be obtained through public hearings. The decision not to base the guidelines on prison population capacity, and not to include corrections representatives on the commission, demonstrated the lack of concern for the impact of the guidelines on corrections. This view was maintained well into the 1990s, when legislators rejected a proposal by the executive director of the PCS (Kramer) that the secretary of corrections and the chair of the Board of Probation and Parole be added to the commission.[3]

Second, the membership debate focused on the size and relative composition of the commission. The initial Scirica-Berson bill had proposed a fifteen-member commission composed of eight legislators and seven judges. But this was viewed as too large a body for achieving consensus. In May 1978, when the legislation was being debated on the floor of the House, membership of the commission was reduced to thirteen, including four legislators, six judges, and three governor-appointed positions—a district attorney, a defense attorney, and a criminologist or law professor. Finally, the six judicial appointments were further reduced to four, leaving the commission at eleven members. The final vote on the legislation was unanimous in both the House and the Senate. The chair of the Senate Judiciary Committee, Senator Michael O'Pake, noted that the bill was supported by the Pennsylvania Trial Judges Association and the District Attorneys Association.[4] The purpose of the guidelines was, according to Senator O'Pake, to alleviate two major problems with sentencing:

1. The problem of "judge-shopping," which in some counties resulted in soft or lenient sentences, even for repeat violent offenders.
2. The lack of uniformity in sentences in all counties of the commonwealth. (*Senate Journal,* November 14, 1978, p. 1075)

Neither the federal commission nor the Minnesota commission, as models for Pennsylvania's guideline legislation, proposed that legislators be included on the PCS. The tenor of sentencing politics in Pennsylvania at the time, however, required legislative representation. In fact, the debate was not whether there should be legislative representation, but who should have more votes.

Another key way in which the Pennsylvania process departed from the national movement was in the role of the parole board and parole supervision. Senator Kennedy and sentencing reform that was emerging in California, Illinois, and Maine followed the criticisms of Andrew von Hirsch (1976) and others in rejecting the rehabilitative model and the indeterminate sentence. In Pennsylvania these concerns were never a significant part of the dialogue in creating the sentencing commission.

The important point to take away from this history is that the PCS's sociopolitical environment and legislative mandate strongly influenced its role, the quality of its sentencing guidelines, and its ability to effectively implement them. Researchers have found that the most frequently cited reasons for creating sentencing commissions are to increase sentencing fairness, reduce unwarranted disparity, control prison populations, and establish truth in sentencing (Bureau of Justice Assistance [BJA] 1996, p. 31). The PCS's enabling legislation and its lack of consideration for prison resources and truth in sentencing reflected to a great extent Pennsylvania's marginality in adopting sentencing reform.

Getting Started

The Pennsylvania Commission on Sentencing was established on November 26, 1978, with a budget of $200,000 to cover staff salaries and operating and travel expenses. However, no commissioners had been appointed, nor had staff and offices been set up in preparation for commission decisionmaking. In addition, getting commissioners appointed proved to be a slow and unfortunate process in terms of the gubernatorial appointments. In November 1978, Richard Thornburgh was elected governor of Pennsylvania, replacing Milton Shapp. The three gubernatorial appointments were a law professor or criminologist, a district attorney, and a defense attorney. Technically, these appointments rested with Governor Shapp, whose term would not end until Thornburgh took the oath of office in late January 1979. It was expected that Governor Shapp would defer the appointments to his successor. However, Governor Shapp decided to move forward with his appointments to the commission, which meant that Thornburgh would not have the power to appoint commissioners for two years, after expiration of the initial terms. Ultimately, Governor Thornburgh did not make appointments to the commission until 1982, after the guidelines had been adopted by the General Assembly and after passage of his legislation requiring five-year mandatory minimum sentences for violent crimes committed with a firearm (42 Pa. C.S. § 9714[g]: third-degree murder, voluntary manslaughter, aggravated assault, rape, involuntary

deviate sexual intercourse, kidnapping, and robbery), and a five-year mandatory minimum sentence for a second conviction for any of such offenses, or
any of these offenses committed on public transportation. For the PCS, this
meant that it initially operated with no direct ties to the governor's office. Although Governor Thornburgh did not oppose the work of the commission, he
basically ignored it early in his tenure.

Other appointments to the PCS came slowly, with its full membership of
eleven commissioners not attained until the spring of 1979. The final appointments included Representative Anthony Scirica, one of the prime sponsors of
the legislation. The other state representative was Norm Berson, who at that
time was chair of the House Judiciary Committee. From the Senate, George
Gekas, chair of the Judiciary Committee, was appointed.[5] However, the commission did begin the process of hiring an executive director by conducting a
nationwide search. Ten individuals were interviewed by the search committee,
two of whom were forwarded to the commission for final consideration. Ultimately, the commission hired John Kramer, professor of criminal justice at
Penn State University.

The first meeting of the PCS was held on April 27, 1979. The commission's mandate was to write sentencing guidelines and submit them to the
General Assembly within eighteen months. The problem the commission
faced was negotiating the divided political environment, which provided the
strong but conflicting endorsement of the guideline legislation. Some viewed
the guidelines as a means to constrain judicial discretion, and others saw them
as a way of preserving judicial discretion. Further, it remained to be seen
whether the judicial and legislative members of the commission could reach
agreement.

The commission also faced practical constraints as it began to navigate
the troubled waters of sentencing policy. First, many commissioners, particularly the legislative appointments, had never sentenced before, and they had
little experience with criminal justice procedure. Second, the commission had
to determine the appropriate process and timeline for developing the guidelines. Of the many decisions required, the key issues concerned the information that the commissioners needed to begin building the guidelines, and
whether the commissioners were comfortable building the guideline structure
without data to inform their judgments. The first meetings were organized
around these two issues.

To build a common appreciation for the complexity and issues involved
in sentencing, pre-sentence reports were sent to the commissioners, including
sentencing forms for them to complete and bring to commission meetings. The
sentencing forms asked commissioners to sentence sample defendants, and to
identify and rank the information that influenced their decisions on incarceration, including length of prison sentences. These cases provided several important foundations for the functioning of the commission. First, they gave

nonjudicial commissioners a greater appreciation of the complexity of the two-stage sentencing decision (see Kress 1980), and of the factors that were important in determining sentences. Second, they provided for a team-building exercise in which disagreements could be discussed, which almost always resulted in commissioners finding common ground in the role of particular factors in the sentencing decisions. This exercise portended many similar discussions as the commission drafted the guidelines and decided which factors should be considered when making sentencing decisions. The ensuing discussions demonstrated that while the outcomes sometimes varied, they were not far apart in terms of sentencing factors, with disagreements seen as opportunities to present alternative views.

Another key decision was the development of a list of tasks and a timeline for their completion. This was difficult, requiring several iterations as staff became more familiar with assembling the data needed to build and assess the impact of sentencing guidelines. One of the first decisions by the commission was to separate the construction of the guideline structure from the construction of the information base. This was done for two reasons. First, the eighteen-month timeline provided in the enabling legislation was insufficient for building and analyzing the database before constructing the guideline structure and guideline sentences. Second, the discussions had also raised the issue of whether the commission should write descriptive or prescriptive guidelines. Based on the time pressure, but particularly on the legislative members' view that the commission's mandate was to change sentencing practices, the commission decided to write prescriptive guidelines, which freed it to move forward while the data was being compiled. With this decision behind it, the commission set out to determine what form the guidelines should take and what factors should be included in the structure. However, rather than moving forward in isolation, the commission decided to include broad-based input from key actors in the criminal justice system by undertaking a survey of judges, district attorneys, and public defenders

The survey had two formal objectives and one informal purpose. The first formal objective was to obtain input on the form of the guidelines. To do this, the survey presented respondents with a matrix model like those adopted in several local guideline projects around the country and an alternative ladder model. The matrix model was similar to the Minnesota guidelines, and the ladder model was based on a combined measure of the seriousness of the current offense and the seriousness of the offender's prior convictions. Second, the survey asked respondents about the appropriate role of offense factors, criminal history, and offender characteristics such as age, employment, and educational status. Regarding the form of the guidelines, respondents clearly preferred the matrix model. Regarding what should be incorporated into the guidelines, the two key factors were offense severity and criminal history. The informal purpose of the survey was to alert the respondents to the work of the commission so they would not be surprised when the guidelines were presented for public comment.

Offense Severity

Constructing a meaningful measure of offense severity required several decisions. The first decision was whether the six statutory grades comprised an appropriate measure. Some commissioners, including one of the authors of the enabling legislation, had assumed that the three felony and three misdemeanor grades were adequate. However, staff suggested that there were problems with relying on the statutory grades. The central argument against doing so was that they were designed to provide statutory maximums for the most serious offense that could occur for any particular crime. It was argued that such a ranking would result in significant contradictions to the goals of sentencing guidelines. For example, third-degree murder and burglary were both first-degree felonies. If they were to receive the same ranking and therefore the same guideline recommendation, the goal of fairness and proportionality implicit in the creation of guidelines would be undermined. Further, this example illustrated for commissioners the fact that guidelines provide sentence recommendations for *typical* offenses, not the most serious possible offense. This discussion resulted in the commission determining that it needed to develop its own offense ranking, one that was to some degree guided by the statutory grading, but that provided further refinement.

The commission considered three options for how best to rank offenses. First, it assessed whether there were sentencing data available from which to derive offense seriousness from past judicial decisions. The commission determined that there was no good comprehensive dataset on which to build the measure of offense severity and thus discarded this approach. A second alternative was to conduct a survey, with respondents asked to rank a list of offenses. This approach was rejected because the commission did not want to delay moving forward until such a survey could be developed and analyzed. Further, because of the large number of statutory offenses, such a survey would have been too time-consuming for respondents. The third alternative, and the approach taken by the commission, was to create a subcommittee to develop the offense ranking. One issue raised by the subcommittee was whether the offense of conviction or the offense behavior as cited in police reports should be the base for the offense severity scale. The commissioners unanimously agreed that conviction facts should serve as the key ingredient of the guidelines. Although research demonstrated that sentencing practices relied on judges' consideration of information that was not part of the conviction offense (as case law permitted), the commissioners felt that many of these factors, such as race, were inappropriate in determining sentencing, and that others should be used to aggravate or mitigate the sentence, when relevant, as opposed to being considered in the guideline measure of offense severity. Thus, from the beginning, the PCS chose not to build its offense severity ranking around "real offense sentencing," as the US Sentencing Guidelines later would.

There was some discussion as to whether using the offense of conviction would provide the prosecutor with too much power to control the sentencing guidelines, but commissioners determined that there was no way to control prosecutors' decisions at any level. Therefore, the commissioners decided to rely on the conviction offense. Later, after the ranking of offenses had been created, the commission returned to the issue of factors that were not a part of the conviction offense when it faced the challenge of establishing guidelines for broadly defined statutes such as burglary, and when it had to meet its statutory mandate to increase penalties for offenses involving possession of a deadly weapon.

The offense severity subcommittee ranked all criminal and drug offenses on a scale of 1 to 10, with 10 being the most serious offense. As the commissioners worked through the ranking of offenses on the ten-point scale, clear principles emerged that would later serve as the basis for ranking offense severity, including new offenses. The principles provided a clear rationale to others who might question the commissioners' ranking of the offenses. The principles were basically that the severity ranking of the offense should be commensurate with the culpability of the offender, and the injury to the victim.

After the subcommittee proposed a set of offense rankings to the full commission,[6] the latter (in a full meeting, with Andrew von Hirsch attending as a consultant) developed a set of principles that represented the factors used in developing the offense rankings. Staff spent considerable time comparing the principles with the offense rankings. These comparisons revealed incongruities and stimulated much debate, but they provided an important opportunity for commissioners to thoroughly review and apply the principles to the offense rankings and reconcile conflicts. This process continued for the duration of the development of the guidelines as staff and others uncovered inconsistencies and presented new issues, despite occasional disgruntlement over what sometimes seemed an endless task.

The ten-point offense scale was the major component of the commission's offense score, and was based on the offense of conviction. However, the commission had a legislative mandate to enhance the guideline recommendation for offenses involving possession of a deadly weapon, which meant that in such instances the commission had to consider offense behavior, not just the offense of conviction. Determining how to best address such offenses was a difficult task for the commission, and also raised concerns among commissioners about offenses involving the infliction of serious bodily injury that was not part of statutory definitions. Consequently, the commission determined to incorporate actual offense behavior for these factors, and to add one point to the offense rank for deadly weapon use, and one point for infliction of serious bodily injury, if they were not already considered in the statutory definition of the offense. Thus this resulted in a twelve-point scale, with the most serious offense of conviction still ranked 10, but with the potential for two points to be added. In addition, the commission lowered the score by one point when the offense was attempted, solicited, or conspired. This decision was supported by statute in that inchoate offenses were ranked one grade lower than the attempted, solicited, or conspired offense if such offense was a first-degree felony (this grading was later dropped). Further, the commission reasoned that there was usually less potential for damage or injury in such inchoate crimes, and that the ranking principles of victim injury supported lower scores for such inchoate offenses compared to completed offenses.

The last phase of the offense ranking occurred during the final days of the guideline development, when the commission was still wrestling with the problem of broadly defined offenses that consequently created inherent unfairness and disproportionality. As the commission reached its closing days before submitting the final guidelines to the General Assembly, it brought in outside commentators to provide critical analysis, including Andrew von Hirsch. Together with the commission's chair, vice chair, and executive director, von Hirsch considered how best to rank the broadly defined burglary statute. Burglary was statutorily graded equal to the most serious felonies, which included rape, third-degree murder, robbery, aggravated assault, and kidnapping, but was viewed as less serious than these offenses because it generally posed less risk of victim injury.

Von Hirsch suggested that the commission subcategorize burglary based on the type of structure burglarized and whether the structure was occupied. The commission's chair and vice chair both supported the idea. The proposal resulted in a four-category measure of the seriousness of burglaries, reflecting whether the burglarized structure was a home, and whether it was occupied. The commission adopted the proposal, which later served as an important model when confronting other broad offenses that challenged the establishment of fair guideline sentences, at the risk of labeling dissimilar offenses similarly.

The PCS's ranking of offenses represents an interesting process of commissioners focusing on the offense of conviction, but subsequently moving toward accommodating offense behavior beyond statutory definitions when confronted with complex fairness issues, such as for burglary, and when statutorily mandated to do so for offenses involving possession of a deadly weapon. The importance of this from the offender's point of view is that, at sentencing, the factors required under the guidelines but not part of the conviction offense would only have to be proven by a preponderance of the evidence. Many years later the US Supreme Court would confront this issue in *Blakely v. Washington* and in the *Booker* and *Fanfan* decisions, which we will discuss later.

Criminal History

The Pennsylvania Commission on Sentencing unanimously agreed that its guidelines needed to incorporate offender characteristics, but debated which offender characteristics should be included. The enabling legislation mandated that the guidelines should consider prior record, but some argued that the guidelines should also incorporate "social stability" factors, such as educational record and employment history. Whether to require consideration of such factors raised considerable debate among commissioners. The argument for incorporating some of these social stability factors rested on the view that the guidelines were not taking in account any positive, mitigating attributes of the offender, and as a consequence were becoming too severe. After a contentious debate, the commission rejected motions to include these factors in the guidelines, for two reasons:

1. They were highly correlated with race, social status, and economic advantage, thereby incorporating disparity into the guidelines.
2. Judges responding to the commission survey did not endorse these factors as universally important at sentencing.

Act 319 required a range of sentences of increased severity for persons "previously convicted of a felony or felonies." The challenge was how to do this and whether prior misdemeanors should also be considered. In Pennsylvania this was more important than in most states, because misdemeanors can be given maximum sentences of five years, two years, or one year, depending on their statutory grading. Developing a fair measure of prior criminal convictions required several key decisions. First, the PCS had to determine whether to weight the value of the offenses depending on their severity and whether and how to consider prior misdemeanor convictions. Second, the commission had to address the controversial issue of including juvenile adjudications.

Creating a prior record measure required considerable discussion. Staff drafted several alternative models, ranging from a simple tabulation of prior felony convictions to a more complex model providing weights to prior offenses depending on their severity. The commission considered using prior sentences as an indicator of the severity of prior offenses. This debate was stimulated by concerns that the offense of conviction did not accurately reflect the offense behavior, because of charge bargaining. But the debate ended quickly because commissioners were convinced that if their key responsibility was to reduce disparity, then use of prior sentences to determine the seriousness of prior records would incorporate past disparities into the guidelines. Ultimately the commission divided prior felonies into three categories, reflecting the severity of the previous conviction, and divided prior misdemeanor convictions into two categories. These were combined into a seven-point scale measuring the frequency and gravity of the prior record. The final measure incorporated the following calculation rules:

1. One point was assigned for a prior record of two or three misdemeanors.
2. Two points were assigned for a prior record of four or more misdemeanors.
3. One point was assigned for each prior felony and each prior weapon misdemeanor, with a maximum of four points for the prior record score.
4. One point was assigned for any prior conviction for an offense ranked 6 or 7 by the commission.
5. Two points were assigned for any prior conviction for an offense ranked 8 or higher by the commission.

The final prior record scoring system did not consider the first prior misdemeanor unless it was a weapon misdemeanor. One much debated issue was whether prior convictions should lapse if the offender had not committed any crimes for a substantial amount of time. The Minnesota sentencing commission's lapse provision helped stimulate discussion among Pennsylvania's commissioners. The Pennsylvania Commission was never comfortable with letting offenses lapse, but did adopt a lapse provision of six years for prior convictions for less serious offenses. This left more serious prior convictions as permanent ingredients in the prior record. But the toughest criminal history issue facing the commission was how to treat juvenile adjudications.

Juvenile Adjudications
Whether to consider juvenile adjudications in the sentencing guidelines raised much debate. In fact, the PCS initially rejected the inclusion of juvenile adjudications because several commissioners argued that the nature of juvenile courts and their focus on "helping" juveniles undermined the rule of law and the legal safeguards inherent in adult convictions. For example, three commissioners argued that this focus on helping juveniles rather than punishing them resulted in a lower standard in determining guilt. In addition, one judicial member of the commission argued that juvenile court recordkeeping was inadequate to use in the guidelines. However, the issue was reopened when Chairman Richard Conaboy, after returning from the 1980 summer meetings of the Trial Judges Association, reported that judges strongly criticized the exclusion of juvenile adjudications.

This empowered those who had initially argued for including juvenile adjudications. Their rationale was that excluding juvenile adjudications would result in the exclusion of information that current judges consider extremely relevant as an important culpability indicator in sentencing. Despite this reversal from exclusion to inclusion, the commission still had to decide which circumstances and which juvenile adjudications to include in the prior record. One of the judges who had argued for exclusion of prior juvenile adjudications convinced the commission that it needed to require an "express finding" that the juvenile was being adjudicated for a particular offense. The express finding was intended to eliminate adjudications where the record failed to indicate clearly that the court had found "beyond a reasonable doubt" that the juvenile had committed a particular offense. This policy imposed a standard on the juvenile courts that the commission felt would limit the use of juvenile adjudications in the guidelines, and improve juvenile courts' adjudicating procedures.

Beyond requiring an express finding, the PCS also imposed two other restrictions on the use of juvenile adjudications in the sentencing guidelines. The primary concern of the Trial Judges Association, as expressed to Judge Conaboy, was that courts needed to consider juvenile adjudications for serious offenses. To address the judges' concern, and accommodate those on the commission who preferred no consideration of juvenile adjudications, the commission decided to limit juvenile adjudications to offenses ranked 6 or higher on the offense gravity score. This limited juvenile adjudications to serious felonies. The second issue was whether to impose an age limit on juvenile adjudications that would be considered in the guidelines. The commission decided that it would only count adjudications of offenses committed at age fourteen and above.

Legal Status Factors

Another important decision faced by the PCS was whether to include "legal status" factors, such as probation or parole status at the time of the current offense, in the measure of offender characteristics. The commission determined that these factors were already included as part of the prior record score in terms of the conviction offense, and therefore determined that to include them would result in "double counting." Further, some commissioners argued that revocations of probation or parole already resulted in punishment, and thus that any further punishment would be unfair. In fact, Senator George Gekas, chair of the Senate Judiciary Committee, expressed particular concern regarding the fact that offenders were punished for parole violations and then were also punished for the violation offenses; he believed that further punishment, under the sentencing guidelines, would exacerbate the problem.

By the spring of 1980 the PCS had developed its guideline matrix. The next challenge was to establish sentence recommendations that would fit within this newly created matrix, which required the commission to assemble and analyze data on current sentences.

Developing Sentence Recommendations

The PCS's guideline matrix—comprising twelve categories of offense severity, ranked according to the offense gravity score, and seven categories of prior record—provided eighty-four cells in which to structure sentences. While the commission was developing the matrix structure, staff worked with consultants, including Kay Knapp from the Minnesota sentencing commission, in designing a data collection effort to compile information on past sentencing practices. These data were seen as crucial to ensuring an informed discussion of the appropriate penalties to include in the guideline matrix, and of the likely impact of guideline sentences. Although the commission was not instructed in Act 319 to consider correctional resources, it recognized that it was necessitary to inform the General Assembly, the Department of Corrections, and the Board of Probation and Parole of the potential impact on correctional resources. But early on, the major role of the data was to guide decisionmaking. While the judges on the commission had sentenced many offenders, no one had any sense of overall sentencing patterns, nor did individual judges have a good sense of their own overall sentencing practices. The data proved crucial in this phase, reining in the commission as it began to decide for whom it wanted to recommend incarceration and how long the sentences should be.[7]

To build a base of information, the commission compiled a dataset of 1977 sentencing decisions.[8] A 12 percent county-based random sample from each of Pennsylvania's sixty-seven counties was identified. Trained data collectors traveled to each county and collected information on offenders and sentences given from court records, including pre-sentence reports. By the time the commission started discussions about setting sentences, staff had compiled the sentencing information to guide the development of an in/out line (Parent 1988) and establish sentence length ranges.

Although the PCS had sought to develop a prescriptive guideline model, it used the sentencing data as a base from which to establish its actual recommendations in the sentencing guideline matrix. Staff prepared many charts based on the data from the statewide sample, indicating where cases fell within the matrix, the proportion of cases that resulted in incarceration sentences, and the average minimum and maximum sentences.[9]

There were several key sentencing issues facing the commission. The first was to establish how the guidelines would approach the incarceration decision. This raised several important questions. First, would there be an imprisonment demarcation as well as an overall incarceration jail line? That is, would incarceration be differentiated by state prison or by county jail? (Our sentencing analyses in later chapters illustrate the empirical importance of this state prison versus county jail decision for disparity and sentencing differences between county courts.) Second, would the matrix allow for nonincarceration as a presumptive sentence?

Incarceration Guidelines
The in/out guidelines. The Minnesota guidelines provided an important benchmark for the PCS as it tried to determine how detailed the guidelines

should be (see Parent 1988 for a detailed discussion of Minnesota's decision-making process). The Minnesota sentencing commission had developed a guideline system that presumptively set which combination of offense severity and prior record should result in imprisonment, but that did not specify who should *not* be incarcerated, nor did Minnesota's guidelines provide guidance for county jail sentences (likely because Minnesota's guidelines did not apply to misdemeanors).[10] However, Pennsylvania's commissioners thought it necessary to provide a more comprehensive set of guidelines that would cover misdemeanors as well as felonies, because Pennsylvania statute labeled as misdemeanors crimes that would be punished as felonies in most other states. To illustrate, in Pennsylvania, first-class misdemeanors are eligible for statutory maximums of up to five years, and second-class misdemeanors are subject to statutory maximums up to two years. In most states these offenses would typically be classified as felonies, making offenders eligible for state incarceration. The statutory grading of many traditional felonies as misdemeanors means that the vast majority of sentences in Pennsylvania are for misdemeanants, and thus that sentencing provisions for misdemeanants can have substantial impact on local and state resources. The commissioners felt that, given their responsibility to reduce sentencing disparity, it would be irresponsible not to provide guidelines for these offenses. Ultimately, this decision would present political problems for the commission. Judges and prosecutors thought the guidelines severely restricted their discretional authority. Defense attorneys thought the guidelines severely restricted their charge-bargaining options.

The sentencing data collected by PCS staff provided strong benchmarks for building the guideline sentences. The first set of analyses demonstrated that the key factor in determining both the decision to incarcerate and the incarceration length was the current conviction offense. Less significant than seriousness of the offense, but a powerful predictor of sentencing decisions, was the defendant's prior record. Importantly, the ranking developed by the commission was very consistent with the scaling of offenses based on sentencing decisions. This reinforced the validity of the commission's rankings.

The assignment of sentences to cells in the guideline matrix first focused on the incarceration versus probation decision. Staff provided information on the distribution of type of sentence for each cell in the guideline matrix. The goal was to determine if past practices could substantially guide their decision-making. As expected, at the extremes of increased offense severity, state incarceration was the typical sentence; for the least serious offenses, probation was the predominant sentence. Fortunately, there were clear breaks between the cells that represented majority incarceration for offenders, and the neighboring cells that represented below-majority incarceration. Using this natural break as an incarceration line created a natural relationship between offense severity and criminal history in structuring the incarceration decision. This in turn emulated the modified "just desert" model created by the Minnesota sentencing commission, in which the primary sentencing factor was the offense of conviction, with prior record playing an important but secondary role.

Since prior record is primarily used to identify offenders who are at increased risk of committing future crimes (implying the focal concern of "community protection"), prior record is generally used as a tool to incapacitate and deter offenders (also see von Hirsch 1976 for a discussion of a retributive role of prior record). Thus the relationship between severity of the offense and prior record expresses the focus on fair retributive punishments, along with concern for incapacitation and deterrence, in the Pennsylvania sentencing guidelines. The flatter the slope of the in/out line, the greater the emphasis on the offense and the lesser the emphasis on prior record.

Pennsylvania sentencing data supported the commission's inclination to emphasize severity of the offense over prior record. Thus the demarcation between cases in which 60 percent of offenders were sentenced to imprisonment, and cases in which less than 40 percent of offenders were imprisoned (according to the sentencing data) established a benchmark for a modified "just desert" model. Figure 2.1 shows there were two incarceration lines in the initial guideline matrix. The upper line was an imprisonment line, with state incarceration recommended for all offenders above that line. The second line was a jail line, with jail sentences recommended for all offenders above that line and below the state incarceration line. Below the jail line were thirteen cells in which the PCS recommended alternatives to incarceration. Establishing presumptive nonincarceration guideline cells was bound to raise concerns that judges would have to aggravate the sentence in order to incarcerate the offender, although sentencing practices supported the argument that nonincarceration was the typical sentence in those cells.

Setting guideline sentence lengths. The setting of sentence lengths began with staff presentations on past sentencing practices. One key decision was how to establish guidelines for indeterminate penalties that were retained under Pennsylvania's guideline legislation. Commissioners deliberated on whether to establish guidelines for both the minimum sentence and the maximum sentence, or just the minimum or the maximum sentence. Because there is no "good time" (i.e., early release for good behavior) in Pennsylvania, and because the minimum sentence sets parole eligibility, judges on the PCS and judges at conferences had argued that the minimum sentence was the key, because they viewed the minimum as the fair term of incarceration absent misconduct in prison. Also, judges generally presumed that offenders would be released at the expiration of the minimum. The second piece of information came from the Board of Probation and Parole, which reported that the average time served was 102 percent of the minimum sentence.[11] This meant that the minimum sentence, at the time of the initial drafting of the guidelines, was the presumptive term of confinement. With judges seeing that the minimum sentence was predictive of the desired

Figure 2.1 Proposed Guidelines Matrix, 1980

Offender Score

Offense Score		0	1	2	3	4	5	6
	12	78–84	84–90	90–96	96–102	102–108	108–114	114–120
	11	60–66	66–72	72–78	78–84	84–90	90–96	96–102
	10	48–54	54–60	60–66	66–72	72–78	78–84	84–90
	9	36–42	42–48	48–54	54–60	60–66	66–72	72–78
	8	24–30	30–36	36–42	42–48	48–54	54–60	60–66
Prison line	7	8–11.5	12–17	17–22	22–27	27–32	32–37	37–42
	6	4–7	6–9	8–11.5	12–17	17–22	22–27	27–32
	5	0–3 / *	3–6	5–8	8–11.5	12–15	15–18	18–21
Jail line	4	*	0–3 / *	0–5 / *	5–8	8–11.5	12–15	15–18
	3	*	*	*	0–3 / *	2–5	5–8	8–11.5
	2	*	*	*	*	0–3 / *	2–5	5–8
	1	*	*	*	*	*	0–3 / *	0–3 / *

Source: Pennsylvania Bulletin 10 (43), October 25, 1980.
Notes: All sentence ranges are in months. For cells containing both an asterisk (indicating alternatives to incarceration, including probation or probation with special conditions) and a range of months, the guidelines allow either an incarceration sentence within the specified range or any alternative to incarceration.

period of confinement, and the parole board releasing offenders very close to the minimum sentence, it made sense to focus guideline sentence lengths on the minimum sentence, as the PCS consequently did (importantly, this also provides our rationale for focusing on the guideline minimum as the presumptive sentence in our empirical analyses in later chapters).

One of the key debates that played out further when the guidelines were before the General Assembly was the width of the ranges. Those commissioners who believed that the primary focus of the guidelines was to limit discretion, in order to reduce disparity, argued for narrow ranges. The countervailing view came from the commissioners who viewed the guidelines as having an unexpressed purpose of maintaining judicial discretion (versus mandatory minimums). These commissioners argued for wider ranges. In the development of the initial guidelines, the group who supported narrower ranges prevailed. The commission chose to create ranges that increased in width as the length of incarceration increased. Thus the upper tier of the matrix contained cells with a range of twelve months being most common, and the lower tier of the matrix contained cells with a range of three months being most common. Ranges across the measure of prior convictions did not increase in severity as substantially as they did with increases in the offense rankings, because the commission was emphasizing the conviction offense rather than prior convictions.

Aggravating and mitigating under the guidelines. The legislation that created the PCS required that the guidelines "prescribe variations from the range of sentences applicable on account of aggravating or mitigating circumstances." The initial proposed guidelines did this by specifying that the court may increase the sentence for aggravation by moving one cell to the right (or one cell up if the defendant scores 6 on the Offense Gravity Score [OGS]), and may decrease the sentence by one cell to the left for mitigation (or one cell down if the defendant scores 0 on the OGS).

The development of ranges for aggravating and mitigating circumstances opened debate as to whether the commission should specify reasons for aggravating and mitigating sentences, or should leave the reasons to the discretion of the judge and ultimately the appellate courts. The commission ultimately decided to provide a list of exclusive reasons for sentencing in the aggravated and mitigated ranges. Commissioners argued that the list needed to be exclusive because, under Pennsylvania statute, judges' sentencing in the aggravated and mitigated ranges was not a departure from the guideline ranges, but rather an extension of the guideline ranges. The use of a nonspecified rationale for sentencing in the aggravated and mitigated ranges would be a departure from the guidelines.

The exclusive reasons for aggravating and mitigating sentences, included unusual harm to the victim, culpability of the offender, payment of restitution, and cooperation with law enforcement. The first three items were offense-related factors intended to allow the judge to "correct" offense severity rankings. Several commissioners (notably those who had supported inclusion of offender characteristics in the offender score) argued that payment of restitution was a mitigating factor in that it reflected reduced culpability. Cooperation with law enforcement was intended to encourage mitigation of the sentence for plea bargains as well as other forms of cooperation, although there was some concern that decreasing the offense gravity score by one point would be insufficient to encourage negotiated pleas.

The final key issue was how to address concurrent and consecutive sentences. The commission adopted rules that prohibited the use of consecutive sentences under the guidelines except when the multiple conviction arose from different crime episodes or from a series of criminal transactions, and when the most serious offense involved a felony against a person that carried a maximum sentence of twenty years, and the second offense was ranked at least 7 by the commission. Under these circumstances the court was expected to sentence consecutively, but it was "guided" to treat the prior record score as 0 so as to not "double count" that record against the defendant. Overall, then, the guidelines, as originally adopted by the commission for public hearings, represented an ambitious agenda with relatively strict calculation rules, incorporating differentiations between state prison and county jail sentences, and even establishing nonincarceration rules for the least serious offenses.

Projected Guideline Impact

PCS staff projected, based on a comparison of 1977 sentences, that the initial guidelines would likely result in a slight decrease in the number of offenders incarcerated, but in an increase of the minimum sentence of 16.3 months for those incarcerated. It was projected that the guidelines would increase incarceration sentences most dramatically in urban areas, and decrease incarceration sentences in rural counties, reflecting the more lenient sentences that had been the historical pattern in the urban areas.

Public Reaction to the Initial Guidelines

The PCS scheduled five public hearings on these draft guidelines in December 1980. Generally, the tenor of reaction was negative. Legislators, judges, the attorney general–elect, and district attorneys attacked the concept of guidelines themselves, and also their leniency. On the other hand, the private defense bar, the state, and the Public Defenders Association supported the guidelines.

The public hearings unveiled the difficult hurdles the commission faced in attempting to balance severe intercounty disparity (a theme we return to in our empirical analysis and in our concluding chapter), which required it to reduce sentences in the nonurban counties in order to increase them in the urban counties. Without a capacity constraint, the commission had no leverage to counter the arguments for increased penalties. The seven district attorneys who testified all attacked the guidelines as being too lenient and too restrictive of discretion. Judges, although less strident, but no more supportive, were also concerned with the loss of discretion. However, even groups such as the Governors Council on Alcohol and Drug Abuse, which had been consulted extensively and had not raised any concerns regarding sentences for drug offenses or driving under the influence, now opposed the guidelines. Clearly the commission would continue to face considerable opposition unless it acquiesced to the pressure to increase severity and enhance judicial discretion.

The Commission Reconsiders the Guidelines

The PCS's response to the suggestions and the criticisms expressed at the public hearings was hampered by a lack of appointments from the sitting governor. Even though the governor could have replaced the commissioners whose terms had expired, he chose not to do so. This allowed Governor Thornburgh to stay outside the conflicts encircling the commission.

Staff prepared synopses of the concerns raised by the seventy-six individuals who testified before the commission at its public hearings. The chair, Judge Richard Conaboy, began a two and a half day meeting by stating that, from his vantage point, the criticisms were focused on the leniency of the guidelines, their mandatory language, and their failure to allow for different community standards. These three general areas were the focus of the commissioners' discussions as they debated revisions to the proposed guidelines. The commission made numerous changes in the guidelines to address the concern with leniency, but as Susan Martin concluded, "Such a proposal, while arguably equitable and ostensibly responsive to the legislative mandate, was politically unpalatable" (1983, p. 293).[12]

In response to the criticism that the guidelines overly constrained judicial discretion, the commission increased the width of the guideline sentencing ranges. In the upper tier, sentencing ranges were generally changed from six to twelve months, with six months being added to the upper number in each cell in the guideline matrix. This created overlapping ranges between cells in the matrix. The ranges in the middle tier of the matrix were also increased, although not as much as in the upper tier.

The changes were minor, the result of largely invisible tinkering. The guidelines still maintained their fundamental structure, despite the stridency of the law and order argument that sentencing severity should be increased. To address the criticism that the guidelines overly constrained judicial discretion, and that they provided nonincarceration guidelines for 15 percent of matrix cells (representing more than 15 percent of the convicted offenders), the commission merely widened the ranges and reduced the number of cells calling for presumptive nonincarceration from thirteen to five. For the cells that now allowed incarceration, the range became 0–1, so that minimal incarceration would be allowed within the guidelines. However, it was unlikely that this change would chill the criticism that the guidelines were too restrictive and too lenient.

It was clear that the guidelines would face an uphill, if not impossible, struggle to gain acceptance by the General Assembly. The District Attorneys Association, judges, and others were marshaling their forces to stimulate a legislative backlash, characterizing the sentencing recommendations as too lenient.

Guidelines Submitted to the General Assembly

The general consensus on the PCS began to fall apart as the time to submit the guidelines to the General Assembly approached. Three members of the commission—two gubernatorial appointments (a defense attorney and a law professor) and a Philadelphia judge—indicated they did not support the proposed guidelines. The primary reason for their rejection was that the guidelines were too severe and did not consider factors such as education and employment to mitigate sentences. The Philadelphia judge was also concerned with the inclusion of juvenile adjudications in the prior record score. The remainder of the commission supported the guidelines and generally felt that the dissent might be beneficial to the debate. The commission submitted the guidelines to the General Assembly on January 24, 1981, and awaited legislative response.

Without appointments by the sitting governor, Richard Thornburgh, the commission had no access to him, nor to agencies under his authority, such as the Department of Corrections, the Board of Probation and Parole, and the Pennsylvania Commission on Crime and Delinquency. Then the governor sent to the General Assembly his own sentencing proposal, recommending the establishment of five-year mandatory minimums for serious violent felonies committed with a firearm.

This bill presented two problems for the guidelines. First, it emphasized their leniency. Second, it sent the message that the governor did not support the guidelines as proposed. This message was important coming from Governor Thornburgh, who had campaigned for office on a law and order platform and who had a strong law enforcement track record as a US attorney. The governor's indirect assessment amplified the criticisms expressed by the judiciary and the district attorneys.

The guidelines generated controversy in the General Assembly, with many judges criticizing them as too constrictive of judicial discretion and too lenient. They were also criticized by the District Attorneys Association, which was emerging as a strong law and order voice in Pennsylvania. The fate of the guidelines, and perhaps the existence of the commission, was seriously in doubt. According to Susan Martin (1983), the commission could not argue that sentencing leniency was guided by fiscal responsibility and consideration of prison capacity. Nor were the guidelines politically acceptable for any of the groups involved. Judges would lose sentencing discretion and, contrary to determinate sentencing provisions such as in Minnesota and California, they were not getting control over time served. That control continued with the parole board. And district attorneys across most of the state perceived that the guidelines provided more lenient sentences than they were already getting.

The commission silently recognized the problem of prison capacity as an important consideration, even though the legislature had not given it a mandate to consider prison populations. There are many examples of other state sentencing commissions, such as those in Minnesota, Washington, and North Carolina, whose consideration of capacity constraints garnered fiscally conservative support, but no such voices were to be heard in Pennsylvania.

In response to growing criticism, some of the legislative members of the PCS began to work on a rejection resolution that would ensure continuation of the commission and provide revisions to the guidelines, including increased judicial discretion and sentence severity for violent offenders. The resolution was presented to the House and Senate, both of which, by strong majorities, passed it. Interestingly, the concurrent resolution was never presented to the governor, but his silence, his failure to make appointments, and his interest in mandatory minimum legislation clearly indicated his support for a concurrent resolution to reject the guidelines.

With the guidelines rejected, the commission went back to work to respond to the mandate to increase severity for violent offenses and to provide judges greater discretion. The commission prepared for the revisions by collecting more recent sample data with a greater focus on violent offenses, especially those committed in the counties that were most vociferous in their criticism of the leniency of the guidelines. PCS staff collected data from the metropolitan and suburban counties on offenses such as robbery, burglary, aggravated assault, and rape to provide more detailed information to counter the arguments from these counties (Kramer and Lubitz 1985). The commission was also helped in this process by the governor, who now took the opportunity to appoint a district attorney, a defense attorney, and a criminologist to the PCS. With the input of these members, the commission set about the task of responding to the resolution.

The commission widened the ranges in the matrix (see Figure 2.2) to provide more discretion. In order to keep the impact on prison populations at a minimum, the commission left the initial low figures in the ranges the same as in the previous submission, but raised the upper figures. This allowed for both tougher sentences and greater judicial discretion, but also meant that if judges sentenced in the lower part of a guideline range, prison populations would not be significantly impacted. The commission also backed off the restrictive guidelines for the less serious offenses and ultimately provided almost unlimited judicial discretion for misdemeanor offenses. For example, sentences for misdemeanors with a statutory maximum of one year were changed from nonconfinement to ranges of zero to six months, with the zero meaning nonincarceration options. Thus the commission effectively backed away from providing

Figure 2.2   Adopted Guidelines Matrix, 1982

Offense Gravity Score	Prior Record Score	Minimum Sentencing Range (months)
10 Third-degree murder	0 1 2 3 4 5 6	48–120 54–120 60–120 72–120 84–120 96–120 102–120
9 For example: rape, robbery inflicting serious bodily injury	0 1 2 3 4 5 6	36–60 42–66 48–72 54–78 66–84 72–90 78–102
8 For example: kidnapping, first-degree arson, voluntary manslaughter	0 1 2 3 4 5 6	24–48 30–54 36–60 42–66 54–72 60–78 66–90
7 For example: aggravated assault causing serious bodily injury, robbery threatening serious bodily injury	0 1 2 3 4 5 6	8–12 12–29 17–34 22–39 33–49 38–54 43–64
6 For example: robbery inflicting bodily injury, third-degree theft by exertion	0 1 2 3 4 5 6	4–12 6–12 8–12 12–29 23–34 28–44 33–49

continues

Figure 2.2   Cont.

Offense Gravity Score	Prior Record Score	Minimum Sentencing Range (months)
5 For example: third-degree criminal mischief, third-degree theft by unlawful taking, third-degree theft by receiving stolen property, bribery	0 1 2 3 4 5 6	0–12 3–12 5–12 8–12 18–27 21–30 24–36
4 For example: theft by receiving stolen property, less than $2,000, by force or threat of force, or in breach of fiduciary obligation	0 1 2 3 4 5 6	0–12 0–12 0–12 5–12 8–12 18–27 21–30
3 Most first-degree misdemeanors	0 1 2 3 4 5 6	0–12 0–12 0–12 0–12 3–12 5–12 8–12
2 Most second-degree misdemeanors	0 1 2 3 4 5 6	0–12 0–12 0–12 0–12 0–12 2–12 5–12
1 Most third-degree misdemeanors	0 1 2 3 4 5 6	0–6 0–6 0–6 0–6 0–6 0–6 0–6

Source: Pennsylvania Bulletin 12 (4), January 23, 1982.

Notes: These offenses are listed here for illustrative purposes only; offense scores are given in § 303.7. Weapon enhancement: At least twelve months and up to twenty-four months confinement must be added to the above lengths when a deadly weapon was used in the crime.

almost any guideline direction or constraint for the least serious offenses. To further expand judicial discretion, the commission dropped the provisions that restricted consecutive sentences, the list of aggravating and mitigating reasons, and the lapsing of prior convictions. The guidelines were submitted to the legislature and adopted with little fanfare. They became effective for all offenses committed after July 12, 1982.

The Commission Rests

The mid-1980s were a time of consolidation and relative quiet after the turbulence of the late 1970s and the early 1980s. However, there were two developments that are important to the history of the Pennsylvania Commission on Sentencing: a constitutional challenge to the 1982 concurrent resolution that rejected the initial guidelines, and the national move to toughen drug sentences. These developments, briefly reviewed in the next chapter, provide important backdrop to the commission's guideline revisions in the 1990s.

Notes

1. The 1870 meetings of the National Prison Association (later to become the American Correctional Association) adopted the Declaration of Principles, which declared that the purpose of incarceration was to reform the offender. The organizational model proposed was a division of labor whereby the court would determine whether an offender was to be incarcerated, but the length of time served would be determined by a parole authority, which would be informed by recent behavior of the offender as an indication of readiness for release.

2. This sentiment was particularly strong in the suburban counties surrounding Philadelphia, where district attorneys frequently cited cases in which a defendant, on being arrested and discovering that they were being taken to the county seat of a suburban county, was heard to exclaim, "Where are you taking me?" followed by "Oh, no!" when told where, given the defendant's awareness of the tougher sanctions they would receive. In fact, many times during the implementation training sessions, judges publicly expressed criticism of the sentencing guidelines, pointing out that the only reason that guidelines had been developed was to counter the weak sentences given by Philadelphia's judges.

3. As of this writing there is proposed legislation (HB 3, 4, and 5) that would broaden the commission's mandate to write parole revocation guidelines and parole release guidelines and that would add the secretary of corrections and the chair of the Board of Probation and Parole to the commission as ex officio members.

4. The efforts of Judge Richard Conaboy were instrumental in garnering the support of the Trial Judges Association. Judge Conaboy was a strong supporter of the guideline concept and of the legislation. He viewed guidelines as providing judges with a benchmark for the calculation of the sentence, but as permitting the judge great latitude in setting the actual sentence. Further, the guidelines were viewed as a lesser threat to judicial discretion than mandatory minimums.

5. The full membership of the commission included Senators George Gekas (Dauphin County) and James Kelley (Westmoreland County); Representatives Anthony Scirica (Montgomery County) and Norman Berson (Philadelphia County); Judges

Richard Conaboy (Lackawanna County), Curtis C. Carson (Philadelphia County), Myrna Marshall (Philadelphia County), and John W. O'Brien (Allegheny County); District Attorney Robert Colville (Allegheny County), defense attorney Michael Minney (Lancaster County), and law professor Albert Palaez (Duquesne University).

6. One commissioner, a sponsor of the enabling legislation, argued for using the statutory rankings rather than the proposal. However, given the strong arguments of commissioners, staff, and consultant Andrew von Hirsch, he ultimately supported the commission's ranking system.

7. Susan Martin (1983) reported in her analysis of the PCS that Judge Conaboy and a couple other commissioners were mistrustful of statistics and reluctant to rely on PCS staff. This is true in some respects, but it oversimplifies the relationships. Overall, commissioners understood the importance of statistics and relied upon them considerably as the data were reported during the development of guideline sentences. Data from past sentencing practices became crucial in crafting where to establish presumptive incarceration sentences and where an appropriate demarcation between county jail and state prison sentences might be drawn. Also, she reported that the PCS did not follow the staff work plan. This is also a mischaracterization of the staff-commissioner relationship. Actually, the commissioners' process and timeline for collecting data and developing the guidelines were very consistent with the staff work plan. In fact, one of the criticisms is that the commission tried to go too far in the guidelines. For example, the presumptive nonconfinement in several guideline cells that later resulted in criticism of the commission was a staff proposal based on data indicating that most offenders to whom these guideline cells applied received nonincarceration sentences.

8. Although a more recent sample would have been preferable, the Administrative Office of Pennsylvania Courts, which collected the case-processing information that was needed to identify cases, did not have access to post-1977 data at the time the sample was being developed.

9. One of the important debates within the staff was whether to quantify nonincarceration sentences as "zero" in calculating the average sentences, or to provide an average only for those who received incarceration sentences. Because sentences in the guidelines would apply to all offenders categorized within a particular cell of the matrix, staff chose the former option.

10. Dale Parent (1988) reviewed the decisions of Minnesota's sentencing commission, particularly its decision to focus the initial guidelines on state imprisonment.

11. Personal communication, February 1980, from the chair of the Board of Probation and Parole to the executive director of the PCS. This average time served before release increased substantially in the 1990s and early 2000s, up to 127–133 percent of minimum by 2002 (as shown by data provided by the Pennsylvania Department of Corrections).

12. The commission increased the penalty if the offender possessed or discharged a firearm; raised the rank of rape and assaults; and denied application of the guidelines to white-collar crime and major drug dealers in response to criticism from district attorneys regarding leniency of sentences for these offenders.

3

Pennsylvania's Commission Meets New Challenges

WRITING GUIDELINES AND getting them implemented is perhaps viewed as the key role of a sentencing commission, but it could be argued that the real challenge is for a newborn sentencing commission to take its position as a significant player in the criminal justice system. The viability of sentencing commissions as institutional actors is a key issue, and there are examples of states that created commissions only to have them abolished, such as Wisconsin and Tennessee, or that developed guidelines but failed to get them implemented, such as Massachusetts. Another significant disappointment is that, in general, sentencing commissions have been relatively unsuccessful in leading change after the initial development and implementation of sentencing guidelines. For example, the two most heralded guideline systems, those in Minnesota and Washington, have changed little since their inception. In this chapter, we review some of the challenges that the Pennsylvania Commission on Sentencing (PCS) faced after implementation of its initial guidelines, with the key question concerning whether it began to play an important leadership role and the factors that assisted or hindered that emergence.

Mandatory Drug Sentences and Sentencing Guidelines

The mid-1980s were marked at the national level by dramatic and hardening reactions to drug offenses. The states, Pennsylvania in particular, played a role in the attempt to curb drug use and drug trafficking by increasing penalties for drug crimes. At the federal level, Congress passed legislation creating the US Sentencing Commission (USSC) in 1984. But, too impatient to wait for the submission of sentencing guidelines to address drug penalties, Congress passed mandatory minimums for drug trafficking in "crack" and powder cocaine, also in 1986. The attention generated by the federal action stimulated states, including Pennsylvania, to pass mandatory minimums in order to attack the drug problem. The Pennsylvania Commission on Sentencing, in response

41

to the increasing pressure for sentences targeting drug trafficking, developed a separate set of guidelines for drug offenses. But while these guidelines were before the General Assembly, the Pennsylvania Supreme Court ruled in *Commonwealth v. Sessoms* (532 A.2d 775 [1987]), declaring the concurrent resolution to reject the 1981 guidelines (described in the previous chapter) unconstitutional, because the governor had not signed it. The *Sessoms* decision effectively vacated the current guidelines and any subsequent revisions to those guidelines, so the commission quickly withdrew its separate set of guidelines for drug offenses, which were then before the legislature.

With no guidelines in effect, and no clear sense of when they would come into effect, the path was open to push through a mandatory minimum bill that had been before the legislature, but had shown no signs of passage. This bill now quickly passed both houses and was signed by the governor. Notably, it established relatively low thresholds (compared to the federal level) for the application of mandatory minimums, with a two-year mandatory minimum for trafficking in 2–10 grams of heroin, and a three-year minimum if the person had a prior record for drug trafficking. Other mandatory minimums targeted cocaine and marijuana, and later methamphetamine.

While this was occurring, some argued that the rejected 1981 guidelines were actually still in effect, and others argued that no guidelines were in effect. Some judges considered the guidelines and some did not. The PCS immediately began to rectify the problem by resubmitting the current (1987) guidelines, with the proposed changes to drug sentences, to the General Assembly.

With the normal time line for passage, this would have required the commission to submit the guidelines for public hearings, readopt the guidelines, and then resubmit them to the General Assembly. The General Assembly would then have had ninety days to reject by concurrent resolution. But the commission had requested another ninety-day period, following the initial ninety-day rejection period, so that it could train judges and others in applying the guidelines, prior to their implementation. The General Assembly had accepted the commission's request and enacted legislation to allow for a training period.

However, in view of the *Sessoms* decision, the General Assembly wanted to speed the process of reimplementation of the guidelines, and quickly passed legislation to revoke the ninety-day training period, so that the guidelines would go into effect at the end of the ninety-day rejection period. The commission republished the guidelines, held public hearings, revised the guidelines, and quickly resubmitted them for consideration by the General Assembly. The guidelines went back into effect in June 1988.

This legislative response to reenact the guidelines and speed their implementation reflected an important change in the political stature of the commission and the guidelines in the middle to late 1980s, as compared to the early 1980s. No one called to let the guidelines die as a result of the *Sessoms* decision; rather, legislative and gubernatorial support were quickly reinforced.

As with the 1982 guidelines, the sentencing recommendations under the revised guidelines were not set to track mandatory minimums. In all other guideline systems of which we are aware, mandatory penalties are used as baselines for sentences. Pennsylvania's sentencing commission determined that there were valid reasons to establish penalties different from (and generally more lenient than) mandatory minimums. The commission argued in the early 1980s that its guidelines were appropriately independent of the legislatively adopted mandatory minimums, because they represented more complex and comprehensive sentencing standards. The commission argued, for example, that whereas mandatory minimums generally only consider the offense, the guidelines consider prior convictions and deadly weapon use. Further, the commission believed that in order for the guidelines to be fair, they had to be inherently proportional; to adjust the guidelines to be commensurate with mandatory minimums would either distort all sentences or violate the commission's ranking principles. For example, while the commission distinguished in its ranking between completed offenses and attempted offenses, the mandatory minimum legislation made no such distinction. This was a difficult decision, because establishing guidelines different than the mandatory minimums effectively resulted in sentencing disparity. Second, it empowered the prosecutor to determine whether to file a motion to impose the mandatory minimum or let the guidelines provide the sentencing recommendation. Surprisingly, there was no backlash from the legislature, the governor, judges, or the district attorneys. This contrast of sentencing provisions is still maintained in Pennsylvania (we examine sentencing under the guidelines and mandatory minimums as alternative sentencing provisions in Chapter 8).

Guideline Revisions in the 1990s

An increase in Pennsylvania prison populations from 8,000 in 1980 to more than 22,000 in 1990 led to major growth in the budget of the Bureau of Prisons, and garnered the General Assembly's attention. Within this context there were innovative developments in other state guideline systems to divert offenders to "intermediate punishments" (Tonry 1996), and research on the effectiveness of offender treatment (e.g., drug treatment) was rejecting the view of the 1970s that "nothing works" (Martinson 1974). These changes provided a wedge opportunity for the Pennsylvania Commission on Sentencing to engage in comprehensive review of its sentencing guidelines.

One challenge the PCS faced was turnover of commissioners and how to maintain the energy and commitment of those who had led the enactment, development, and promotion of the sentencing guidelines. The commission undertook periodic reviews of the guidelines in order to educate new commissioners on the subtle and complex decisions on which the guidelines had been built, and to give new commissioners an opportunity to revise the guidelines.

This process was intended to build commitment as well as to ensure that the guidelines reflected the most recent information available.

A major justification for establishing a sentencing commission is to build a dynamic, innovative organization that can continuously evaluate sentencing and ensure informed sentencing policy through guidelines. To this end, the PCS determined in 1990, as the guidelines approached their tenth anniversary, to undertake a comprehensive review. The focus of the review and its resultant revisions centered on (1) narrowing the guideline ranges (including establishing presumptive nonconfinement for the least serious offenses), (2) establishing philosophical premises for guideline sentences, (3) broadening the use of nonconfinement options so as to reduce the reliance on incarceration, and (4) reducing the severity of some of the nonviolent sentencing recommendations, while (5) increasing the severity of the recommendations for violent felonies. In many respects, the key goal of the guideline revisions was to address criticisms expressed by Michael Tonry (von Hirsch et al. 1987) and others (see, for example, Martin 1983). But more importantly, the revisions were intended to reflect a changing political climate in which reliance on incarceration was becoming a fiscal concern, and in which the PCS was viewed as the key agency to address the emerging correctional crisis.

Guideline Ranges

Pennsylvania's guidelines were criticized by many for providing judges too much discretion, because they provided extremely wide sentencing ranges, including ranges for aggravating and mitigating circumstances; this discretion was extended even further by weak appellate review. Tonry observed that "the effect of Pennsylvania's three wide ranges allows enormous scope for variation without departures"; as a result, he concluded that the PCS had failed "to establish meaningful guidelines" (1987, p. 24).

While Tonry's criticism might be an overstatement, it had considerable justification as a result of the commission's revisions in meeting the requirements of House Resolution 24 of 1981, which rejected the initially proposed guidelines. In the face of academic criticism and growing prison populations, and bolstered by eight years of monitoring data, the commission set about systematically reviewing each component of the guidelines.

Increases in Sentencing Severity
for Serious Violent Offenders

As part of its comprehensive review, the PCS compared its guidelines to those in other states (Kramer, Lubitz, and Kempinen 1989). This study revealed that in comparison to Minnesota's and Washington's guidelines, Pennsylvania's were more lenient for violent offenders and harsher for nonviolent offenders. These findings provided a serious challenge to the commission. They raised serious questions about how well the guidelines were protecting the public from violent offenders, and at the same time raised concerns about the invest-ment of correctional resources in confining nonviolent offenders. This study helped stimulate careful reexamination of the guidelines in the early 1990s, eventually resulting in revisions in 1994 and 1997. In another study conducted by the commission, it was found that departures were most frequent for the more serious offenses, as ranked by offense gravity score. These departures were generally downward, particularly for aggravated assaults. Thus the mon-itoring data pointed to inadequacies in the distinctions the commission had made in ranking offenses and determining guideline sentences. The message that judges were sending was that, for many offenses, the guidelines seemed to provide appropriate penalties, but for others, such as aggravated assault, the guidelines prompted inadequate penalties. For each of the more serious of-fenses, the first set of rankings failed to adequately distinguish among them. To do this, the PCS expanded the number of categories that measured offense severity, from three categories to six, thereby expanding the OGS from ten to thirteen categories. This refinement allowed the commission to make impor-tant distinctions among offenses that had previously been grouped together, which had put pressure on judges to depart from the guidelines or to treat dis-similar offenders similarly. Also, it allowed the commission to naturally nar-row the guideline ranges. In 1997 the commission added another offense severity category, resulting in a ranking of these offenses from 9 to 14.

From the focal concerns perspective (described in Chapter 1), judges were in effect telling the commission that the guidelines were failing to address two cru-cial sentencing issues. For offenses with high departures, the guidelines were set-ting sentences that exaggerated the culpability of the offender, or providing penal-ties that failed to protect the public, or both. James MacElree, a district attorney, in 1993 commenting on aggravated assault compared to other violent felonies, stated, "For aggravated assault, often the loser goes to the hospital and the win-ner goes to jail." This comment brought to the commissioners' attention the often mutual culpability of the offender and the victim, and reflected the need to sepa-rate aggravated assault from other serious felonies such as rape and robbery.

Table 3.1 presents 1994 and 1997 changes in the guideline recommenda-tions for major offenses (identified as serious violent offenses in 42 Pa. C.S. § 9714: sentences for second and subsequent offenses).[1] For murder, attempted murder, rape and involuntary deviate sexual intercourse, and robbery with se-rious bodily injury, the commission increased the minimum of the standard guideline range in both 1994 and 1997. For burglary of an occupied home, the recommendation stayed the same—eight months—in 1994, but in 1997 was raised to twelve months.

Establishing Ranges for Less Serious Offenses

Typically, most guideline systems allow almost total discretion in setting the penalties for the less serious offenses. Sentencing commissions leave the

Table 3.1   Change in Sentencing Guidelines for Serious Violent Offenses (in months)

Offense	Pre-1994 Guidelines	1994 Guidelines	1997 Guidelines
Third-degree murder	48–120	60–120	72–240
Attempted murder	24–48	30–48	60–78
Rape/IDSI	36–60	42–60	48–66
Robbery (SBI)	36–60	42–60	48–66
Robbery (ASBI)	8–12	8–20	22–36
Aggravated assault (SBI)	24–48	8–20	22–36
Aggravated assault (ASBI)	24–48	8–20	22–36
Kidnapping	24–48	30–48	22–36
Burglary (occupied structure or home)	8–12	8–20	12–24
Burglary (unoccupied structure)	0–11.5	RS–6	RS–9
Aggravated indecent assault	24–48	8–20	22–36

Note: Sentencing guideline recommendations based on a prior record score of zero.

sanctions for the less serious offenses to judicial discretion for two reasons. First, their mandate frequently requires them to focus on state incarceration and to manage prison populations. Second, commissions find it difficult to write specific guidelines for sentences to probation or local jail due to the wide diversity of local resources across a state. These issues concerned the Pennsylvania Commission on Sentencing as well. Pennsylvania has sixty-seven counties, across which there exists great disparity in local correctional resources. Consequently, although concerned with the disparity that might result from providing broad discretion for these offenses, the commission determined in revising the initial guidelines rejected by the General Assembly to leave almost total sentencing discretion to the judge for these less serious offenses. For example, it set ranges of minimum sentences of zero to six months at OGS 1 (with "zero" meaning probation). The vast majority of these offenses were third-degree misdemeanors for which the maximum sentence possible was six to twelve months. For the rest of the lower part of the guideline matrix, the commission provided ranges of zero to eleven and a half months. The reason for cutting off the range at eleven and a half months was to set a guideline for a county jail sentence, because a typical such sentence in Pennsylvania was eleven and a half to twenty-three months. The effect of these guidelines was that they provided minimal limitations on the court. Thus, judges had almost unlimited discretion in terms of both whether to confine the offender and the length of confinement. The guidelines did indicate that if an offender was confined, the confinement should be in a county facility. Under Pennsylvania statute, if the court sentenced in the aggravated range and set minimums at twelve months or longer, this would be a state sentence (i.e., the sentence would place the release and time-served decisions under the jurisdiction of the state Board of Probation and Parole, and *could* be served in the state prison system).

When the PCS undertook its first comprehensive review of the guidelines in the early 1990s, the political and economic context was considerably different from that of the late 1970s and early 1980s, when the commission was writing the first guidelines. One key change was an escalating prison overcrowding problem, despite tremendous expansion of the prison system during the 1980s and early 1990s. Second, there was growing concern among legislators that state investment in prisons was straining the state budget.[2] Third, the growth in prison populations was primarily being caused by the incarceration of nonviolent offenders. And finally, there was a growing belief that many of these nonviolent offenders, drug offenders in particular, could more effectively be dealt with through nonincarceration sentences, especially drug treatment.

Legislative Support for Diversion

An opportunity to garner support for guideline changes arose when Senator Stewart Greenleaf sponsored a community corrections bill that recognized prison growth as a budgetary issue as well as the fact that many incarcerated offenders were nonviolent offenders who could be as effectively, if not more effectively, sanctioned through nonincarceration options. The problem was that this bill showed no signs of attaining passage in the legislature. However, in the late summer of 1990, numerous Pennsylvania officials attended a corrections conference in Washington, D.C. The conference provided an opportunity for these officials to discuss the problem of the expanding state prison population and the role that sentencing alternatives to incarceration could play in alleviating this problem. Some attendees suggested that Senator Greenleaf's bill provided a possible vehicle to encourage the development of community-based alternatives to imprisonment. The challenge was how to obtain support for the bill. The Pennsylvania contingent included the chair of the PCS, Judge Theodore McKee, as well as its executive director, along with representatives of the attorney general's office and key legislative and gubernatorial staff. This bipartisan group caucused at the conference to consider what they could do, and decided that the Community Corrections bill provided a vehicle for change. But two key changes to the bill would be needed to make it viable. First, the group identified the title of the bill as a problem, because it sounded too "soft" on crime. To address this concern, it was determined that a title such as "intermediate punishment" would be more likely to draw political acceptance. Second, the bill needed to link the current guideline revisions to intermediate punishment, and so an amendment was drafted to mandate that the PCS identify appropriate offenders for intermediate punishment. With a strong, more "punitive"-sounding title, a new mandate, and the commitment of the conference attendees, the bill easily passed as Act 193 of 1990 (Intermediate Punishment Act) before the end of the legislative session.

Act 193 formally created intermediate punishments as a sentencing option and was intended to stimulate the development of a range of penalties between probation and incarceration, such as drug treatment, electronic monitoring, and other nonincarceration options. Many if not all of these options were being used in some counties for some offenders as a condition of probation. Act 193 served as a legislative endorsement of these penalties as appropriate alternatives to incarceration sentences, and removed them from the probation designation, which had been publicly labeled as lenient. Passage of Act 193 was an important endorsement for increasing the available resources for community corrections, and to do so in a way that would not "widen the correctional net" by enhancing the penalties for offenders who historically would have received probation. This responsibility rested with the PCS.

Act 193 directed the commission to identify offenders for "intermediate punishment." But the commission faced a challenge. It was beginning a comprehensive revision of the guidelines, intended to not only divert nonviolent offenders from incarceration, but also to review sentences for violent offenders, the width of guideline ranges, and many of the policies that had been abandoned after the legislative rejection of the initial guidelines. In order to avoid derailing the comprehensive revision of the guidelines, and yet meet the mandate of Act 193, the commission decided to undertake a minor revision to establish presumptive nonconfinement when the offense gravity score was 1 or 2 and the prior record score (PRS) was 0. Then, bolstered by the directive and implicit support given in Act 193, the commission pursued comprehensive revision of the guidelines.

1994 Guideline Changes

In the 1980 guidelines, the PCS had recommended nonconfinement for many less serious offenders. The 1994 guideline revisions reestablished presumptive nonconfinement for eight cells in the guideline matrix (OGS/PRS: 1/0, 1/1, 1/2, 1/3, 2/0, 2/1, 2/2, and 3/1). In addition, whereas under the pre-1994 guidelines the ranges were extremely wide, the 1994 guidelines reduced these ranges considerably. For example, for cell 3/0, where the range was zero to six months, the commission reduced the range to restorative sanction (RS) to restrictive intermediate punishment (RIP); and for cell 4/0, where the range was zero to eleven and a half months, it was reduced to RS to three months. It should be noted that the 1997 changes reversed some of the 1994 changes by allowing some incarceration in several of the cells previously limited to nonconfinement. This 1997 "adjustment" reflected the continuing concerns that resulted in rejection of the 1980 guidelines under the rubric of crime control. From a focal concerns perspective, the arguments against presumptive nonconfinement raised "protection of the public" issues by arguing that taking away the right to incarcerate offenders was undermining deterrence.

Establishing Intermediate Punishment Guidelines for Mid-Range Offenses

The third key goal of the commission in revising the guidelines was to reduce the reliance on incarceration for the "mid-range" offenses (i.e., OGS 6–9 in the 1994 guidelines, and OGS 6–8 in the 1997 guidelines). The offenses targeted in the "mid-range" were the less serious forms of burglary, many theft offenses, and trafficking in small and medium amounts of drugs. Both the 1994 and the 1997 guidelines developed provisions to encourage the use of intermediate punishments as alternatives to incarceration for these offenders. The 1994 changes provided intermediate punishment alternatives to county incarceration sentences, and referred to these as Level 3 offenders. In the 1997 changes, the commission created a fourth level that expanded intermediate punishments to target offenders in guideline ranges that called for state incarceration sentences. Figures 3.1 and 3.2 show the 1994 and the 1997 sentence guideline matrices, respectively.

The PCS had two primary focal concerns in mind in creating these levels. First, it wanted to identify sentencing alternatives that would be more effective at rehabilitating offenders than traditional incarceration. Second, it wanted to maintain fairness, such that similar offenders were treated similarly in terms of the severity of their sentences. The commission balanced the twin goals of effectiveness and equity by narrowly defining the eligible programs as "restrictive intermediate punishment." The commission defined RIP "as programs that provide for strict supervision of the offender" (PCS 1997, 9), and limited their availability to counties that had been granted authority by the Pennsylvania Commission on Crime and Delinquency to use RIP sentencing. The support for structured sentencing alternatives that focus on treatment rested on confidence throughout the Pennsylvania criminal justice system that rehabilitation was often more effective than incarceration. This view was supported by recent findings on the effectiveness of drug treatment (see Anglin and Hser 1990 for a review of research that the commission used to support its position).

Figure 3.1, the 1994 guidelines sentencing matrix, delineates the cells identified as Level 3 and Level 4. The Commission identified Level 3 and Level 4 offenders using a combination of the OGS and the PRS. Offenders of OGS 6–8 with a PRS of 0 are Level 3, but even an OGS as low as 1 can designate an offender as Level 3 if the PRS indicates repeat felony offender (RFEL) status. Similarly, Level 4 offenders may have OGS scores as low as 3 when the PRS indicates RFEL status.[3]

Sentencing Reforms in Pennsylvania

As noted previously, three years after Pennsylvania adopted a broad set of mandatory minimums for drug offenses, it reversed course and passed an inter-

Figure 3.1   Revised Guidelines Matrix, 1994

Level	Offense Gravity Score	Example Offenses	Prior Record Score						RFEL	REVOC	AGG/MIT
			0	1	2	3	4	5			
	13	Third-degree murder	60–120	66–120	72–120	78–120	84–120	90–120	96–120	120	+12 / -12
Level 4 Incarceration	12	Drug delivery resulting in death; PWID cocaine, etc. (> 1,000 grams)	54–72	57–75	60–78	66–84	72–90	78–96	84–102	120	+12 / -12
	11	Rape (IDSI); robbery (SBI); aggravated assault (SBI); PWID cocaine, etc. > 100–1,000 grams)	42–60	45–63	48–66	54–72	60–78	66–84	72–96	120	+12 / -12
	10	Voluntary manslaughter; arson (person inside); PWID cocaine, etc. > 50–100 grams)	30–48	33–51	36–54	42–60	48–66	54–72	60–84	120	+12 / -12
Level 3 Incarceration County Jail/ RIP trade	9	Burglary (home and or person present); aggravated assault (cause BI with weapon); robbery (threatened SBI); robbery (inflict BI); aggravated assault (attempted SBI); aggravated individual assault; PWID cocaine. etc. (> 10–50 grams)	8–20	12–27	15–30	21–36	27–42	33–48	39–60		+6 / -6
	8	Involuntary manslaughter, homicide by vehicle (when DUI); PWID cocaine, etc. (2.5–10 grams); PWID marijuana (> 10–50 pounds); arson (person not inside); burglary (home and or person not present); theft ($50,001–$100,000)	6–18	9–21	12–24	18–30	24–36	30–42	36–48		+6 / -6
	7	Involuntary manslaughter, homicide by vehicle (no DUI); statutory rape; theft ($25,001–50,000)	4–12	7–15	10–18	16–24	22–30	28–36	34–42		+6 / -6
	6	Aggravated assault (attempt BI with weapon); burglary (not a home, person present); arson (property); escape (secure facility); PWID cocaine, etc. (< 2.5 grams)	3–9	6–11	9–15	12–18	15–21	18–24	21–27		+3 / -3

Level	Offense									AGG / MIT
Level 2 Incarceration RIP RS	**5** Burglary (not a home, no one present); theft (> $2,000–25,000); corruption of minors; firearms (loaded); robbery (removes property by force); PWID marijuana (1–10 pounds)		RS-6	1-6	3-9	6-11.5	9-15	12-18	15-21	+3 / -3
	4 Indecent assault; forgery (will, etc.); firearms (unloaded); criminal trespass (breaks into buildings)	RS-3	RS-3	RS-6	RS-9	3-9	6-11.5	9-15	12-18	+3 / -3
	3 Theft ($200–2,000); PWID marijuana (< 1 pound); drug possession; forgery (money, etc.); simple assault; retail theft (third or subsequent offense)	RS-RIP	RS-3	RS-6	RS-9	3-9	6-11.5	9-15		+3 / -3
Level 1 RS	**2** Theft ($50 – < $200); bad checks; retail theft (first or second > $150); retail theft (second offense < $150)	RS	RS	RS-RIP	RS-RIP	RS-6	1-6	3-9		+3 / -3
	1 Most third-degree misdemeanors; drug paraphernalia; small amount of marijuana; theft (< $50)	RS	RS	RS-RIP	RS-RIP	RS-6	RS-6			+3 / -3

Notes: When the offender meets the statutory criteria for boot camp participation, the court should consider authorizing the offender as eligible. Shaded areas of the matrix indicate that restrictive intermediate punishment may be imposed as a substitute for incarceration. When restrictive intermediate punishments are appropriate, the duration of the restrictive intermediate punishment program shall not exceed the guideline ranges. When the range is RS through a number of months (e.g. RS-6). RIP may be appropriate. When RIP is the upper limit of the sentence recommendation (e.g. RS-RIP), the length of the restrictive intermediate punishment programs shall not exceed 30 days.

Key:

AGG	= aggravated sentence addition
BI	= bodily injury
ISDI	= involuntary deviate sexual intercourse
MIT	= mitigated sentence subtraction
PWID	= possession with intent to deliver
REVOC	= repeat violent offender
RFEL	= repeat felony offender
RIP	= restrictive intermediate punishment
RS	= restorative sanction
SBI	= serious bodily injury
11	= county sentence of less than twelve months
<	= less than
>	= greater than

Figure 3.2   Revised Guidelines Matrix, 1997

Level	OGS	Prior Record Score						RFEL	REVOC	AGG/MIT
		0	1	2	3	4	5			
	14	72–240	84–240	96–240	120–240	168–240	192–240	204–240	240	+/–12
Level 5	13	60–78	66–84	72–90	78–96	84–102	96–114	108–126	240	+/–12
State incarceration	12	48–66	54–72	60–78	66–84	72–90	84–102	96–114	120	+/–12
	11	36–54 BC	42–60	48–66	54–72	60–78	72–90	84–102	120	+/–12
	10	22–36 BC	30–42 BC	36–48	42–54	48–60	60–72	72–84	120	+/–12
	9	12–24 BC	18–30 BC	24–36 BC	30–42 BC	36–48 BC	48–60	60–72	120	+/–12
Level 4 State incarceration/ RIP trade	8	9–16 BC	12–18 BC	15–21 BC	18–24 BC	21–27 BC	27–33 BC	40–52	NA	+/–9
	7	6–14 BC	9–16 BC	12–18 BC	15–21 BC	18–24 BC	24–30 BC	35–45 BC	NA	+/–6
Level 3 State/ county incarceration RIP trade	6	3–12 BC	6–14 BC	9–16 BC	12–18 BC	15–21 BC	21–27 BC	27–40 BC	NA	+/–6
Level 2 County incarceration RIP RS	5	RS–9	1–12 BC	3–14 BC	6–16 BC	9–16 BC	12–18 BC	24–36 BC	NA	+/–3
	4	RS–3	RS–9	RS–<12	3–14 BC	6–16 BC	9–16 BC	21–30 BC	NA	+/–3
	3	RS–1	RS–6	RS–9	RS–<12	3–14 BC	6–16 BC	12–18 BC	NA	+/–3
Level 1 RS	2	RS	RS–2	RS–3	RS–4	RS–6	1–9	6–<12	NA	+/–3
	1	RS	RS–1	RS–2	RS–3	RS–4	RS–6	3–6	NA	+/–3

Notes: Aggravated and mitigated ranges add or subtract, respectively, the months shown from the standard range. Shaded areas of the matrix indicate that restrictive intermediate punishment may be imposed as a substitute for incarceration. When restrictive intermediate punishment isappropriate, the duration of the restrictive intermediate punishment program shall not exceed the guideline ranges. When the range is RS through a number of months (e.g., RS–6), RIP may be appropriate.

Key:
AGG   = aggravated sentence addition
MIT   = mitigated sentence subtraction
NA   = not applicable
RS   = restorative sanctions
REVOC   = repeat violent offender
RFEL   = repeat felony offender
RIP   = restrictive intermediate punishment
<   = less than
>   = greater than
BC   = boot camp

mediate punishment bill intended to reduce the state's growing reliance on incarceration. This legislation mandated that the PCS identify offenders to be shifted from incarceration to community-based intermediate punishment. The sentencing guideline revisions in response to this bill took almost three years to implement following passage. Time was needed to gather the necessary information regarding effectiveness of treatment alternatives, and to study the guideline monitoring data for sentencing trends. Further, PCS staff, two commissioners, and representatives of the Pennsylvania Commission on Crime and Delinquency traveled to Oregon and Washington to talk to representatives of those states' sentencing commissions, as well as to prosecuting attorneys, judges, and others regarding alternatives to incarceration in sentencing guidelines. Also, PCS staff were involved in a nationwide study of structured sentencing undertaken by the National Institute of Justice, and this provided them the opportunity to travel to many other states in preparing a report for the Bureau of Justice Assistance (1996).

Sara Steen, Rodney Engen, and Randy Gainey frame one of the conflicts: when guidelines "encourage judicial decision making to move away from the more formal goals of uniformity and just deserts inherent in sentencing guidelines" (2005, p. 451). The issue they raise is the shift from the philosophical premise of retribution to rehabilitation, and the risk that sentencing disparity may result. The PCS's first challenge was to address this very conflict. Consequently, the commission wrestled with distinguishing intermediate punishments from probation and then establishing proportionality among those various punishments. After much deliberation on the issue, the commission established a simple, two-category classification based on the extent of offender monitoring provided.[4]

The less severe category of intermediate punishments was labeled "restorative sanction." The commission (Pa. C.S. Fourth:8) defined RS as

nonconfinement sentencing options that:

(i)   Are the least restrictive in terms of constraint of the offender's liberties;
(ii) do not involve the housing of the offender (either full or part time); and
(iii) focus on restoring the victim to pre-offense status.

Examples of these RS options were community service programs, probation, outpatient treatment, and drug-testing programs.

The guideline revisions primarily focused, however, on diverting incarceration-targeted offenders to community-based alternatives. For these offenders, the commission developed programs it called "restrictive intermediate punishment." The RIP concept was developed to cover alternatives to incarceration that house the offender full- or part-time, significantly restrict the offender's movement, and monitor the offender's compliance (42 Pa. C.S. § 303.12). By narrowly defining the concept, the commission assured the General Assembly that these sanctions were both considerably more severe than traditional probation, and further that the sanctions were relatively equivalent to incarceration.

A key purpose of RIP sanctions was to attack the recalcitrant problem of drug addiction, which was viewed as a major driving force behind the crime problem and the growing pressures of the prison population boom. Consequently, the guideline revisions focused on diagnosis and treatment of drug-addicted offenders.

RIP sanctions included drug and alcohol treatment, house arrest with electronic monitoring, boot camps, or combinations of sanctions that provided for sufficient surveillance and sufficient offender accountability to be equivalent to incarceration. Once the commission had identified these sanctions, it then identified cells in the guideline matrix where RIP sentences would be appropriate replacements for incarceration. In the 1994 guideline revisions, the commission created four levels in the guidelines so that courts could easily identify candidates eligible for RIP. Specifically, the commission created Level 3, for which the guidelines prescribed county imprisonment or short terms of state confinement.

In 1997 the commission revised the guidelines and expanded RIP eligibility by increasing the number of guideline levels to five and crafting Level 4, according to which offenders who had been prescribed state incarceration were eligible for RIP sentences. Figure 3.2, showing the 1997 sentencing guideline matrix, clearly delineates the cells identified as Level 3 and Level 4 for which RIP sentences were provided as substitutes for incarceration. The development of RIP sentences for state prison–bound offenders was important for two reasons. First, it widened the diversion net considerably. Second, it provided an argument to use state funding to support the diversion of offenders from state incarceration.

The state initially provided $7 million in support of the RIP guidelines. Eligibility for funding required that counties develop intermediate punishment programs to assess available and needed correctional resources, review current procedures, and develop goals and objectives for effective utilization of correctional resources (42 Pa. C.S. § 9806). The state criminal justice planning agency (the Pennsylvania Commission on Crime and Delinquency) reviewed these proposals and determined whether to fund them and, if so, the level of support. In the most recently passed budget (July 15, 2007), General Assembly support for RIP sentences grew to $17.9 million.

Implementing Guideline Changes

The 1994 guideline changes were met with two major criticisms. One came from probation officers, who argued that probation already incorporated intermediate punishment and that the changes were of little substantive merit. County-level officials were also concerned with the PCS's push for counties to assume the costs of dealing with prison problems. The other key criticism came from the Philadelphia district attorney's office in the form of a memo detailing that the increases in severity for the more serious offenses had been overstated by the commission, and were inadequate (Eisenberg 1994). While none of these criticisms diverted the General Assembly from adopting the proposed 1994 guidelines, they did raise legitimate concerns that the commission felt needed to be addressed.

The most significant concern was the funding of intermediate punishment, particularly the relatively expensive RIP drug and alcohol treatment. The commission felt that for the guidelines to have a significant impact on diverting offenders, there needed to be financial support for the counties. To do this, the commission joined forces with the Pennsylvania Commission on Crime and Delinquency to develop a funding base. There were many components to this process, but the key aspect was to convince the governor's office that funding of RIP sentences would divert offenders from state prison and thus result in cost savings. A broad-based committee of state and county agencies, including treatment providers, was created to determine how best to establish cost-saving treatment programs, including how best to estimate the number of offenders who be diverted from incarceration.

To undertake such an estimate, the committee decided to survey district attorneys, since they held the key power in diverting offenders. The committee first selected a sample of county cases. The district attorney from each county was then interviewed and asked to review the cases to determine whether he or she would support diversion of the sample offenders from incarceration to RIP sentences if there were RIP programs available. Based on these interviews, the committee compiled a list of characteristics of offenders who could be diverted, and then estimated numbers and costs accordingly.

The governor's budget officer would only support funding if it was likely to divert offenders from state incarceration. Further, the diversion of an offender would save only an estimated $4,000 per year, because there was no anticipation that prisons could be closed. This meant that only the cost savings from food, clothing, and healthcare could be used to form a budget estimate. Ultimately, the governor supported funding that was targeted for RIP drug and alcohol treatment. As indicated above, funding started in 1997 with $7 million, and has since grown with the support of data indicating that changes in the guidelines diverted offenders from state incarceration, and that treatment was effective at reducing recidivism (although data on the latter were limited; see Ulmer and van Asten 2004).

Guideline Changes Since 1997

Since 1997 there have been only minor changes to the guidelines, and no changes to the basic matrix. However, one important policy change did take place: the decision in 1998 to release judge-by-judge sentencing information. Historically, the PCS had recorded the monitoring data by judge, but had not generally released this information. Judges in Pennsylvania are elected to ten-year terms and then stand for retention election. Although it is rare that a judge will lose a retention election, the politics of sentencing, and the potential for sentencing information to be used to portray judges as lenient, raised concerns that PCS data would become a "scorecard" for assessing judges. This caused two concerns. One concern was that if judges feared that information would be released, they might fail to report the data. Second, there was concern that judges might increase the severity of their sentencing practices to appeal to the "tough on crime" stance. Further, there was considerable judicial hostility to the initial guidelines, in terms of both the restriction of judges' discretion and the work of calculating the guidelines and developing the guideline reporting forms. To have released this data would have incurred additional hostility that the commission did not want to face in 1982, after the General Assembly's rejection in 1981. Thus, when developing a comprehensive database to monitor judicial sentencing practices, the PCS determined that it would be best to keep judicial identifiers confidential.

However, in the late 1990s, the commission revisited this issue as a result of three key challenges (Bergstrom and Mistick 2003). First, Philadelphia Newspapers Inc., publisher of the *Philadelphia Inquirer,* requested access to the commission's computer records under the Right to Know Act (P.L. 390, June 21, 1957). Second, a trial judge requested individual sentencing information to defend himself against charges that he had violated the Code of Judicial Conduct. Finally, the US Senate Judiciary Committee requested sentencing information on a trial court judge who had been nominated to the federal bench, and subsequently the judge asked that her sentencing information be provided to the committee.[5] The PCS determined that, as a legislative agency, it was not subject to the Right to Know Act and therefore did not have to release the information. But in the other two cases, the commission disseminated information in deference to a request from the sentencing judge. As a result, the commission was wary that it might face lawsuits regarding release of the information and the pressure on individual judges to request information on their own sentencing records as part of their election campaigns or as a part of their nomination to the federal bench. Thus, to avoid such challenges, the commission decided in 1998 that the information it collected was public information, and that it needed a policy to guide the release of this information. A public hearing on the policy drew concerns regarding the accuracy of the data, the initial promises by the commission to keep information of individual judges confidential, and the increased politicalization of sentencing. Despite this testimony, the commission determined that release of the information was consistent with the fact that adult court records are public information, and consistent with its own status as a publicly funded agency.

This decision had some positive outcomes. Primarily, it improved reporting by judges in the monitoring forms developed by the commission. Since its decision to release judge-specific information, the commission has developed an electronically based reporting system that allows for logical consistency checks to improve the accuracy and enhance the efficiency of the data reporting and compilation process. It also allows for data from other information systems (such as police arrest records) to be linked into the commission's data, further enhancing the compilation process.

Enforcement of Guidelines: Appellate Review

The key enforcement mechanism for sentencing guidelines rests with the appellate review process. There is much focus on enforcement through the appellate courts (see, for example, Reitz 1997), but one caution is in order. It should be remembered that the vast majority of cases are guilty pleas, which means that appeals are unlikely; in the federal system, there is even a growing use of waiver of the right to appeal as a part of negotiated pleas. This does not mean that appellate review does not influence these cases, because it may. For example, in Pennsylvania, appellate review is minimal. Such minimal review means that the sentencing judge has the last word except in very rare cases. This means that defense attorneys know that they have little hope of getting a severe sentence overturned, and may consequently be more prone to encourage clients to plead guilty. On the other hand, in jurisdictions such as the pre–*Booker* era federal system, if the judge sentences above the guidelines, defense attorneys may believe that they will stand a better chance on appeal because of the presumptiveness of the federal guidelines. We do not want to speculate too far in this regard, but merely want to suggest that the appellate review process may affect negotiated pleas as well as the cases that are taken on appeal.

In Pennsylvania, a judge is required to consider the guidelines and to provide a "contemporaneous written statement" supporting the sentence when he or she sentences above or below the standard range. Act 319, which created the PCS, established that sentences can be reversed when the guidelines are erroneously applied, when a sentence within the guidelines is "clearly unreasonable," or when a sentence outside the guidelines is unreasonable (42 Pa. C.S. § 9781[c]). Further, Pennsylvania statute allows appeals "at the discretion of the appellate court where it appears that there is a substantial question that the sentence imposed is not appropriate under this chapter" (42 Pa. C.S. § 9781[b]). The commission decided that it did not have the authority to include in the guidelines any clarification for appellate review.

The result of relatively weak legislative appellate standards and a silent commission resulted in what Kevin Reitz viewed as "overdoing appellate restraint" or a "de minimus role in the enforcement of guidelines" (1997, p. 1471). Actually, this is an oversimplification of appellate review of Pennsylvania's guidelines, as our discussion will reflect. We rely heavily here on two thorough reviews of Pennsylvania appellate history, by Jody Hobbs (1996) and Judge Pat Tamilia and John Hare (2000).

There have been at least two phases to appellate review. The first, which we will call the pre-*Devers* phase, started in 1982 and ended in 1988. The second is the post-*Devers* phase. By way of background, Pennsylvania has two intermediate courts of appeal. The Commonwealth Court's jurisdiction over public sector appeals involves state and local governments, agencies, ordinances, and the like. The Superior Court has appellate jurisdiction over private sector appeals, including criminal law, in cases involving sentencing and, of key interest here, the application of sentencing guidelines (Pa. Act of 1973, 17 PS 211.402, 211.403 [Supp. 1973]).

The PCS anticipated that the Superior Court would effectively develop a common law of sentencing, but, as Judge Patrick Tamilia and John Hare (2000, p. 300) note, there were two opposing conceptions of appellate review of sentencing. One conception strongly respected judicial discretion. The other position, less deferential of judicial discretion, required sentencing judges to carefully document their sentencing decisions and required appellate courts to hold sentencing judges accountable for their decisions and to carefully hold judges to the purposes of the sentencing guidelines, to reduce sentencing disparity. Tamilia and Hare argue that during the pre-*Devers* era, Superior Court reviewed guideline appeals consistent with relatively strong enforcement of the guidelines by holding them to a "reasonable" standard on review.

There are two general areas of review (Tamilia and Hare 2000). One form of review is referred to as procedural: Did the sentencing court follow the proper procedures? Did it apply the guidelines and, if so, apply them correctly? Did it provide a contemporary written justification for the sentence? The second form of review is substantive: the appellate court analyzes the justifications for the sentence as provided by the sentencing court. During the pre-*Devers* phase, Superior Court held the lower courts to both review standards. For example, in *Commonwealth v. Royer* (328 Pa. Super. 60, 476A.2d 453 [1984]), the court held that a contemporaneous written statement must be provided at the sentencing proceeding, in the defendant's presence, and must be recorded and transcribed. The more crucial role in enforcing sentencing guidelines results from a more substantive analysis of sentencing decisions. In this arena, the pre-*Devers* Superior Court moved strongly to fulfill the PCS's goal of creating a common law of sentencing.

Probably the most important appellate issue concerned the departures of sentencing courts from the guidelines. In the guidelines rejected by the legislature, the PCS had provided an exclusive list of reasons for departures, but in the adopted guidelines the commission had dropped the list, in response to a directive that the commission should provide the sentencing courts more discretion. This left the responsibility to the Superior Court to determine appropriate justifications for departures from the guidelines or for aggravating or mitigating a sentence. In *Commonwealth v. Mattis* (352 Pa. Super. 144, 507 A.2d 423 [1986]) and *Commonwealth v. Septak,* (359 Pa. Super. 375, 518 A.2d 1284 [1986]) sentences below the guidelines were remanded for resentencing, rejecting the lower court's support for sentences that rested on the rehabilitative needs of the offender. Further, the pre-*Devers* court held in several cases that deviations based on factors that are already considered in the guidelines were inappropriate. For example, in *Commonwealth v. Stevens* (349 Pa. Super. 310, 503 A.2d 14 [1986)]) and *Commonwealth v. Drumgoole* (341 Pa. Super. 468, 491 A.2d 1352 [1985]), the court rejected the lower court's use of prior record as a reason for departure, because prior record was incorporated into the guidelines. The court did uphold the lower court's support for a departure sentence above the guideline based on prior juvenile adjudications that were not counted in the prior record score. Jody Hobbs (1996) reports that between 1982 and 1988, 321 appeals were filed with Superior Court related to the discretionary aspects of sentencing. In general, Superior Court did not defer to the lower court judges in their reviews, but this frame came to an end with the Pennsylvania Supreme Court's ruling in *Commonwealth v. Devers* (352 Pa. Super. 505 A.2d 1030).

In *Commonwealth v. Devers,* the Pennsylvania Supreme Court rejected the Superior Court's rulings calling for separate written opinions supporting a sentencing decision, and even went so far as to state:

> Where pre-sentence reports exist, we shall continue to presume that the sentencing judge was aware of relevant information regarding the defendant's character and weighed those considerations along with mitigating statutory factors. A pre-sentence report constitutes the record and speaks for itself. . . . Having been fully informed by the pre-sentence report, the sentencing court's discretion should not be disturbed. This is particularly true, we repeat, in those circumstances where it can be demonstrated that the judge had *any* degree of awareness of the sentencing considerations, and there we will presume also that the weighing process took place in a meaningful fashion. It would be foolish, indeed, to take the position that if a court is in possession of the facts, it will fail to apply them to the case at hand. (pp. 18–19)

The *Devers* ruling established a "presumption of reasonableness" (Hobbs 1996, p. 951) when a judge has a pre-sentence report. This decision effectively eliminated the Superior Court's ability to provide substantive review of sentencing judges' sentencing discretion. It should be noted that there have been Superior Court panels who tried to challenge the discretionary aspects of sentencing (see, for example, *Commonwealth v. Jones,* 538 A.2d 497 [1988] and *Commonwealth v. Smart,* 564 A.2d 512 [1988]), but the chilling impact of *Devers* clearly moved appellate review of sentencing to a procedural review and undermined the guidelines' ability to reduce sentence disparity. In fact, the Supreme Court in *Devers* directly rejected the fairness focus of the guidelines and the legislature, seeming to prefer unfettered judicial discretion. In 1996, Hobbs noted the Superior Court's reluctance to give up on substantive review of sentencing, and seemed to signal the potential for a third phase of appellate review in which the Superior Court might resurrect more substantive review of judges' sentencing discretion.

Subsequent to Hobbs's and Tamilia and Hare's assessments of appellate review, there still seems to be a tension between Superior Court's substantive review in the pre-*Devers* phase and the appellate standard set by the Supreme Court in *Devers*. For example, in *Commonwealth v. Diaz* (867 A.2d 1285 [2005]), the court ruled that chronic depression did not warrant reduction of sentence for burglary; and in *Commonwealth v. Stewart* (867 A.2d 589 [2005]), the court found that the trial court had abused its discretion when it enhanced sentences based on charges that were nolle prossed. In *Commonwealth v. Cortez* (860 A.2d 1045 [2004]), the Superior Court also remanded the sentence, because the trial court's reasons did not justify imposition of an aggravated sentence of fifteen to thirty years. In *Cortez*, the Superior Court argued that the defendant's conduct of "spreading his cancer" throughout neighborhoods lacked firm evidentiary support. In *Commonwealth v. Mola* (838 A.2d 791 [2003]), the Superior Court found that the trial court had abused its discretion when declaring that it would give the statutory maximum to "anybody convicted of a drug offense." The Superior Court found in *Mola* that imposing a standardized sentence on all drug offenders is an abuse of discretion. While these cases suggest a return to a more substantive review, the shadow of *Devers* severely constrains the Superior Court's substantive review. For example, *Commonwealth v. Boyer* (856 A.2d 149 [2004]), *Commonwealth v. Pollard* (832 A.2d 517 [2003]), and *Commonwealth v. Cunningham* (805 A.2d 566 [2002]) reflect the constraining effect of manifest abuse of discretion standard.

The US Supreme Court's opinions in *Blakely v. Washington* (124 S. Ct. 2531 [2004]) and *United States v. Booker/Fanfan* (125 S. Ct. 738 [2005]) have had major impact on the federal sentencing guidelines and on many state guideline systems as well. The basic issue at law in *Blakely* and *Booker* was whether judges may increase a sentence based on factors not presented to a jury or proven beyond a reasonable doubt. *Apprendi v. New Jersey* (530 U.S. 466 [2000]) foreshadowed the Supreme Court's view of Sixth Amendment rights at sentencing. In *Apprendi*, the Supreme Court ruled that any factor (other than prior record) "that increases the penalty for a crime beyond that prescribed statutory maximum must be submitted to a jury, and proved beyond a reasonable doubt" (p. 490). In *Blakely*, the Supreme Court extended *Apprendi*, ruling that factors that increase a defendant's sentence under Washington's sentencing guidelines must be presented to the jury. In *Booker/Fanfan*, the Supreme Court applied the ruling in *Blakely* to the federal sentencing guidelines. Subsequent to *Booker/Fanfan*, the Supreme Court has ruled that the appellate courts may use a "presumption of reasonableness" standard for sentencing inside a guideline range (*Rita v. United States*, 127 S. Ct. 2456 [2007]). Additionally, in *Kimbrough v. United States* (128 S. Ct. 558 [2007]), the Supreme Court ruled on the issue of whether the judge could consider the disparity between the federal guidelines' treatment of crack and powder cocaine, and found that such disparity is an appropriate factor for sentencing consideration. Finally, in *Gall v. United States* (128 S. Ct. 586 [2007]), the Supreme Court overturned an Eighth Circuit opinion that required "proportionality review" of departures—that is, the notion that departures greater in magnitude required greater justification.[6] The question is whether these decisions apply to Pennsylvania's sentencing guidelines.

The Pennsylvania Supreme Court addressed the applicability of Blakely to the Pennsylvania guidelines in *Commonwealth v. Yuhasz* (923 A.2d 957 [2007]). Yuhasz pled guilty to one count of statutory sexual assault, a second-degree felony punishable by up to ten years. The guidelines provided a sentencing range for the minimum sentence of six to fourteen months for Yuhasz who had a prior record score of zero. The sentencing court departed above the guideline range and gave a sentence of twenty-four to sixty months. Yuhasz appealed the departure above the guidelines arguing that *Blakely* required that only facts proven by a jury beyond a reasonable doubt can be used to enhance the sentence beyond the guideline range. The court viewed the key issue as whether Pennsylvania's sentencing guidelines were mandatory or advisory and cited its decision in *Mouzon* (812 A.2d 617, 621[2002]), where it concluded that "the trial courts retain broad discretion in sentencing matters, and therefore, may sentence defendants outside the Guidelines." The Court found in *Yuhasz* that the guidelines are "merely advisory" because of the broad discretion retained by judges at sentencing and therefore *Blakely* does not apply.

The Pennsylvania Commission on Sentencing as an Institution

Michael Tonry's assessment of the initial guidelines was that "there appear to be a number of reasons for the Pennsylvania Commission's failure to establish meaningful guidelines" (1987, p. 24). One important purpose of this chapter has been to highlight some significant changes to Pennsylvania's sentencing guidelines since they were implemented and to explore how the role of the commission has changed since Tonry's 1987 assessment. Our review has highlighted changes that, when viewed from broader contexts, reflect a shift in the commission's stature since the 1981 resolution that rejected the initial guidelines. At that point, the future of the commission was much in doubt, and its ability to influence the direction of legislation was certainly unlikely.

But by 1990 there were several key factors indicating that the role of the commission had changed. First, in 1984, the PCS faced and survived sunset review. Unless legislation reestablishing the PCS were passed, the commission would have been eliminated. With no agency to monitor their application, it is likely that the guidelines would have been eliminated as well. After public hearings in which not only the PCS but also other agencies testified, legislation was sponsored that would establish the commission as a permanent agency. At that time, the commission was an independent agency, operating under the budget of the Administrative Office of the Pennsylvania Courts (AOPC).

Interestingly, in the summer of 1984, the total budget of the AOPC was cut 5 percent at the very end of the fiscal year. As a result, the budget of the PCS was cut as well. Subsequently, the PCS's executive director met with Senator Richard Tilghman, the chair of the Senate Appropriations Committee, and inquired about the reason for the budget cut. Tilghman apologized, indicating that the cut had not specifically targeted the commission. The importance of this story is not that the commission's budget was cut, but that as the commission's sunset legislation was moving through the Senate, Tilghman introduced a minor amendment that designated the commission as an agency of the General Assembly. This action, undertaken by the powerful chair of the Appropriations Committee and a senator who represented the counties in a suburban area of Philadelphia that had been particularly hostile to the initial guidelines, represented an important shift in the role of the PCS. With the unanimous passage of the reauthorization legislation, and with its new designation as a legislative agency, the commission entered the mid-1980s in a new role and with new avenues to build a budget for special projects such as guideline revisions.

We have already noted other legislative actions in 1987–1988, when the commission's guidelines were found unconstitutional in *Sessoms,* and the speed with which the guidelines were reconstituted to affirm the General Assembly's commitment to them. We have also noted the PCS's role in revitalizing the Intermediate Punishment Act, and the specification in that act that the PCS was to identify offenders for whom such punishment would be appropriate.

These actions demonstrate how the commission's stature had risen considerably since 1980. Further, the commission's ability to join forces with other agencies, particularly the Pennsylvania Commission on Crime and Delinquency, in obtaining funding for RIP in the mid-1990s, reinforced its proactive role in sentencing policy. During this same time frame, Pennsylvania, like many other states, was contemplating legislation to create boot camps. Again, the sponsor of the legislation, Representative Dwight Evans, met with the Department of Corrections and the executive director of the PCS to discuss the legislation and his desire for the commission to lead research evaluating the effectiveness of boot camps. He selected the commission because it was an agency that had taken on, as one of its major roles, the evaluation of sentencing decisions, and he was distrustful of the Department of Corrections evaluating its own program. As of this writing, there is legislation pending (Pennsylvania HB 4)—with support from the Board of Probation and Parole, the Department of Corrections, the District Attorneys Association, and others—that would extend the PCS's mandate to write parole and re-parole guidelines, broaden its research responsibilities, and enlarge its membership by including the secretary of corrections and the chair of the Board of Probation and Parole in an ex officio capacity. This bill, if passed, will coordinate Pennsylvania's fragmented, indeterminate sentencing system by establishing a single agency, the PCS, as the guideline-developing body, in terms of the incarceration decision, the length of incarceration, and now the release and revocation process. Further, it will correct what we have viewed as an unfortunate oversight in the initial membership of the commission by bringing in correctional representation (see Chapter 2). In addition, while the commission's initial mandate did not direct it to consider correctional resources, passage of this bill will encourage the consideration of correctional resources in the adoption of parole guidelines. The legislation states that the guidelines shall "provide for prioritization of incarceration, rehabilitation and other criminal justice resources for offenders posing the greatest risk to public safety" (HB 4:4). This would result in a major expansion of the commission's purview, mission, and influence. We know of no other sentencing commission at this time that would have similar responsibility and scope.

The question concerns the reason for this apparent change in the stature of the PCS. In Susan Martin's critique of the commission (1983), she raised several reasons for its failure to get the initial guidelines passed, including the chair's lack of political involvement and the executive director's lack of political experience. To some degree, the commission's shifting role may reflect the changing role of its leadership and particularly their increased political connections. For example, when the initial chair left the commission due to his appointment to the federal bench, he was replaced by Judge Anthony Scirica, who was one of the key drafters of the commission's enabling legislation when he was a state representative. Scirica, however, still had strong legislative connections. And as a Republican, he had better access to Governor Thornburgh's office. He was a very important chair for the commission, as he helped establish its credibility.

Further, PCS staff served important roles in using the guideline monitoring data in projecting prison populations and in assessing the impact of proposed legislation. In this role, the commission established its credibility as an agency that can provide helpful and accurate data that have not been available in the past.

Another boost was the fact that, as commissioners served their terms and were replaced, there was a cadre of former and current commissioners who seemed to have developed respect for the commission's function and operation. In part, the commission was constantly evaluating the guidelines. As other states developed guidelines, the decisions of these commissions were used by PCS staff to encourage PCS commissioners to reconsider their sentencing guidelines. This was bolstered by the formation of the National Association of Sentencing Commissions in the 1980s, whose annual meetings provided commissioners and staff opportunities to consider particular approaches to particular problems.

Whether this justifies the PCS being labeled an "institution" is perhaps questionable. It has been institutionalized to the degree that the legislature has established it as a permanent agency; its work has resulted in funding for RIP, and it has been specifically delegated additional responsibility under intermediate punishment and boot camp legislation. Whatever the cause, the commission has become a significant force, and perhaps even a leader in the development of Pennsylvania's sentencing policy.

Notes

1. Both the PCS and the legislature debated about whether burglary was a property crime or a violent crime. When the commission originally attempted to develop an offense severity ranking for burglary, it confronted a single burglary statute that encompassed entering a structure with intent to commit a crime. The extreme breadth of behavior under the burglary statute made it impossible for the commission to comfortably fulfill its responsibility to set fair sentencing standards that captured the risk to victims and the culpability of the offender. To resolve this dilemma, the commission subcategorized burglary depending on whether the burglarized structure was a home or not and whether the structure was occupied. In Act 193 the General Assembly created a second-degree felony burglary category for unoccupied nonhomes that would be eligible for intermediate punishment. The rest of the burglaries were left as first-degree felonies ineligible for intermediate punishment. Subsequently, the General Assembly, in a special session on crime in 1994–1995, identified burglary of an occupied home as a serious violent crime for purposes of three-strikes legislation.

2. In one appropriation hearing for the PCS, a legislator exclaimed to the PCS executive director that Pennsylvania was moving toward a billion-dollar corrections budget and asked what the PCS could do about it.

3. The guideline revisions developed a more refined prior record measure identifying some offenders as repeat violent offenders (REVOC) and some as repeat felony offenders (RFEL).

4. Michael Tonry (1996, chap. 4) provides a very good discussion of the incorporation of intermediate sanctions into sentencing guidelines while maintaining the integrity of the guideline focus on retribution.

5. The PCS executive director met with staff of the Senate Judiciary Committee to request the information. The committee had heard charges that the judge had a lenient sentencing record and wanted to examine the sentencing record to test the claims. Ultimately, with the judge's agreement, the PCS provided general information to the committee.

6. The Supreme Court, in overturning the decision, stated that the court "must consider the extent of the deviation and ensure that the justification is sufficiently compelling to support the degree of the variance . . . but must give *due deference* to the district court's decision that the 3554(a) factors, on a whole, justify the variance" (emphasis added).

4

Sentencing Serious Violent Offenders

IN ITS 1997 revisions, the Pennsylvania Commission on Sentencing intended to make its guidelines more consistent with policy changes that emerged out of the governor's 1994–1995 special session on crime, as described in Chapters 2 and 3. These revisions increased the offense gravity score from thirteen to fourteen points, in order to make finer distinctions among violent offenses, and significantly increased the severity of sentences recommended for serious violent offenders.[1] As will be shown later, in Chapter 9, the 1997 guidelines did indeed increase average sentencing severity for serious violent offenders, most dramatically for third-degree murder and attempted murder. However, as will be shown first, in this chapter, local courts also departed below the guidelines in cases involving serious violent offenders, at substantial rates. Leslie Wilkins and colleagues (1978) posited that departure rates of 20 percent or more would suggest that guidelines are not adequately constraining sentencing discretion. In Pennsylvania, downward departures occurred for 19 percent (615 out of 3,243) of serious violent offenders sentenced between 1997 and 1999.

We focus here on several important research questions about these downward departures for the kinds of serious violent offenses targeted for more severe sentences under the 1997 guidelines. Under what situational and contextual circumstances do downward departures for serious violent offenders occur? Which criminal justice agents (e.g., judges, prosecutors) are the key actors in these decision processes? Is there a mismatch between guideline recommendations for serious violent offenders, and the realities of sentencing in local courts? What can we learn about the locus and use of sentencing discretion under guidelines by examining departures for serious violent offenders? Finally, are guideline departures for serious violent offenders a locus of race, gender, or age disparity—the kind of disparity that guidelines aim to reduce?

Discretion, Departures, and the 1997 Guideline Revisions

Pennsylvania presents a particularly instructive context in which to study guideline sentencing—and sentencing in general—for two reasons. First, its local courts are extremely diverse in terms of size, political contexts, socio-cultural features, and crime concerns. Second, unique features of its sentencing guidelines and their history present a situation that throws into bold relief the universal dilemma of sentencing: the dilemma between the goal of uniformity and logically formal-rational rules and the goal of individualized justice, which necessitates local discretion and substantively rational considerations (see Savelsberg 1992; Ulmer and Kramer 1996). We will return to this dilemma again and again throughout our various analyses of sentencing under Pennsylvania's guidelines.

As discussed in Chapter 2, the Pennsylvania Commission on Sentencing intentionally created guidelines with relatively wide standard ranges and, pursuant to its legislative mandate, further expanded discretion through aggravated and mitigated ranges. In comparison to guidelines in other states such as Minnesota and Washington, Pennsylvania's ranges are extremely wide. As one Pennsylvania sentencing commissioner put it, "It's frustrating to have departures from the planet Earth's widest guidelines."[2] Another issue is the right to appeal the discretionary aspects of sentencing, and the standard of review when such appeals are made. Under Pennsylvania's guidelines, both downward departures and upward departures can be appealed by the prosecution or defense, respectively. However, the Pennsylvania Supreme Court has determined that, "absent a manifest abuse of discretion, judges' sentencing discretion shall be left undisturbed" (*Commonwealth v. Devers*, 1988). This standard provides for only minimal enforcement of the guidelines by the appellate court (Del Sole 1993, p. 499). Thus, in Pennsylvania, there is little threat of sentences being appealed and, if appealed, remanded for resentencing. This sets the presumption not in favor of the guidelines, but in favor of local sentencing discretion. Thus, even though the PCS strove to increase sentencing severity for serious violent offenders through its 1997 guidelines, and did so to some extent, substantial postconviction sentencing discretion still remains for judges (and for prosecutors and their plea agreements). In addition, departures from the guidelines present few practical constraints and consequences (a focal concern of sentencing).

Empirical Research on Guideline Departures

While a number of studies have examined sentencing under guidelines in general (see Spohn 2000 for a review), fewer have focused on explaining departures from sentencing guidelines. Research on guideline departures has mostly focused on Minnesota, the federal court system, and Pennsylvania. One of the goals of the Minnesota sentencing commission was to increase the severity of penalties for serious violent offenders. Terence Miethe and Charles Moore's research (1985) concluded that the Minnesota guidelines had successfully changed sentencing patterns as intended, although later research indicated that the early high levels of guideline conformity had eroded over time (Frase 1993; Knapp 1987). In addition, Richard Frase (1993) found that sentencing for black offenders had lower rates of downward departures, controlling for relevant legal factors, and found that the guidelines had not eliminated gender, geographic, and plea versus trial disparities.

A few studies of conformity and disparity under the federal sentencing guidelines exist, and contain mixed results (see Nagel and Schulhofer 1992; Albonetti 1997, 1998; Smith and Damphousse 1998). For example, Ilene Nagel and Stephen Schulhofer (1992) studied three federal districts and found that prosecutors were plea bargaining around the guidelines in 25–33 percent of the cases (especially drug cases), but did not find that these decisions were linked to race or gender. By contrast, Celesta Albonetti, in research on federal guideline sentencing (1997, 1998), found departure rates of 16–20 percent for certain kinds of offenses, and found that departures interacted with defendant race and gender to produce disparities in sentence severity. Furthermore, David Mustard (2001) found that downward departures were a primary source of disparity under the federal guidelines.

Regarding guideline departures in Pennsylvania between 1985 and 1992, we found that legally prescribed factors such as offense severity and criminal history were the primary predictors of departure decisions, and were inversely related to downward departures (Kramer and Ulmer 1996; Ulmer 1997). However, both of these studies also found that departures were the locus of disparity based on mode of conviction, gender, and race. Specifically, offenders who pled guilty, females, and white offenders were significantly more likely to receive sentences that departed below the guidelines. Furthermore, qualitative research (Ulmer and Kramer 1996, 1998; Ulmer 1997) found that downward departures were very often implicit or explicit concessions in plea bargaining between prosecutors and defense attorneys, and judges sometimes used them as rewards for pleading guilty even in the absence of a bargained plea agreement.

Theoretical Expectations

As Joachim Savelsberg (1992) and others (e.g., Ulmer and Kramer 1996) have described, sentencing guidelines represent an attempt to institute a greater degree of logically formal rationality in sentencing (approximating what Max Weber called a "gapless system of rules" that are to be applied universally and uniformly, with a minimum of decisionmaker discretion—see Ewing 1987; Marsh 2000). In the "real world" of sentencing, however, substantive rationality coexists with such formally rational policies (Ulmer and Kramer 1998). That is, sentencing is a complex, localized, interpretive process, and formally rational sentencing policies like guidelines cannot cover all possible situations.

Guideline departures represent deviations—albeit legally permissible ones—from such logically formal sentencing rules. The key questions we raise are: What factors cause these departures, and what decision processes produce them? We focus on two possible answers below. One set of expectations emphasizes the pervasiveness of substantive rationality in the form of focal concerns of sentencing embedded in local court communities. Another perspective emphasizes organizational efficiency as an overriding goal of court decisionmaking.

Court Communities and Focal Concerns of Sentencing

In Chapter 1, we outlined the court community and focal concerns perspectives and described their importance to understanding sentencing under guidelines. According to focal concerns, judges and other court community actors make such situational imputations and attributions about defendants' character and expected future behavior, and assess the implications of these imputed characteristics for three focal concerns: blameworthiness, dangerousness and community protection, and practical constraints and consequences. In the abstract, the use of and reliance on these focal concerns are said to be universal, but the meaning, relative emphasis and priority, and situational interpretation of them are embedded in local court community culture, organizational contexts, and politics.

In the sentencing of serious violent offenders, it is very likely that the focal concerns of community protection and blameworthiness would be paramount. Just what blameworthiness means, however, and what kinds of offenders are seen as especially dangerous, might vary according to local court community culture and politics. In addition, the nature and salience of practical concerns and consequences (e.g., prosecutorial and court time and resources, jail and prison resources, political and organizational ramifications, and impact on victims, offenders, and offenders' families) would vary according to local court community contexts. From the focal concerns perspective, then, we would predict that the guidelines' offense severity and prior record scores (and both in combination) would be strongly positively associated with sentence severity and negatively related to leniency, but only to the extent that they match *local court actors' interpretations* of blameworthiness and dangerousness.

We do not have a direct measure of local court actors' interpretations of blameworthiness and dangerousness, and how these interpretations match those represented by guidelines, but one way to infer this potential mismatch in specific cases is through departures. In other words, a departure may imply that guideline recommendations did not match local courts' perceptions of blameworthiness and dangerousness for that case, or that practical considerations overrode the guideline recommendations. Later in this chapter, we present qualitative evidence from interviews that suggest how local judges' definitions of blameworthiness and dangerousness can conflict with those represented by the guidelines in departure cases for serious violent offenders.

Court community actors make these attributions and interpretations regarding the focal concerns mostly on the basis of legally relevant factors, but they may also draw on racial, ethnic, gender, or age stereotypes about defendants (Albonetti 1991, 1997; Bridges and Steen 1998; Steen, Engen, and Gainey 2005), particularly given the latitude provided under Pennsylvania's guidelines. For example, both Albonetti's attribution and uncertainty avoidance framework (1991) and the focal concerns perspective predict that some judges may perceive young black or Hispanic males as particularly dangerous or lacking rehabilitative potential compared to other types of defendants, and sentence accordingly. Practical considerations may also affect judges' decisions, such that they may perceive that certain types of offenders can handle imprisonment better than others (Kramer and Steffensmeier 1993). Further research empirically supports this argument, finding consistently that young black and Hispanic males are sentenced more severely than any other groupings of race, age, and gender (Bridges and Steen 1998; Spohn and Holleran 2000; Steffensmeier and Demuth 2000, 2001; see also Zatz 2000). Thus, downward departures among serious violent offenders may be a locus of unwarranted disparity (Johnson 2005).

Another set of issues centers around the practical constraints and consequences of downward departures for serious violent offenders. Such departures present a political risk for judges and prosecutors alike, in the sense that they are leaving the "safe harbor" of the guidelines and indicating that the offense, offender, or risk of future serious crime warrants a more lenient sentence. They risk the twin criticisms of being soft on crime and failing to protect the community if the offender later violates this trust. In a state like Pennsylvania, where judges and prosecutors face partisan election, these considerations are not trivial. A key question, then, is why judges would ever take such risks in the face of uncertainty about the defendant.

One possible answer is that departures may be more likely when judges and prosecutors have localized court community sentencing norms like "going rates" to fall back on. In the case of a mismatch between guidelines and local interpretations of blameworthiness or dangerousness, local going rates legitimize deviations from guidelines (Ulmer 1997). We suspect that large urban courts are particularly likely to have relatively high rates of downward departure, since such courts have been consistently found to sentence more leniently than small and medium-sized ones (Eisenstein, Flemming, and Nardulli 1988; Ulmer 1997). Several possible explanations exist for this pattern: (1) it could be that with larger volumes of crimes, and more serious crimes in particular, the tolerance for criminal behavior is higher in large urban courts; (2) if crime concentrates in lower social status areas of large cities, victims and offenders might be of very similar social status, and this may diminish the perceived seriousness of the offense (see Wooldredge and Thistlethwaite 2004 for an argument with similar logic); and (3) the caseload pressures on the courts in urban areas may present practical considerations of moving cases as well as using limited correctional resources (we control for these latter two factors themselves in later chapters' analyses). Departures might also be more likely in large courts, since there may be less public visibility for such cases, and there may also be less public scrutiny when downward departures result in the offender committing a new offense. Furthermore, local organizational culture, or situational practical constraints and consequences, may make downward departures attractive in particular counties of any size.

Organizational Efficiency

Another potential practical constraint is the need to process cases in an efficient manner. Rodney Engen and Sara Steen (2000) focus on the concern of organizational efficiency (see also Dixon 1995). Organizational efficiency may be a key goal in criminal sanctioning, one that may supersede formally rational rules like sentencing guidelines. The chief way in which court actors achieve efficiency is by inducing guilty pleas (Engen and Steen 2000, p. 1363).

While their analysis focuses primarily on aggregate changes in charging, convictions, and sentence severity in drug cases, Engen and Steen (2000) clearly imply that efficiency is similarly important at the individual case level, and that guilty pleas will be similarly rewarded among individual offenders. In addition, the need to move cases, avoid backlogs, and conserve resources is a significant theme in prior research from the court community and focal concerns perspectives (Nardulli, Eisenstein, and Flemming 1988; Eisenstein, Flemming, and Nardulli 1988; Flemming, Nardulli, and Eisenstein 1992; Ulmer 1997; Ulmer and Kramer 1996, 1998). Further, the single largest and most consistent extra-guideline sentencing difference found in these studies has been between those who plead guilty and those convicted by trial (a form of disparity that we further investigate in Chapter 7). As a result, we expect that those who plead guilty—and especially those who negotiate plea bargains—would be more likely to receive downward departures than those convicted by trial.

Additionally, in the language of focal concerns, judges and prosecutors may interpret guilty pleas as evidence of remorse and rehabilitative potential, and plea agreements are also sometimes rewards for cooperation with law enforcement (e.g., confessing to additional crimes, informing on others, etc.). Both of these circumstances can mitigate perceived blameworthiness and perhaps even increase perceived rehabilitative potential, thus affecting perceptions of the offender's dangerousness to the community. Furthermore, trials not only consume time and resources, but also risk that the defendant might be acquitted—an unattractive risk for prosecutors (see Smith 1986 and Albonetti 1987 for treatments of plea bargaining and prosecutorial rationality). Downward departures might be used as concessions in plea bargaining, especially when prosecutors are uncertain about the strength of their evidence against the defendant. Thus, we would expect downward departures to be more likely following negotiated guilty pleas compared to open guilty pleas (guilty pleas without a negotiated agreement with the prosecutors—see Ulmer 1997).

Research Methods

We use the sentencing data maintained by the Pennsylvania Commission on Sentencing, which contain detailed information on type and length of sentence, prior record, offense type and severity, mode of conviction, as well as other variables such as age, race, and gender of the defendant. The first part of our analysis in this chapter focuses on these data. Further information about the quantitative data is provided in the Research Methods Appendix.

Then we go beyond the quantitative data on sentencing outcomes to explore qualitative data from semistructured, open-ended interviews with judges, conducted in the spring and summer of 2000. These qualitative data suggest some possible patterns to the situations and reasons for downward departures for serious violent offenders, and thus illuminate some of the quantitative findings. Our interpretations of the quantitative and qualitative data are also informed by several conversations about this project, and about guideline conformity in general, with various PCS commissioners and staff members from 2000 to 2001.

Downward Departures

A previous study of guideline departures in Pennsylvania examined dispositional departures (situations where courts gave nonincarceration sentences when the guidelines called for incarceration) and durational departures below and above the guidelines (Kramer and Ulmer 1996). Here, however, we narrow the focus to downward departures, generally the most typical situation, in which departures represent leniency for these serious violent offenders.[3] We also do not distinguish between whether the sentence was a dispositional departure (i.e., courts giving nonincarceration sentences when guidelines call for incarceration) or a durational departure (incarceration sentences that are less than the length recommended by the guidelines). Because we are focusing on very serious offenses, there are hardly any dispositional departures from the guidelines for these cases. For our purposes, a downward departure refers to any sentence that is less than the lowest sentence in the mitigated range of the guidelines.

Results

Table 4.1 presents descriptive statistics for the variables used in the quantitative analysis and the rates of departure for the specific offenses. As the table shows, 19 percent of the serious violent offenses we focus on resulted in downward departures.

Table 4.1 Serious Violent Offenses and Offenders, 1997–1999

Variables	Frequency (%)	Mean (standard deviation)
Downward departures	615 (19.0)	
Aggravated assault with attempted SBI	246 (7.6)	
Aggravated assault with SBI	229 (7.0)	
Arson	97 (3.0)	
Attempted third-degree murder	58 (1.8)	
Burglary/occupied home	432 (13.3)	
Inchoate offenses	293 (9.0)	
Involuntary deviant sexual intercourse	170 (5.2)	
Kidnapping	13 (0.4)	
Third-degree murder	153 (4.7)	
Rape	167 (5.2)	
Robbery	1,256 (39.0)	
Voluntary manslaughter	40 (1.2)	
Offense severity		10.3 (1.41)
Prior record score		1.7 (2.11)
Mandatory minimum applied	504 (15.5)	
Nonnegotiated guilty plea	1,028 (31.6)	
Negotiated guilty plea	1,612 (49.7)	
Bench trial	210 (6.5)	
Jury trial		393 (12.2)
Male	2,977 (91.8)	
Female	266 (8.2)	
White	1,439 (44.3)	
Black	1,581 (48.8)	
Hispanic	223 (6.9)	
Age		28.0 (9.8)
Black males 25 and under	809 (25.0)	
Hispanic males 25 and under	130 (4.0)	
White males 25 and under	616 (19.0)	
Black males 26 and over	677 (21.0)	
Hispanic males 26 and over	77 (2.4)	
White males 26 and over	662 (20.5)	
Black females 25 and under	41 (1.0)	
Hispanic females 25 and under	9 (0.28)	
White females 25 and under	63 (2.0)	
Black females 26 and over	50 (1.5)	
Hispanic females 26 and over	7 (0.22)	
White females 26 and over	94 (3.0)	
Sentenced in a large court (2 counties)	1,285 (39.6)	
Sentenced in a medium court (14 counties)	1,337 (41.2)	
Sentenced in a small court (51 counties)	621 (19.2)	
Sentenced in County A	920 (28.4)	
Sentenced in County B	365 (11.3)	
Sentenced in County C	151 (4.7)	
Sentenced in County D	121 (3.7)	
Sentenced in County E	102 (3.2)	
Sentenced in County F	60 (1.9)	

Table 4.2 presents logistic regression models of the likelihood of downward departures for serious violent offenses. We first discuss the main effects (Models 1–3), then turn to an examination of important interaction effects (Models 4–5). Models 1–3 show the main effects on downward departures for serious violent offenders. For reasons we discuss later, Model 2 is our preferred specification, and we will base our discussion of main effects on its coefficients.

Offense severity and prior record both have the strongest effects on the odds of departures. Surprisingly, offense severity and prior record, in their main effects, *increase* the likelihood of downward departures. That is, those convicted of more severe offenses are more likely to receive sentences that are below those recommended by the guidelines, and the same is true of those with more serious prior records. A one-point increase in offense severity multiplies the odds of a departure below the guidelines by 1.56. In cumulative terms, this means that an offender with an offense severity score of 13 (and a prior record score of 0), for example, would have about nine times greater odds of receiving a departure below the guidelines than an otherwise similar offender with a severity score of 8. Each one point increase in prior record score multiplies the odds of a departure below the guidelines by 1.3. So, an offender with a prior record score of 5, for example, would have 3.7 times greater odds of receiving a departure than an otherwise similar offender with a prior record score of 0. Also, the application of a mandatory minimum decreases the odds of a downward departure by 76 percent. The odds associated with applying a mandatory minimum are not zero because in rare cases, the mandatory minimum can be less than the guideline lower boundary. In such cases, applying the mandatory minimum rather than giving the (higher) guideline sentence would result in a downward departure.

Four of the thirteen offense dummy variables were significant compared to the reference category of robbery with serious bodily injury. Offenders convicted of aggravated assault with threatened serious bodily injury have 3.1 times greater odds of receiving a downward departure. Aggravated assault with serious bodily injury is associated with about 2.4 times greater odds of receiving a downward departure. Two offenses are particularly less likely to receive downward departures: third-degree murder and rape.

Type of disposition is coded with nonnegotiated pleas ("open" guilty pleas that do not entail an explicit plea agreement) as the reference category. Interestingly, negotiated guilty pleas (those with explicit plea agreements over sentence or charges) yield only a modest advantage in the chances for downward departures over open guilty pleas. However, offenders convicted at bench and jury trials are much less likely to receive downward departures than those convicted by guilty pleas. Those convicted by bench trials have their odds of receiving a downward departure reduced by 72 percent, and those convicted by jury trial have 74 percent lower odds. What seems to make the real

Table 4.2   Likelihood of Downward Departures for Serious Violent Offenses and Offenders, 1997–1999 (odds shown)

	Model 1	Model 2	Model 3	Model 4	Model 5
Constant	.001	.002	.0005	.001	.006
(block of 13 offense dummy variables, significant offense dummies shown)					
Aggravated assault with attempted SBI	3.25**	3.10**	2.96**	3.12**	2.92**
Aggravated assault with SBI	2.42**	2.39**	2.22*	2.31**	2.32**
Third-degree murder	.23***	.25**	.21***	.25***	.24***
Rape	.36**	.37**	.35**	.39**	.35**
Offense severity	1.59***	1.56***	1.79***	1.57***	1.39**
Prior record score	1.31***	1.31***	2.47***	1.31***	1.32***
Mandatory minimum applied	.24***	.24***	.24***	.24***	.24***
Negotiated guilty plea	1.13	1.16	1.15	1.17	.13**
Bench trial	.27***	.28***	.28***	.28***	.29***
Jury trial	.25***	.26***	.28***	.25***	.29***
Sex (male = 1)	.55***	.52***	.51***		.52***
Black defendant	.80*	.88	.90		.90
Hispanic defendant	.49**	.61*	.59*		.60*
Age	1.001	1.001	.99		1.00
Large court	3.43***				
Medium court	1.83***				
Philadelphia		2.39***	2.46***	2.41***	2.47***
Allegheny		2.97***	3.08***	2.98***	3.03***
Bucks		3.16***	3.25***	3.16***	3.22***
Chester		1.89*	2.03**	1.88*	1.97**
Westmoreland		2.58**	2.68**	2.48**	2.71**
Offense severity × prior record			.94***		
Black males 25 and under				.91	
Hispanic males 25 and under				.48*	
Black males over 25				.78	
Hispanic males over 25				.59	
White males over 25				1.06	
Black females 25 and under				3.80***	
Hispanic females 25 and under				3.18	
White females 25 and under				1.74	
Black females over 25				1.43	
Hispanic females over 25				1.51	
White females over 25				1.31	
Offense severity × negotiated plea					1.24**
Chi-square	458	484	494	502	490
p-value	.0001	.0001	.0001	.0001	.0001
N	3,243	3,243	3,243	3,243	3,243

Notes: Robbery with serious bodily injury (SBI) is the reference category for the offense dummy variables.

Nonnegotiated guilty pleas are the reference category for mode of conviction.

Small courts are the reference category for court size.

All other courts are the reference category for the individual court dummy variables.

White males 25 and under are the reference category for race, ethnicity, age, and gender categories.

* significant at .05 or less; ** significant at .01 or less; *** significant at .001 or less.

difference in chances for downward departures, then, is pleading guilty (and not being convicted by trial), with or without a negotiated plea agreement. These odds are shown graphically in Figure 4.1.

Turning to defendant characteristics, we do not find a significant direct difference in the departure chances of whites and African Americans among these serious violent offenders. However, Hispanic serious violent defendants are moderately disadvantaged in terms of receiving downward departures (odds = .61). In addition, men's odds of receiving a downward departure are about half those of women.

To examine the differences between counties, we first entered dummy variables for county size (medium and large, with small counties as the reference category), shown in Model 2. Large counties have almost 3.5 times greater odds for granting downward departures than small counties, while medium counties exhibit about 1.8 times greater downward departure odds than small counties. Thus the likelihood of downward departure definitely increases with county size.

In addition to examining the effect of county court size, we wanted to investigate which specific counties were distinctive in terms of their likelihood of downward departures for serious violent offenders. We therefore entered dummy variables for all individual counties.[4] Out of sixty-seven counties, five significantly differed from the rest of the state in their odds of granting

Figure 4.1   Effects of Mode of Conviction on Departure Odds

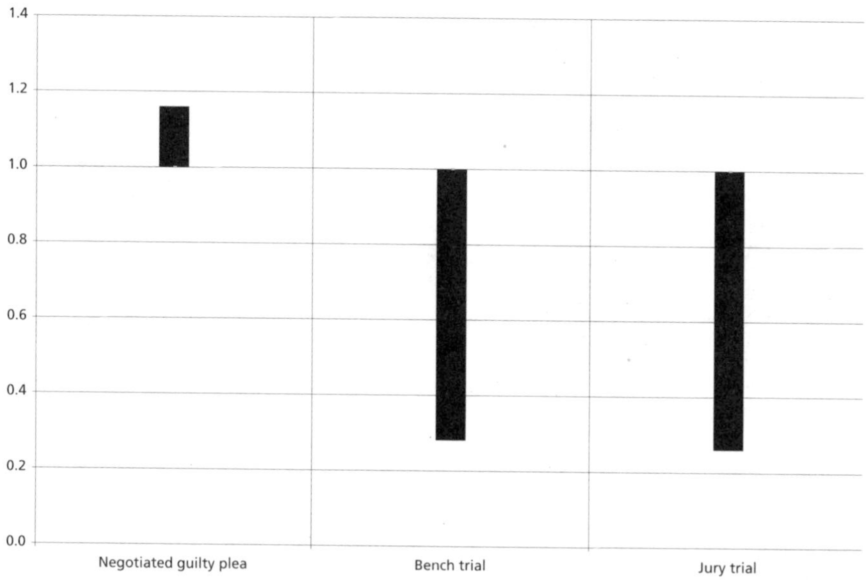

downward departures for serious violent offenders, and these are shown in Model 3 and in Figure 4.2. Allegheny and Bucks counties especially stand out, each exhibiting about three times greater odds of downward departures compared to all other counties. Philadelphia and Westmoreland have roughly two and a half times greater odds, and Chester has almost two times greater odds of downward departure than the rest of the state. Furthermore, the five distinctive counties account for 50 percent of the serious violent offenders convicted in the state, and Philadelphia and Allegheny counties by themselves account for 40 percent of the state's serious violent offenders. Thus, half of the serious violent offenders in the state are sentenced in five counties that are particularly likely to grant downward departures. Interestingly, the five counties share some contextual characteristics, but differ on others. They vary widely in terms of their minority populations (from over 40 percent black to 2 percent black, for example), violent crime rates (from 1,465 to 162 per 100,000, for example), and other sociodemographic characteristics. Philadelphia and Allegheny each comprise major metropolitan areas (but lie at opposite ends of the state) and are in fact the two counties that make up the "large counties" category. Bucks, Chester, and Westmoreland are medium-sized suburban counties that border on one of the two large metropolitan areas. Bucks and Chester border on Philadelphia, and Westmoreland shares a border with Allegheny. Beyond geographic proximity, all of the five counties have Democratic ma-

Figure 4.2   Key County Differences in Departures

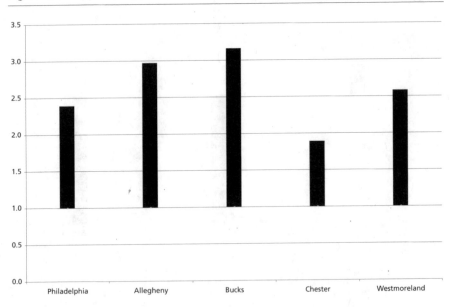

jorities or pluralities among their voters (Chester County's voters were roughly evenly split between George W. Bush and Al Gore in the 2000 presidential election, but went solidly for John Kerry in 2004).

Combined Effects of Race/Ethnicity, Gender, and Age

First, as shown in Model 4, offense severity and prior record interact. Downward departures are less likely in the high prior record and high offense severity portion of the guideline matrix (see Chapter 3). Thus, while the direct effects of offense severity and prior record increase downward departure odds, in combination they significantly reduce them. In practical terms, this means that a serious violent offender who has committed a relatively severe offense, but has a less serious prior record, would be relatively more likely to receive a downward departure, and vice versa. However, an offender who has committed a very severe offense, and has an extensive prior record, would be much less likely to receive a downward departure.

Research demonstrates that young minority males face particularly severe sentences compared to other race, gender, and age categories (Steffensmeier, Ulmer, and Kramer 1998; Bridges and Steen 1998; Spohn and Holleran 2000; Spohn and DeLone 2000; Steffensmeier and Demuth 2000; Steen, Engen, and Gainey 2005). To investigate this, instead of a hard-to-interpret three-way interaction term (race/ethnicity × gender × age), we included a set of dummy variables for race/ethnicity, gender, and age categories, with white males aged twenty-five and under excluded as the reference category. The results single out young Hispanic males as being particularly less likely to receive downward departures, and young black females as considerably more likely to receive them, compared to the reference category of young white males. Young Hispanic males have 52 percent lesser downward departure odds compared to young white males. Older Hispanic males are also moderately, but not significantly, less likely to receive downward departures. These patterns are shown in Figure 4.3.

On the other hand, young black females' downward departure odds are nearly four times those of young white males, and also exceed those of any other race, gender, and age groups. Furthermore, the slopes for black males and females are in opposite directions. Younger and older black males are slightly (and not significantly) less likely to receive downward departures. On the other hand, young black females are much more likely to receive downward departures (older black females are also slightly more likely to receive them as well).

In addition, while we expected that guilty pleas would be rewarded with greater odds of downward departure, Model 5 shows that the effect of negotiated pleas is conditional on offense severity. Negotiated pleas bring a greater advantage over nonnegotiated pleas at higher levels of offense severity. To illustrate this further, we estimated partitioned models for offenders with

Figure 4.3   Differences in Departure for Race, Ethnicity, Gender, and Age Groups

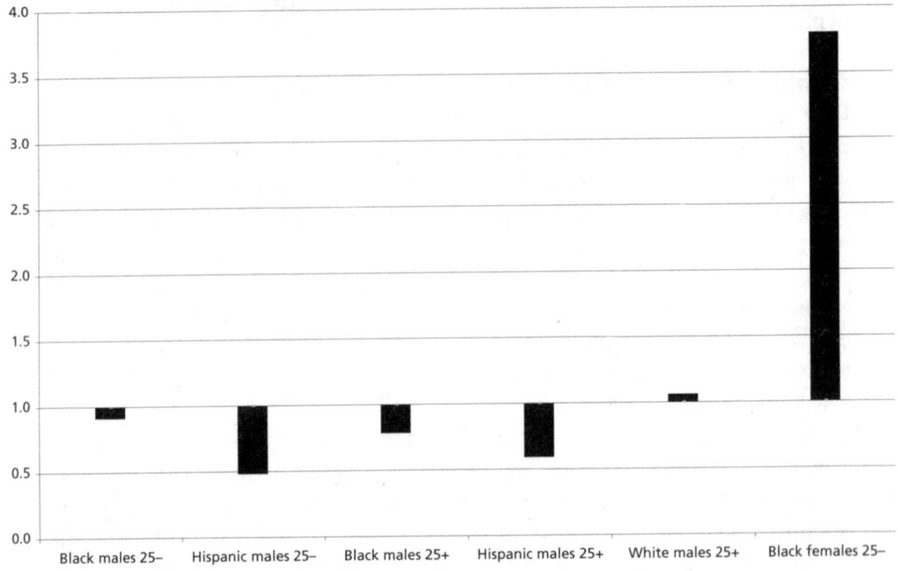

Note: – indicates ages 25 and under; + indicates ages over 25.

offense severity scores of 8–11 versus 12 or more on one hand, and offenders with negotiated pleas versus those with all other modes of conviction on the other. The downward departure odds associated with negotiated pleas are a nonsignificant 1.12 among cases with offense severity scores between 8 and 11. Among cases with offense severity scores of 12 or more, the departure odds associated with negotiated pleas are 1.86 (z-score test for equality of co-efficients = 1.82, p = .03; see Paternoster et al. 1998). On the other hand, this interaction also indicates that increases in offense severity increase the chances of a downward departure, *especially* when there is a negotiated guilty plea. The effect of offense severity on the odds of downward departure is 1.96 among negotiated plea cases, but only 1.20 among all other modes of conviction (z-score test for equality of coefficients = –2.45, p = .007).

Judicial Interview Themes

To supplement the findings from the quantitative data, we selected a purposive theoretical subsample (see Strauss 1987) of 134 cases from the serious violent offenses analyzed above. In terms of our selection criteria, we selected offense types in proportion to their downward departure rates. We also oversampled cases with minority offenders and cases with jury trials, due to the low base rates for these kinds of cases. We examined the number of relevant departures by county and found that only twelve out of sixty-seven counties accounted for 80 percent of the departures for serious violent offenses. In each of these twelve counties (which include the five counties that, as shown in our multivariate analyses below, have significantly greater odds of downward departure), we then examined all sentences for the identified offenses by judge. We then selected judges with multiple relevant departures for interviews, omitting judges for whom the case sampled was an isolated, single downward departure, in favor of interviewing judges with at least two or more departures, so as to maximize our case coverage. We wanted to shed light on this question: When downward departures occur, what are the situational characteristics and reasons given for such decisions? The Research Methods Appendix provides further information about the collection of these interview data.

Interviews with judges uncovered several distinguishable but also somewhat overlapping themes regarding substantively rational considerations in downward departure decisions among serious violent offense cases, as shown in Table 4.3.

Evidence Strength

One of the overarching views that emerged in our interviews was the court's interest in forging and maintaining a working relationship within the court community, especially prosecutors. In fact, judges framed their decisionmaking as being very sensitive to prosecutorial concerns in these kinds of cases. One of these chief prosecutorial concerns was the issue of securing a conviction for a potentially dangerous offender in the face of weak or legally questionable evidence strength. Judges frequently expressed their support of prosecutors' goals in such situations. For example, one judge commented, when asked about a departure below guidelines that involved a negotiated plea agreement in which the prosecutor agreed not to seek a mandatory five-year prison sentence: "When a district attorney comes in and says, 'Judge, the defendant is willing to

Table 4.3   Judicial Considerations and Departure Decisions for Serious Violent Offenders

Theme	Percentage of Cases Mentioned
Evidence strength	14
Judicial deference to plea agreements	47
Victim-offender relationship	10
Crime was less onerous than it appeared	10
Offender showed remorse	6
Offender needs drug treatment	8
Offender has mental problems	6
De-mandatorizing	30

Note: Theme categories are not mutually exclusive. Interviews about a particular case could mention one or more of these themes.

plead to 4–8 years and I think that the public is better off with that than me running the risk of losing this case because I think we have some evidentiary problems. The witness against him is a convicted felon that told two different stories.' What are you going to do? Sounds like the best deal to me for everybody [is to accept the plea]." This statement not only emphasizes the interconnectedness between the judge and the prosecutor, but also highlights the shared emphasis on getting a conviction. For the judge and the prosecutor in situations like these, the focal concerns of perceived dangerousness and practical constraints and consequences (in the form of trial uncertainty due to weak evidence) are both highly salient and interrelated. One may question the legal ethics of such a view, but it is clear that in situations like that described above, judges and prosecutors appeared to share a "crime control" orientation as opposed to a "due process" one, as described by Herbert Packer (1968).

In 14 percent of the cases about which judges were interviewed, they explicitly elaborated on the issue of plea agreements to secure convictions of serious violent offenders in the face of questionable evidence strength and trial uncertainty. In the most severe evidentiary problem that arose in our interviews, one judge indicated that in an armed robbery where the victim shot the defendant, the police had gone to the hospital and forced the defendant to undergo surgery to have the bullet removed from his leg, so that the police could collect the bullet as evidence. In the course of the surgery, the police also had a blood sample taken from the defendant to allow for comparison with blood at the scene of the crime. The judge said that the prosecutor did not think the evidence was admissible and was concerned about losing the case if it went to trial. The judge accepted a plea agreement to a sentence that was a downward departure, noting that there were an "amazing number of constitutional violations" in this case.

Judicial Deference to Plea Agreements

Overlapping the above theme, the judges we interviewed mentioned deference to plea agreements in 47 percent of the cases as a reason for downward departure. The judges were unanimous in noting that they were very reluctant to reject plea agreements. In discussing an aggravated assault case that was a negotiated plea, a particular judge's comments are representative: "When the parties have agreed, then my personal scope of review is very limited. The standard is whether the sentence 'shocks my conscience.'"

In the aggravated assault case in question, the judge indicated that after accepting the plea, he found that the defendant and the victim had been married for forty-six years, that the defendant was eighty-eight years of age, that this was the defendant's first episode of violence, and the serious bodily injury had resulted in a few stitches on the forehead. In another county, a judge reinforced this commonly heard view: "Often the judge knows little about the case. The prosecutor has negotiated a penalty and we merely concur with this result." However, judges still must learn enough about the case to give reasons for departures in the legal sentencing record, even if this learning takes place after accepting a plea.

Several judges indicated that they had rejected guilty plea agreements in the past, but only in rare instances. Never did they cite a downward departure case as a specific example of the circumstances that would prompt the rejection of a plea. They also commonly indicated that to reject guilty pleas would (a) slow down case processing (an organizational efficiency theme), and (b) undermine the ability of prosecutors to work with defense attorneys (a court community theme).

"De-Mandatorizing"

In creating mandatory minimum sentences, the Pennsylvania legislature gave the discretion to apply mandatory minimums to the prosecutor. That is, in Pennsylvania (42 Pa. C.S. § 9712[b]), mandatory minimums apply only if the prosecutor files a motion seeking to apply them. Our interviews unveiled a very important interaction between the guidelines and mandatory minimums that applied to many of these cases. Often, judges indicated (in 30 percent of cases) that the prosecutor had *de-mandatorized* the case. In fact, this was a term we heard in most of the counties we visited, even if it was not mentioned as a reason for downward departures. What judges meant by this was that the facts of the case supported application of a mandatory minimum, but the prosecutor did not file a motion to apply it. Of the 109 cases covered by our interviews, 41 were eligible for the application of mandatory minimums. However, in only 19 of these 41 cases (46 percent) were the mandatory minimums actually applied.

Judges indicated that when prosecutors did not move to apply the mandatory minimums, it was a clear "message" that the prosecutor thought the appropriate sentence was less than what the mandatory minimums called for. This reflects two important issues. First, it suggests that mandatory minimums may have been avoided in some cases for evidentiary reasons (the case described previously, of the armed robbery defendant who was allegedly coerced into having surgery and giving a blood sample, was one such case), and for perceived fairness reasons (where prosecutors perceived that the sentence was too harsh relative to the severity of the crime). For example, a prosecutor de-mandatorized an armed robbery offense to which a mandatory minimum could have been applied because (1) the defendant used a "starter" pistol that could not fire a bullet, and (2) the item stolen was a hat.

Other Substantive Considerations

Another common reason for departing below the guidelines seems to be the role of the victim. In 10 percent of the departure cases, the judge mentioned the victim-offender relationship as an important factor. For example, in the aggravated assault case discussed above, the victim was the spouse of the offender.

In another downward departure case, the victim of an occupied-home burglary was the grandparent of the offender. In these cases, the judges indicated that the link between offender and victim was an important consideration in their defining the offense as less serious than typical aggravated assaults and burglaries. Specifically, the judges viewed the offender as less culpable because the victim and the offender were closely related.

In another 10 percent of cases, judges argued that the offense was less onerous than the charges and the guidelines' offense severity scores indicated.[5] This theme overlaps with several examples mentioned above, and was usually reflected as a reason accompanying plea agreements to departures and demandatorizing cases. Other substantive considerations that were sometimes mentioned as reasons for downward departures in these serious violent offense cases were that the offender showed remorse (6 percent), the offender needed drug treatment (8 percent), and the offender had mental problems (6 percent).

Discussion

The quantitative analysis revealed that the most important factors in affecting the likelihood of departures below the guidelines for serious violent offenses were offense severity and prior record. However, these relationships were more complex than we expected. The main effects for offense severity and prior record increased the odds of downward departures, but the interaction of prior record and offense severity reduced them. This means that offenders who were convicted of a particularly severe offense (an offense severity score of 13 or 14, for example), but had a modest or no prior record, were especially likely to receive downward departures. In such cases, there may have been a mismatch between guideline sentence recommendations and local courts' "going rates," and between local actors' definitions of offender blameworthiness and dangerousness. Consequently, local courts—especially in five particular counties—*corrected* the guidelines by departing below them. It appears that judges and prosecutors tended to agree with guideline recommendations on serious violent offenses at severity levels of 8–11, and for offenders with less serious prior records, but they tended to disagree with the punitiveness of sentences associated with higher severity offenses (12 or more), *or* for those with extensive prior records (but not both).

We found that male serious violent offenders were about half as likely to receive downward departures as females. Our analyses of race/ethnicity showed no significant main effects for being black, but Hispanic offenders were less likely to receive a downward departure than non-Hispanic whites. The patterns for race/ethnicity, gender, and age groupings complicate this picture, however. Young Hispanic males were much less likely to receive downward departures, while young black females were much more likely to receive them. We can only speculate, but the results are consistent with the notion that young Hispanic males tend to be seen as particularly dangerous and blamewor-thy, with fewer practical considerations that might foster a downward depar-ture. Young black females, on the other hand, may be perceived as particularly less dangerous and blameworthy—even more so than young white females. We would also speculate that, to the extent that young black women are more likely to be single parents, courts may be more concerned about the "collateral dam-age" of the sentence to the children—a practical consideration that may encour-age downward departures. Another possibility is that many of the cases involv-ing black females may be about "mutual combat" with husbands, domestic partners, or others, and judges view the guideline sentences as simply too se-vere for such cases. Future research—especially qualitative research—is sorely needed, however, to move beyond the realm of speculation on the "gendered" differences in sentencing processes within racial and ethnic groups.

These findings contrast considerably with findings from prior research on departures in Pennsylvania in the 1989–1992 period. In these earlier years, and among *all offenders,* offense severity and prior record were associated with decreased—not increased—odds of downward departures (Kramer and Ulmer 1996). We replicated the analysis of serious violent offenders here using the Pennsylvania data from 1989 to 1992 in our earlier study of departures for all offenses (Kramer and Ulmer 1996), in which we did not separate out serious violent offenders. Similar to the 1997–2000 data, we found that offense sever-ity and prior record were associated with greater odds of downward departures among serious violent offenders in the 1989–1992 period (though the effect for prior record was less strong in the latter period).

Interestingly, race, ethnicity, and gender were much more strongly associ-ated with downward departures among serious violent offenders in 1989–1992: women were 2.7 times more likely to receive downward depar-tures, and blacks' odds of departure were 18 percent less than whites. Hispanic serious violent offenders were also less likely to receive downward departures in these earlier years, with 48 percent lesser odds than whites. These contrasts from earlier findings suggest that among serious violent offenders, black ver-sus white distinctions may be less influential in departure decisions than in previous time periods. At the same time, however, these contrasts also suggest that Hispanics may have become increasingly defined as a dangerous minor-ity, and these definitions may be reflected in sentencing (see Spohn and Holleran 2000; Steffensmeier and Demuth 2001).

We also found strong evidence of local court variation in the probability of downward departures. First, county court size affects the probability of downward departures, which are least common in Pennsylvania's many small rural counties, moderately more common in medium-sized counties, and most common in the two large urban counties. More specifically, nearly 80 percent of the departures came from only twelve of Pennsylvania's sixty-seven coun-ties. Five of these twelve counties (two large urban ones and three medium-sized suburban ones that border on the two large urban ones) accounted for a very disproportionate share of serious violent offender cases in general, and downward departures for serious violent offenders in particular. These five counties varied widely in terms of sociodemographic characteristics, but four of the five had Democratic majorities or pluralities among their voters (data from 1999 Pennsylvania City and County Extra). We can only speculate, but perhaps Democratic Party political strength in these counties encourages comparatively less punitive sentencing views among judges and prosecutors (both of whom are elected by popular, partisan vote in Pennsylvania).

In sum, these findings suggest that (1) important interjurisdictional disparities exist in downward departures for serious violent offenders, (2) county size is positively associated with sentencing leniency, and (3) individual court communities seem to vary in their local cultural interpretations and prioritizations of the focal concerns of sentencing vis-à-vis the guidelines, as reflected in their probability of granting downward departures.

Regarding mode of conviction, we find that conviction by trial—especially by jury—considerably reduces a defendant's chances of a departure below the guidelines. In other words, most downward departures occur following guilty pleas, whether or not there is a negotiated plea agreement. In terms of main effects, we find little substantial difference between negotiated or nonnegotiated guilty pleas—both of these modes of conviction are much more likely to result in a departure below the guidelines when compared to a jury or bench trial. However, negotiated pleas and offense severity interact, and negotiated pleas offer more benefit to defendants in the upper levels of offense severity.

One shared goal of all key court actors is the need to process cases efficiently, and guilty pleas can be a key mechanism for pursuing this goal—even sometimes among serious violent offenders—just as the organizational efficiency model depicts. Efficiency is likely to play an even bigger role in the disposition of cases that are less serious. In fact, courts often implement procedures such as "fast tracking" or "rocket dockets," putting less serious cases into highly efficient court processing modes so that more time can be spent on serious cases (for example, see Ulmer 1997; Flemming, Nardulli, and Eisenstein 1992; Eisenstein and Jacob 1977). However, we do not want to imply that in serious violent offense cases, prosecutors, defense attorneys, and judges produce downward departures only out of an interest in organizational efficiency. Our qualitative data suggest that sentences following guilty pleas represent sometimes unilateral and sometimes negotiated decisions that reflect focal concerns of offender dangerousness and blameworthiness, as well as a variety of practical constraints and consequences (like evidence strength, trial risks, *and* case-processing efficiency).

That other concerns besides organizational efficiency are involved in the rewarding of guilty pleas with more lenient sentences should be no surprise.

This practice has been a feature of US criminal justice since at least the post–Civil War period. Plea rewards exist in a variety of cross-national contexts (Fisher 2003; Tonry and Frase 2001), and most importantly, exist and thrive in the absence of heavy caseloads (see Church 1979; Mather 1979; Feeley 1979; Flemming, Nardulli, and Eisenstein 1992). In other words, the goal of organizational efficiency may be a *sufficient cause* of plea bargaining and plea rewards, but it is probably not a *necessary cause* of them (a theme we return to in Chapter 7).

We interviewed the judges who sentenced the subsample of departure cases in order to explore the reasons and situations behind downward departures for these kinds of serious violent offenders. The interviews suggested these key points:

1. Judges revealed that a variety of substantively rational considerations supporting the role of focal concerns of sentencing in their decisions to depart below guidelines for serious violent offenders. Namely:

   a. *Perceived dangerousness and community protection* constituted a key consideration in downward departure decisions. Ironically, downward departures appeared to sometimes be a mechanism for incapacitating offenders seen as dangerous, by ensuring a guilty plea and thus conviction and incarceration.
   b. The victim-offender relationship was sometimes seen as a factor that reduced the *perceived blameworthiness* or culpability of offenders, and thus encouraged a downward departure.

2. A variety of guilty plea considerations related to *practical constraints and consequences* also came into play, both singly and interrelated to substantive considerations above:

   a. Court actors often seemed mindful of the desirability of efficiently moving cases through the system and avoiding undue delays, even for serious violent offenders.
   b. In these serious violent cases, judges seemed particularly willing to defer to prosecutors' sentencing concerns and the plea agreements they negotiated. Among the prosecutorial concerns that influenced judges were:

      • securing the conviction and incarceration of offenders seen as dangerous, in the face of weak evidence and trial uncertainty; and
      • the need to avoid undermining prosecutor–defense attorney negotiations and working relations.

    c. The practice of "de-mandatorizing" seemed to be a particularly important mechanism generating downward departures for serious violent offenders. In such cases, prosecutors chose not to apply a statutorily available mandatory penalty, and instead pursued a guilty plea to a sentence within or below the guidelines.

Local Court Corrections to Guidelines

Departures are often used as a barometer to determine whether the guidelines are constraining judicial discretion. In the view of local decisionmakers, departures reflect the use of discretion to "correct" the guidelines. In fact, guideline departures capture the most visible local corrections to sentencing guidelines, but our quantitative data missed those situations where guideline-relevant factors themselves, such as the offense of conviction or deadly weapon enhancement, are negotiated as part of plea agreements. Thus our findings regarding departures probably underestimate the true amount of local guideline manipulation or correction.

    Local guideline corrections may indicate offense behavior that is less serious than reflected in the guideline ranking, or factors not considered in the guidelines but viewed as important to the court at sentencing. The findings here once again raise the perennial dilemma between logically formal rationality and substantive rationality in sentencing. Guidelines can provide a benchmark for courts, but there are distinct limitations to their ability to capture the full complexity of individual cases. This seems to be true for the serious violent crimes we focused on. For example, one judge pointed out that what the criminal code and the guidelines call "serious bodily injury" might range from an injury that results in stitches on the forehead to a firearm injury that results in a wound the size of a soda can in the victim's leg. Thus, local situational interpretations of focal concerns would seem to make departures inevitable, especially from relatively simple guideline systems found in the states, as opposed to the federal system. On the other hand, this same local discretion can be the locus of disparity, such as the racial, ethnic, and gender disparity (alone and in combination), as well as interjurisdictional disparity.

    From the perspective of judges like the one who confronted the wide variety of injuries covered by the statutory term "serious bodily injury," would ritualistic conformity to the guidelines be fairer? Or is it more important for judges and other court actors to "correct" the guidelines on a case-by-case basis, with the concomitant risk of disparity (including interjurisdictional disparity)? This issue has been unfortunately lost in attempts to decide whether guidelines are "successful," using departure rates as an indicator of success or failure.

    Guidelines may also play an interesting role in the guilty plea process in situations like that in Pennsylvania, where the legislature has enacted mandatory minimums that are in general more severe than guideline sentences—*but has given prosecutors the discretion and formal responsibility to apply the mandatory minimums.* We found that the mandatory minimums were commonly dropped as part of a plea agreement ("de-mandatorized") when the defendant pled guilty to the less severe guideline sentence, or a downward departure. In this respect, the ability to apply the mandatory minimum or not (with no "safety valve" provision in Pennsylvania's law) empowers the prosecutor (and perhaps the defense attorney, who must sell the plea to the client) with concrete tools with which to secure convictions. We return to this theme in Chapter 8, where we examine prosecutorial discretion and mandatory minimum sentences.

Like all guidelines, Pennsylvania's sentencing guidelines single out serious violent offenders for the most severe sentences. In our quantitative and qualitative data, we find that judges often reject these guideline sentencing recommendations and give lesser sentences. However, an important policy concern is to determine how much danger is posed to the community when local courts choose to grant downward departures to offenders convicted of serious violent offenses.

This is a testable question. Future research should study the recidivism of offenders who receive downward departures to test the consequences of such departures for community protection. In addition, researchers should study the recidivism of offenders in general, and compare serious violent offenders to this more general population. This would provide valuable information about the recidivism of the "dangerous" offender as well as other kinds of offenders, and the incapacitative effect (if any) of the guidelines. In our view, research that connects analyses of sentencing outcomes to analyses of subsequent offender behavior will constitute one of the next major advances in our understanding of courts and their sentencing practices.

Notes

1. As indicated in Chapter 3, the Pennsylvania District Attorneys Association had lodged a serious critique of the 1994 commission's argument that it had increased the guideline recommendations for violent offenders.

2. Personal communication to the authors, December 2000.

3. We defined upward departures as minimum sentences that exceeded the guideline aggravated range. Among the 3,243 serious violent offender cases considered here, there are 372 upward departures (11.5 percent of sentences for serious violent offenders). Basically, the upward departure results are the inverse of the downward departure results, with the exception that offense severity is not significantly related to the likelihood of upward departure. Interestingly, Hispanics are 1.86 times more likely than whites to receive departures above guidelines. Also, negotiated pleas *and bench trials* reduce the odds of departure above guidelines (odds of .72 and .82, respectively). The results also illustrate the importance of intercounty variation. Nearly 60 percent of all departures above guidelines for serious violent offenders occur in Philadelphia and Allegheny. However, these two counties exhibit *opposite* patterns with respect to upward

departures: upward departures are modestly more likely in Philadelphia (odds = 1.33) than in the rest of the state, but are considerably less likely in Allegheny (odds = .43).

4. We entered sixty-six county dummy variables (with one county left out as a reference category) into the logistic regression equation (with the other variables shown in Model 1 of Table 4.2). Then we deleted the county dummy variables that were not statistically significant and that did not have logit coefficients twice the size of their standard errors. We reestimated the model with these significant variables included. Model 3 of Table 4.2 shows the five county dummy variables that remained statistically significant and whose coefficients were twice their standard errors.

5. This may be one reason why large urban jurisdictions like Philadelphia and Allegheny (Pittsburgh) tend to sentence less severely in general. Perhaps court actors in large urban jurisdictions see a higher proportion of comparatively more serious cases, and develop a court community culture that defines a comparatively higher standard of offense severity and offender blameworthiness.

5

Racial, Ethnic, Gender, and Age Disparity

THE ONE GOAL shared by all sentencing guideline systems is to reduce or eliminate unwarranted disparity in sentencing outcomes based on the status characteristics of defendants. In fact, some consider this *the* major goal and rationale for guidelines. Naturally, then, research assessing the extent of such disparity will always be a fundamental and essential part of assessing sentencing guidelines themselves. Whatever else guidelines do (e.g., raising the severity of punishments for violent offenders, increasing the use of alternatives to incarceration for other offenders), sentencing commissions, in order to be true to their mandate, must continuously monitor and address unwarranted disparity related to legally irrelevant offender characteristics like race, ethnicity, and gender, and—some would argue—age. The previous chapter on guideline departures for serious violent offenders discussed departures as a locus of disparity, including how locally embedded focal concerns of sentencing can condition such disparity. In this chapter, we address these themes further by examining the direct and combined influences of race, ethnicity, gender, and age on sentencing in Pennsylvania under the 1997 guidelines, and then compare these analyses with similar data from the pre-1994 guidelines period in order to examine changes in the amount and bases of disparity.

Focal Concerns and Status-Related Sentencing Disparity

Eduardo Bonilla-Silva (1997) developed the concept of "racialized social systems," in which racial and ethnic ideologies and disadvantage are embedded in social structures, even though the behavior of actors in the system might be ostensibly race- or ethnicity-neutral and directed toward other, nonracist goals. As a central mechanism of formal social control, a society's criminal justice system could be considered a racialized social system if its apparently race- and ethnicity-neutral and organizationally rational pursuit of crime control and punishment disadvantage racial and ethnic minorities. In the contemporary

89

United States, blacks and Hispanics tend to be objects of crime fear and are seen as particularly threatening (Steffensmeier and Demuth 2001; Britt 2000; Spohn and Holleran 2000; Spohn 2000). Racial ideology and stereotypes can be the "organizational map that guides actions of racial actors" in racialized social systems (Bonilla-Silva 1997, p. 474).

Aaron Beim and Gary Fine (2007) explicitly incorporate the perceived threat of deviant or undesirable activity (such as crime) from minority out-groups as an element of racial and ethnic (or other out-group) prejudice. Specifically, they propose that racial or ethnic prejudice stems from beliefs that (1) the targeted group is more likely to engage in deviant or undesirable actions than other groups (that the group is "uniquely disreputable"), (2) the harmful actions of the group are not balanced by positive actions or attributes, and (3) the in-group benefits of discriminating against the target group are perceived to be greater than the costs of such discrimination (p. 377).

Racially charged decisions and actions often become "embedded in normal operations of institutions" (Bonilla-Silva 1997, p. 476). One example of such a process might be the everyday sentencing decisions of courts, and decisions of prosecutors. Prosecutors' interpretations and assessments of focal concerns such as dangerousness and blameworthiness, as well as the salience of relevant practical constraints and consequences, might be influenced by race, ethnicity, and gender (e.g., Steffensmeier, Ulmer, and Kramer 1998; Spohn 2000; Engen et al. 2003). In particular, some prosecutors and judges may perceive black or Hispanic males as particularly dangerous or lacking rehabilitative potential compared to other types of defendants. They may also see fewer practical costs of incarceration for minorities, who might be perceived as being more adaptable to prison, and as having less conventional social capital (Kramer and Steffensmeier 1993).

In sum, then, the focal concerns perspective argues that those who are viewed as more threatening and dangerous, lacking in rehabilitative potential, or more morally blameworthy will receive more severe treatment at the hands of criminal justice officials. In turn, racial threat theory and other research on racism implies that in the contemporary United States, blacks and Hispanics are likely to be seen as especially dangerous, morally blameworthy, lacking in conventional social capital, and better able to manage the personal impact of incarceration.

Research on Status-Related Disparity Under Guidelines

A very large literature exists on sentencing disparity based on defendant social statuses (see Hagan and Bumiller 1983; Steffensmeier, Kramer, and Streifel 1993; Spohn 2000; Zatz 2000; Steffensmeier and Demuth 2000; Bushway and Piehl 2001). The published research on disparity under guidelines tends to overwhelmingly focus on a handful of guideline jurisdictions: Minnesota, Washington, and the federal system, along with Pennsylvania. Overall, studies uniformly show that the primary determinants of sentencing under guidelines are the guideline-approved ones: offense severity, offense type, offense-related conduct, and criminal history. Guideline jurisdictions have apparently had mixed experiences with defendant status-related disparity, with some jurisdictions characterized by comparatively less disparity (Minnesota, Washington) and some experiencing more (Pennsylvania, the federal system). Also, at least one study has found evidence that blacks are sentenced more harshly than whites under Maryland's voluntary, advisory guidelines (Bushway and Piehl 2001).

Terence Miethe and Charles Moore's 1985 research concluded that the Minnesota guidelines had successfully changed sentencing patterns as intended, although later research indicated that the early high levels of guideline conformity had eroded over time (Frase 1993; Knapp 1987). Generally, Miethe and Moore's studies of Minnesota's guidelines (Miethe and Moore 1985, 1988; Moore and Miethe 1986) found that race, gender, and class disparity greatly decreased in the early years of implementation, but increased moderately in later years, though they did not return to pre-guideline levels. In a later analysis, Jo Dixon (1995) also concluded that Minnesota's guidelines significantly reduced racial sentencing differences (though she did not examine the influence of gender or class). On the other hand, Richard Frase (1993) found that black offenders had lower rates of downward departures, controlling for relevant legal factors, and found that the guidelines had not eliminated gender, geographic, and plea versus trial disparities.

More recently, Barbara Koons-Witt (2002) examined the role of the combined gender, race, and family situation in imprisonment decisions before and after the implementation of Minnesota's guidelines. She found that women overall were not more or less likely to be imprisoned, but that women with dependent children were significantly less likely to be imprisoned before the guidelines had been implemented as well as for several years after the guidelines had been implemented. More relevant to our research, Koons-Witt (2002) further found that the Minnesota guidelines strongly decreased the combined impact of race and gender (e.g., differential sentencing of nonwhite males, white males, nonwhite females, and white females) on imprisonment in the early years of implementation. In fact, the guidelines strongly increased the likelihood of all groups being imprisoned. However, in later years, the probability of imprisonment decreased to levels comparable to those before the guidelines, for all groups. More to the point, nonwhite males and females became more likely to be imprisoned than their white counterparts. Like Frase (1993) and Moore and Miethe (1986), then, Koons-Witt's more refined and updated analysis also showed an early and strong disparity reduction impact of Minnesota's guidelines, followed by the reappearance of disparity. It is important to note, however, that absolute levels of disparity in Minnesota were smaller than in studies of Pennsylvania or the federal system.

A series of studies of sentencing in Washington state has generally shown less evidence of direct racial disparity, but moderate evidence of disparity based on gender and Hispanic ethnicity (Engen and Gainey 2000; Engen et al. 2003). Rodney Engen and Randy Gainey (2000) found no significant differences in sentence lengths between blacks and whites when controlling for the influence of presumptive guideline sentence recommendations, but found moderate differences between Hispanics and whites, and between males and females. In a later study focused on guideline departures and structured sentencing alternatives, though, Engen and colleagues (2003) found that blacks, Hispanics, younger offenders, and males were significantly disadvantaged in guideline departure decisions and in the granting of treatment-oriented alternatives to incarceration.

A number of studies of sentencing under the federal guidelines have found evidence of extralegal disparity related to defendant social statuses. Celesta Albonetti's studies of federal drug offenders (1997) and white-collar offenders (1998) found that women received more lenient sentences overall, and that gender conditioned the impact of federal guideline departures on sentence outcomes. In addition, Albonetti (2002) found that certain guideline provisions (a "safety valve" for first-time nonviolent offenders) conditioned the effects of race and ethnicity on sentence lengths. Darrell Steffensmeier and Stephen Demuth's study of male defendants in the federal system (2000) found that Hispanic defendants, and particularly Hispanic drug defendants, received significantly longer sentences. In addition, they found that Hispanic drug offenders' sentencing disadvantage was especially pronounced in prosecutor-controlled "substantial assistance" departure decisions. R. S. Everett and R. A. Wojtkiewicz (2002) found that blacks, Hispanics, and Native Americans received more severe sentences under the federal guidelines, and these disparities were not fully explained by offense-related characteristics. As mentioned in the previous chapter, David Mustard (2001) found substantial racial, gender, and ethnic disparities under the federal guidelines, and found that most of these disparities were attributable to guideline departures.

Furthermore, Paula Kautt and Cassia Spohn's analysis of federal drug sentences (2002) found that defendant race (being black) conditioned the effects of drug types and amounts on sentences, and did so differently between guideline sentencing cases and mandatory minimum cases. Kautt's multilevel analysis of federal drug sentences (2002) also found modest but significant sentence length disadvantages for black, Hispanic, and male federal defendants, and found that the effects of race, ethnicity, and gender on sentence length varied considerably between federal district courts.

Taken together, all of these studies suggest that defendant status-related disparity remains a challenge for many guideline systems. As the older and more recent research reported below shows, Pennsylvania is certainly no exception.

Prior Research on Race, Ethnicity, and Gender in Pennsylvania Sentencing

Previous studies of race, ethnic, and gender disparity in Pennsylvania have analyzed quantitative and qualitative data from 1977, 1985–1994, and 1997–2000. It should be noted that most of these studies were not explicitly framed as studies of guideline implementation or disparity per se, but rather as theoretically oriented studies of sentencing as a key criminal justice decision. Table 5.1 briefly summarizes the most prominent of these studies in chronological order and lists their data sources, variables included as statistical controls, and major findings. In addition, some of these studies also investigated sentencing differences connected to mode of conviction (type of guilty plea or trial) and court contextual features as variables of interest in their own right.

The findings of this literature can be summarized by the following general patterns. First, the strongest and most consistent predictors of sentencing outcomes in the Pennsylvania studies are the legally prescribed ones relevant to the sentencing guidelines. No study finds a general pattern in which extra-legal, non-guideline-relevant factors *outweigh* legal, guideline-relevant factors. This is an important point, because it suggests that whatever else may be influencing sentencing decisions in a secondary way, courts are primarily relying on the guideline framework to fashion sentences. To that extent, the guidelines do seem to produce a degree of consistency, predictability, and structure in Pennsylvania sentencing.

Second, modest to substantial sentencing advantages consistently exist for women. The majority of studies of Pennsylvania sentencing, like studies of sentencing in other jurisdictions, find that women (1) are significantly less likely to be incarcerated, (2) are more likely to receive shorter sentences, and (3) are more likely to receive downward departures from the guidelines.

Third, race and ethnicity exert small to moderate effects on sentencing. These effects are typically found for incarceration decisions and downward departures rather than sentence length decisions. However, the effects of race are conditioned by gender and age (see the Steffensmeier, Ulmer, and Kramer 1998). In addition, later studies of Pennsylvania sentencing (Steffensmeier and Demuth 2001; Kramer and Ulmer 2002; Ulmer and Johnson 2004) find that Hispanics are often disadvantaged in sentencing outcomes, including incarceration decisions, length decisions, downward departures, and upward departures. In addition, Kathleen Auerhahn's analysis of homicide sentencing (excluding first- and second-degree murder) in Philadelphia (2007) found that young black and Hispanic males who were also detained before trial received notably longer sentences, supporting the notion that the degree of disparity is conditional on multiple defendant social statuses and even on case-processing factors.

Fourth, defendant age has been found to exert a curvilinear relationship to sentencing (Steffensmeier, Kramer, and Ulmer 1995; Steffensmeier, Ulmer,

Table 5.1 Review of Selected Literature on Statewide Disparity in Pennsylvania Sentencing

Researchers	PCS Data Years	Key Variables	Key In/Out Findings	Key Length Findings	Other Findings
Austin and Kempf (1986)	1977 PCS data (2,907 cases)	Bail status, offense seriousness, prior record, urban, etc.	Blacks more likely than whites to be incarcerated for all-size counties; bail status the most powerful predictor of in/out	Blacks receive longer sentences in suburban counties	
Kramer and Steffensmeier (1993)	1985–1987 PCS data (61,294 cases)	Severity of offense (10-point severity scale), 20 offense dummy variables, multiple concurrent convictions (yes or no), race, age, sex, mode of conviction, county contextual factors	Blacks are 8 percent more likely to be incarcerated than white defendants	No race effect on sentence length	
Steffensmeier, Kramer, and Streifel (1993)	1985–1987 PCS data	Same as above	Males 12 percent more likely to be incarcerated	On average, men receive slightly shorter sentences (–1.6 months); black female defendants receive sentences about three months longer than those of white females; females receive shorter sentences for robbery (22 months), and shorter sentences for drug violations	

continues

Table 5.1 Cont.

Researchers	PCS Data Years	Key Variables	Key In/Out Findings	Key Length Findings	Other Findings
Steffensmeier, Kramer, and Ulmer (1995)	1989–1991 PCS data	Same as above	Effect of defendant age on sentencing outcomes is curvilinear—an "inverted U-shaped" relationship; the youngest and oldest offenders are sentenced more leniently, while offenders in their late twenties and middle to late thirties are sentenced most severely	Results largely parallel in/out findings	
Kramer and Ulmer (1996)	1985–1987, 1989–1991 PCS data (41,925 cases in guideline cells where departure below is possible)	Same as above	Blacks and males less likely to receive departures below guidelines	No significant race or gender differences in departures above guidelines	
Ulmer and Kramer (1996)	1985–1987, 1989–1992 PCS data for three counties (small, medium, and large; 39,476 cases)	Same as above	Blacks significantly more likely to be sentenced to jail and especially state prison in large and medium-size counties, but not in small counties; females less likely to be incarcerated in all-size counties, but size of difference varies	Results largely parallel in/out results	

continues

Table 5.1   Cont.

Researchers	PCS Data Years	Key Variables	Key In/Out Findings	Key Length Findings	Other Findings
Ulmer (1997)	1985–1987, 1989–1992 PCS data (166,677 cases)	Same as above	Results parallel Kramer and Ulmer (1996) and Ulmer and Kramer (1996), plus race effects moderately concentrate among offenders with less serious priors state-wide, but the exact opposite pattern is found in some counties; blacks moderately more likely to be incarcerated after conviction by trial than comparable whites		
Steffensmeier, Ulmer and Kramer (1998)	1989–1992 PCS data (139,000 cases)	Same as above (10 percent offense gravity score)	Main effects of gender result in women 15 percent less likely to be incarcerated; blacks are 10 percent more likely to be incarcerated; white males aged 18–29 12 percent less likely than corresponding black males 18–29 to be incarcerated	Women receive 6.5-month shorter sentences; blacks receive two-month longer sentences; white males aged 18–29 receive three-month shorter sentences than corresponding black males	
Steffensmeier & Demuth (2001)	1991–1994 PCS data (96,000 cases with 8,500 Hispanic offenders)	Same as above	Blacks 6 percent more likely and Hispanics 18 percent more likely to be incarcerated for nondrug offenses than whites—net of controls	Blacks receive three-month longer sentences than whites, and Hispanic defendants receive ten-month longer sentences	

continues

Table 5.1 Cont.

Researchers	PCS Data Years	Key Variables	Key In/Out Findings	Key Length Findings	Other Findings
Britt (2000)	1991–1994 PCS data (with data on county racial population composition)	Same as above	Significant variation in sentencing severity between counties; racial disparities vary by court jurisdiction; measures of social context do not explain the variation in racial disparity between counties	Results largely parallel in/out findings	
Kramer and Ulmer (2002)	1997–1999 PCS data (3,243 serious violent offenses)	Same as above, but with a 14-point offense gravity score and an 8-point prior record score, reflecting the 1997 guideline changes			Those convicted by trial, blacks, men, and Hispanics are less likely to receive downward departures; downward departures are much more likely in large urban county courts, and 51 percent of downward departures come from just five counties
Johnson (2003)	1996–1998 PCS data (cases sentenced under the 1994 guidelines)	Same as above, but with a 13-point offense gravity score reflecting the 1994 guidelines; dependent variables were the likelihood of upward and downward departures			Blacks, Hispanics, and males are more likely to receive upward departures and less likely to receive downward departures; the effects of race and ethnicity vary significantly across modes of conviction (nonnegotiated pleas, negotiated pleas, bench trials, jury trials)

continues

Table 5.1 Cont.

Researchers	PCS Data Years	Key Variables	Key In/Out Findings	Key Length Findings	Other Findings
Ulmer and Johnson (2004)	1997–1999 PCS data (108,169 cases covering a broad range of offenses, as well as county and court contextual data)	Same as above, with guideline presumptive sentence recommendation as an additional control	Blacks, Hispanics, men, and those convicted by trial are all significantly more likely to be incarcerated; county court size and caseload decrease the likelihood of incarceration; local jail capacity increases odds of incarceration; size of in/out trial penalties increases with court caseload	The degree of racial and ethnic (Hispanic) disparity in sentence length depends on the racial and ethnic composition of the local population	Sentencing severity varies between counties; the effects of all individual defendant and case-level predictors vary between counties
Holleran and Spohn (2004)	1997 PCS data (4,026 cases sentenced in Philadelphia County)	Similar to above	Multinomial models of county jail versus state prison versus noncarceration show that effects of race, ethnicity, and gender differ for jail as compared to prison incarceration; blacks, Hispanics, and males are more likely to be sentenced to state prison than to county jail		Many other effects differentially affect jail versus prison outcomes as well; authors recommend modeling these two incarceration outcomes separately in future studies

continues

Table 5.1 Cont.

Researchers	PCS Data Years	Key Variables	Key In/Out Findings	Key Length Findings	Other Findings
Johnson (2005)	1997–1999 PCS data (185,427 cases covering a broad range of offenses, as well as county and court contextual data)	Same as above, with additional contextual variables			Several significant contextual effects on downward and upward departures, including court size, caseload, departure rate, trial rate, and percent Hispanic (which decrease the likelihood of downward and increase the likelihood of upward departures); in addition, the effects of most individual-level predictors of departures, including race/ethnicity and gender, vary significantly between counties
Johnson (2006)	1997–1999 PCS data (148,590 cases covering a broad range of offenses, as well as county and court contextual data)	Same as above, with judge characteristics added as a contextual level of analysis	Older judges less likely to incarcerate; minority judges less likely to incarcerate; judges with military experience more likely to incarcerate	Older judges give shorter sentences; minority judges give shorter sentences	Minority judges less likely than white judges to incarcerate blacks and Hispanics
Auerhahn (2007)	1,137 homicide cases (excluding first- and second-degree murder) sentenced in Philadephia County 1995–2000	Homicide type, characteristics, number of charges, mode of conviction, type of attorney, pretrial detention, defendant race, ethnicity, age, and gender, various victim characteristics		Young blacks and Hispanics detained pretrial receive substantially longer sentences	Those convicted by trial receive longer sentences; offenders under age twenty-five receive longer sentences

and Kramer 1998). Offenders in their late teens and early twenties as well as offenders over age fifty are sentenced more leniently, and those in their late twenties and in their thirties are sentenced most severely.

Fifth, mode of conviction consistently and strongly affects sentencing outcomes. Compared to those who plead guilty, those convicted by trial are consistently and significantly more likely to be incarcerated and to receive longer sentences, and are less likely to receive downward departures. In addition, Brian Johnson (2003) showed that the effects of race and Hispanic ethnicity on the likelihood of downward or upward departures varied across modes of conviction (i.e., nonnegotiated guilty pleas, negotiated guilty pleas, bench and jury trials). We will return to the sentencing differences between guilty pleas and trials, and how defendant statuses relate to these differences, in Chapter 7.

Sixth, substantial differences in sentencing severity exist between court jurisdictions, a pattern that can be called geographical or contextual disparity. In addition, we found (Ulmer and Kramer 1996; Ulmer 1997) that the amount and nature of racial and gender disparity varied widely throughout the state, a theme later substantiated in other studies (Britt 2000; Ulmer and Johnson 2004; Johnson 2005, 2006). We elaborate on this point later, after presenting our empirical analysis of defendant social statuses and sentencing.

More specific highlights of these studies include the following:

• We found in our analysis of 1991–1994 sentencing in Pennsylvania (Steffensmeier, Ulmer, and Kramer 1998) that the effect of race on sentencing outcomes depended on the defendant's age and gender, and the effect of gender on sentencing varied depending on the age and race of the offender. Specifically, we found that young, black males received the most severe penalties compared to other age, race, and gender categories. Interestingly, this analysis found that older black offenders received less severe penalties than other age, race, and gender categories. A key implication is that models of the overall effect of race (or ethnicity) mask substantial variation in the way that gender and age condition the effect of race, and mask substantial sentencing differences between certain race, age, and gender categories.

• We found (Kramer and Ulmer 1996; Ulmer 1997) that while legally prescribed factors such as offense severity and criminal history were the primary predictors of departure decisions, females and white offenders were significantly more likely to receive dispositional departures (nonincarceration sentences when the guidelines call for incarceration) below the guidelines. In other words, certain departures presented a pattern of differential leniency that favored certain kinds of offenders.

• David Holleran and Cassia Spohn (2004) separately examined the decision to sentence an offender to state prison versus county jail (versus no incarceration) rather than including both decisions in one overall incarceration variable. They found that the effects of gender, race, and ethnicity differed substantially for the state prison as compared to the county jail decision. Specifically, they found that whites and women, when they were incarcerated, were more likely to be sent to county jail as opposed to state prison, whereas blacks, Hispanics, and men were more likely to be sent to state prison.

Thus the literature presents a picture in which legally relevant, guideline-prescribed factors (offense type and severity, prior record, presumptive sentence recommendation) most strongly determine sentences in Pennsylvania. However, important types of disparity appear to remain. Gender, mode of conviction, race/ethnicity, and court context tend to produce significant sentencing differences. In addition, defendant social statuses tend to mutually condition one another's influence on sentencing—that is, the effect of race or ethnicity appears to depend on gender, and to a lesser extent on age. Furthermore, different case-processing decisions and sentencing outcomes condition different degrees of defendant social status disparity.

Older and More Recent Data on Social Status Disparity in Pennsylvania Sentencing

To further examine overall disparity connected to defendant social status (race and ethnicity, gender, age), we analyzed data on sentencing outcomes in Pennsylvania for the periods 1989–1992 and 1997–2000. These analyses used sentencing data from the Pennsylvania Commission on Sentencing, as in Chapter 4. Our analysis focused on three key decisions: the jail and prison incarceration decisions, the length of incarceration (in months), and departures from the sentencing guidelines. More information about these data and our research methods can be found in the Research Methods Appendix.

Our analysis here begins by examining descriptive statistics for the sentencing outcome variables, the defendant characteristic variables, and the control variables we used in our 1989–1992 and 1997–2000 analyses, as shown in Table 5.2. Of particular note in this table is that there are 128,557 (about 64 percent) white defendants, 58,541 (29 percent) black defendants, 12,732 (6.3 percent) Hispanic defendants, and 1,330 (.7 percent) defendants of other races or ethnicities (racial and ethnic data were missing for 6,567 cases). Men constitute 83 percent (170,396) of the defendants, while women constitute 17 percent (34,658). Table 5.2 also shows the number of defendants in race/ethnicity, gender, and age categorizations—for example, young black males, young white males, and older Hispanic males. These categorizations will be used in our later analyses of the interactive effects of race/ethnicity, gender, and age.

Jail, Prison, and Length of Minimum Incarceration

Several previous scholars have suggested analyzing jail and prison incarceration separately (Holleran and Spohn 2004; Kramer and Steffensmeier 1993;

Table 5.2   Descriptive Statistics for Individual Sentencing Cases, 1997–2000

Variable	Frequency	Percentage
In/out		
Not Incarcerated	94,845	45.6
Incarcerated	113,137	54.4
Downward departure	8,884	4.3
Upward departure	9,878	4.7
Sentencing year		
1997	5,137	2.5
1998	57,995	27.9
1999	71,689	34.5
2000	73,161	35.2
Offense type		
Homicide	956	.5
Rape	315	.2
IDSI	301	.1
Robbery	4,793	2.3
Weapons	4,103	2.0
Aggravated assault	4,035	1.9
Simple assault	19,324	9.3
Arson	454	.2
Burglary	6,519	3.1
Criminal trespassing	3,792	1.8
Theft	37,407	18.0
Forgery	4,109	2.0
Drug felony	21,862	10.5
Drug misdemeanor	18,884	9.1
DUI	45,767	22.0
Mode of conviction		
Negotiated guilty pleas	133,309	73.4
Bench trials	5,435	3.0
Jury trials	2,891	1.6
Nonnegotiated guilty pleas	39,895	22.0
Race/ethnicity		
Black	58,541	29.1
White	128,557	63.9
Hispanic	12,732	6.3
Other	1,330	.7
Gender		
Male	170,396	83.1
Female	34,658	16.9

continues

Ulmer 1997). We therefore estimate a multinomial regression model of the likelihood of receiving these two incarceration options. Table 5.3 shows multinomial regression models for jail and prison incarceration, and an ordinary least squares (OLS) regression model for minimum sentence length (logged). It shows the effects of combined categories of race, ethnicity, and gender on incarceration and length, along with the effects of all the other control variables.

Table 5.2   Cont.

Variable	Frequency	Percentage
Age		
White males 18–29	49,303	24.8
Black males 18–29	25,967	12.5
Hispanic males 18–29	6,707	3.2
White males 30 and over	55,567	26.7
Black males 30 and over	22,043	10.6
Hispanic males 30 and over	4,274	2.1
White females 18–29	8,679	4.2
Black females 18–29	3,781	1.8
Hispanic females 18–29	754	.4
White females 30 and over	13,703	6.6
Black females 30 and over	5,710	2.7
Hispanic females 30 and over	710	.3

	Mean	SD	Median	N
Offense severity score (1–14)	3.39	2.119	3.00	207,727
Prior record score (0–8)	1.29	1.831	.00	207,876
Minimum incarceration length (in months, incarceration cases only)	8.15	16.39	3.00	111,711

Offense severity and prior record are the strongest predictors of the two types of incarceration and sentence length, just as the guidelines intend, along with particular offense types. Offense gravity score and prior record score are particularly strong predictors of prison sentences. While each increase in OGS increases the odds of going to county jail by 22 percent, each increase in OGS increases the odds of going to state prison by 104 percent. Similarly, each increase in PRS increases the odds of a county jail sentence by 29 percent, but the odds of a state prison sentence by 93 percent. Presumptive disposition predicts jail incarceration significantly, but not state imprisonment (not surprising, since the presumptive disposition variable does not distinguish between the two types of incarceration). Homicide and robbery offenses are especially likely to result in prison sentences. Jury trial convictions are more likely to result in jail sentences, but are *much* more likely to result in prison sentences. In fact, jury trial conviction far outweighs any one offense type as a predictor of prison. Jury trial convictees also have sentence lengths almost 160 percent greater than those convicted by nonnegotiated guilty pleas. We will return to the issue of trial penalties in Chapter 7.

The race/ethnicity and gender categories reveal several interesting findings. Figures 5.1 and 5.2 show bar graphs of the various groups' jail and state prison odds. In parallel to the results above for overall incarceration, Hispanic and black males (in that order) appear to be disadvantaged in the county jail

Table 5.3   Sentencing Outcomes, 1997–2000

	Jail Odds	Prison Odds	Incarceration Length (logged)	
			Log (b)	Antilog (b)
Constant			2.004***	100.877
Offense gravity score	1.22***	2.04***	0.258***	1.810
Prior record score	1.29***	1.93***	0.154***	1.426
Presumptive disposition/	1.57***	1.05		
presumptive minimum				
Mode of conviction				
Negotiated guilty plea	.92**	.94*	−0.060***	0.872
Bench trial	1.17***	1.69***	0.148***	1.405
Jury trial	2.13***	13.8***	0.414***	2.597
Offense type ("other offenses" is reference category)				
Homicide	1.28	3.65***	0.485***	3.053
Rape/IDSI	.43*	1.08	0.299***	1.993
Robbery	2.30***	3.33***	0.271***	1.867
Weapons	.81***	.77***	−0.050*	0.891
Aggravated asssault	1.59***	1.28*	−0.035	0.923
Simple assault	.99	.89	0.041***	1.099
Arson	1.25	1.54*	0.033	1.080
Burglary	1.57***	2.00***	0.107***	1.280
Criminal trespassing	1.43***	1.56***	0.096***	1.247
Theft	1.18	.85	−0.012	0.973
Forgery	1.17***	2.30***	0.097***	1.251
Drug felony	.88***	1.49***	0.100***	1.260
Drug misdemeanor	.55***	.34***	−0.158***	0.696
Race and gender				
Black male	1.36	1.02	.04***	1.04
Black female	.83***	.41***	−.09***	.91
Hispanic male	1.42**	1.47***	.10***	1.10
Hispanic female	.79*	.49**	−.17	.84
White female	.70***	.55***	−.17***	.84
Age	.99***	.98***	−.001	.999
N		178,110		60,892

Notes: Reference category is all white/other male defendants in Pennsylvania.
*** p < .0001; ** p < .001; * p < .01.

decision. That is, black males' odds of jail incarceration compared to white males are 1.36, while Hispanic males' odds are 1.42. On the other hand, women, particularly white women (who have moderately lower odds of jail incarceration than black or Hispanic women), are modestly advantaged in jail decisions—they are all less likely to go to jail than white men.

The picture is somewhat different for state prison incarceration. Here, black and white males' odds of state imprisonment are virtually identical. No black versus white race disparity among men is evident for state prison sentences. Hispanic males, on the other hand, have significantly greater odds of going to state prison than white or (indirectly) black men. Hispanic men's odds

Figure 5.1   Effects of Race and Gender Categories on Jail Incarceration

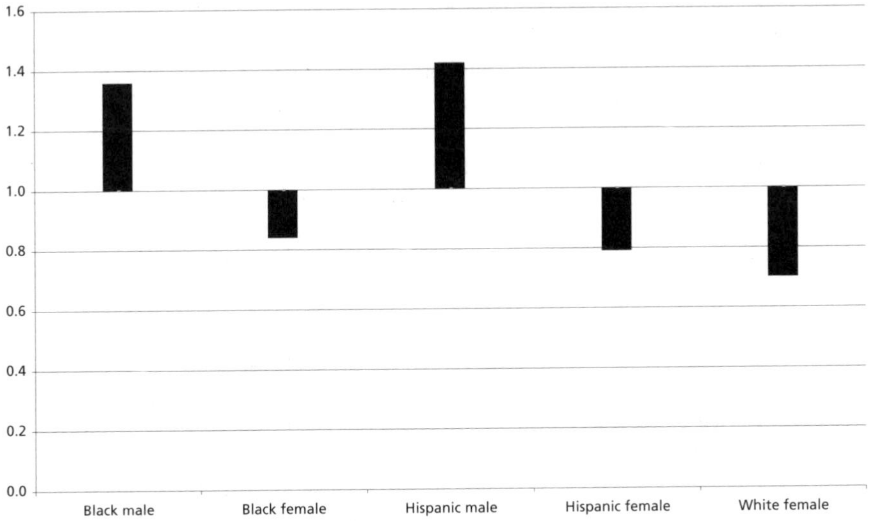

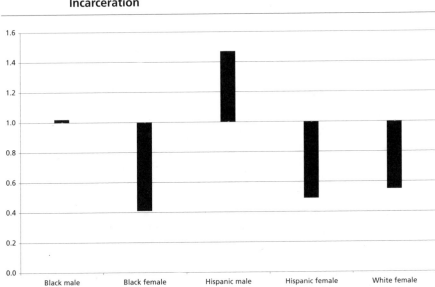

Note: Based on multinomial regression analyses in Table 5.3.

Figure 5.2   Effects of Race and Gender Categories on State Prison Incarceration

Note: Based on multinomial regression analyses in Table 5.6.

of state prison are 47 percent greater than white men's. This implies that 1.47 Hispanic men go to state prison for every one white man, even though Hispanics make up only 1.5 percent of the state's population and Hispanic males comprise only 5.3 percent of the state's court caseload. Clearly, Hispanic males are overrepresented in state prison sentences, even controlling for guideline-relevant and case-processing factors.

Finally, women in all categories are about half as likely, or less, to go to jail than white men. In contrast to the jail decision (where white women were the most advantaged), the group least likely to go to state prison is black women, followed by Hispanic women. White women are moderately more likely to go to state prison than either group of minority women. In sum, we conclude from the multinomial analysis that (1) black versus white disparity among males, such as it is, concentrates in the county jail decision, (2) disparity is evident for Hispanic males in both the county jail and the state prison decision, and (3) women are especially less likely to go to state prison, with black women being the least likely. Women are also moderately less likely to go to county jail, with white women being least likely by a slight margin.

The sentence length results in Table 5.3 show that Hispanic males' sentences are about 10 percent longer than white males' but black males' sentences are about 4 percent longer than white males'—a very modest black versus white difference. White and Hispanic females' sentence lengths are about 16 percent shorter than white males'. Black women's sentences are about 9 percent shorter than white men's. Thus, in terms of sentence length, white and Hispanic women are more advantaged vis-à-vis white men than are black women.

Age, Race, Ethnicity, and Gender in Combination

Earlier research uncovered the need to examine offender subgroups based on categories of race, ethnicity, and gender. Table 5.4 shows logistic and OLS multivariate regression models of overall incarceration and incarceration length that focus on the combined effects of race, ethnicity, gender, and age (there is too little variation in types of incarceration among the race/ethnicity, gender, and age categories to run multinomial models differentiating jail and prison). That is, the variables for defendant status characteristics in these models examine the effects of these characteristics in combination. We compare the following race/ethnicity, gender, and age categories, with young (age eighteen to twenty-nine) white males being the reference category: young white females, older (age thirty and over) white females, older white males, young black males, young black females, older black males, older black females, young Hispanic males, young Hispanic females, older Hispanic males, and older Hispanic females. The effects of the control variables are also presented in Table 5.4, to show whether they stay the same when the defendant status factors are combined into race/ethnicity, gender, and age categories.

Table 5.4   Combined Effects of Race, Ethnicity, Gender, and Age on Sentencing Outcomes, 1997–2000

	Incarceration Odds	Incarceration Length		
		Log (b)	Standard Error	Antilog (b)
Young white female defendant	0.494***	−0.167***	0.018	0.681
Older white female defendant	0.670***	−0.066***	0.014	0.859
Older white male defendant	1.183***	0.008	0.007	1.020
Young Hispanic male defendant	1.288***	0.056***	0.013	1.138
Older Hispanic male defendant	1.416***	0.062***	0.015	1.152
Young Hispanic female defendant	0.609***	−0.136*	0.042	0.731
Older Hispanic female defendant	0.702***	−0.040	0.041	0.912
Older black female defendant	0.608***	−0.051*	0.016	0.890
Older black male defendant	1.180***	−0.020	0.009	0.954
Young black female defendant	0.469***	−0.161***	0.022	0.691
Young black male defendant	1.215***	0.038***	0.008	1.091
N	173,333		59,344	

Notes: Reference category is young white male defendants.
*** $p < .0001$; ** $p < .001$; * $p < .01$.

In Table 5.4, the effects for the legally prescribed variables largely stay the same, as in Table 5.3, the only exception being that the effects on incarceration of rape and involuntary deviate sexual intercourse change slightly. The four strongest determinants of incarceration and length are, in order: prior record, offense gravity score (whose effects are cumulative), offense type, and jury trial conviction.

Turning to the race, ethnicity, gender, and age categories, it is evident that the effects of race/ethnicity on sentencing vary not only by gender, but also by age. Figure 5.3 displays bar graphs of the relative incarceration odds and lengths for these different groups. Compared to the reference category of young white males, older Hispanic males are the most likely group to be incarcerated, and for the longest periods. Older Hispanic males have about 1.42 greater odds of incarceration than young white males. In other words, regardless of the effects of the other legally prescribed, case-processing, and court size factors in the model, about 1.5 older Hispanic men are sentenced to jail or prison for every one young white male, and older Hispanic men have about a 9 percent greater probability than 50/50 of incarceration. In addition, older Hispanic males are sentenced to incarceration terms that are on average 15 percent longer than those for young white males. Young Hispanic male defendants are also more likely to be incarcerated than young white males: 1.29 young Hispanic males are incarcerated for every one young white male, and older black males have a 6 percent greater probability than 50/50 of being incarcerated. Older and young Hispanic males are followed by young black males, who have 1.21 times greater odds of incarceration and receive incarceration sentences that are about

Figure 5.3   Sentence Lengths by Race, Ethnicity, Gender, and Age

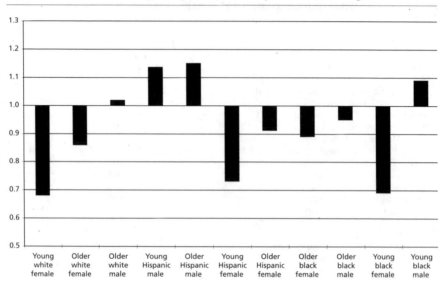

9 percent longer. Older black males and older white males are about equal in their incarceration chances and sentence lengths.

All female groups are sentenced more leniently than young white males, and indirectly, more leniently than all males. In particular, young black females are sentenced most leniently. Young black females' incarceration odds are less than half (.47) those of young white males, and they are 18 percent less likely than 50/50 to be incarcerated. Young black females are also sentenced to incarceration terms that are 31 percent shorter than those for young white males.

Our analyses here confirm that courts primarily rely on the type and seriousness of the offense and prior record, as intended by Pennsylvania's guidelines. However, we conclude that defendant status characteristics of race, gender, and age definitely affect a variety of sentencing outcomes, apart from guideline-relevant factors and mode of conviction. Exactly *how* these statuses affect sentencing becomes quite complicated.

First, gender is the most consistently influential variable among defendant status characteristics. We found that women were less likely to be incarcerated overall than men, and received shorter sentences than men. The role of gender in sentencing particularly emerged, however, when we analyzed how it combines with race, ethnicity, and age. Black and white women received the least severe penalties (measured in terms of both the likelihood of jail or prison incarceration, and length). The other female offender groups also received less serious penalties. This suggests that gender is important across various age, race, and ethnicity categories.

Based on the analyses above, we conclude that gender is a crucial variable in the sentencing decision. This does not necessarily reflect *unwarranted* disparity, since there are factors that we could not include in the models, such as having childcare responsibilities, having a minor role in the offense, and other factors that might legitimately (at least to some observers) account for the fact that women receive less severe penalties.

Second, concern about sentencing disparity has historically centered around race. When we combined race, age, and gender categories, we found that gender specified the relationship for blacks, with black men sentenced more severely than whites (of both sexes), while black women tended to be sentenced more leniently (particularly for state prison sentences). In other words, the *role of race* in sentencing outcomes *depends on gender*, and to a lesser extent on *age*. Race is important in sentencing, but its exact role depends on the age and gender of the defendant. Furthermore, the "black male" effect concentrates around county jail sentences. Black males were significantly more likely to go to county jail than white males, but their odds of state prison sentences were virtually equal to those of white males.

Third, when we explored how the sentencing for Hispanics was differentiated by age and gender, we found that older Hispanic males were the most severely punished category, followed by young Hispanic males. Hispanic females, on the other hand, received less severe penalties, though not as lenient as those for young black and white females. Among females as with males, it is the older Hispanics who are at the top of the severity rankings, though all females are punished more leniently than all males. As with race, then, gender and age differentiate the effect of Hispanic ethnicity on sentencing. Also, unlike for black males, the Hispanic male sentencing disadvantage characterizes both county jail and state prison decisions.

Departures from Guidelines

We also replicated the above analyses for downward and upward departures from Pennsylvania's sentencing guidelines as dependent variables. The logistic multivariate regression results are shown in Table 5.5.

Older Hispanic males are the least likely to receive sentences that depart below the guidelines (i.e., sentences that are more lenient than those called for by guidelines), and young black females are the most likely to receive them. Furthermore, both younger and older Hispanic males are significantly more likely to receive departures above the guidelines (i.e., sentences that are more severe than called for by the guidelines), while young black, white, and Hispanic females are less likely to receive them.

Variation in Disparity over Time

Finally, we examined changes in race, ethnicity, and gender sentencing patterns between the early and late 1990s. We ran identical models of incarceration and

Table 5.5   Departures from Sentencing Guidelines, 1997–2000

	Downward Departure Odds	Upward Departure Odds
Constant	0.005**	0.037***
Offense gravity score	1.700**	0.979
Prior record score	2.257**	0.862**
Mode of conviction		
Negotiated guilty plea	1.077	0.910*
Bench trial	0.395***	0.933
Jury trial	0.170***	2.717***
Offense type ("other offenses" is reference category)		
Homicide	0.083***	1.291
Rape	0.113***	2.794***
IDSI	0.207***	1.683
Robbery	0.193***	2.755***
Weapons	0.838	0.831
Aggravated assault	0.775*	1.081
Simple assault	1.338***	1.098
Arson	0.735	1.766*
Burglary	0.353***	1.926***
Criminal trespassing	0.728*	1.257*
Theft	0.780***	1.034
Forgery	0.838	1.759***
Drug felony	0.562***	1.176*
Drug misdemeanor	1.408***	0.929
Age, race, and gender		
Young white female defendant	1.070	0.754***
Older white female defendant	1.033	0.942
Older white male defendant	1.144*	0.966
Young Hispanic male defendant	0.638***	1.230*
Older Hispanic male defendant	0.542***	1.341***
Young Hispanic female defendant	1.438	0.664
Older Hispanic female defendant	0.800	0.898
Older black female defendant	1.022	0.867
Older black male defendant	1.002	1.033
Young black female defendant	1.583***	0.571***
Young black male defendant	0.741***	1.098
Sentencing year	0.847***	0.950***
N = 169,245 persons		

Notes: Reference category is young white male defendants.
*** $p < .0001$; ** $p < .001$; * $p < .01$.

length for the period 1989–1992, and compared them with our main analyses above (all previous control variables were included, but are not shown). In the interests of parsimonious presentation and ease of comparisons, we do not differentiate between jail and prison incarceration in these analyses. We tested whether the direct and combined effects of race, ethnicity, and gender were different, and whether the differences were statistically significant. The statistical test we used to determine the statistical significance of differences was the z-score test for equality of regression coefficients (for details, see Paternoster et al. 1998). The results for the direct effects of race, Hispanic ethnicity, and gender are shown in Table 5.6, and the combined effects are shown in Table 5.7. The tables show time period differences for both incarceration decisions and sentence lengths.

Table 5.6 shows that the effects of race and ethnicity differed significantly between 1989–1992 and 1997–2000. There was significantly less racial disparity in 1997–2000 than in 1989–1992. The effect of being Hispanic on incarceration was also significantly less in the more recent years than in 1989–1992. Thus, overall black versus white and Hispanic versus white disparity in incarceration have significantly and meaningfully declined with time. This implies that overall racial and ethnic disparity is less under the recent 1997 version of the guidelines than under the older, pre-1994 version. The effect of gender on incarceration, however, has remained the same. In both time periods, women had odds of incarceration that were about half those of men. This suggests that gender differences in incarceration are relatively durable.

There do not appear to be meaningful differences between the time periods in the effects of race or ethnicity on sentence lengths. But gender disparity in sentence lengths was somewhat decreased in the more recent time period. Women's sentence lengths were about 14 percent less than men's in the earlier time period, and were about 10 percent less than men's sentences in the later guideline period. Still, gender disparity was significant in both periods.

Turning now to the combined effects of race, ethnicity, gender, and age (Table 5.7), we see that nine of the twenty-two comparisons display significant differences. Incarceration disparity affecting young black males, young Hispanic males, older Hispanic males, and young black females was also less in the later time period. In other words, the incarceration disadvantages of these groups decreased between the two time periods, with less disparity in the recent guidelines than under the old guidelines. The biggest declines were for young black and Hispanic males, whose incarceration odds dropped by .60

Table 5.6   Differences in Direct Effects of Race, Ethnicity, and Gender on Sentencing Patterns, 1989–1992 and 1997–2000

	Black	Hispanic	Gender (female = 1)
Odds of Incarceration			
1997–2000	1.06	1.20	0.52
1989–1992	1.73	1.95	0.52
Difference	–0.66***	–0.74***	.00
Length of Incarceration			
1997–2000 (logged)	.006	0.047	–.102
1989–1992 (logged)	.003	0.29	–.152
Difference	0.003	0.018	–.05***

Note: *** Indicates that the difference between the effects in the two time periods is statistically significant at $p < .001$.

Table 5.7 Differences in Combined Effects of Race, Ethnicity, Gender, and Age on Sentencing Patterns, 1989–1992 and 1997–2000

	Odds of Incarceration			Length of Incarceration		
	1997–2000	1989–1992	Difference	1997–2000 (logged)	1989–1992 (logged)	Difference
Young black males	1.215	1.81	−0.60*	0.038	0.044	−.006
Young Hispanic males	1.288	1.94	−0.65*	0.056	.049	.009
Older black males	1.180	1.28	−0.10	−0.020	−.033	.013
Older Hispanic males	1.416	1.87	−0.45*	0.062	.037	.025
Older white males	1.183	0.804	0.38*	0.008	.043	−.035*
Young white females	.494	0.51	−0.01	−0.167	−.126	−.04
Older white females	.670	0.40	0.27*	−0.066	−.197	.13*
Young black females	.469	0.96	−0.49*	−0.161	−.150	−.01
Older black females	.608	0.74	−0.13	−0.051	.053	.02
Young Hispanic females	.609	0.84	−.23	−0.136	−.061	0.15
Older Hispanic females	.702	0.534	0.17	−0.040	−.252	.21*

Note: * Indicates that the difference between the effects in the two time periods is statistically significant at p < .05.

and .65 respectively. Incarceration differences involving young black females versus young white males were notably greater in the more recent period than in the past, and in the more recent period young black females were the group least likely to be incarcerated (especially in state prison, see Table 5.3).

Older white males and females show an opposite pattern to the young minority groups above. Older white males went from a position of slight relative advantage to one of disadvantage in incarceration. The incarceration effects for older white females were also greater in the past than in 1997–2000. This is noteworthy because older white females were the group least likely to be incarcerated in 1989–1992.

Overall, then, the trend for incarceration decisions has been one of decreasing incarceration disparity for Hispanic males, and for young black men and women. In fact, young black women have supplanted older white women as the group least likely to be incarcerated. Black versus white disparity has dampened among older men, too. Once a somewhat advantaged group, older white men now have virtually the same incarceration chances as both groups of black men (though all three groups are more likely to be incarcerated than young white males).

Three groups' effects on sentence length were significantly different in 1997–2000 versus 1989–1992: older white males, older white females, and older Hispanic females. Being an older white male had less of an effect on sentence length in later years than it did in the past. Older white males received slightly longer sentences relative to young white males in the past, but in the more recent period, white males received sentences of about the same length, regardless of age. Older white females were less advantaged in the more recent period than in the past. In the 1989–1992 period, older white females received sentences that were 18 percent shorter than those for young white males; but in the 1997–2000 period, their sentence lengths were 6 percent shorter. Similarly, older Hispanic women (a very small group in the 1989–1992 data) had a greater sentence length advantage in the earlier period than under the most recent guidelines.

In sum, trends in racial, ethnic, and gender sentencing patterns over time arguably present a story of overall decreasing race/ethnic incarceration disparity between males, and stability in the moderate race/ethnic length differences that do exist. In no comparison was there significantly greater disparity in the later guideline years. In particular, Hispanic male and young black male sentencing disadvantages have significantly shrunk. This is heartening for proponents of guidelines as a way to reduce unwarranted disparity.

Still, in the earlier years, just as now, Hispanic males (especially older ones) were the most severely sentenced group. Thus the disparity findings for Hispanics are mixed. Though Hispanic males of all ages remain the most severely sentenced groups, the Hispanic versus white disparity has decreased from the early 1990s—sometimes dramatically.

The trend for race is one of a moderately decreased black versus white sentencing disadvantage for men, but a greater relative sentencing *advantage* for black women (especially young black women). Blacks were and still are actually less disadvantaged in sentencing than Hispanics, and black versus white disparity among men has shrunk modestly but significantly. Black men still receive somewhat more severe sentences than their white counterparts, but young black women receive the least severe sentences of all. Thus the effect of race on sentencing was and still is strongly differentiated by gender. Furthermore, overall gender differences seem to be relatively durable.

Conclusion

Concern about unwarranted sentencing disparity based on status characteristics like race, ethnicity, gender, and age will always be central to the ongoing project of sentencing guidelines. Guidelines seek to treat legally similar offenders alike through logically formal rationality—a consistent set of rules (e.g., offense severity, prior record, other formal guideline mechanisms) that should determine sentences. However, the focal concerns perspective suggests that substantive rationality in the form of locally and subjectively interpreted focal concerns guides sentencing as much as formal policies. To the extent that local court community actors stereotype blacks, Hispanics, and men as more blameworthy and threatening, and perceive the practical consequences of sentencing as linked to race, gender, and age (in combination), disparities based on such social statuses will persist, even under guidelines.

Our data here are consistent with this focal concerns view, even as they offer hope that some disparities may be decreasing over time. Hispanic males and young black males receive more severe sentences overall. Interestingly, young black females receive the least severe sentences. This parallels a little-noticed finding by Koons-Witt (2002)—black females were the most leniently sentenced group in Minnesota's pre-guidelines era. On the other hand, we have found that racial and especially Hispanic versus white disparities appeared to decrease overall from 1989–1992 to 1997–2000 (the exception to this pattern is black males, for whom black versus white disparity increased somewhat).

It is important to note that the above analysis, as well as nearly all of the Pennsylvania sentencing studies, share some limitations that need to be considered. First, we do not have information on charging decisions, and these decisions can have a very important impact on sentencing. For example, the decision on what to charge, and the decision as to whether to file a motion for the application of a mandatory minimum, rest in the hands of the prosecutor. We do not know how this discretion is being used, but we do know that it could have a significant impact on the sentencing. Second, we lack information on factors such as offenders' employment, socioeconomic status, role in the offense, and family status and responsibilities, which may affect sentencing. This is especially important because these factors are probably correlated with gender, race, and ethnicity. We cannot rule out the possibility that the race, ethnicity, and gender differences we find here are actually attributable to the above factors.

We are therefore cautious in our interpretation that the disparities we uncovered are "unwarranted," since it is possible that other factors seen by some as legitimate, such as family responsibilities, employment, or similar considerations, create differences between racial, ethnic, and gender groups. Court actors sometimes consider characteristics of defendants' biography, situational life circumstances, and social resources that are likely linked to race, ethnicity, and gender (see Ulmer 1997). Some might argue that such factors are legitimate, while others would disagree. For example, the Minnesota sentencing commission finds the use of employment status inappropriate in determining sentencing, because it would result in racial disparity. Moreover, the US Sentencing Commission determined that family responsibilities and employment are "not ordinarily relevant" at sentencing. The US Sentencing Commission concluded that such factors would undermine a fair system of justice and make penalties disproportionate to the severity of the crime.

The Pennsylvania Commission on Sentencing has not addressed the appropriate role of such factors in sentencing, but it is possible that our findings of disparity might merely reflect our lack of information on the appropriate social circumstance and resource variables that might explain away the race/ethnicity, gender, and age differences. Even so, reasonable observers may disagree as to whether sentencing on the basis of employment, family status, or other factors constitutes warranted or unwarranted disparity.

We also found that the groups most likely to receive longer sentences were, not surprisingly, less likely to receive departures below the guidelines. This raises important policy concerns about the degree that departures above and particularly below the guidelines are a site of disparity. We cannot determine for certain whether this disparity is unwarranted, because there are factors such as employment, role in the offense, and family responsibilities, which we cannot control for, but which judges might consider and which may account for the effects of race, ethnicity, and gender. However, as long as we find these differences, it will raise questions about the potential for discrimination in guideline departures.

We would make two suggestions regarding the reduction of disparity in Pennsylvania. The first concerns the formal standards of accountability to which judges are held. Pennsylvania's standards of appellate review of sentencing decisions allow the most judicial discretion of any state that uses sentencing guidelines. In the *Commonwealth v. Sessoms* decision, the Pennsylvania Supreme Court applied the standard that, "absent a manifest abuse of discretion," a sentence will not be remanded. This standard strongly discourages appellate review of sentencing, as our research in the early 1990s documented (Kramer and

Ulmer 1996). The key result is that judges are practically unaccountable for the sentencing decision. A review of the statement of reasons provided to the Pennsylvania Commission on Sentencing for departures from the guidelines reveals that the most common rationale given is the vague one of "plea agreement," and that for a majority of the departures no rationale is provided to the PCS at all. Other states with sentencing guidelines, such as Minnesota and Washington, have established higher standards for departure, with no obvious deleterious effect on the number of appeals.

Finally, when we speak of sentencing, we often make the assumption that it is under the sole jurisdiction of the judge. This is a profound error. The reality is that, as our previous research has found, the prosecutor plays a key role in sentencing. In all cases, prosecutors control the charging process, and they solely control the application of mandatory minimums. Furthermore, over 95 percent of all sentencing cases are guilty pleas (see Table 5.2). Thus, prosecutors' plea agreements are crucial in determining sentences, including departures from guidelines, in the overwhelming majority of cases. For example, our analysis in Chapter 4 found that negotiated plea agreements were the key factor in determining whether serious violent offenders received departures below the guidelines, and our analysis in Chapter 8 demonstrates the importance of extralegal factors in prosecutors' decisions to apply mandatory minimums. Thus it is not enough to focus on judges in addressing unwarranted disparity. Prosecutors are a crucial ingredient in sentencing, and are also key to attacking concerns about racial and gender bias in sentencing.

6

Location Matters:
Variation Between Counties

A NEW AND important direction of sentencing research is the analysis of between-court variation in sentencing. This type of contextual disparity has received relatively less attention than overall levels of disparity based on social statuses of defendants (race, for example) in the sentencing literature or in guideline policy discussions. Three recent studies, however, suggest that contextual disparity may be sizable and important in Pennsylvania sentencing.

Chester Britt (2000) examined between-court variation in racial disparities, and was the first to apply hierarchical linear and logistic modeling (HLM) techniques to Pennsylvania sentencing. Britt found that not only did overall sentencing severity (as measured by the odds of incarceration and sentence lengths) differ significantly between counties, but also that the level of racial disparity varied substantially between counties.

Jeffery Ulmer and Brian Johnson (2004) also applied HLM techniques to 1997–1999 Pennsylvania data. Like Britt, they found that sentencing severity and the effect of race on sentencing varied between counties. They also found that the effects of a variety of other defendant and case-related factors, such as Hispanic ethnicity, gender, trial conviction, and even offense type and severity and prior record, varied between counties. In addition, court size and caseload were negatively related to incarceration, while local jail capacity increased incarceration odds. Furthermore, contextual features of courts interacted with individual case characteristics and defendant social statuses. Courts with heavier caseloads punished defendants convicted by trial more severely than courts with lighter caseloads. In addition, blacks and Hispanics received longer sentences in counties with greater concentrations of blacks and Hispanics, respectively. In other words, the percentage of the local population consisting of blacks or Hispanics influenced the degree to which blacks or Hispanics were disadvantaged in sentence length decisions. In this chapter, we extend this analysis by Ulmer and Johnson, with some key changes explained below.

The propensity to depart from guidelines also appears to vary considerably between county courts. We found (Kramer and Ulmer 1996) that county court size was associated with the likelihood and size of downward departures, with large urban courts being much more likely to depart below guidelines, and to grant larger downward departures. Furthermore, we found (Kramer and Ulmer 2002) that 80 percent of downward departures for serious violent offenders occurred in twelve out of Pennsylvania's sixty-seven counties, and five counties accounted for 51.3 percent of these departures.

The main messages from these recent studies, then, are that (1) sentencing severity varies according to court and place, (2) the presence and strength of extralegal effects on sentencing vary by place, and (3) certain contextual characteristics such as caseload, local jail capacity, and racial and ethnic composition of the local population can affect sentencing, especially in interaction with individual case or defendant characteristics. Therefore, it makes little sense to talk about *the* effects of race, ethnicity, and the like. The presence and amount of disparity between individual defendants tend to depend on *where* defendants are sentenced. Such variation occurs even in a state with a sentencing guideline system that is supposed to make sentencing outcomes more uniform. This means that what kind of sentence one gets in part depends on where one is sentenced.

Is contextual disparity unwarranted disparity? Such disparity would seem to undermine the principle of equal justice valued in most modern legal systems. However, some might argue that principles of democracy, local autonomy, and decentralized government demand that local jurisdictions be able to fashion punishments as they see fit, at least within broader legal parameters. Should small, rural Bradford County, Pennsylvania, be required or expected to sentence the same way as Philadelphia? It seems that criminal punishment presents a situation in which key principles of US democracy may foster unequal sentencing.

Law and legal policies may be mediated by local contexts and culture. In particular, distinctive organizational and legal cultures of local courts may foster distinctive substantive rationalities that shape the nature of sentencing decisions (Savelsberg 1992; Ulmer and Kramer 1996). This embeddedness of law and legal policy in local organizational contexts means that the level and criteria for punishing criminal defendants might vary from place to place (see Ulmer 1997; Ulmer and Kramer 1998; Kautt 2002). The possibility of locally varying justice presents a dilemma between fundamental civil rights issues on the one hand, and notions of democracy on the other. If the sentence one receives, and the grounds for that sentence, depend on location, then the valued notions of equal justice that underlie most Western legal systems may be undermined.

On the other hand, local autonomy and decentralized government are also valued features of US democratic philosophy, and are certainly central features of US criminal justice. Such autonomy implies that local jurisdictions would have the right to shape criminal punishments according to local culture, concerns, and constituencies. In this chapter, we simultaneously examine county- and individual-level influences (as well as cross-level interactions) on local court decisions to incarcerate criminal defendants, and if incarcerated, on the length of sentence, using hierarchical modeling methods appropriate for multilevel data analysis. Importantly, our analysis here goes beyond that presented in Ulmer and Johnson's 2004 study in three ways: (1) we include data from more Pennsylvania counties and an additional year of individual-level data (2000), but omit cases involving miscellaneous offenses such as driving under the influence, (2) we present multinomial regression models differentiating jail and prison incarceration, and (3) we make some different methodological choices than were made in the earlier study.

Existing Research

The effects of legal, case-processing, and extralegal variables on sentencing have been studied extensively at the individual case level (for definitive reviews, see Spohn 2000; Zatz 2000; Steffensmeier and Demuth 2000). While contextual influences on sentencing and other formal social control processes and outcomes have also been investigated before, until recently these studies have been limited in at least one of three ways. First, the large majority of sentencing studies are limited to one level of analysis. Such studies either analyze individual sentencing cases (e.g., Nardulli, Eisenstein, and Flemming 1988; Albonetti 1991; Steffensmeier, Ulmer, and Kramer 1998; Engen and Gainey 2000; Steffensmeier and Demuth 2000) or aggregate jurisdictions (e.g., Bridges and Crutchfield 1988; Engen and Steen 2000), but do not assess individual-level and contextual-level influences simultaneously. Such studies therefore cannot tell us the *relative importance* of contextual- versus individual-level factors.

Second, older studies that do simultaneously examine contextual- and individual-level influences on sentencing typically use traditional OLS or logistic regression techniques, which are inappropriate for multilevel data (e.g., Myers and Talarico 1987; Steffensmeier, Kramer, and Streifel 1993; Ulmer 1997; Kramer and Ulmer 1996). Such analyses risk misestimating the role of contextual factors, individual-level factors, or both (Bryk and Raudenbush 1992).

Third, a number of other studies take what Britt (2000) calls the cross-jurisdictional approach. This approach compares a relatively small number of jurisdictional contexts with each other, either by comparing the results of separate regression models for each jurisdiction, or by including dummy variables for each jurisdiction in regression models (e.g., Nardulli, Eisenstein, and Flemming 1988; Dixon 1995; Ulmer and Kramer 1996; Albonetti 1997, 1998; Ulmer 1997; Spohn and Holleran 2000; Steffensmeier and Demuth 2001). While often useful and informative, this approach has two weaknesses: (1) it precludes broad, large-scale comparisons across a large number of jurisdictional contexts (most studies only compare three or fewer), and (2) simply comparing the effects of jurisdictional dummy variables on sentencing outcomes does not tell us anything about the *specific social or organizational features* of jurisdictional contexts that might condition variation in sentencing. However, this problem is mitigated when such studies also rely on ethnographic data (e.g., Nardulli, Eisenstein, and Flemming 1988; Nagel and Schulhofer 1992; Ulmer 1997; Ulmer and Kramer 1996).

Court Communities and Their Embedded Focal Concerns

Jo Dixon (1995), in an organizational perspective on sentencing, argues that the predominant mix of formal and substantive rationality and decision criteria in sentencing varies between courts according to the organization of judicial and prosecutorial activity and interests. These kinds of local variations are especially likely in states (such as Pennsylvania) where judges and prosecutors are locally elected. Furthermore, court communities typically have locally distinctive, informal, and ever-evolving case-processing and sentencing norms, or "going rates" (Eisenstein, Flemming, and Nardulli 1988; Ulmer 1997). These going rates often provide members of courtroom workgroups with "templates" for case-processing strategies, typical plea-bargaining terms, and sentences. The court community perspective predicts that all of these factors above produce significant interjurisdictional variation in sentencing.

As Paula Kautt puts it, the embeddedness of sentencing law, policies, and processes in the social worlds of court communities "suggests that the impact of case-level factors should be conditioned by the characteristics of the court in which a case is adjudicated" (2002, p. 642). Thus the court community perspective implies not only that sentence severity will vary across courts, but also that the effects of key predictors will vary. This is because sentencing processes and workgroup members' interpretations of sentencing criteria, such as focal concerns of sentencing (Steffensmeier, Ulmer, and Kramer 1998), are embedded in court community culture and interpersonal and interorganizational relationships (Ulmer and Kramer 1998).

One particular variable hypothesized to be crucial is *jurisdiction size,* since size is said to be associated with distinctive organizational and cultural features of court communities, and thus with court decisions such as conviction patterns and sentencing (see Eisenstein, Flemming, and Nardulli 1988, p. 285; Ulmer 1997). In particular, research in the tradition of court communities and social worlds consistently finds that sentencing severity is inversely related to court community size (e.g., Ulmer 1997; Kramer and Ulmer 2002). The court community perspective predicts that sentencing will be relatively less severe in large urban court communities in particular (Eisenstein, Flemming, and Nardulli 1988). This is said to be caused by several factors directly related to large court community size: (1) a relatively high degree of autonomy of the court community from external controls of other community institutions, (2) relatively low public visibility of *routine* case-processing matters and sentences,[1] and (3) amount and diversity of social deviance in general, which tend to be greater in large urban areas, producing more tolerance and less punitiveness (Eisenstein, Flemming, and Nardulli 1988, pp. 278–285; but see our analyses in Chapters 7 and 8 for interesting exceptions to this tendency).

Local electoral politics is another important factor predicted to affect sentencing, especially since judges and prosecutors are locally elected by partisan vote in Pennsylvania and other states. For example, courts in which the electorate holds more conservative ideologies about "law and order" and getting "tough on crime" would be expected to sentence more severely than a court in a more politically liberal county.

The focal concerns perspective we have been using to frame our conception of sentencing emphasizes particular kinds of substantive rationalities (Savelsberg 1992) at work in sentencing decisions, which are in turn embedded in the culture and organization of court communities. Recall that Figure 1.1 listed a variety of court environmental factors and how they are linked to interpretations of focal concerns. Two focal concerns that particularly interest us in this investigation of court communities' contextual effects on sentencing are community protection and perceived offender dangerousness, and the practical constraints connected to sentencing decisions. These two focal concerns seem to be the most likely points through which court community contextual features might influence individual-level sentencing decisions. The focal concern of practical constraints invokes issues of case-processing efficiency and local jail capacity. The focal concern of community protection invokes the notion of racial threat and the relative size of minority populations, which may be perceived as more of a crime threat by court actors.

Practical Constraints: Jail Capacity

Jurisdictional correctional resources such as jail capacity may be a potential practical constraint that influences sentencing (see also Peterson and Hagan 1984, p. 68). Counties with plentiful jail space would be more likely to incarcerate offenders than counties with smaller jail capacity, other things being equal. Of course, defendants may be sentenced to either local county jails or state prison. While local jail capacity would be expected to affect jail incarcerations, state prison capacity would be a constant for all counties in a state. In Pennsylvania, approximately 79 percent of the incarceration sentences are county jail sentences, so we expect jail space to be an important influence on the overall probability of incarceration. If local space for jail-eligible offenders is lacking, this might decrease the overall likelihood of incarceration.

Furthermore, in the name of protection of the community, one would expect that local courts would conserve their jail space for more serious, more violent offenders, and for those with lengthier criminal histories. Thus, offense severity, violent offenses, and prior criminal records might be more influential on incarceration decisions in counties with more constrained jail resources.

Practical Constraints: Organizational Efficiency

Another important practical constraint on sentencing is the need to process cases in an efficient manner, or at least to avoid case backlogs (Engen and Steen 2000; Dixon 1995). The chief way in which court actors achieve efficiency is by inducing guilty pleas (Engen and Steen 2000, p. 1363). Therefore, one should expect a fairly uniform pattern of more lenient sentences accompanying guilty pleas, and more severe sentences accompanying trials (at both aggregate and individual levels), across courts of all types.

However, this "trial penalty" is likely not uniform across court communities. In addition to possible influences of court community culture and going rates, sentencing differences between guilty pleas and trials may be aggravated by court caseload pressure (Dixon 1995). The greater the ratio of caseload to personnel, the greater the need to process cases efficiently, the greater the need to induce guilty pleas, and the greater the potential sentencing disparity between guilty pleas and trials (see Dixon 1995). Trial rates may also be related to sentencing differences between guilty pleas and trials, and existing research provides insufficient guidance on this issue. Trial rates may be negatively related to plea versus trial sentencing disparity. That is, low trial rates may be found among jurisdictions with high sentencing costs for defendants who go to trial and lose. These high costs would tend to deter defendants (and especially defense attorneys) from taking cases to trial. Conversely, higher trial rates are likely found among jurisdictions with comparatively lower sentencing costs of going to trial and losing.

Organizational efficiency also suggests interaction effects between caseload pressure and mode of conviction (whether someone pled guilty or was convicted by trial), and trial rate and mode of conviction. "Trial penalties" would be relatively greater in jurisdictions with greater caseload pressure, and greater in jurisdictions with lower trial rates.

Sentencing and Racialized Threat

As we pointed out in Chapter 5, the court community and focal concerns perspectives are also compatible with racial threat theory. In particular, criminal law and punishment may be tools for containing racial or ethnic minority groups defined as threatening by those in positions of privilege and power. In the contemporary United States, blacks and Hispanics tend to be objects of crime fear and are seen as particularly threatening (Steffensmeier and Demuth 2001; Britt 2000; Spohn and Holleran 2000; Spohn 2000; Barkan and Cohn 2005).

In Chapter 5, we focused on racial threat and how it might influence decisionmakers' interpretations of focal concerns at the individual level. At the contextual level, racial threat theory clearly predicts that the size of the local black or Hispanic population will be positively associated with sentencing severity. In particular, we highlight the possible connections implied in the literature between black and Hispanic population size, white fear of minority crime, and protection of the community from offenders perceived as dangerous.

Furthermore, racial threat theory also implies a cross-level interaction effect. Black or Hispanic defendants may be sentenced more severely in places where their populations are larger. That is, individual black or Hispanic offenders might be seen as especially threatening in counties that have larger black or Hispanic populations, if they are taken to embody white fears of minority criminals, and thus stereotypically represent "dangerous offenders." In this way, the effect of defendant race or ethnicity might be conditioned by county proportions of blacks or Hispanics.

Little research exists on the role of racial or ethnic composition in individual sentencing decisions. Jeffery Ulmer (1997) found no direct relationship between county percent black and individual sentencing decisions, but Martha Myers and Susette Talarico (1987) found that all offenders were more likely to be imprisoned in jurisdictions with larger black populations (both studies used traditional OLS regression methods). At the aggregate level, George Bridges and Robert Crutchfield (1988) found that percent black jurisdictional population was positively related to black versus white disparity in aggregate sentencing severity. On the other hand, Chester Britt (2000) found that percent black was unrelated to incarceration odds and modestly negatively related to sentence length, and that percent black did not condition the effect of offender race on sentencing. Paula Kautt (2002) found that the racial and ethnic composition of district court jurisdictions did not substantially affect sentencing among federal drug offenders. Clearly, these mixed findings warrant further examination.

Research Context

Pennsylvania is a particularly interesting and valuable jurisdiction for examining organizational social contexts as they relate to criminal sentencing. The presence of its sentencing guidelines, and the fact that they have been in place for over two decades, may therefore represent a force for uniformity among jurisdictions.

However, Pennsylvania is also characterized by wide variations in local contextual characteristics. For example, Pennsylvania is home to two of the largest cities in the United States (Philadelphia and Pittsburgh), but also home to numerous medium-sized cities (e.g., Harrisburg, Erie, Reading, Scranton, Allentown) and a large number of small rural counties. The state is politically diverse as well, with the eastern and western ends of the state tending to have a stronger organized labor presence, more racial, ethnic, religious, and cultural diversity, and a higher percentage of voters registered as Democratic. Central Pennsylvania's counties tend to be more conservative, less diverse, and dominated by Republican voters. Political party composition is potentially important, since both judges and district attorneys in Pennsylvania are selected through partisan elections. Finally, Pennsylvania's counties vary widely in terms of the prosperity and resources of their populations, local governmental resources, crime rates, and racial and ethnic diversity.

Data and Methods

We draw on the same overall dataset as the last chapter, PCS files for most serious convictions per criminal transaction, for the years 1997–2000 (as before, the data only include cases sentenced under the 1997 guidelines). We supplement these individual-level data with contextual data from the 2000 US Census, Uniform Crime Reports, and the 1999 County and City Extras, as well as aggregate case-processing data per county (such as caseloads and trial rates, for example). Fuller information about our data, procedures, and methodological choices for this chapter's analysis can be found in the Research Methods Appendix.

We make three different methodological choices in this chapter's analysis compared to the earlier analysis by Ulmer and Johnson (2004, see Table 5.1). First, we log the sentence length variable (as in the previous chapter and all subsequent analyses of sentence length) to address the skewed distribution of this outcome. Second, while Ulmer and Johnson combined bench and jury trials into one category, our greater number of cases and our additional year and counties of data enable us to split these kinds of trials into distinct variables. Third, as we explain below (and in a more extended way in Chapter 7), we present sentence length results that do not include a Heckman two-step correction for selection bias from the incarceration decision. As mentioned, we also present multinomial models that differentiate jail and prison incarceration.

Results

Because our focus in this chapter is on county contextual effects, we use an estimation procedure designed for multilevel data, hierarchical modeling (HLM). Basically, HLM allows us to appropriately estimate the effects of individual case level and county court and contextual variables simultaneously, and also to estimate variation in individual-level variables' effects between counties, including cross-level interaction effects. The Research Methods Appendix presents further information about our use of HLM in this and subsequent chapters. Table 6.1 presents descriptive statistics for both our individual (level-one) and contextual (level-two) explanatory variables.

The descriptive statistics for our individual-level variables are different from the previous chapter (see Table 5.2), because in this analysis, and Chapter

Table 6.1 "Core Crimes" Data, 1997–2000

Variable	Frequency	Percentage
In/out		
Not incarcerated	62,891	50.7
Incarcerated	61,050	49.3
Prison/jail incarceration		
No incarceration	62,891	51.0
County jail	41,857	34.0
State prison	17,829	14.5
Offense type		
Homicide	918	.7
Rape/IDSI	600	.5
Robbery	4,531	3.7
Weapons	3,958	3.2
Aggravated assault	3,849	3.1
Simple assault	18,938	15.3
Arson	443	.4
Burglary	6,339	5.1
Criminal trespassing	3,704	3.0
Theft	36,798	29.7
Forgery	4,046	3.3
Drug felony	21,309	17.2
Drug misdemeanor	18,569	15.0
Mode of conviction		
Negotiated guilty plea	80,047	65.0
Bench trial	4,260	3.4
Jury trial	2,038	1.7
Nonnegotiated/other guilty plea	37,596	30.0
Race/ethnicity		
Black	45,751	37.0
White	68,371	55.0
Hispanic	9,819	8.0
Gender		
Male	103,548	83.5
Female	20,393	16.5

	Mean	SD	Min	Max
Offense severity score (1–14)	4.04	2.3	1	14
Prior record score (0–8)	1.5	1.93	0	8
Guideline minimum	5.12	11.8	0	240
Minimum incarceration length (in months, incarceration cases only)	12.9	20.4	1	300
Logged length	2.01	1.08	0	5.70
County level variables				
Total index crime rates	2,386	968	682	7,518
Violent crime rates	231	189	67	1,465
Caseload	5.9	1.4	2.6	8.8
Jail space	24	16	0	87
Jury trial rate	1.7	1.2	0	6.3
Percent Republican	45	8.1	16	60
Percent black	3.2	6.0	.1	43.3
Percent Hispanic	1.5	1.7	.1	7.3

Court Size	Frequency	Cases	Percentage of Total
Large court	2	34,252	28
Medium court	14	59,004	48
Small court	49	30,681	24

7, we omit cases involving miscellaneous offenses such as driving under the influence, escaping from custody, and disorderly conduct. We do this because such cases may be interpreted and sentenced in particularly idiosyncratic ways from court to court, and may muddy our picture of how courts vary in sentencing cases that involve more unambiguously criminal behavior. Thus, our data for analyses in this chapter and in Chapter 7 involve only the following offenses: third-degree homicide, aggravated assault, robbery, rape and involuntary deviate sexual intercourse, burglary, simple assault, arson, criminal trespassing, thefts, drug felonies, drug misdemeanors, forgeries, and weapon offenses. This is also the reason our numbers of cases differ here from those reported in Ulmer and Johnson's study (2004). The other descriptive statistics are also sometimes different from Table 5.2 because the data here come from counties with valid data on county characteristics, since HLM cannot tolerate missing level-two data.

We first ran an unconditional model (which allows us to compare the amount of between- versus within-county variation in sentencing outcomes), and found that in both the incarceration and sentence length models, significant variation exists between counties.[2] The intraclass correlation for logged sentence length was .07, indicating that 7 percent of the variation in length existed at the between-county level. Thus, individual-level variation accounts for a much greater proportion of the total variance in sentence length outcomes than do between-county and contextual differences. This does not mean, however, that between-county variations in sentencing outcomes are not substantively meaningful. In fact, Allen Liska (1990) argues for the theoretical importance of contextual factors in understanding individual-level outcomes, even when their predictive power is less relative to individual-level factors. Furthermore, contextual factors might condition important variation in individual-level predictors (i.e., cross-level interaction effects).

Table 6.2 presents the main effects on prison and jail incarceration and sentence length for our individual- and contextual-level predictors (using hierarchical, multinomial, and linear models). In evaluating the county-level predictors' effects, it is important to remember that the number of cases on which the statistical tests of significance are based constitutes the sixty-five counties with viable data, and not the 121,364 (for incarceration) or 51,788 (for length) individual cases. This means that the conventional statistical significance levels of .05 or .01 are much more meaningful for the county-level effects. The individual-level variables explain over 60 percent of the total variance in sentence lengths. The county-level variables explain 4 percent of the total variance, and 50 percent of the between-county (or level-two) variance.

As in Chapter 5, offense severity and prior record are the strongest predictors of the two types of incarceration, just as the guidelines intend, along with particular offense types. As before, offense gravity score and prior record score are particularly strong predictors of prison sentences. Presumptive disposition predicts jail incarceration to a stronger degree than it does state imprisonment

Table 6.2   Jail and Prison Incarceration and Length: Fixed and
Random Effects

Models	Odds Ratios		Logged Length	
	County Jail	State Prison	b	Antilog of b
Intercept (B_0, G_{00})	2.20***	.78***	.34***	1.40
Level 1 predictors				
Negotiated plea (r)	.87***	.76***	-.02	.98
Bench trial (r)	1.21***	1.92***	.27	1.31***
Jury trial (r)	1.92***	9.61***	.36	1.43***
Homicide	1.35	2.74***	.52	1.68***
Aggravated assault	1.51***	.98	.004	1.004
Robbery	2.53***	3.43***	.30	1.35***
Rape/IDSI	.40**	.66	.28	1.32***
Simple assault	1.002	.85**	-.07	.93**
Arson	1.11	1.01	.01	1.01
Burglary	1.56***	1.78***	.15	1.16***
Criminal trespassing	1.52***	1.63***	.13	1.14***
Drug felony	.87***	1.34***	.14	1.15**
Drug misdemeanor	.55***	.35***	-.32	.73***
Forgery	1.25***	1.96***	.21	1.23***
Weapons	.85***	.87	-.06	.94
Offense gravity score (r)	1.28***	2.27***	.38	1.46***
Prior record score (r)	1.34***	2.08***	.28	1.32***
Presumptive disposition (r)	1.55***	1.17***		
Guideline minimum (r)			-.01	.99***
Black (r)	1.48***	1.52***	.06	1.06 ***
Hispanic (r)	1.36***	1.65***	.12	1.13***
Female	.66***	.45***	-.17	.84***
Age	.994*	.98***	-.001	.99
Level 2 predictors				
Mean annual court caseload	.87*	.73***	-.04	.96*
Jury trial rate	.92ᵗ	.99	.01	1.01
Jail space	1.02***	1.01***	.001	1.001
Percent black	.97*	.98***	-.02	.98***
Percent Hispanic	1.01	.97**	.02	1.02ᵗ
Percent Republican	.99	.99**	.0004	1.0004
Crime rate	1.0001	1.0001**	.0001	1.0001
Large court	.43*	.17***	.18	1.20***
Small court	1.26ᵗ	1.84***	.04	1.04
Level 2 R-squared			.50 (.04 of total variance)	
Level 1 R-squared			.60	
Level 2 N		65	65	
Level 1 N		121,364	51,788	

Notes: Theft is the reference category for offense type, nonnegotiated guilty pleas are the reference category for mode of conviction, medium courts are the reference category for court size. The models also include dummy variables for missing data on race/ethnicity and gender.
(r) = significant random effects; slopes allowed to vary randomly.
ᵗp < .10; *p < .05; **p < .01; ***p < .001.

(again, the presumptive disposition variable does not distinguish between the two types of incarceration). Jury trial convictions are again much more likely to result in sentences to state prison, and this variable far outweighs any one offense type as a predictor of prison. Women are also less likely to go to jail, and especially less likely to go to prison. Race and ethnicity effects are more pronounced for the state prison decision—blacks and Hispanics have 52 percent and 65 percent greater odds of going to prison, respectively, than whites. Recall from the previous chapter that these overall race and ethnicity effects mask variation by gender, and that sentencing disadvantage for jail and prison primarily characterizes men (for prison, particularly Hispanic men). It is also noteworthy that these stronger race and ethnicity effects characterize this more restrictive subsample of "core" crimes.

A number of interesting contextual effects appear when the incarceration decision is differentiated between jail and prison. First, court caseloads reduce the odds of both jail and prison, and the effect is especially strong for prison. Thus, courts with heavier caseloads appear more reluctant to sentence offenders to jail, and especially to state prison. Available jail space surprisingly predicts both outcomes significantly. Understandably, increases in jail space increase the odds of jail incarceration, but this effect appears to slightly spill over to the state prison decision as well. Also, county crime rates predict greater odds of state prison sentences, possibly representing an effort at general or specific deterrence in higher-crime counties.

County percent black reduces the odds of offenders going to both jail and prison by about equal amounts. Percent Hispanic also notably reduces the odds of offenders going to prison. Note that these results refer to the effects of percent black and percent Hispanic on the odds of all offenders, not just these minorities, going to jail or prison. In themselves, then, these results do not precisely test the racial threat hypothesis we discussed previously, which really specifies that it is minority defendants who are punished more harshly as percent minority increases (perhaps up to a certain threshold).

Finally, the effects of the court size variables are more pronounced for the state prison decision. That is, court size appears to more specifically affect state prison sentences. The directions of the effects are the same for jail and prison—with large courts sentencing more leniently and small courts more severely. However, the odds of large courts meting out state prison sentences are 83 percent less than those of medium-size courts (and indirectly, less than those of small courts), while small courts' odds of giving prison sentences are almost double those of medium-size courts. Thus, court size seems to especially differentiate counties in the degree to which they hand out state prison sentences.

Table 6.2 also shows some notable influences of county and court characteristics on sentence lengths. First, court size is related to incarceration length. Large courts, when they incarcerate offenders, give sentences that are about 20 percent longer than those of medium-size courts. Local jail capacity and caseloads are significantly related to sentencing outcomes. Caseload pressure is negatively related to the length of incarceration. Higher caseloads increase the need to process cases quickly and efficiently, and this efficiency appears related to sentencing severity, as suggested by the finding that incarceration is shorter in higher-caseload counties. Specifically, average sentence lengths decrease by 4 percent for every unit increase in caseload. Percent Republican has a slight but significant negative relationship with state prison incarceration—counties that have larger Republican populations are slightly less likely to send offenders to state prison.

We find that percent black significantly predicted shorter, not longer, sentences. That is, a 1 percent increase in county black population is associated with a 2 percent decrease in average sentence length. Percent Hispanic is also a marginally significant predictor of sentence length in the opposite direction—a 1 percent increase in county Hispanic population is associated with a 2 percent increase in sentence length.

Random Effects

The random effects provide information about the degree to which the effects of different variables vary across county contexts. We allowed the slopes to vary randomly for the variables marked "(r)" in Table 6.2, for the sentence length model and a hierarchical logistic model of overall incarceration.[3] The random effects of key predictors are shown graphically in Figures 6.1 and 6.2., and the actual values are shown in the Research Methods Appendix.

The standard deviation of the variance component for the random effects shows the degree of variation in the given effects. For example, the effect of presumptive disposition on the odds of incarceration varies by plus or minus .52 among two-thirds of the counties (those within one standard deviation of the mean effect), meaning that among two-thirds of the counties, the effect of presumptive disposition varies from .95 to 1.99. Variation in the other random effects in Table 6.2 can be interpreted similarly.

We find strong support for our expectations about how influences on sentencing vary between court communities. Several key predictors exhibit statistically significant random effects for both the incarceration and sentence length decisions. In other words, decisionmakers in different courts differentially weight the importance of these various individual-level case characteristics at sentencing. In particular, the effects of OGS, PRS, guideline presumptive dispositions, race, Hispanic ethnicity, and the modes of conviction all vary significantly between counties.

It is particularly interesting that the guideline factors themselves vary in their effects between counties. In other words, the very use of, or weight given to, OGS, PRS, and the guideline minimum recommendations varies considerably between counties. The variation in the effects of guideline presumptive dispositions is especially interesting: apparently, courts react quite differently to the

Figure 6.1   Variation in Effects of Key Predictors of Incarceration

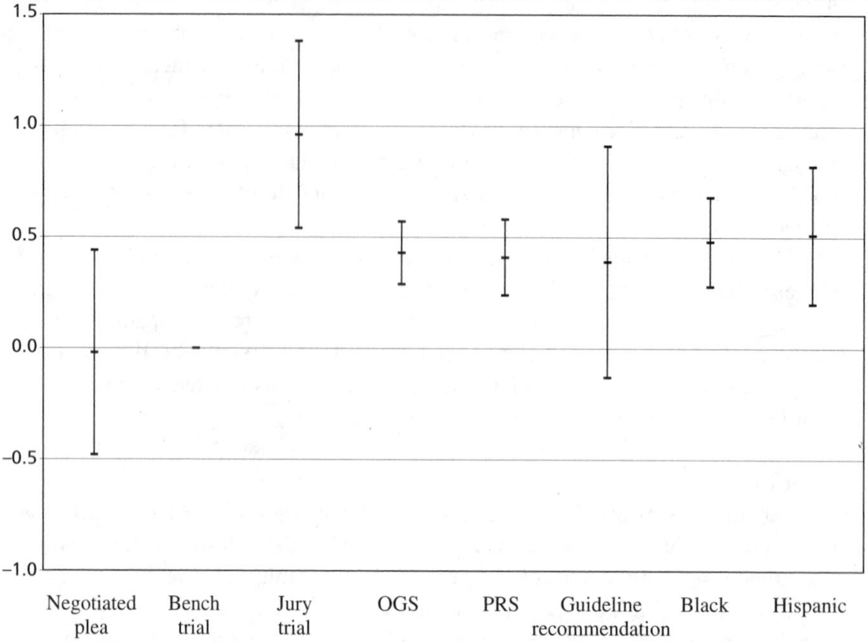

Note: Based on random effect analyses in Table 6.2.

guideline recommendations about incarceration. This certainly provides substantial support for our argument in Chapter 1 that the implementation and use of guidelines are shaped by and embedded in distinctive court communities.

The effect of going to jury trial (especially for sentence length) exhibits considerable variation, suggesting that trial penalties and their size are strongly shaped by the court community. This is a topic we will return to in Chapter 8. Also, negotiated pleas have widely divergent effects between counties, probably reflecting the differential prominence and norms about plea bargaining and plea concessions between counties. The effect of negotiated pleas on incarceration odds varies from .52 to 1.44. Clearly, negotiated plea agreements provide substantial benefits over open (nonnegotiated) pleas in some counties, provide almost no benefits in others, and harm defendants' chances of avoiding incarceration in still others. Similar patterns are evident for negotiated pleas and sentence lengths.

Cross-Level Interaction Effects

The results to this point suggest that individual factors clearly dominate the incarceration and sentence length decisions, but county-level contexts also exert

Figure 6.2   Variation in Effects of Key Predictors of Sentence Length

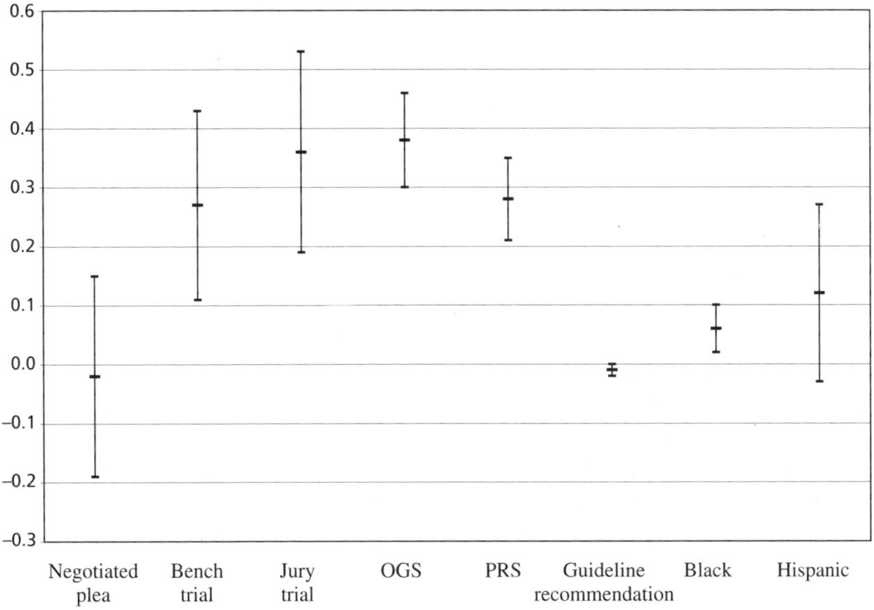

Note: Based on random effect analyses in Table 6.2.

significant influences on sentencing. While the individual and contextual effects we have described to this point are noteworthy in and of themselves, at the outset of this chapter we discussed several expectations about interactive relationships between individual and contextual factors. We therefore estimated a series of models specifying cross-level interactions between these two units of analysis for overall incarceration, county jail, state prison, and sentence length outcomes. The results from these models are presented in Table 6.3.

We predicted that available jail capacity would condition the effects of offense severity and prior record. We found no support for this prediction regarding offense severity, but we did find a significant (but quite small) interaction between available jail space and the impact of prior record on county jail incarceration. An offender's prior criminal record has a greater, not lesser, effect in courts with greater jail capacity. We reasoned that courts with constrained jail space would reserve that space for more serious and repeat offenders, and thus that courts with fewer jail resources would put relatively greater emphasis on offense seriousness, violent offenses, and repeat offenders. Instead, it may be that greater jail space liberates courts to be more punitive toward those with more extensive prior records. We do not want to overstate the importance

Table 6.3   Significant Cross-Level Interaction Effects (interaction terms added separately)

	In/Out Odds Ratio	County Jail Odds Ratio	State Prison Odds Ratio	Length b	Length (antilog of b)
PRS × jail space	1.003***	1.003***			
Bench trial × caseload				.04	(1.04)**
Jury trial × jury trial rate			.75***	−.06	(.94)*
Black × percent black			.99*		
Hispanic × percent Hispanic	.95***	.93***			

Note: *p < .05; **p < .01; ***p < .001.

of this effect, though, since it is so small: a prior record's positive effect on in-carceration odds increases by .003 for every one-unit increase in jail space.

We do not find very much support for the notion that caseload pressure increases trial penalties (see also Chapter 7, where we find that caseloads also generally fail to affect the size of trial penalties). The only evidence for this that we found was a significant interaction between caseloads and bench trial. Each increase in caseload is associated with a 4 percent increase in the sentence length impact of bench trials.

On the other hand, the jury trial rate is significantly related to jury trial penalties for state prison decisions and sentence length. State prison sentences become progressively less likely among those convicted by jury trial as court trial rates increase, and jury trial defendants' sentence lengths similarly decline in relatively high-trial counties. In other words, the costs of jury trial in terms of going to state prison and sentence lengths are less in counties that conduct more jury trials.

According to racial threat theory, larger percentages of minorities in the county should be associated with increased severity of minorities' sentences. We found some significant interactions between county minority populations and the incarceration variables, but in the opposite direction predicted by racial threat. These results suggest that the positive relationship between minority status and the incarceration variables, especially state prison (see the previous chapter, and Table 6.2), cannot be explained by the percentage of the population belonging to the respective minority group.

The interaction effects for Hispanics are noteworthy, especially for county jail incarceration. A 1 percent increase in county Hispanic population is associated with a 7 percent *decrease* in the odds of Hispanics going to county jail. A similar but smaller effect is seen for blacks and state prison sentences. A 1 percent increase in county black population yields a 1 percent decrease in the odds of blacks going to prison. Both of these interaction effects are not explainable by the racial threat perspective.

Summary

As our theoretical framework in Chapter 1 envisions, significant variation exists in sentencing severity between counties. More importantly, considerable variation exists between counties in the effects of key individual-level predictors. Especially noteworthy is variation in the impact of key guideline factors, which are always the chief influences, particularly guideline-recommended dispositions. In other words, *courts vary considerably* in their responses to the guideline recommendations about incarceration. These findings support the notion of court communities with distinctive norms and practices, even within guidelines. They also suggest that guideline use and implementation are embedded in and shaped by local court communities.

Beyond the guideline variables, modes of conviction consistently play a big role in shaping sentences. The impact of negotiated pleas and jury trials also widely varies between counties. In some courts, negotiated plea agreements help defendants a great deal in securing more lenient sentences, and in other courts (and on average throughout the state), negotiated pleas carry no meaningful sentencing benefits beyond nonnegotiated (open) guilty pleas. Furthermore, jury trials vary a great deal in their impact on sentencing outcomes, though as a rule they foster substantially greater sentencing severity. Furthermore, the size of jury trial penalties in some ways is associated with county jury trial rates—counties with higher trial rates exhibit notably smaller jury trial effects on state prison sentences and, to a lesser extent, smaller sentence length trial penalties. The causal direction of such a relationship is ambiguous. However, we could reasonably argue that some counties might have comparatively higher trial rates because they view trials as more normatively acceptable and discourage them less.

Our main focus here, though, is on contextual variation in sentencing. We find that court caseloads consistently predict decreased odds of incarceration (both jail and especially prison) and shorter sentences. Caseloads do not, however, condition the size of jury trial penalties or plea rewards. The sentence length cost of bench trials does moderately increase with caseloads.

Local jail space predictably increases the odds of jail sentences, but also state prison sentences, which is not readily explainable. Furthermore, jail space slightly influences the premium placed on prior record as a sentencing factor, and does so in a direction opposite what we expected. We reasoned that scarce jail space would encourage courts to husband their jail space by reserving it for those with more serious criminal histories (and those committing more serious offenses). Instead, there is a slight tendency in the opposite direction. The positive influence of prior record on jail incarceration actually increases in counties with more jail space. In other words, counties with more jail space seem to weigh prior record more heavily than counties with less space in deciding whom to send to jail.

Court size's relationship to sentencing is complex. The two large courts (Philadelphia and Pittsburgh) are very much less likely to incarcerate offenders, and are especially unlikely to send people to state prison. When they do, however, they incarcerate people for moderately (20 percent) longer sentences. Small courts, in turn, are significantly more likely to send people to state prison. Also, county percent Republican is associated with moderately decreased odds of state prison—that is, more heavily Republican counties are less, rather than more, likely to send people to state prison.

We find three significant ways in which the minority population percentage conditions the effects of race and ethnicity—each of them the *opposite* of that predicted by racial threat theory. The degree to which Hispanic ethnicity predicts greater chances of jail incarceration *decreases* as the Hispanic population percentage increases. In other words, Hispanic defendants are less likely to go to county jail in counties with more Hispanic residents. Similarly, the degree to which blacks are more likely to go to state prison declines modestly but definitely as county percent black increases; that is, black defendants are sentenced to state prison less often in counties with more black residents. In addition, percent black is associated with overall decreases in the odds of jail and prison incarceration (that is, for offenders of all races, not just blacks). We find some similar patterns in the next two chapters as we look at trial penalties and mandatory minimum sentences in more depth.

Discussion

Our analysis shows that most of the "action" is at the individual case level in criminal sentencing. But we also find that local contextual features, such as caseloads, jail space, court size, and county minority composition, affect sentencing outcomes both directly and in interaction with individual-level case factors. We thus concur with Liska (1990) that contextual effects can be substantively and theoretically important, even though contextual variables may explain relatively less variation in individual-level outcomes than individual-level predictors. Our findings support insights from a variety of different yet compatible theoretical perspectives in the sentencing literature (like organizational efficiency and organizational context models, as well as Albonetti's causal attribution and uncertainty avoidance framework [1991]), which we integrated under the umbrella of the court community and focal concerns perspectives in Chapter 1.

Our findings support the importance of focal concerns of sentencing, and guidelines as a codification of blameworthiness and community protection, as these are interpreted in the contexts of local court communities. These focal concerns also invoke the importance of constraints like organizational efficiency and local correctional resources, and also the potentially racially or ethnically influenced perceptions of criminal threat and dangerousness to the community (though in a different way than that depicted in racial and ethnic threat theories).

The findings above, that the effects of key individual-level predictors of sentencing vary between counties, are quite supportive of the court community perspective's prediction that local courts will vary in their informal case-processing and sentencing norms, or "going rates." This apparently even extends to the use of the guideline factors themselves. Furthermore, the findings support the court community perspective's prediction that court size produces distinctive sentencing patterns.

Sentencing appears to be particularly affected by court communities' distinctive practical constraints and consequences, a key focal concern of sentencing. Local jail capacity and organizational efficiency appear to be two of these important constraints. They directly affect sentencing outcomes. This set of findings expands on other studies that highlight the importance of organizational contexts and organizational efficiency (e.g., Dixon 1995; Engen and Steen 2000).

Percent Republican has no significant effect on jail incarceration and sentence length, and a significant effect on state prison, in the opposite direction expected. Our inconsistent, and mostly null, findings regarding the direct effects of percent Republican could indicate that a county's political context has little to do with sentencing, once the many other important predictors of sentencing are controlled, even though judges and prosecutors in Pennsylvania are chosen in partisan elections at the county level. On the other hand, a county's political context might influence court community sentencing norms and outcomes in more subtle ways, and county percent Republican may be too crude a measure to capture the influence of political context. Another possibility is that the lack of effect for percent Republican reflects a lack of real ideological differences between local Republicans and Democrats regarding their stances on criminal justice issues. In Pennsylvania as in the rest of the United States, for example, many Democrats routinely run for office as advocates of crime control through "tough" sentencing. Furthermore, recall from Chapter 3 that many prominent Republican politicians, including district attorneys, were strong supporters of restrictive intermediate punishments and associated drug and alcohol treatments, and supported their incorporation into the guidelines. This suggests that partisan affiliations are probably not monolithic and predictable influences on criminal justice policy stances. Our finding that more Republican counties are less likely to send people to state prison certainly suggests that one should not make simplistic attributions about counties' punishment practices based on their partisan electoral patterns.

Other recent research on contextual effects on sentencing under Pennsylvania's guidelines extends our findings here. A pair of studies by Brian Johnson (2005, 2006) examined contextual variation in guideline departures, and then added judicial characteristics as an intermediate contextual level, between individual cases and county and court characteristics, in an examination of incarceration and length (see also Table 5.1). As we showed in Chapters 4 and 5, departures from guidelines are an important window of sentencing discretion, and a potential window of disparity as well. Johnson (2005) examined between-county variation in the likelihood of upward and downward guideline departures, using similar data and models as we use here. Highlights of his findings about the effects of court context on departures include:

1. Court size is strongly related to both kinds of departures: downward departures are more likely and upward departures are less likely in large courts. Downward departures are moderately less likely in small courts.
2. Caseloads are strongly predictive of downward departures. Every increase in caseload raises the odds of downward departures by 16 percent.
3. Trial rates are positively related to upward departures: every increase in jury trial rate raises the odds of upward departures by 11 percent.
4. County percent Hispanic moderately lowers the odds of downward departures, and raises the odds of upward departures, for all offenders.
5. Court context features condition the effects of individual-level predictors of departures: (a) jury trial convictees are more likely to receive downward departures in counties with higher trial rates (an interesting parallel with our findings about trial rates here); (b) jury trial convictees are less likely to receive downward departures in counties with heavier caseloads; (c) jury trial convictees are less likely to receive upward departures in large courts; (d) violent crimes were more likely to receive downward departures and less likely to receive upward departures as the caseload's percentage of violent crimes increases; (e) blacks are more likely to receive upward departures as percent black increases, and Hispanics are less likely to receive downward departures as percent Hispanic increases; (f) Hispanics are less likely to receive upward departures as percent Republican increases.

Not surprisingly, then, decisions about guideline departures vary according to features of local court communities, just as other sentencing decisions do.

Earlier research on the role of judge characteristics in sentencing in Pennsylvania and elsewhere has generally found that judge characteristics like race or gender are sometimes significantly related to sentencing patterns, but their influence is quite small relative to the effects of factors such as offense characteristics, prior record, and conviction by trial (e.g., Steffensmeier and Hebert 1999; Spohn 1990; Myers and Talarico 1987). This research, however, shares the same methodological shortcoming as other investigations of contextual influences on sentencing—the use of methods that are not appropriate for multilevel data. However, more recently, Johnson (2006) published the first hierarchical analysis of the role of judge characteristics on sentencing. He investigated the effect of judge characteristics by treating them as an intermediate contextual level, between individual case and defendant-level factors on the one hand, and county court and community contextual factors on the other. The highlights of his findings include:

1. Sentencing severity and effects of predictors on sentencing severity vary significantly by judge.
2. Minority judges sentence more leniently overall than white judges.
3. Minority judges are less likely to incarcerate black and Hispanic offenders.
4. Male judges are less likely to incarcerate women.

Johnson's analysis, applying appropriate methodology for multilevel data to the question for the first time, clearly confirms what many have long suspected—that judge characteristics matter, in addition to individual and county contextual characteristics, in influencing sentencing decisions (after all, the concept of guidelines was invented as a way to control unwarranted between-judge variation in sentencing). Future research, however, needs to further expand our understanding of *how* judges "matter." Johnson's work can serve as an important template for such research, which would be especially valuable if it includes data on judges' attitudes and ideologies about crime and criminal justice in multilevel analyses.

Our findings and those of Johnson discussed above join those of Kautt (2002) and others on sentencing under the federal guidelines in suggesting the potential importance of local organizational and legal culture of courts, as the court community perspective emphasizes. Clearly, local variation in sentencing practices and processes is a major issue for sentencing commissions and their guidelines to explicitly consider. Is such variation warranted or unwarranted? How much uniformity in sentencing is possible or desirable under guidelines? In our concluding chapter, we will return to these questions.

Notes

We acknowledge Brian Johnson's contribution as coauthor of an earlier version of this chapter.

1. This is not true in nonroutine, sensational cases, which can make court community activities highly visible in large urban areas.

2. In unconditional models, the variance component for incarceration was .21 ($p < .0001$). The variance component for logged length was .12 ($p < .0001$).

3. Random effects could not be computed for the multinomial models differentiating jail and prison incarceration.

7

Guilty Pleas vs.
Trial Convictions:
Unwarranted Disparity?

THE RIGHT TO a jury trial is fundamental to the US legal system. Thus the practice of punishing those convicted by trial more severely than similar offenders who plead guilty constitutes an important potential form of sentencing disparity (Uhlman and Walker 1979; 1980; LaFree 1985; King et al. 2005), one that presents a tension between legally recognized rights and organizational realities of courts. Compared to the amount of research on racial, ethnic, or gender disparity in sentencing, or on sentencing guideline issues, relatively few studies examine plea/trial sentencing differences per se, or try to unpack their variation and meaning. More typically, in most studies the mode of conviction (type of plea or trial) is included as a control variable while focusing on the effects of other variables such as defendant characteristics (e.g., race, gender). We saw in our analyses in previous chapters several ways in which different modes of conviction result in sharply different sentences: conviction by trial, especially jury trial, results in considerably greater odds of incarceration, longer sentences, much lower chances of downward departures, and greater chances of upward departures. Also, Chapter 6 showed that the degree to which trial convictions increase sentence severity varies significantly between counties. We take these earlier findings as our starting point in this chapter, and investigate how such "trial penalties" might vary according to offense types, defendant characteristics, and court contextual features.

As a matter of policy, Pennsylvania's guidelines neither formally encourage nor discourage plea versus trial sentencing differences, or trial penalties. Unlike the federal guidelines, which have built-in sentencing discounts for "acceptance of responsibility" and departures for "substantial assistance to law enforcement," which at least indirectly encourage pleading guilty, Pennsylvania's guidelines provide no *formal* inducements to plead guilty. However, we have seen in previous chapters that pleading guilty benefits defendants at sentencing in a variety of ways under Pennsylvania's guidelines. Different observers can and do take divergent positions on whether such differences constitute warranted or unwarranted disparity, and whether plea bargaining and trial penalties constitute coercive compromises of due process or rational and necessary features for case-processing efficiency and crime control (see, for example, Rosett and Cressey 1976, compared to Smith 1986). In this chapter, we are primarily concerned with empirically investigating variation in trial penalties. We return to a more philosophical discussion about plea rewards, trial penalties, and guidelines in the book's concluding chapter.

These analyses are an extension of those found in a previously published article by Jeffery Ulmer and Mindy Bradley (2006). This chapter improves on this prior article in four ways: (1) we consider two additional contextual variables, local jail space and trial rates, (2) our measure of caseload is standardized by the number of judges in a county (as in the previous chapter), (3) we include multinomial analyses that examine county jail and state prison as distinct decisions, and (4) we add analyses of trial penalties among less serious offenses as well as among serious violent offenses.

Prior Research on Sentencing Differences

Although we found in previous chapters that a variety of trial penalties do exist, the prior literature, including studies of other states, and of jurisdictions with and without guidelines, presents somewhat mixed findings as to whether significant trial penalties exist, and only a handful of studies examine how they might vary. Probably the majority of studies that focus on the sentencing effects of different modes of conviction show that those convicted by trial, especially jury trials, receive more severe sentences (e.g., Uhlman and Walker 1979; 1980; Brereton and Casper 1982; Zatz and Hagan 1985; Ulmer 1997; Johnson 2003). In one recent analysis, Nancy King and colleagues (2005) even found significant "process discounts," or plea/trial sentencing differences in five sentencing guideline states. Numerous other studies not focused on the plea/trial sentencing issue find that those convicted by trial are sentenced more severely than those who plead guilty when mode of conviction is treated as a control variable (see, among many other examples, Zatz 1984; Peterson and Hagan 1984; Spohn, Gruhl, and Welch 1982; Albonetti 1991, 1998; Steffensmeier, Kramer, and Streifel 1993; Dixon 1995; Ulmer and Kramer 1996; Steffensmeier, Ulmer, and Kramer 1998; Steffensmeier and Hebert 1999; Steffensmeier and Demuth 2000, 2001; Spohn and Holleran 2000; Kautt 2002; Holleran and Spohn 2004; Engen and Gainey 2000; Kurlychek and Johnson 2004).

Many studies suggest that the size of any plea/trial sentencing differences likely varies by jurisdiction (Eisenstein and Jacob 1977; Brereton and Casper 1982; Nardulli, Eisenstein, and Flemming 1988; Ulmer 1997; King et al. 2005). Specifically, scholars have debated the relationship between trial penalties and plea rewards, and court caseloads, with some arguing that heavy caseloads drive mode-of-conviction differences, and others arguing that such differences are independent of caseload pressure (for reviews, see Brereton and Casper 1982; Farr 1984; Meeker and Pontell 1985; Nardulli, Eisenstein, and Flemming 1988; Wooldredge 1989; Holmes, Daudistel, and Taggart 1992; Dixon 1995). Furthermore, trial penalties have been found to be stronger for defendants with more substantial criminal histories (e.g., Ulmer 1997; Smith 1986), and to be stronger for blacks (Ulmer 1997). In addition, Brian Johnson (2003) also found that racial disparity varies by mode of conviction in Pennsylvania—blacks are least likely to obtain downward guideline departures following trials, especially jury trials.

Other studies, typically older ones from the 1970s and mid-1980s, fail to find significant plea rewards or trial penalties (Hagan 1975; Eisenstein and Jacob 1977; Smith 1986). William Rhodes (1979) found that the size of plea/trial sentencing differences varies by offense type, with meaningful differences in robbery cases but not assault, burglary, or larceny. Rhodes, along with Douglas Smith (1986) and Gary LaFree (1985), argued that the chances of acquittal may offset the potential for a greater penalty after losing at trial, and may also offset the potential for a more lenient sentence through plea bargaining (leniency that Rhodes argued is largely illusory).

Smith and Rhodes, in particular, hinged the assessment of trial penalties on a comparison of sentences defendants received after pleading guilty, with those they *would have* received had they gone to trial, adjusted for the probability of conviction at trial (in other words, the chance of being acquitted, which defendants forgo if they plead guilty). Using this approach, both Smith and Rhodes found limited evidence for trial penalties. On the other hand, Marjorie Zatz and John Hagan (1985) found the opposite—significant plea/trial sentencing differences appeared only after they controlled for the likelihood of conviction versus acquittal.

Relatedly, James Eisenstein and Herbert Jacob (1977) and David Brereton and Jonathan Casper (1982) noted that trial penalties need not be significant in the aggregate to meaningfully shape what court participants believe about the punishment costs of going to trial and losing. Rather, penalizing those who lose at trials may not need to be done often to be effective, since courthouse grapevines may rely only on unusually visible cases that "send a message" to the court community.

Overall, then, the literature mostly supports the notion that those convicted by trial are more likely to be incarcerated, and are more likely to receive longer incarceration sentences. However, some important studies do not find trial penalties, or else they only find limited ones. A few studies also suggest that plea/trial differences may vary by jurisdiction, with caseload being especially important in conditioning such differences. Finally, a few studies suggest that trial penalties may vary by offense type, prior record, or race/ethnicity. To the extent that the findings regarding trial penalties are mixed, this may be the result of different modeling choices (such as controlling for the odds of conviction or acquittal, or not). Mixed findings could also result from the possibility that trial penalties might vary between court contexts, and between different kinds of cases and offenders. The analyses in this chapter address these latter potential sources of confusion about trial penalties and their variation. Here, we examine not just whether trial penalties exist and how large they are, but how they vary according to court contextual characteristics, as well as by offense and offender characteristics.

In keeping with the theoretical themes running throughout this book, we view the issue of trial penalties and their possible variation from an integrated perspective, comprising focal concerns as well as court communities and social worlds, to make theoretical sense of jury trial penalties. In this chapter, we investigate how factors suggested by this integrated perspective affect variation in trial penalties.

Focal Concerns of Sentencing and Their Embeddedness in Court Communities

The interesting and seldom examined questions we address here are: How might trial penalties vary between individual cases and between jurisdictions? What might such variation suggest about which of the focal concerns are most related to trial penalties? Are trial penalties primarily driven by practical constraints like caseload pressure? Or are there variations produced by factors plausibly linked to social identities and person constructions that are relevant to blameworthiness and dangerousness? What jurisdictional characteristics besides caseloads might be associated with variation in trial penalties?

As already argued, court participants' situational definitions of defendants vis-à-vis focal concerns (defendant blameworthiness, defendant dangerousness and community protection, and practical constraints and consequences connected to the punishment decision) determine sentencing decisions. This chapter focuses on the following questions: If going to trial and losing, especially losing at jury trial, results in more severe sentences for convicted defendants, what is associated with variation in such effects? Which focal concerns, if any, might be related to variation in such trial penalties, as evidenced by particular interaction effects?

A practical constraint that would be highly relevant to the issue of plea rewards and trial penalties is *organizational efficiency*. Most commonly, researchers explain differences between guilty plea and trial sentences as the product of courts rewarding those who plead guilty for behavior or attitudes that courts organizationally value. Most researchers argue that rewarding those who plead guilty and penalizing those who lose at trial reflects the need for efficiency in case processing. This organizational efficiency model (see Uhlman and Walker 1980; Holmes, Daudistel, and Taggart 1992; Dixon 1995; Engen and Steen 2000) views rewarding people who plead guilty and avoiding time- and resource-intensive trials as an effort by courts to keep cases moving smoothly and avoid docket backlogs. Relatedly, those who focus on interorganizational and interpersonal relations between court actors, such as adherents of the court community perspective, suggest that court actors often view trials as unpleasant, conflictive, and disruptive of court community working relations, and thus seek to discourage them (Flemming, Nardulli, and Eisenstein 1992; Ulmer 1997).

Pleading guilty as opposed to losing at trial might also be associated with differences in perceived *blameworthiness*. Rewarding those who plead guilty with lighter sentences is widely seen as necessary to encourage defendants' "remorse," "acceptance of responsibility" for crimes, and perhaps cooperation with law enforcement. In fact, these kinds of guilty plea rewards are explicitly built into the US Sentencing Guidelines, according to which federal defendants receive guideline-based sentencing discounts or departures for "acceptance of responsibility" and "substantial assistance to law enforcement" (US Sentencing Commission 2001). A quote from a Pennsylvania judge illustrates how going to trial and losing may signal a defendant's lack of remorse, and therefore greater blameworthiness, to judges:

> People who plead guilty always argue that remorse is a mitigating factor, and one cannot deny that. They are saying 'I am sorry, I did it.' I consider that a mitigating factor. If you don't plead guilty and go to trial, then there is the absence of a mitigating factor. Sure enough after a trial at the time of sentencing he will be remorseful. He might have taken the stand and said he didn't do it, now he is remorseful. I ask what he is remorseful about. He will say that he hates to be in this situation. I say that I am sure you do, and maybe I don't want to be in this position either. You could look at it as a penalty but there is no other way of doing it. You have to give people credit for pleading guilty and expressing remorse. It is that simple. I choose not to call it a sentencing penalty. (Ulmer 1997, p. 88)

Finally, trials may bring out "bad facts," or facts about crimes or defendants that increase perceived blameworthiness. Such facts could be covered up, or at least not have as much visceral impact, in a guilty plea agreement (see Brereton and Casper 1982; Flemming, Nardulli, and Eisenstein 1992; Ulmer 1997). As Brereton and Casper note: "In addition, the trial is likely to produce more publicity and attendant public scrutiny, *as well as providing the sentencer with much more detail about the nature of the harm done by the defendant.* Both of these may militate against the leniency that often attends the privacy and flexibility of the plea bargain" (1982, p. 68, emphasis added). A quote from a Pennsylvania defense attorney provides another example of this reasoning: "Sure, there is a plea discount, but the trial penalty you have to worry about is that the judge is going to learn too much when you go to trial that he wouldn't otherwise, *because you can present a much better sentencing case if the judge doesn't learn all the ugly facts*" (Ulmer 1997, p. 99, emphasis added).

Harold Garfinkel (1956) explicitly identified criminal trials (at least those where the defendant loses) as a special type of "status degradation ceremony" in modern societies, and in fact argued that these degradation practices are professional role expectations for court officials. In the course of such degradation ceremonies, unsuccessful trials may mobilize more negative attributions about blameworthiness toward convicted defendants than would guilty pleas, and this then may influence subsequent sentencing decisions.

The salience of organizational efficiency versus other concerns probably varies by the seriousness of the offense. For example, sentencing stakes would be higher for all parties involved in serious violence cases, which often entail more salient victim-related considerations, and which are relatively more visible to the news media and public. In serious violent offense cases, judges and prosecutors tend to take blameworthiness, protection of the community, and public perceptions of criminal punishment very seriously (Kramer and Ulmer 2002). Consequently, all serious offenders may tend to face relatively severe sentences, regardless of whether they plead guilty or go to trial.

On the other hand, organizational efficiency might be a more dominant concern in less serious cases, both because they make up the bulk of the caseload, and because the potential punishments are much less severe. If so, taking up the time of prosecutors and courts by insisting on a trial, especially when the punishment stakes are less severe, may be met with more substantial trial penalties, in proportional terms, than in serious cases. Prosecutors and even judges may not always presume innocence, and might resent taking court personnel's time and resources for a trial that may not be seen as necessary (Nardulli, Eisenstein, and Flemming 1988).

Thus, one would expect significant plea/trial sentencing differences based on both notions of organizational efficiency and differential constructions of blameworthiness of those who plead guilty compared to those who go to trial. We would anticipate this effect to be especially pronounced for jury trials, which are typically longer, more elaborate, and more visible, and entail the disclosure of more information than bench trials (Eisenstein and Jacob 1977; Mather 1979; Brereton and Casper 1982; Nardulli, Eisenstein, and Flemming 1988; Ulmer 1997). Bench trials typically tend to resemble "slow guilty pleas," are relatively short, and entail less information disclosure (Eisenstein and Jacob 1977; Ulmer 1997).

If, as Garfinkel argued, unsuccessful trials are a type of status degradation ceremony (with the subsequent sentencing hearing constituting another, second status degradation ceremony), the effects of such ceremonies on sentences may be more severe for those with more extensive criminal histories. Garfinkel (1956) argued that status degradation ceremonies are occasions where the past (and prospective future) behavior of the accused is reinterpreted by authorities in light of his or her present degradation. Erving Goffman (1963) described a similar process in which the biography of the stigmatized is reinterpreted retrospectively, and past negative events or behaviors intensify the "spoiled identity" of the deviant.

A prior record of criminality then, especially an extensive one, might be a resource to be used by the prosecution following a trial conviction to dramatize the criminality, and thus the blameworthiness, of the defendant. Trials, and the sentencing hearings before the judge that follow them, would likely provide an opportunity for prosecutors to "dirty up" defendants (to use a phrase common among defense lawyers). In fact, Douglas Smith (1986) found that defendants with no prior felony or drug arrests reduced their odds of incarceration by pleading guilty, whereas those with more extensive criminal records did not. Further, Jeffery Ulmer (1997) found that plea/trial sentencing differences increased as criminal histories increased. Thus, we suspect that those with more extensive prior criminal records will experience a greater trial penalty.

Race, Ethnicity, and Gender:
Trial Penalties and Social Status–Related Disparity?

Court actors' interpretations and assessments of focal concerns such as perceived dangerousness or blameworthiness, as well as the salience of relevant practical constraints and consequences, might be influenced by race, ethnicity, and gender (Peterson and Hagan 1984; Steffensmeier, Ulmer, and Kramer 1998; Spohn and Holleran 2000). After jury trials, marginalized racial or ethnic identities might mobilize more negative emotional responses than whites, especially fear (which implicates perceived dangerousness, or the focal concern of community protection), and their trial penalties might then be correspondingly greater than those for whites. In fact, in two studies of broad samples of offenses in Pennsylvania, Jeffery Ulmer (1997) found that trial penalties were greater for blacks, and Brian Johnson (2003) found that blacks convicted by jury trial were especially less likely to receive sentencing leniency (in the form of downward guideline departures).

In contrast, female defendants tend to arouse less fear, are often seen as less crime-prone and less morally blameworthy, and tend to be the objects of more sympathy (see Steffensmeier, Kramer, and Streifel 1993; Koons-Witt 2002). Therefore, trials involving women defendants might arouse more sympathy and less negative feelings toward the defendant, and their trial penalties would be correspondingly less severe.

Court Contexts: The "Caseload Controversy"
Trial penalties and plea rewards have most frequently been discussed in relation to court caseload pressure. Scholars debated throughout the 1980s and

early 1990s about whether the pressure to keep cases moving and avoid docket backlogs was the major reason for the existence and variation in plea/trial sentencing differences (see Meeker and Pontell 1985; Nardulli, Eisenstein, and Flemming 1988; Holmes, Daudistel, and Taggart 1992; Dixon 1995; Engen and Steen 2000). As far as we can tell, the "caseload controversy," as Peter Nardulli, James Eisenstein, and Roy Flemming (1988) called it, seems to have faded away in the late 1990s with little resolution or consensus in the literature. An organizational efficiency perspective would suggest that differentially punishing pleas and trials was an organizationally rational response to the need to keep cases moving efficiently. Trials consume scarce prosecutorial and judicial time and resources. Presenting incentives to plead guilty, and imposing costs on going to trial and losing, would seem to be a rational organizational strategy for prosecutors and judges alike. The greater the caseload pressure, the more a court would rely on such costs and incentives. On the other hand, several have argued that plea bargaining and its potential for plea/trial sentencing differences persist, despite variations in caseload pressure, because they are sustained by other courtroom incentives and culture (Eisenstein and Jacob 1977; Church 1979; Meeker and Pontell 1985; Nardulli, Eisenstein, and Flemming 1988).

Douglas Smith (1986) argued that plea bargaining is a rational rather than a coercive process. He argued that from the perspective of defendants, plea/trial sentencing differences must be weighed against the possibility of acquittal that a trial affords. He found little difference, on average, between the sentences of people who pled guilty and those who went to trial. Even though plea bargaining is neutral in its sentencing consequences, Smith argued, guilty pleas are rational for prosecutors to pursue: "Perhaps the primary advantage of a system of negotiated pleas is that it allows prosecutors to pursue more cases than otherwise would be possible" (p. 966).

Smith's logic is at least congruent with the idea that caseloads might produce variation in plea/trial sentencing differences, as the organizational efficiency hypothesis suggests. In fact, Smith's study found that plea/trial sentencing differences varied substantially between jurisdictions, and that "we need to know more about the factors which may contribute to this inter-jurisdictional variation" (p. 967). Variations in caseload might be just such a factor, and a key one at that.

A strong version of the organizational efficiency hypothesis would be that trial penalties are primarily driven by caseloads. Thus caseload should be the only factor that conditions variation in trial penalties. A weaker version would suggest that caseload would be one of several factors that might significantly interact with trial penalties.

Court Community Context: Other Factors

Beyond court caseload pressure as a practical constraint that may interact with jury trial effects, the literature provides little guidance. We know of no published studies that have investigated contextual variation in trial penalties with multilevel statistical methods. However, it is reasonable to suspect that court size, violent crime rate, percent black, and percent Hispanic would be associated with variation in trial penalties.[1] James Eisenstein, Roy Flemming, and Peter Nardulli (1988) paid particular attention to court community size, and argued that large urban courts are typically more lenient than smaller courts, and that their routine case processing (that is, their guilty plea process) is relatively invisible to the public. However, such courts receive greater scrutiny from the media (perhaps even newspapers and television stations with national visibility), and serious violent offense jury trials might receive relatively more public attention. Due to this atypical scrutiny, judges and prosecutors might feel more pressure to sentence defendants more severely after such trials (compared to more routine and less visible guilty pleas) in order to politically demonstrate their seriousness and "toughness" regarding violent crime. This would be especially true in jurisdictions where judges and prosecutors are elected by partisan vote, as in Pennsylvania. However, to our knowledge, this proposition has never been empirically tested. Thus we expect that large court communities will apply greater jury trial penalties than smaller court communities for serious violent offenses. For less serious offenses, we expect little variation in trial penalties in relation to court size.

Relatedly, a community's violent crime problem might condition variation in trial penalties. Again, if trials are relatively more publicly visible than guilty pleas (regardless of county size), and a county has a more serious crime problem (and for serious violent cases the rate of violent crime might be especially salient), this would create political pressure on prosecutors to push for more substantial sentences in trial cases, and on judges to mete out those sentences, in order to visibly demonstrate their concern for public safety and retribution.

Percent black has been found to be an important factor in previous multilevel analyses of sentencing (Britt 2000; Ulmer and Johnson 2004). Given the arguments above regarding racial threat and trial penalties, it is reasonable to expect that trial penalties will be greater in counties with larger black populations. This is because more publicly visible trials, especially serious violent crime trials, present an opportunity to "send a message" to the local (majority white) electorate that crime, which prejudiced whites tend to equate with *black* crime (Barkan and Cohn 2005), will be dealt with severely.

Finally, we examine whether effects of trial conviction on sentencing vary by the county trial rate. As mentioned in Chapter 6, we suspect that trial penalties are less substantial in courts with higher trial rates. That is, low trial rates may be found among jurisdictions with high sentencing costs for defendants who go to trial and lose. Courts with low trial rates might have particularly strong informal norms that encourage guilty pleas and discourage trials, and norms that foster stronger trial penalties. These norms would tend to deter defendants, and defense attorneys, from taking cases to trial. Conversely, higher trial rates are likely found among jurisdictions with comparatively lower sentencing costs of going to trial and losing. Higher trial rates might suggest that such courts lack informal norms that discourage trials but that do not condone strong trial penalties.

Data

We test these expectations using aggregate and individual-level sentencing data from county criminal trial courts in Pennsylvania. We use the same dataset and contextual data sources as in the previous chapter—that is, the subset of "core crimes." The Research Methods Appendix provides more detail on the data and the analytic procedures used in this chapter.

The dependent variables we use here are the same as in Chapters 5 and 6: (1) the decision whether or not to incarcerate, (2) the decision between county jail and state prison incarceration, and (3) the decision about sentence length for incarcerated defendants.

In addition to the data limitations we listed in previous chapters, another important limitation is that since the PCS does not collect preconviction data, we cannot control for the likelihood of conviction or acquittal at trial as the studies by William Rhodes (1979), Douglas Smith (1986), and Gary LaFree (1985) do. Thus our analysis is limited to convicted offenders only, and we cannot generalize our findings to all individuals charged with crimes.

We know from Chapters 5 and 6 that those convicted by jury trial are sentenced more severely, and so are, to a lesser extent, those convicted by bench trials. We also know that negotiated pleas benefit defendants to a greater extent than nonnegotiated or open pleas. We find here, in preliminary analyses, that trial penalties and their variation differ between more serious and less serious offenses, just as we suspected. In our analyses below, we therefore split the data into serious violent offenses (the same offenses analyzed in Chapter 4) and less serious offenses, and present separate but similar sets of models for the two groups of offenses.

Findings

Serious Violent Offenses

Table 7.1 summarizes the descriptive statistics for the variables included in our analyses of the serious violent offenses. Approximately 88 percent of the sample received incarceration sentences, with an average minimum length of confinement of about twenty-eight months (the mean for logged length is about 2.9, with a standard deviation of about 1.1; logging sentence length thus considerably normalizes its distribution). The large percentage of incarceration is not surprising, considering that the data consists only of serious violent offenses. In addition, this table shows that trials are relatively rare; bench trials

Table 7.1   Select Descriptive Statistics: Serious Violent Offenses, 1997–2000

Variables	Frequency	Percentage	Mean	Standard Deviation
Incarceration (1 = yes)	7,643	88.1		
Type of incarceration				
None	1,084	12.5		
County jail	3,401	39.2		
State prison	4,200	48.4		
Logged sentence length (includes incarceration cases only)			2.9	1.1
Sentence length (includes incarceration cases only)			27.6	35.4
Level 1 predictors				
Bench trial	781	9.0		
Jury trial	608	7.0		
Black	4,256	49.0		
Hispanic	608	7.0		
Female	869	10.0		
Age			28.9	9.9
Offense gravity score			8.4	2.3
Prior record score	1		.6	2.0
Presumptive disposition (1 = incarceration)	8,250	95.1		
Presumptive guideline minimum sentence length			24.7	25.5

and jury trials constitute roughly 9 percent and 7 percent of convictions, respectively. Table 7.2 presents HLM models of jail and prison incarceration decisions and logged incarceration length.

How does trial conviction affect the chances of incarceration, and do trial penalties vary depending on whether one considers county jail or state prison? We immediately see that the sentencing consequences of trial convictions are much more substantial for the state imprisonment decision. Bench trials increase the odds of county jail, while jury trial conviction actually has a negative (and not significant) relationship with going to jail. In the prison model, it is clear why this is true—those convicted by jury trial and incarcerated are very much more likely to go to prison rather than jail (recall that a similar finding was reported in Chapter 6). Jury trials increase the odds of going to state prison almost five and a half times. Bench trials also increase the odds of prison by more than three times.

The state prison incarceration trial penalty here is slightly larger than that found by Marjorie Zatz and John Hagan (1985) in their sample of convicted offenders (they found incarceration odds of 2.16 associated with jury trial conviction). Of course, our findings are quite different from those of Smith (1986), who found no significant overall difference between pleas and trials in

Table 7.2   Incarceration Odds and Length for Serious Violent Offenses: Fixed Effects

Models	Odds Ratio		Logged Length	
	County Jail	State Prison	b	Antilog of b
Intercept (B_0, G_{00})	2.46***	3.27***	1.20	3.32***
Level 1 predictors				
Bench trial	*1.83******	*3.13******	*.24*	*1.27******
Jury trial	*.90*	*5.40******	*.48*	*1.62******
Homicide	.66*	.69	.08	1.08*
Rape/IDSI	.54*	.56***	−.05	.95
Aggravated assault	.79**	.40***	−.28	.76***
Offense gravity score	1.32***	2.36***	.34	1.40***
Prior record score	1.41***	2.26***	.20	1.22***
Presumptive disposition	3.08***	2.02***		
Guideline minimum			−.01	.99***
Black	1.22*	1.45***	.08	1.08***
Hispanic	1.75***	1.75***	.09	1.10*
Female	.51***	.30***	−.24	.79***
Age	.996	.98***	−.003	.997**
Level 2 predictors				
Mean annual court caseload	NS	.76	−.07	.93***
Jury trial rate	NS	NS	NS	
Jail space	1.03**	NS	NS	
Percent black	NS	.90**	−.03	.97**
Violent crime rate	NS	¹1.003***	.001	1.001*
Large court	NS	.40**	NS	
Small court	1.82*	2.40**	NS	
Level 2 R-squared			.43	
Level 1 R-squared			.57	
N		8,685	7,643	

Notes: Robbery is the reference category for offense type, guilty pleas are the reference category for mode of conviction, medium courts are the reference category for court size. The models also include dummy variables for missing data on race/ethnicity and gender.

NS = variable not significant and deleted from model.

¹$p < .10$; *$p < .05$; **$p < .01$; ***$p < .001$.

their probabilities of being sentenced to at least a year in prison, after accounting for the likelihood of being convicted.

In the model of logged sentence length in Table 7.2, trials result in significantly longer sentences than guilty pleas. On average, those found guilty by bench trials received roughly 27 percent longer incarceration sentences than those who pled guilty. Being convicted by jury trial increased sentence lengths by roughly 62 percent. Thus, trial convictions for serious violent offenses apparently carry considerable sentence length costs.

Table 7.3 shows the cross-level interactions with jury trial as well as the significant level-one interaction effects, for overall incarceration, jail and prison incarceration, and sentence length.

Table 7.3 Significant Interaction Effects: Serious Violent Offenses (interaction terms added separately)

	In/Out Odds Ratio	County Jail Odds Ratio	State Prison Odds Ratio	Length b	(antilog of b)
Cross-level interaction effects					
Jury trial rate × jury trial				−.11***	(.90)
Large courts × jury trial				.28***	(1.32)
Violent crime × jury trial				.0002**	(1.0002)
Percent black × jury trial				.01**	(1.01)
Level 1 interaction effects					
Offense gravity score × jury trial	1.36**				
Prior record × jury trial	.69***	.60***	.57***	−.03*	(.97)
Aggravated assault × jury trial				.16**	(1.17)
Rape/IDSI × jury trial	n/v			−.19**	(.83)
Black × jury trial	n/v			.12**	(1.13)

Notes: Robbery is the reference category for offense type; guilty pleas are the reference category for mode of conviction.

n/v = insufficient variation existed in the incarceration outcomes of certain categories. For example, all rape/IDSI offenses convicted by jury trial resulted in incarceration, and 97 percent of blacks convicted by jury trial (all but nine offenders) were incarcerated.

*p < .05; **p < .01; ***p < .001.

None of the county-level characteristics exhibit significant cross-level interaction effects with jury trial for overall incarceration, or for county jail versus state prison. Contrary to our expectations, court caseloads do not significantly affect variation in trial penalties. However, as expected, jury trial exhibits a significant and negative cross-level interaction with jury trial for logged sentence length. A 1 percent increase in courts' jury trial rates is associated with a 10 percent decrease in the length of jury trial penalties.

We expected that serious violent offenses in large urban courts would result in greater jury trial penalties than in other courts, and this is supported for sentence length. The length trial penalty for such offenses in the large counties is 32 percent greater than in medium-sized courts (and indirectly greater than in small courts). We also expected that counties with more violent crime would have greater trial penalties for serious violent offenses, and this idea receives support in our models of sentence length as well. Each unit increase in violent crime rate increases the trial penalty by .02 percent, a seemingly small effect, but one that would add up to meaningful cumulative differences between counties with substantially different crime rates. A county with a violent crime rate of 800 per 100,000 would have a 12 percent greater length trial penalty than a county with a violent crime rate of 200 per 100,000.

We reasoned that counties with larger black populations would have greater trial penalties for serious violent offenses, and the sentence length analysis also supports this idea. A one unit increase in percent black increases the trial penalty by 1 percent. Thus the trial penalty for a county with a 30 percent black population would be 20 percent greater than that for a county with a 10 percent black population. Interestingly, this cross-level interaction "washes out" the individual-level black–jury trial effect (discussed below). To the extent that percent black is correlated with defendant's race (the correlation between county percent black and black defendant is .36), an interaction effect between percent black and jury trial might eliminate the interaction effect between black and trial.

We expected the jury trial penalty to be greater for those with more extensive criminal records. Contrary to our prediction, these terms were significant and negative for all four of our sentencing decisions, indicating that the jury trial penalty *decreases* as the prior record score of the defendant increases. Each increase in prior record score decreases the size of overall incarceration trial penalty by .31, while each increase in prior record decreases the sentence length trial penalty by 3 percent. Also, each increase in prior record decreases the jury trial effect on county jail by .40, and its effect on prison by .43. Thus, contrary to our expectations, jury trials "hurt" those with more serious criminal histories less than those with less serious and extensive criminal histories.

We thought that jury trial penalties would increase as offense severity increased. This term was not significant in the length model, but it was in the overall incarceration model (it was also borderline significant and in the expected direction for jail and prison), indicating that the jury trial penalty in terms of incarceration increases substantially as offense severity increases. This effect of offense severity–jury trial interaction on the odds of incarceration is 1.36. In other words, for each one-point increase in offense severity, the odds of incarceration following a jury trial conviction go up by .36.[2]

None of the offense categories varied significantly in their jury trial penalties for overall incarceration or jail versus prison. Insufficient variation in incarceration outcomes prevented assessing an interaction term for rape and involuntary deviate sexual intercourse; all jury trial convictions for such offenses resulted in incarceration. However, we find that those convicted of rape or involuntary deviate sexual intercourse at jury trial received 17 percent shorter sentences compared to those convicted of robbery. By contrast, those convicted of aggravated assault received 17 percent longer sentences than those convicted of robbery.

We expected that the jury trial penalty would be greater for blacks and Hispanics. Hispanic–jury trial interactions were not significant for incarceration, prison versus jail, or sentence length. Thus the size of the jury trial penalty did not differ significantly between Hispanics and whites. Black–jury trial interactions present a more complicated picture. In a model that excludes the cross-level caseload–jury trial interaction (the last column of Table 7.3), the black–jury trial interaction is significant at p < .05, and indicates that the length trial penalty for blacks is 13 percent greater than for whites. Thus it would first appear that among these serious violent offenses, the effect of jury trial is conditioned by race. However, when we control for the conditioning effect of percent black on trial penalty, the black–jury trial interaction drops to a nonsignificant .06 (antilog = 1.06). Thus it appears that the modest black–jury trial interaction is explained away by between-county differences in trial penalties. Most plausibly, the individual-level black–jury trial interaction is spurious in the face of the percent black–jury trial interaction.

Although gender has a direct effect on odds of incarceration and sentence length, we found no significant gender–jury trial interaction effect. That is, the jury trial penalties for women did not differ significantly from those of men with regard to either outcome. In supplemental analyses, we also found no evidence that gender significantly interacted with offense type to condition trial penalties. Apparently, then, gender does not condition the size of trial penalties, at least for these serious violent offenses.

Less Serious Offenses

Patterns of trial penalties are somewhat different for less serious offenses. Here we replicate the analyses above for crimes such as simple assault, burglary, theft, drug felonies and misdemeanors, and others. Table 7.4 shows the descriptive statistics for this subsample of cases. Table 7.5 shows the main effects of bench and jury trial and the other predictors for county jail and state prison incarceration, and sentence length.

Significant contextual effects for the jail decision include jail space (which increases the likelihood of jail sentences), and large court size (large courts are substantially less likely to jail defendants). Caseload and court size, in turn, affect the imposition of prison sentences. Higher caseloads are associated with fewer prison sentences, small courts are more likely to send people to prison, and large courts less so (the effect is marginally significant). The only significant county-level predictor of sentence length is caseload—heavier caseloads are associated with shorter sentences. As with the analysis of serious violent offenses, offense severity and prior record are more strongly predictive of prison sentences than jail sentences. At the individual case level, the guideline-relevant variables are, as usual, the strongest predictors of the incarceration decisions and length in the models. Burglary and drug misdemeanors are associated with the longest and shortest sentences, respectively. Also, more black versus white and Hispanic versus white disparity is evident for the state prison decisions than for jail outcomes. Blacks do not receive significantly longer sentences than whites, though, and Hispanics receive only modestly longer sentences.

Of central relevance here, both bench and jury trials increase the odds of both types of incarceration. The effects are much stronger for prison, however.

Table 7.4   Select Descriptive Statistics: Less Serious Offenses, 1997–2000

Variables	Frequency	Percentage	Mean	Standard Deviation
Incarceration (1 = yes)	49,970	45		
Type of incarceration				
None	60,958	55		
County jail	38,761	35		
State prison	11,305	10		
Logged sentence length (includes incarceration cases only)				
Sentence length (includes incarceration cases only)			9.0	9.3
Level 1 predictors				
Bench trial	3,332	3.0		
Jury trial	1,111	1.0		
Black	39,976	36.0		
Hispanic	8,884	8.0		
Female	18,878	17.0		
Age			30.0	9.7
Offense gravity score			3.6	1.8
Prior record score			1.5	1.9
Presumptive disposition (1 = incarceration)	39,975	36.0		
Presumptive guideline minimum sentence length			5.9	8.3

In particular, jury trial conviction raises the odds of going to state prison 9.7 times. In other words, offenders convicted of less serious crimes by jury trial have almost ten times the odds of going to prison than comparable offenders who plead guilty. Bench trials do result in about 19 percent longer sentences, and jury trials yield about 57 percent longer sentences than guilty pleas.

In addition, the two trial variables exhibited significant random variation in their effects for overall incarceration and length. In the length model, the standard deviations for the variance components for bench and jury trial effects were .18 and .14, respectively. This means, for example, that among two-thirds of the counties, sentences associated with bench trials ranged from about 20 percent greater to 20 percent less than the effect shown in Table 7.5. The standard deviation of the variance components for overall incarceration were .49 for bench trial and .33 for jury trial. So, among two-thirds of the counties, the incarceration odds for bench trial varied by 63 percent plus or minus the odds in Table 7.5, while the jury trial effect on incarceration odds varied by plus or minus 39 percent. Clearly, trial penalties vary a great deal between counties for less serious offenses.

Finally, Table 7.6 shows the significant interactions with jury trial effects for the less serious offenses. More cross-level interaction effects occur for the incarceration variables here than in the serious violent offenses analysis. In

Table 7.5   Factors Affecting Incarceration Odds and Length for Less Serious Offenses: Fixed and Random Effects

Models	Odds Ratio		Logged Length	
	County Jail	State Prison	b	antilog of b
Intercept (B_0, G_{00})	1.31***	.18***	.47	1.60***
Level 1 predictors				
Bench trial (r)	*1.32*	*2.22**	*.17*	*1.19***
Jury trial (r)	*2.09****	*9.73****	*.45*	*1.56****
Simple assault	.99	.81***	.04	1.04***
Arson	1.05	1.42*	.19	1.21***
Burglary	1.42***	1.96***	.21	1.23***
Criminal trespassing	1.49***	1.48***	.10	1.10***
Drug felony	.82***	1.25***	.18	1.20***
Drug misdemeanor	.56***	.36***	−.17	.84***
Forgery	1.16***	1.94***	.11	1.12***
Weapons	.82***	.95	.02	1.02
Offense gravity score	1.31***	2.23***	.25	1.28***
Prior record score	1.35***	2.13***	.19	1.21***
Presumptive disposition	1.56***	1.27***		
Guideline minimum			.02	1.02***
Black	1.55***	1.61***	.001	1.001
Hispanic	1.44***	1.77***	.05	1.05***
Female	.67***	.50***	-.09	.91***
Age	.99***	.98***	-.001	.999*
Level 2 predictors				
Mean annual court caseload	NS	.77**	−.04	.96*
Jury trial rate	NS	NS	NS	
Jail space	1.02**	NS	NS	
Percent black	NS	NS	NS	
Crime rate	NS	NS	NS	
Large court	.40*	.84ᵗ	NS	
Small court	NS	1.92*	NS	
Level 2 R-squared				
Level 1 R-squared				
N	110,994	42,483		

Notes: Theft is the reference category for offense type, guilty pleas are the reference category for mode of conviction, medium courts are the reference category for court size. The models also include dummy variables for missing data on race/ethnicity and gender.

NS = variable not significant and deleted from model.

(r) = effects allowed to vary randomly.

ᵗp < .10; *p < .05; **p < .01; ***p < .001.

terms of overall incarceration, jury trial penalties increase with county percent black. Incarceration odds associated with jury trials increase 1 percent with every 1 percent increase in percent black. The jail versus prison analysis shows that this effect is specified for, or concentrates around, the prison decision. The percent black–jury trial effect is not significant for jail, but a one point increase in percent black increases the jury trial penalty odds by 3 per-

Table 7.6   Significant Interaction Effects: Less Serious Offenses (interaction terms added separately)

	In/Out Odds Ratio	County Jail Odds Ratio	State Prison Odds Ratio	Length b	Length (antilog of b)
Cross-level interaction effects					
Jury trial rate × jury trial			.81*	–.09***	(.91)
Large courts × jury trial			.88*	.27***	(1.31)
Crime rate × jury trial			.0002**		
Percentage black × jury trial	1.01*		1.03*	.01***	(1.01)
Level 1 interaction effects					
Offense gravity score × jury trial				.03*	(1.03)
Prior record × jury trial	.85***	.77***	.76***		
Offense gravity score × prior record × jury trial	.97**	.93***	.94***		
Simple assault × jury trial	1.40*	1.92***	1.63*		
Drug misdemeanor × jury trial	.59*	n/v	n/v		
Weapons × jury trial			4.63**	.20*	(1.22)
Criminal trespassing × jury trial		4.75*			
Black × jury trial	1.38*		2.01**		

Notes: n/v = insufficient variation existed in the incarceration outcomes of certain categories to estimate effects.
*p < .05; **p < .01; ***p < .001.

cent. In other cross-level interactions, large courts are less likely to send those convicted by trial to prison, but (as in the serious violent offenses analysis) the jury trial sentence length penalty is greater in large courts.

The prior record–trial effect is significant and similar for overall incarceration and the jail versus prison decision. As with the serious violent offenses, and unexpectedly, increases in prior record score substantially decrease the trial penalty for these outcomes. Also, simple assault offenders convicted by trial receive both prison and jail incarceration more often. Weapon offenders convicted by jury trial are much more likely to go to prison and receive longer sentence lengths than theft offenders (the reference category), and criminal trespass cases that go to jury trial are much more likely to result in jail sentences. Clearly, plea/trial differences differ between offenses.

Interestingly, there is evidence that the jury trial penalty decreases as offense gravity score and prior record score jointly increase. That is, among these less serious offenses, when offense severity and prior record are both relatively higher, and the guideline recommendations for punishment become comparatively more severe, the trial penalty odds decline. Perhaps judges and prosecutors are more likely to view trials as having merit when the sentencing stakes are higher for defendants, and are less inclined to penalize defendants as much for exercising their trial rights in such cases.

Finally, blacks who go to trial for less serious offenses are more likely to be incarcerated, and this effect concentrates around the prison decision. Blacks convicted of less serious offenses by jury trial have twice the odds of going to prison as similar whites. Unlike with the serious violent offender analyses, this race–jury trial effect stays strong and significant even when the percent black–jury trial effect is included in the model—the cross-level interaction does not render the individual-level race interaction effect spurious. So, among less serious offenses: (1) blacks convicted by trial are more likely to go to prison, and (2) counties with relatively more blacks are more likely to send all offenders convicted by jury trial, regardless of race, to prison.

Trial Penalties or Plea Rewards?

Are the plea/trial differences reflective of additional punishment for those convicted by trial, or reduced punishment for those who plead guilty? That is, are these differences plea rewards or trial penalties? Of course, it depends on how one looks at the issue—it is something of a "glass half-full or empty" question, and one's answer depends on one's value stances toward plea rewards and trial penalties. However, one way to empirically address the question is to determine the degree to which those convicted by guilty pleas versus trial end up with sentences that are above or below the presumptive guideline disposition or incarceration minimum (recall from Chapter 2 that the minimum has been considered the most common "benchmark" to represent the typical presumptive guideline recommendation). If guilty pleas more likely yield sentences that are below guideline recommendations, and if those convicted by trials typically receive sentences equal to the guideline minimums, then plea/trial sentencing differences would typically represent *plea rewards*. That is, trial convictees receive sentences commensurate with guideline minimum recommendations, while those who plead guilty are rewarded with more lenient sentences than called for (e.g., through guideline departures or mitigated range sentences, perhaps). If, however, trial convictees receive sentences that are above the guideline minimum recommendations, while guilty pleas yield sentences that are commensurate with the minimums (or even below them), this would arguably reflect *trial penalties*. Those convicted by trial would receive more severe sentences than called for by the guideline minimums (e.g., sentences in the upper parts of the standard ranges, aggravated range sentences, or even departures above the guidelines), while those pleading guilty would receive the guideline minimum sentences.

In Table 7.7, we estimate multinomial regression models with all cases included together (with the same predictors as above except the county-level variables) predicting where the actual sentences fall relative to guideline minimum recommendations.[3] For the incarceration decision, we categorize sentences as

Table 7.7   Recommended vs. Actual Sentences by Modes of Conviction, All Offenses

	Bench Trials	Jury Trials
Incarceration Disposition (odds)		
Below Guideline Minimum	.42***	.19***
Above Guideline Minimum	.69***	1.69***
Sentence Length (odds, nonincarceration cases not included)		
Minimum Below Guideline Minimum	.66***	.23***
Minimum Above Guideline Minimum	1.68***	4.57***

Notes: Models include all control variables from previous analyses.
***p < .001.

(1) falling below the presumptive minimum disposition (i.e., guidelines call for incarceration but a nonincarceration sentence is given—in other words, a "dispositional departure"; see Kramer and Ulmer 1996), (2) equal to the guideline disposition (guidelines call for incarceration and incarceration is given), or (3) falling above the guideline disposition (guideline minimum is zero months of incarceration but an incarceration sentence is given). For the length decision, we categorize sentences as (1) falling below the presumptive minimum length (in other words, a downward length departure), (2) equal to the guideline minimum length, or (3) falling above the guideline minimum length. The models compare the likelihood of receiving a sentence below the guideline minimum recommendations versus one above the recommendations, as compared to a sentence equal to the recommendations. Only the effects for the trial variables are shown.

Not surprisingly, given our findings throughout this chapter, bench and especially jury trials are considerably less likely to result in nonincarceration sentences when the guidelines call for incarceration. Those convicted by bench trials are also significantly less likely to receive dispositions sentences that are above the minimums, meaning that bench trials are most likely to yield incarceration dispositions that are commensurate with the guideline minimums. Jury trials, however, are significantly (odds = 1.69) more likely than guilty pleas to produce dispositions that are more severe than called for by guideline minimums. The pattern is even stronger when considering decisions about sentence length decisions. Jury trial convictees' odds of receiving a sentence length that is lower than the guideline minimum are 77 percent less than for those who plead guilty, and bench trials are also less likely to result in such sentences. Also, those convicted by bench trial have 1.67 times the odds of receiving a sentence length that is greater than the guideline minimum. Jury trials are strikingly more likely to result in sentences above the guideline minimum than guilty pleas. Compared to guilty pleas, jury trial convictees have four and a half times greater odds of receiving a sentence above, as opposed to equal to, the guideline minimum.

The serious violent offenses and less serious offenses subsamples do not differ much from the overall pattern when we replicate the above analysis for each of them separately (see the Research Methods Appendix). In both subsamples, both bench and jury trial cases are less likely than guilty pleas to result in incarceration dispositions that are more lenient than those recommended by guidelines. Bench trial cases are also less likely to result in incarceration dispositions when the guidelines do not call for them, meaning that bench trial cases are most likely to result in dispositions commensurate with the guidelines. For both subsamples of offenses, jury trial convictees are especially likely to receive incarceration when the guidelines call for nonincarceration. It should be noted that this dispositional analysis is less meaningful for the serious violent offenses, because the guidelines almost always call for incarceration.

The sentence length findings for both sets of offenses are also very similar to the overall pattern. Bench and especially jury trial cases are less likely than guilty pleas to result in sentence lengths that are at or below the guideline minimums, and more likely (very likely, in the case of jury trials) to result in more severe sentences than called for by the guideline minimums. This overall pattern is actually exacerbated among the less serious offenses, where a jury trial conviction raises the odds of a sentence above the guideline minimum by 5.20 (as opposed to odds of 2.24 for serious violent offenses, a significant difference based on a z-test for equality of regression coefficients).

On balance, these findings seem to suggest that the plea/trial differences we have observed most typically constitute trial penalties rather than plea rewards, as we have operationalized these terms. Consistently, guilty pleas strongly tend to eventuate in sentences at or below the guideline minimums, while jury trials are highly likely to yield sentences above the minimums. Bench trial sentences tend to be commensurate with the guidelines in terms of dispositions, but like jury trials, do tend to produce sentence lengths above the guideline minimums. These patterns characterize both serious violent and less serious offenses, and in fact the patterns are somewhat stronger for less serious offenses.

Again, we recognize that the terms "trial penalty" and "plea reward" are not objective, and that others might disagree with our operationalization of them. We also recognize that reasonable observers might disagree about whether such differences are commensurate with the goals of sentencing guidelines. What we can say empirically is that trials, especially jury trials, typically result in more severe punishment than called for by guideline minimums, while guilty pleas typically result in sentences that are at or frequently below those minimums.

Discussion

This chapter's analyses have some consequential limitations. First, although the PCS offense gravity score incorporates elements of victim harm, loss, and impact, we have no *direct* information beyond this about victims in our data, which is a potentially important omission. It is quite likely that the identities, social statuses, and characteristics of victims condition the assessment of focal concerns and the type of interpretive work that occurs in trial and guilty pleas (see Black 1976; Loseke 1993). Assessing the role of victim characteristics on trial penalties must await future research.

Also, our analyses hinge on the premise that guilty pleas, bench trials, and jury trials are comparable and can be modeled together. The large majority of sentencing studies in the past two decades have taken a similar approach and included these different modes of conviction in the same models. However, the authors of at least one important study have argued against this practice: Steven Klepper, Daniel Nagin, and Luke-John Tierney (1983) argued that guilty pleas and trials are qualitatively different and are generated by inherently different processes, and that this makes it inappropriate to lump modes of conviction together in the same models and compare the way they are sentenced. On the other hand, we argue that any criminal case can potentially end up as a guilty plea or a trial at any point in the preconviction process—people plead guilty the night before a trial is set to begin, and people withdraw their guilty pleas at colloquy hearings and insist on trials. In principle, at least, one should be able to compare the ensuing sentences following the different modes of conviction. Furthermore, US legal ideology holds that every defendant has the right to a trial, and that guilty pleas should not be coercive. Some commentators argue that the practice of punishing those who lose at trial more severely than those who plead guilty constitutes just such coercion (Rosett and Cressey 1976; Uhlman and Walker 1979). To us, the importance of presenting evidence, imperfect as it is, on plea/trial sentencing differences and their variation outweighs the methodological caution of Klepper and colleagues.[4] We realize, however, that others might take the opposite position.

Most seriously, these analyses were limited to data on convicted offenders. We cannot control for potential selection bias stemming from conviction or acquittal. Since we cannot control for the likelihood of conviction, we cannot rule out the possibility that our findings might reflect differences in conviction rates by offense severity and type, prior record, or court contexts. Furthermore, we are controlling for offense gravity score and the presumptive guideline minimum, but both of these factors may be the subject of guilty plea negotiations: attorneys may charge bargain with an eye to reducing the OGS or the guideline sentence exposure.

Smith (1986), LaFree (1985), and Rhodes (1979) showed that these limitations are potentially important—all three studies showed that trial penalties were not substantial once balanced against the chances of acquittal at trial. On the other hand, Zatz and Hagan (1985) found that trial penalties appeared only after they controlled for the likelihood of conviction. Similarly, we lack a measure of evidence strength, which, according to some of the prior literature, is important in the decision to go to trial, and influences the attractiveness of prosecutors' plea-bargain offers for defendants (Mather 1973; Farr 1984; Albonetti 1986; Flemming et al. 1992).

What we can say is that *once convicted,* those who plead guilty and those who *lose* at trial tend to face very different sentencing outcomes, and that the size of plea/trial conviction sentencing differences varies by offense characteristics, criminal history, and court and county-level factors. In this way, our findings closely parallel those of LaFree (1985), who found that while those who pled guilty lost out on the chance of an acquittal, those who went to trial and lost received more severe sentences. Nevertheless, future research of guilty plea/trial sentencing differences should strive to incorporate preconviction data and determine whether such differences are meaningful even when accounting for the chances of avoiding conviction at trial.

That said, our findings are consistent with the notion that differential attributions of blameworthiness and dangerousness—along with differences in perceived group threats and in practical political constraints and incentives between court community contexts—are key reasons behind the patterns in jury trial penalties we have found. Our findings about trial penalties cannot be attributed to a simple organizational efficiency argument, because while caseloads sometimes affected overall sentence severity, they did not condition important variation in trial penalties for either serious violent offenses or less serious offenses.

Increased offense severity seems to provide occasions for constructing offenders in the trial courtroom as particularly more morally repugnant, blameworthy, or dangerous, and these "types of person constructions" (Loseke 1993) may then affect judges' sentences. That is, trials, particularly the trials in our data in which the defendants are always the losers, can be seen as status degradation ceremonies (Garfinkel 1956). Judges, who witnessed in detail all the evidence, characteristics of the crimes, and depictions of the defendants that were presented to the jury, may assess defendants as more blameworthy or more of a danger to the community, and administer much harsher sentences than they would have if the case had involved a guilty plea. Recall the quote from the judge, presented earlier, who told of how his direct experience with the human consequences of violent crimes during trials affected the subsequent sentences he gave. As the defense attorney quoted previously said, a guilty plea lets one hide the "ugly facts" of a case, while a lost jury trial (or even a lost bench trial) puts the ugly facts right out in the open, where they can influence judges' constructions of the blameworthiness or dangerousness of defendants (see Ulmer 1997). Furthermore, as another quote presented previously illustrates, judges (and prosecutors) often consider a guilty plea as an indicator of remorse, and a trial as an indicator of a lack of remorse (Ulmer 1997; Kramer and Ulmer 2002). Perhaps the more severe the offense, the more salient such remorse or lack thereof could be to judges. This position also reflects the presumption that defendants are guilty, which is a common assumption behind the application of trial penalties.

In addition, trial penalties differed between offense types. Crimes like aggravated assault, simple assault, weapon offenses, and criminal trespass all are occasions of greater trial penalties of one form or another. On the other hand, drug misdemeanors and cases involving rape and involuntary deviate sexual intercourse yield lesser trial penalties. One additional possible explanation for our findings regarding rape and involuntary deviate sexual intercourse may lie in differences in blame attribution. Rape trials may be more likely to involve disputes over consent, and thus over believability, than other trials (for example, if both sides acknowledge that sex occurred, but are trying to establish whether consent was present). Also, it is well known that the character of the victim may be subjected to more intense scrutiny in rape trials than in other kinds of trials. The defense has the opportunity to construct the victim in a negative light (i.e., she is promiscuous, spurned, intoxicated, manipulative, irresponsible, or negligent) as well as to evoke sympathetic feelings toward the offender so as to downplay his responsibility (i.e., he was intoxicated, there was a misunderstanding, he is being humiliated by "false charges"). On the other hand, defense counsel may hesitate to portray the victim too negatively because of the risk that the court may hold verbal attacks on the victim against the defendant at sentencing. Future qualitative research is necessary to explicitly capture the construction of defendants and victims during trials, and to connect these constructions to sentencing consequences.

Our finding that trial penalties increased slightly but significantly with violent crime rates suggests that trial sentencing may be a vehicle by which prosecutors and judges communicate their seriousness about violent crime to the larger community. As we hypothesized, if trials are relatively visible, and a county has a more substantial violent crime problem, this may create political pressure on prosecutors to push for more substantial sentences in serious violent trial cases, and on judges to mete out those sentences.

Our findings about court size and trial penalties are complex. Research typically finds large urban courts to be more lenient, as our findings mostly do here. However, while such courts might be more lenient overall, our data also show that large courts sentence jury trial defendants (both in serious violent cases and in less serious cases) to substantially longer sentences than do other counties. We interpret the effects for sentence length as support for Eisenstein, Flemming, and Nardulli's description (1988) of how court community politics differ according to court size. Large courts receive more media scrutiny by larger media markets, and trials might receive significant public attention. Due to this public attention, judges and prosecutors might feel more pressure to sentence defendants more severely after such trials. Severe sentencing may be a tool to politically demonstrate their seriousness and "toughness" regarding crime, at least in jurisdictions where judges and prosecutors are elected, as in Pennsylvania.

Our data also point to the possibility that such a process may not be completely racially neutral. The jury trial penalty for the serious violent offenses we examined here was moderately larger in counties with relatively greater numbers of black residents. For less serious offenses, individual blacks convicted by trial were considerably more likely to go to state prison than their white counterparts. This is an especially troubling implication for the guidelines' goal of reducing disparity. Apparently, trial penalties are a window of black versus white racial disparity, at least among less serious offenses. Furthermore, counties with more blacks have stronger trial penalties. Whatever the explanation for this puzzling finding, it is an outcome not envisioned or intended by the guidelines.

Given the strong positive link between anti-black stereotypes and concern about black violence demonstrated by Steven Barkan and Steven Cohn (2005), jury trial penalties for serious violent crimes may present a new twist for racial threat theories of criminal justice. Barkan and Cohn's research implies that when prejudiced whites hear about violent crime, they conjure up offender images with black faces. Since serious violent crime trials are relatively visible to the public through heightened media coverage, the stiffer punishment of trial defendants in such serious cases might be a way that judges and prosecutors signal their "toughness" in dealing with violence, and this process could be exacerbated by racial threat and white fear. However, we find it puzzling that increases in percent black increase trial penalties for *all* defendants, not just blacks (as a racial threat argument would predict), and that the effect of percent black washes out the individual-level interaction effect of race and jury trial for the serious violent offenses analysis. The causal processes by which the racial context of a county might condition trial penalties for serious violence among both blacks and whites are certainly intriguing and deserve further research.

We expected prior record to condition greater trial penalties as prosecutors took the opportunity to "dirty up" defendants, and convincingly dramatize the repeated criminality of defendants to judges. Instead, trials, and sentencing hearings following trials, may provide defense attorneys whose clients have extensive prior records with an opportunity to argue that defendants' prior convictions were actually less serious than they appeared (an argument supported by some ethnographic research—see Kramer and Ulmer 2002; Ulmer 1997). Such trial and post-trial circumstances might provide defense attorneys with the opportunity to tell a story of the defendant's biography and circumstances. This information may counterbalance his or her prior record score and deflect more negative attributions from judges. Alternately, it could be that prosecutors offer smaller plea discounts to those with extensive prior records (Ulmer 1997; see also Smith 1986). That is, prosecutors might be less willing to offer attractive sentence-bargaining terms to those who have more serious criminal histories, and who might therefore be seen as more blameworthy or dangerous.

Rather than this finding being explained by a pattern in which defendants with extensive prior records at jury trial receive more lenient sentences, it might be explained by their counterparts who plead guilty and receive less leniency. In other words, it might not benefit defendants with extensive prior records to go to trial so much as it *fails to benefit them as much* to plead guilty.

In addition, the finding of lesser trial penalties for those with more extensive prior records could be explained by a pattern in which such defendants are more likely to be convicted. That is, such defendants might exhibit smaller sentence differences between guilty pleas and trial convictions if they have greater likelihoods of conviction, and if this likelihood offsets potential plea discounts they might receive. We cannot rule this possibility out, but qualitative interview data show that greater exposure to more severe and certain punishment, as the result of an extensive criminal history, can actually dampen defendants' enthusiasm for pleading guilty (Ulmer 1997, p. 96). Significant criminal records also tend to reduce the willingness of prosecutors to offer attractive plea concessions (Ulmer 1997, pp. 94–96). Thus a criminal history raises the punishment stakes higher, and such defendants might think they are better off "taking their chances at trial." If so, it may be that those with higher prior record scores might go to trial more often, not less, given the possibility for acquittal that trial entails.[5]

Conclusion

Our findings regarding trial penalties and their variation have important implications for sentencing guidelines and legal ethics. The US legal system guarantees every criminal defendant the right to a jury trial, yet we find that defendants are substantially penalized if they exercise this right and then lose. Furthermore, this jury trial penalty is not evenly assessed, but depends on the seriousness and type of offense, the offender's prior record, several court contextual characteristics, and, more troubling for the spirit of the guidelines, sometimes race. It is also worth pointing out that Pennsylvania is a "truth in sentencing" state, meaning that offenders cannot be released prior to serving at least their minimum sentence lengths. It is also noteworthy that incarceration trial penalties so strongly center around the decision to send offenders to state prison. In each multinomial analysis, jury trial convictees' odds of going to state prison dwarfed those of other defendants. Therefore, these sentence length trial penalties and their variations represent very real and meaningful differences in the amount of punishment and loss of liberty experienced by offenders.

Notes

We acknowledge Mindy Bradley's contribution as coauthor of an earlier version of this chapter.

1. We would have liked to test the association of percent Hispanic with trial penalties among serious violent offenses, but with this relatively small serious violent offense sample (compared to other sentencing studies that include a broader range of offenses), we lost too many counties from the analysis that had negligible numbers of Hispanics and very few serious violent offenses. In general, Hispanics are clustered in about fifteen of the sixty-seven counties in Pennsylvania.

2. Due to some collinearity between offense severity and guideline minimum, we also ran alternative sentence length models assessing the interaction between offense severity and jury trial—one omitting guideline minimum and including offense severity and the interaction between offense severity and jury trial, and one including guideline minimum and omitting offense severity and prior record and the interaction between guideline minimum and jury trial. In each case, the interaction term was strong and significant. This increases our confidence in the robustness and integrity of the offense severity–jury trial interaction.

3. We also estimated ordinal logistic regressions, treating the two actual sentence versus guideline minimum variables as ordered categories, and obtained substantively the same results. Bench and jury trial cases were significantly more likely to yield sentences that were above guideline recommendations.

4. In an admittedly imperfect attempt to address Klepper and colleagues' point about the comparability of guilty pleas and trials, and the channeling of cases into one category or the other, we estimated a series of incarceration and sentencing length models in which we performed the Heckman two-step correction for the likelihood of cases being in different mode-of-conviction categories (bench trial, guilty plea, jury trial). We included correction factors for each mode of conviction in the models both separately and together. As covariates of mode-of-conviction categories, we used offense type, offense severity, prior record, race/ethnicity, age, and gender. Thus, within the limits of our data, we attempted to control for the likelihood of membership in one mode-of-conviction category or another. In no case did the results differ meaningfully from those presented here.

5. It is noteworthy that prior record score and jury trial are modestly positively correlated (.10, p < .001). Also, prior record has a positive association (prior record score odds = 1.25, p < .0001) with membership in the jury trial conviction category in a logistic regression model predicting jury trial versus other convictions (and controlling for OGS, offense type, guideline minimum, age, race, ethnicity, and gender). Similar positive associations exist between prior record and bench trial. This does not tell us whether those with greater prior record scores are more or less likely to be convicted, but it does tell us that there is a moderate tendency for those convicted by trial to have more substantial criminal histories.

8

Guidelines and
Mandatory Minimums

IN DISCUSSING THE history of the development of Pennsylvania's sentencing guidelines, we reviewed the passage of mandatory minimums for serious violent offenses under Governor Thornburgh and later, in the 1980s, mandatory minimums for drug convictions. These mandatory minimums were supported by the district attorneys. Further, we have often noted throughout this book the importance of prosecutors in sentencing under guidelines, and the importance of not overlooking the implications of their discretion for disparity of various kinds. Prosecutors have long been viewed as important decisionmakers in criminal justice, but research has tended to focus on judicial discretion. Scores of studies examine sentencing decisions and outcomes, but only a handful examine prosecutorial decisions, such as charging, charge reduction, sentence recommendations, or in some contexts, the imposition of mandatory minimum sentences. In part, this is because the use of prosecutorial discretion is a far less visible act than judicial sentencing. Yet the relative invisibility of prosecutorial discretion, coupled with the considerable formal and informal power of the prosecutor's office, are exactly the reasons it is important to study such discretion. In particular, Rodney Engen and colleagues (2003, p. 126) argue that decisions by prosecutors can considerably affect sentencing, but comparatively little is known about the effects of such prosecutorial discretion.

In Chapters 2 and 3, we also described how mandatory minimums were enacted in the 1980s and 1990s in Pennsylvania as a parallel sentencing structure alongside (and to some extent competing with) sentencing guidelines. Mandatory minimum sentencing policies and the consequent displacement of discretion from judges to prosecutors reflect a larger political trend toward distrust and disempowerment of judges, and simultaneously, growth in the trust in and empowerment of prosecutors (Stith and Cabranes 1998). This trend can be seen especially in the federal criminal justice system and in recent developments regarding federal mandatory minimum sentences and the US Sentencing Guidelines (Stith and Cabranes 1998; Hartley, Maddan, and Spohn 2007).

For example, recent US Department of Justice policy and congressional acts (such as the Feeney Amendment to the 2003 Child Protection Act) have bolstered prosecutorial control over guideline sentence reductions, and have attempted to restrict the ability of judges to depart below the guidelines when prosecutors oppose such departures.

Mandatory minimum sentences are found in almost every state and in the federal system, and some argue that they represent a fundamental change in the formal apparatus of punishment, shifting discretion from judges to prosecutors through a process of "hydraulic displacement of discretion" (see Miethe 1987; Tonry 1992; Savelsberg 1992; Engen and Steen 2000).

The application of mandatory minimums vests prosecutors with sentencing discretion. In Pennsylvania, the decision to pursue most mandatory minimum sentences belongs solely to the prosecutor.[1] First, the prosecutor decides whether to charge an offense that is eligible for a mandatory minimum. Then the prosecutor decides whether to move for the *application* of the mandatory minimum. If the prosecutor so moves, and the offender is convicted, then the court *must* sentence accordingly (42 Pa. C.S. § 9714[d]). If the prosecutor does *not* pursue the mandatory minimum, the offender is sentenced pursuant to the Pennsylvania sentencing guidelines, which are almost always less severe than the mandatory minimums. As we discussed in Chapter 2, the Pennsylvania sentencing guidelines are not coupled to the mandatory minimums. That is, the PCS did not set the guideline minimums according to any applicable mandatory minimums. Rather, in Pennsylvania, guidelines and mandatory minimums are two alternative sentencing structures. Given a pool of offenders who are convicted of crimes for which the prosecutor can choose to apply the mandatory minimum, the outcome of whether or not they receive a mandatory minimum is solely a product of prosecutorial discretion.

Because of the statutory authority vested in Pennsylvania's prosecutors to move for the application of mandatory minimums, to isolate a sample of offenders convicted of mandatory-eligible offenses and then to investigate their likelihoods of actually receiving mandatory minimums (which is up to the prosecutor) is to study prosecutorial sentencing. We present in this chapter a multilevel analysis of the prosecutorial decision to impose a mandatory minimum among a sample of mandatory-eligible offenders.

In addition, many observers argue that mandatory minimums target offenses disproportionately committed by minorities (see Kautt and Spohn 2002; Farrell 2003; Beckett and Sasson 2000; Reiman 1995). Since extralegal disparity is of general concern for sentencing reforms in general, it becomes important to ask whether mandatory minimums are differentially imposed based on social statuses like race, ethnicity, gender, or age, singly or in combination. Furthermore, we investigate the effects of guideline-relevant and case-processing factors as well as court contextual characteristics.

The logic of our analysis resembles Charles Crawford's studies (Crawford, Chiricos, and Kleck 1998; Crawford 2000) of the application of habitual offender sentencing provisions in Florida, except that we are isolating prosecutorial discretion over a sentencing outcome, whereas prosecutors apparently do not have total discretion over the application of Florida's habitual offender sentencing provision.[2] We isolate a sample of offenders eligible for drug-trafficking or three-strikes mandatory minimums, and then investigate whether the factors predict actual imposition of the applicable mandatory minimums.

Research on Prosecutorial Discretion and Sentencing

Research on prosecutorial discretion has focused on its history (Ferdinand 1992; Fisher 2003; Vogel 1999), the role of victims in prosecutorial charging decisions, charging decisions in general (e.g., Albonetti 1986, 1987; Schmidt and Steury 1989; Kingsnorth and MacIntosh 2004; Spears and Spohn 1997; Spohn and Holleran 2001; Spohn, Beicher, and Davis-Frenzel 2001), stereotypical conceptions of case appropriateness for prosecution (Adams and Cutshall 1987; Spears and Spohn 1997; Stanko 1981–1982), and the social organization of prosecutors' offices (Jacoby 1979; Flemming, Nardulli, and Eisenstein 1992). Attempts to isolate prosecutorial discretion over sentencing outcomes per se are less common than studies that focus on judicial discretion (see Zatz 2000; Spohn 2000; Free 2002). Notable studies of prosecutorial discretion, almost all of which focus on charging decisions, include those by Celesta Albonetti (1986, 1987), Celesta Albonetti and John Hepburn (1996), Peter Nardulli, James Eisenstein, and Roy Flemming (1988), Terence Miethe (1987), JoAnn Miller and John Sloan (1994), N. O. Alozie and C. W. Johnston (2000), Rodney Engen and Sara Steen (2000), Rodney Kingsnorth, Randall MacIntosh, and Sandra Sutherland (2002), and Jill Farrell (2003), and we note relevant findings from these studies in the discussion below. Marvin Free (2002) reviewed twenty-four studies of prosecutorial charging decisions and nineteen studies of prosecutors' decisions to seek the death penalty. This review found convincing evidence that race affected whether prosecutors sought the death penalty, but mixed evidence on whether extralegal factors affected charging decisions. Fifteen of the twenty-four charging studies found no significant effects of race (or sometimes ethnicity) on charging decisions, but noted that other social status factors like gender and age sometimes affect these decisions. In discussing gaps in the literature on prosecutorial discretion under sentencing reforms, Free states that little is known about whether race and other extralegal characteristics affect prosecutors' decisions regarding the application of three-strikes and other mandatory minimums (2002, p. 226). Furthermore, Free notes that no studies examine "outside" or contextual influences on prosecutorial decisionmaking (exceptions published after Free's review are studies by John Wooldredge and Amy Thistlethwaite [2004] and Timothy

Griffin and John Wooldredge [2006], who include multilevel analyses of charging decisions, but do not focus on mandatory minimums).

Studies of the predictors of prosecutorial decisions to apply mandatory minimums are thus very scarce. The large majority of pieces published on mandatory minimums are found in law journals and consist of commentaries about legal issues surrounding them. However, research does show that prosecutors do not apply mandatory minimum sentences in all eligible cases. For example, the US Sentencing Commission (1991) estimated that 20 percent of all federal defendants in 1990 were potentially subject to mandatory minimums, but only 54 percent of this pool of eligible offenders actually received a mandatory minimum sentence (see also Kautt and Delone 2006). Also, four studies have found that mandatory minimums or sentencing enhancements for firearm violations were applied in only a fraction of eligible cases (Bynum 1982; Loftin, Heumann, and McDowall 1983; Hofer 2000; Farrell 2003).

Most directly relevant to our focus are the findings of David Bjerk (2005) and Jill Farrell (2003). Bjerk found that prosecutors used their charge reduction discretion to circumvent three-strikes mandatory minimums for some defendants. He found that this kind of circumvention was moderately less likely to occur for men, Hispanics, and to a lesser extent, blacks. Farrell found that blacks, males, and those convicted by trial were more likely to receive firearm mandatory minimums. Also relevant to our analysis, as mentioned, are the findings of Crawford and colleagues (Crawford, Chiricos, and Kleck 1998; Crawford 2000), who isolated a sample of offenders eligible for designation as habitual offenders and thus for enhanced sentences, and then analyzed whether offenders actually were so designated (a decision that involved both prosecutorial and judicial discretion, see endnote 1). These studies found that race significantly and substantially affected the decision to sentence similarly eligible offenders as habitual offenders. In addition, Paula Kautt and Miriam Delone (2006) separately modeled outcomes for federal drug cases sentenced under the US Sentencing Guidelines versus those sentenced under federal mandatory minimums. They found that gender had a greater impact on sentence severity (with females receiving less severe sentences) among cases sentenced under federal mandatory minimums than among those sentenced under the guidelines, though the same was not true for other extralegal factors (e.g., race, ethnicity). Together, these studies point to the potential for extralegal disparity in the application of mandatory minimums, but also present mixed findings.

Thus the application of mandatory minimums is clearly an important potential site of prosecutorial discretion, with implications for extralegal sentencing disparity. While we know that prosecutors choose to apply mandatory minimum sentences in only a fraction of eligible cases, we do not know a great deal about what influences these decisions, because there are very few studies where the predictors of these decisions have been explicitly modeled. We also know little about contextual effects of court characteristics on the application of mandatory minimums.

A Normative/Legalistic Perspective

The engraving on the facade of the US Supreme Court sets forth an important foundation to the US legal system in the phrase of "equal justice under law." In some respects, mandatory minimums reflect this goal by emphasizing legal factors in the setting of criminal penalties and severely restricting judicial discretion. There is also a strong crime control rationale for mandatory minimums, since they are supported as means to increase penalties and are often accompanied by criticisms of judicial leniency. Offenses subject to mandatory minimum penalties, such as three-strikes offenses or possession with intent to deliver illegal drugs, are particularly singled out by legislatures for more severe punishment, and judges do not have the discretion to decrease those punishments.

The *normative/legalistic perspective* reflects the merger of the "equal justice" view with a crime control goal. The merging of these two perspectives has been one of the interesting features of the move to determinate sentencing. The focus on "equal justice under law" was the theme of the "just deserts" proposals of the early 1970s (von Hirsch 1976; Dershowitz 1976; Singer 1978). Then, political conservatives combined equity issues with controlling crime and protecting the community. The outcome of this merger was an overt policy emphasis on tough but equal sentencing, as epitomized by the federal sentencing guidelines and mandatory minimums throughout the United States.

As such, this perspective views criminal sanctions as straightforward normative strategies to punish, exact moral retribution, and control crime. The perspective represents the criminal law and its enforcers' attempts to fulfill its instrumental goals: to deter crime and to incapacitate offenders (Bennett, DiIulio, and Walters 1996; see also Dixon 1995; Engen and Steen 2000; Britt 2000). The normative/legalistic perspective argues that legal or crime-relevant factors should account for most, if not all, of the variation in sentencing severity. The extent to which such factors explain sentencing decisions is a measure of the applicability of the normative/legalistic perspective.

Mandatory minimums effectively represent a legislative enactment of the normative/legalistic perspective, in that the law establishes the legal criteria to be used in determining the applicability of the mandatory minimum. For example, mandatory minimums are sometimes based on the offense of conviction, or the offense of conviction combined with other criteria such as prior convictions (three-strikes mandatory minimums) or drug amounts (for drug-trafficking mandatory minimums).

This perspective would also predict that prosecutors, who are law enforcement's voice in the court community, would rely on mandatory minimums as a mechanism of crime control, and that court caseload composition (i.e., the percent of violent, drug, or property offenses) would be related to the imposition of mandatory minimums. Given that crime control is a prominent goal of mandatory minimums, prosecutors would therefore apply them in an effort to achieve general deterrence and also to incapacitate eligible offenders. This would be especially true regarding violent crime, which has a high degree of political and normative salience. Therefore, we would expect that the application of mandatory minimums would be positively related to the proportion of the court caseload made up of violent crime.

Uncertainty, Attribution, and Focal Concerns of Sentencing

There is general agreement in the sentencing literature that offense character-istics and criminal history are nearly always the strongest predictors of pun-ishment outcomes (Spohn 2000; Zatz 2000). The question is whether these are the only meaningful influences, as law and policy intend. As we have ex-plained throughout the book, the focal concerns perspective argues that three interpretively defined focal concerns of punishment—blameworthiness, pro-tection of the community, and practical constraints—shape and frame punish-ment decisions. In contrast to a strictly normative/legalistic perspective, the decision process that focal concerns describes is one in which legal, organiza-tional (such as conviction by guilty plea versus trial), and extralegal consider-ations affect the interpretation and prioritization of focal concerns through local substantive rationality (Savelsberg 1992; Kramer and Ulmer 2002). Local substantive rationality and definitions of focal concerns, in turn, are shaped by distinctive case-processing and sentencing norms, political con-straints, and social characteristics of court communities (Eisenstein, Flem-ming, and Nardulli 1988; Ulmer 1997; Ulmer and Johnson 2004). This per-spective envisions court actors starting with legal factors such as the offense and prior record as benchmarks, but then making further situational attribu-tions about defendants' character and risk based on case characteristics and so-cial statuses (among other factors). Moreover, recent statements of the focal concerns perspective argue that it is enhanced by joining it with a court com-munity perspective (Eisenstein, Flemming, and Nardulli 1988; Ulmer 1997). Interpretations of focal concerns are locally variable because they are embed-ded in local court community contexts (Ulmer and Johnson 2004; Ulmer and Bradley 2006; Johnson 2006).

Albonetti (1986, 1987), in presenting her uncertainty avoidance and causal attribution theory, argued that prosecutors (and judges—see Albonetti 1991) face an uncertain decisionmaking environment. Prosecutors want to be effective in controlling crime in the community, to be efficient in processing offenders, and to influence subsequent decisionmakers (judges, juries, defense attorneys—see Frohmann 1991). In particular, Lisa Frohmann's research on prosecutorial charging decisions in sexual assault cases (1991) emphasizes the "downstream orientation" of prosecutors, and how they make charging decisions with an eye toward the projected decisions of judges and juries. This points to the importance of conviction certainty as a key concern of prosecutors.

Prosecutors must engage in uncertainty management and satisficing behavior that attempts to balance out these competing pressures. In addition, Albonetti and Hepburn (1996) combine this earlier uncertainty avoidance perspective with causal attribution, etiology of bias, and labeling theories to argue that prosecutors, like judges, make attributions from stereotypes based on ascribed characteristics of defendants in order to reduce decisionmaking uncertainty.

Only one set of studies (Spohn, Beicher, and Davis-Frenzel 2001; Spohn and Holleran 2001; see also Spears and Spohn 1997) has applied the focal concerns perspective to prosecutorial activity, and in doing so has extended Frohmann's emphasis on the downstream orientation of prosecutors by articulating a link between the goal of certainty of conviction and the focal concerns of punishment. Cassia Spohn, Dawn Beicher, and Erika Davis-Frenzel (2001) found that prosecutors' charging decisions in sexual assault cases were guided by the likelihood of conviction (a practical consideration) and whether the victim suffered significant harm (blameworthiness and community protection focal concerns).[3] Recent work also encourages such extensions of focal concerns beyond judicial sentencing (Kramer and Ulmer 2002; Ulmer and Johnson 2004), such as Beth Huebner and Timothy Bynum's application (2006) of the perspective to parole decisions, or Stephen Demuth and Darrell Steffensmeier's analysis (2004) of focal concerns and pretrial detention. Like these earlier works, and in keeping with the theoretical framework of Chapter 1, we use the focal concerns perspective as a heuristic framework to guide our examination of prosecutorial decisions to apply mandatory minimums, because it is congruent with and builds on the themes of uncertainty reduction and causal attribution in Albonetti's work, and because it can integrate themes of organizational efficiency and racial threat as well, rather than treating these theories as mutually exclusive competitors (see Curry, Lee, and Rodriguez 2004 for a discussion of the compatibility of these theories and their potential for integration).

Practical Constraint and Consequences: Efficiency and Certainty

As we discussed in the previous two chapters, one important practical constraint on case processing and sentencing is the need for *organizational efficiency*. Convictions are also seen as a measure of prosecutors' effectiveness, and guilty pleas are a method of obtaining more certain convictions than might be the result if cases went to trial (Albonetti 1986, 1987; Smith 1986; Spohn, Beicher, and Davis-Frenzel 2001). Therefore, a chief way in which prosecutors might both achieve efficiency and demonstrate effectiveness (e.g., high conviction rates) is by inducing guilty pleas. Thus, pleading guilty is likely a way for defendants to avoid mandatory minimums. Farrell's finding (2003) that those convicted by trial were more likely to receive mandatory minimums for firearm crimes in Maryland supports this idea.

Similarly, in Chapter 4, we described a process of "de-mandatorizing" eligible cases as a part of plea agreements (Kramer and Ulmer 2002). This term came from interviews with judges and others, and is apparently widely used by judges, prosecutors, and others in Pennsylvania. To de-mandatorize a case means that prosecutors choose not to apply the mandatory to an eligible charge (rather than reducing the charge to one not eligible for a mandatory minimum). If they choose not to apply the minimum, this allows the defendant to be sentenced by the judge under the guidelines (which are mostly less severe), typically with an implicit or explicit sentence agreement as a part of a plea bargain (see also Ulmer 1997) while maintaining the higher level of offense severity for its future potential impact on the defendant's prior record score should she or he be convicted of another offense later.

This process of de-mandatorizing also points to the *certainty of conviction,* another strong practical concern for prosecutors (Albonetti 1986; Frohmann 1991; Spohn, Beicher, and Davis-Frenzel 2001; Spohn and Holleran 2001). For a variety of reasons, prosecutors often value obtaining a relatively certain conviction more than sentencing eligible offenders to mandatory penalties (Kramer and Ulmer 2002). In such situations, prosecutors might trade severity for certainty of punishment, a scenario in line with Albonetti's arguments (1986, 1987). The rationality of de-mandatorizing is also consistent with Douglas Smith's description of the rational choice dynamics of plea bargaining (1986). For example, in the interview data presented in Chapter 4, many cases exhibited evidentiary problems (a practical consideration connected to the probability of conviction) that encouraged prosecutors to forgo applying the mandatory in exchange for a plea agreement. In addition, prosecutors also de-mandatorized cases because the offender was not perceived as a danger to the community (reflecting community protection). For all these reasons, we expect negotiated pleas to be associated with a decreased likelihood of mandatory penalty imposition.[4]

Racial Threat and Status-Based Attributions About Focal Concerns

As discussed in previous chapters, the focal concerns perspective is also compatible with the notion of *racial threat* (Blumer 1955; Bobo and Hutchings 1996; Steffensmeier and Demuth 2000, 2001). We expect offense characteristics and criminal history, along with mode of conviction, to be the strongest predictors of mandatory minimum application, but we do expect race/ethnicity and gender to exert significant influence, apart from these other predictors.

A sizable literature also shows that females are often seen as less blameworthy, less dangerous, and more amenable to rehabilitation, and that they often present practical problems for the criminal justice system (e.g., if they have children). The preponderance of research shows that women are typically sentenced more leniently than men (see Zatz 2000; Curry, Lee, and Rodriguez, Lee, and Rodriguez 2004; Griffin and Wooldredge 2006). If prosecutors as well as judges view women in this way, then we would expect to see eligible women receive mandatory minimums less often than men. One piece of evidence for this hypothesis is Miethe's investigation (1987) of the degree to which extralegal factors affected initial charging, charge reductions and dismissals, and sentence bargaining in Minnesota. He found that males were charged with more severe offenses and received less favorable sentence bargains from prosecutors. Furthermore, Alozie and Johnston (2000) found that female drug arrestees were more likely to be diverted by prosecutors into alternative programs, and that race and ethnicity interacted with gender in such decisions.

Additionally, Darrell Steffensmeier, Jeffery Ulmer, and John Kramer (1998) argued that the influence of offender status characteristics are likely to be joint and situationally contingent (see also Spohn and DeLone 2000; Kautt and Spohn 2002; Demuth and Steffensmeier 2004). That is, the effect of race or ethnicity likely depends on gender or age, for example. Consistent with this reasoning, sentencing research has often found that young black and Hispanic males are sentenced more severely than other race, age, and gender groupings (Bridges and Steen 1998; Spohn and Holleran 2000; Steffensmeier and Demuth, 2000; Kramer and Ulmer 2002; see also Zatz 2000). In partial support of this idea, Farrell (2003) found that firearm mandatory minimums in Maryland were more likely to be applied to blacks, males, and younger offenders.

As an extension of our discussion of racial and ethnic threat theory in Chapter 6, we suggest that the minority composition of the surrounding community might influence the odds of mandatory minimums being applied to individual minority defendants. We expect that prosecutors might differentially apply mandatory minimums in counties with larger minority populations in order to assuage white fear of minority crime, and to be seen as protecting the community from offenders whom the majority public perceives to be dangerous. The key contextual-level prediction of racial threat theory is that as minority populations become larger and seem more threatening, individual minorities will be subjected to greater punishment, at least until the proportion of minorities becomes large enough to exert greater relative political power (Jacobs, Carmichael, and Kent 2005).

Finally, we expect mandatory imposition to vary with court community size. The court community perspective predicts that sentencing will be relatively less severe in large urban court communities in particular. This is said to be caused by several factors directly related to large court community size: (1) a relatively high degree of autonomy of the court community from external controls of other community institutions; (2) the relatively low public visibility of *routine* case-processing matters and sentences;[5] (3) the generally greater amount and diversity of social deviance in large urban areas, which may produce more tolerance and less punitiveness, and (4) greater efficiency concerns due to large caseloads, which press prosecutors and other court actors to provide inducements, generally in the form of reduced penalties, for guilty pleas (Eisenstein, Flemming, and Nardulli 1988, pp. 278–285). We expect this reasoning to apply to prosecutors and their decisions about mandatory minimums in large courts as well.

Data and Methods

To examine the application of mandatory minimums, we identified and extracted all cases from 1998–2000 PCS data that were eligible to receive a mandatory minimum sentence (too few cases sentenced in 1997 under the 1997 guidelines were eligible for mandatory minimums) based on their conviction charges and offense characteristics (e.g., drug amounts), or prior records, in which the application of the mandatory minimum was dependent upon a motion from the prosecutor. Because the mandatory minimum provisions are based upon the current offense, the offender's prior record, and, in cases of drug offenses, amount of drug possessed, the PCS data include all variables needed to isolate those convictions in which a prosecutor could have made a motion to apply a mandatory sentence. These offenses include certain drug-trafficking offenses, such as possession of a variety of illegal drugs over certain threshold amounts, or in specific circumstances (e.g., near a school), as well as convictions of certain serious or violent felonies (the same serious violent offenses examined in Chapter 4) for the second or third time. In other words, with this subsample, we can distinguish the cases where the prosecutor could have applied the mandatory minimum and did not, from those in which the prosecutor did. This decision thus represents a situation of prosecutorial discretion over sentence outcomes. Our dependent variable is a dichotomous outcome of whether or not a mandatory-eligible offense actually received the applicable mandatory. More information on how we coded the data and performed the analyses for this chapter can be found in the Research Methods Appendix. As in the previous three chapters, we use hierarchical modeling procedures to account for the nesting of cases within counties.

From the prosecutor's viewpoint, the guidelines and the mandatory minimums are two alternative sentencing structures under which the defendant could be sentenced. In this chapter's analysis, we therefore want to control for the difference between the guideline minimum and the mandatory minimum rather than simply controlling for the guideline-recommended sentence itself. We suspect that the size of the difference between the mandatory minimum and the guideline minimum may figure into the prosecutor's calculus about the trade-off between applying the mandatory and allowing the offender to be sentenced under the guidelines. For example, a prosecutor might be more willing to impose the mandatory minimum when it is considerably greater than the guideline minimum—he or she might believe that the guideline recommendation is not severe enough.

Findings

Table 8.1 shows descriptive statistics for all of the variables used in this chapter's analyses. As shown, many eligible offenders avoid the imposition of mandatory minimums. Put another way, prosecutors choose to apply the mandatory minimum to eligible offenses in relatively few cases—18.4 percent in the overall sample and 16.2 percent in the drug subsample. Prosecutors apply the mandatory minimums relatively more often for second- and third-

Table 8.1   Full, Drug, and Three-Strikes Samples

Independent Variables	Full Sample		Drug Eligible		Three-Strikes Eligible	
Individual level	*n = 4,534*		*n = 3,739*		*n = 795*	
Mandatory						
Applied (1)	836	18.4%	607	16.2%	229	28.8%
Not applied (0)	3,698	81.6%	3132	83.8%	566	71.2%
Gender						
Male (1)	3,991	88.0%	3229	86.4%	762	95.8%
Female (0)	497	11.0%	471	12.6%	26	3.3%
Missing	46	1.0%	39	1.0%	7	0.9%
Race						
White (0)	1,249	27.5%	1054	28.2%	195	24.5%
Black (1)	2,297	50.7%	1811	48.4%	486	61.1%
Hispanic (1)	861	19.0%	769	20.6%	92	11.6%
Other (0)	38	0.8%	36	1.0%	2	0.3%
Unknown (0)	89	2.0%	69	1.8%	20	2.5%
Age						
Mean, standard deviation	29.8, 9.6		29.4, 9.2		32.0, 10.9	
Age, race/ethnicity, and gender						
Young black males	1,086	24.0%	942	25.0%	144	18.1%
Young Hispanic males	305	6.7%	249	6.7%	56	7.0%
Young white males	334	7.4%	279	7.5%	55	6.9%
Older black males	1,034	22.8%	703	18.8%	331	41.6%
Older Hispanic males	470	10.4%	448	12.0%	22	2.7%
Older white males	762	16.8%	608	16.0%	154	19.4%
Young black females	67	1.5%	59	1.6%	8	1.0%
Young Hispanic females	21	0.5%	21	0.6%	0	
Young white females	60	1.3%	60	1.6%	0	
Older black females	109	2.4%	106	2.8%	3	0.4%
Older Hispanic females	61	1.3%	47	1.3%	14	1.8%
Older white females	179	3.9%	178	4.8%	1	0.1%
Offense gravity score						
Mean, standard deviation	8.06, 1.7		7.58, 1.4		10.3, 1.4	
Prior Record Score						
Mean, standard deviation	2.08, 2.2		1.43, 1.8		5.1, 1.26	

continues

Table 8.1   Cont.

Independent Variables	Full Sample		Drug Eligible		Three-Strikes Eligible	
Offense Type						
Personal	795	17.5%			795	100.0%
Cocaine	3094	68.2%	3,094	82.7%		
Heroin	312	6.9%	312	8.3%		
Methamphetamines	24	0.5%	24	0.6%		
Narcotic	32	0.7%	32	0.9%		
PCP	9	0.2%	9	0.2%		
Marijuana	268	5.9%	268	7.2%		
Convictions						
Single (0)	1,209	26.7%	1,086	29.0%	123	15.5%
Multiple (1)	3,325	73.3%	2,653	71.0%	672	84.5%
Disposition						
Trial (0)	467	10.3%	258	6.9%	209	26.3%
Nonnegotiated (1)	827	18.2%	677	18.1%	150	18.9%
Negotiated (1)	2,593	57.2%	2,264	60.6%	329	41.4%
Other/unknown (1)	647	14.3%	540	14.4%	107	13.5%
Mandatory length	mean	s.d.	mean	s.d.	mean	s.d.
Length above guideline minimum	30.18	46.61	14.79	12.4	101.98	73.0
Length below guideline minimum	−1.10	6.3	−0.87	4.1	−2.17	12.2

Contextual-level variables (N = 59)	Mean	Standard Deviation	Minimum	Maximum
Court size				
Large	3.39	0.183	0	1
Medium	22.03	0.418	0	1
Small	74.58	0.439	0	1
Violent crime caseload	0.15	0.04	0.07	0.33
Percent black	3.51	6.24	0.10	43.30

strike offenders, though they are still applied in only a minority (29 percent) of cases. Table 8.1 also shows that most of the females in the sample are drug offenders, with approximately 13 percent of the population eligible for drug mandatory minimums being female (compared to 3 percent of the population eligible for three-strikes mandatory minimums being eligible). Furthermore, blacks comprise approximately half of mandatory-eligible offenders in the full and drug-eligible samples, but over 60 percent in the three-strikes subsample.

Table 8.2 shows hierarchical models for the full sample (Model 1), the drug offense subsample (Model 2), and the second- and third-strike offense subsample (Model 3). As shown, prosecutors' application of mandatory minimums in the full sample is increased, sometimes substantially, by several of our legally relevant control variables: offense severity, prior record, and having multiple concurrent convictions. The negative effect for the mandatory distance above the guideline in the full sample is particularly interesting. For

Table 8.2 Predicting the Application of Mandatory Minimums

	Full Model			Drug Model			Three-Strikes Model		
	b	Standard Error	Odds	b	Standard Error	Odds	b	Standard Error	Odds
Level 1 variables									
Reason eligible (other drug reference)									
Second strike	.194	.328	1.214				-1.359	1.699	.257
Third strike	1.181	.65	3.258						
Cocaine	.472	.241	1.603*	.558	.249	1.747*			
Heroin	-.599	.419	.549	-.499	.421	.607			
Age at sentencing	-.011	.005	.989*	-.014	.006	.986*	-.003	.011	.997
Male	.396	.169	1.486*	.541	.185	1.718**	1.181	.706	3.258
Race (white and other race reference)									
Black	.199	.118	1.220	.099	.134	1.104	.359	.283	1.432
Hispanic	.686	.149	1.986***	.389	.168	1.476*	1.501	.425	4.486***
Disposition (trial reference)									
Negotiated plea	-.752	.200	.471**	-.959	.223	.383***	-.075	.442	.928
Nonnegotiated plea	-.466	.268	.628	-.533	.295	.587	-1.160	.326	.313***
Other	.646	.528	1.908	.856	.561	2.354	-1.110	1.404	.330
Prior record	.125	.026	1.133***	.130	.027	1.139***	.282	.166	1.326
Offense gravity score	.099	.033	1.104**	.067	.038	1.069	.640	.170	1.896
Multiple conviction	.285	.107	1.330**	.252	.116	1.287*	.620	.315	1.859
Distance of mandatory above guideline	-.007	.003	.993**	-.007	.004	.993	.011	.009	1.011
Level 2 variables									
Constant	-1.8840	.164	.15***	-2.043	.188	.13***	-1.496	.333	.23***
Court size									
Large	1.099	.690	3.001	-.373	.663	.689	1.152	1.325	3.165
Medium	.441	.299	1.554	.053	.303	1.054	.586	.588	1.797
Percent black	-.040	.027	.961	.018	.025	1.018	-.127	.053	.881*
Percent violent crime	.057	.046	1.059	.005	.005	1.005	.197	.096	1.218*

Note: * p < .05; ** p < .01; *** p < .001.

every one month by which the mandatory exceeds the guideline minimum, the odds of prosecutors applying the mandatory *decline* by .007. Thus, when prosecutors face a situation in which the mandatory minimum substantially exceeds the guidelines, they tend not to apply it. In the drug subsample, the effect size for mandatory distance above the guideline is identical to that in the full sample, but does not attain statistical significance at p < .05 (it is significant at p < .10), perhaps due to a slight loss of power because of the somewhat smaller number of cases in the subsample. The mandatory distance variable has no substantive effect among the three-strikes cases. This suggests that the pattern in which prosecutors opt for guideline sentencing when the mandatory substantially exceeds the guideline pertains largely to drug cases.

In Model 1 (full sample) we find that offenders convicted through a negotiated plea have only about half the odds of offenders going to trial of having a mandatory minimum applied. Offenders convicted through nonnegotiated pleas or other types of dispositions, however, did not differ significantly in the odds of receiving a mandatory minimum compared to offenders going to trial. The effect is even stronger in the drug subsample, with those convicted through a negotiated plea about 60 percent less likely to receive a mandatory sentence. However, the effect is much smaller and fails to reach significance in the subsample of three-strikes offenders. Interestingly, in this sample, it is nonnegotiated pleas that result in a reduction in the odds of receiving a mandatory sentence. It should also be noted that the effect of negotiated pleas exhibits significant random variation between counties in all three models, and the effect of nonnegotiated pleas also has a random effect in Models 1 and 2. Thus, counties significantly vary in how different types of guilty pleas affect mandatory application.

While we do not find a significant race effect for black offenders, we find that Hispanic offenders have almost twice the odds (1.95) of receiving a mandatory sentence compared to white offenders in Model 1 (full sample). This effect is slightly smaller (1.5) in Model 2 (drug subsample), but remains significant. In Model 3 (three-strikes subsample) the effect increases to over four times the odds of receiving a mandatory. Specifically, Hispanic offenders have about four and a half times greater odds of having a mandatory applied compared to white offenders in the three-strikes subsample.

Also, we find males' odds to be considerably greater (about 1.4 times in the full model and 1.7 times in the drug subsample) for receiving a mandatory than female offenders. Again our findings differ for the three-strikes subsample, with the effect of gender—regardless that it is larger in size—failing to reach statistical significance. This finding is likely due to the low number of females eligible for three-strikes mandatory minimums. In fact, we leave gender in the model for the three-strikes subsample only for comparability purposes, and removing gender from this model does not change any of our other findings. Also, age moderately reduces the odds of mandatory application in the full sample and in the drug subsample.

Overall, Model 1 (full sample) and Model 2 (drug subsample) show quite similar results, which is not surprising given the large portion of the full sample that is composed of drug offenders. However, the only defendant status characteristic that achieves significance in Model 3 is Hispanic ethnicity. Striking differences also exist regarding some of the control variables across the three models that are worth mentioning. First, type of offense, age, multiple convictions, prior record, and offense gravity score all fail to achieve significance in the three-strikes subsample. Regarding prior record, it is plausible that the significance of this relationship is reduced by a concentration of offenders in this sample in the upper-half portion of the prior record scale, due to the underlying nature of the sample. Obviously, to be eligible for a second- or third-strike mandatory minimum, the offender must have prior convictions for violent felonies, locating him or her in the upper ranges of the prior record score. The loss of significance for the other control variables may reflect a true difference across models, or possibly reflect the loss of power in this model, as the sample size is less than one-fourth of the original sample.

We proposed that young, male, black, and Hispanic offenders would have a higher probability of receiving a mandatory minimum. Table 8.3 presents the findings from our analyses (with the predictors listed in Table 8.2 included but not shown). The results are mixed. We find young Hispanic males to be much more likely than young white males to receive mandatory sentences in the full sample and in the drug-eligible subsample, and older Hispanic males to be moderately more likely to receive mandatory minimums in the full sample. However, we find that young black males are not particularly disadvantaged in prosecutors' decisions to apply mandatory minimums. No significant effects are found for female offenders. However, this is likely due to the small number of females in each age, race, and gender category. Given this, there were insufficient data to test the corresponding race, ethnicity, and age groupings for females in this model.

At the contextual level, we expected that county racial composition would interact with offender ethnicity such that minorities would be punished more severely in counties with larger minority populations. The findings are more complex than we envisioned. In Table 8.4, the race by percent black interaction reaches significance in the full sample and the three-strikes subsample. For the full sample, while the main effect of percent black decreases the overall odds of receiving a mandatory minimum, the interaction effect between county percent black and offender's race (being black) is positive.[6]

Figure 8.1 shows this relationship graphically, revealing that in the full sample, the odds of receiving a mandatory minimum decrease for both white and black offenders as percent black in the county increases. However, the mandatory odds decrease *less* for black offenders than for white offenders (the figures cut off at 50 percent black, since no county exceeds about 44 percent black). This leads to larger gaps in the likelihood of a mandatory application

Table 8.3 Effects of Age, Race/Ethnicity, and Gender Categories on Application of Mandatory Minimums

	Full Model			Drug Model			Three-Strikes Model		
	b	Standard Error	Odds	b	Standard Error	Odds	b	Standard Error	Odds
Older white male	-.064	.197	0.938	-0.114	0.223	0.892	1.079	0.664	2.942
Young black male	.287	.181	1.332	0.186	.201	1.204	-0.309	1.039	0.734
Older black male	.138	0.183	1.148	-0.077	.211	0.926	0.536	0.653	1.709
Young Hispanic male	1.034	0.217	2.812***	0.648	0.247	1.912**	-1.748	1.788	0.174
Older Hispanic male	0.450	0.216	1.568*	0.262	0.233	1.300	0.381	1.525	1.464
Young white female	-0.819	0.640	0.441	-1.001	0.642	0.368			
Older white female	-0.237	.314	0.789	-0.373	0.323	0.689			
Young black female	-.285	0.462	0.752	-0.065	.482	0.937			
Older black female	-0.336	0.357	0.715	-0.456	0.367	0.634			
Young Hispanic female	-.562	1.067	0.570	-0.649	1.081	0.523			
Older Hispanic female	.472	0.391	1.603	-1.421	0.758	0.241			

Table 8.4 Cross-Level Interaction Effects: Offender's Race with Racial Composition of County

	Full Model			Drug Model			Three-Strikes Model		
	b	Standard Error	Odds	b	Standard Error	Odds	b	Standard Error	Odds
Intercept	-1.89	0.17		-2.1	0.19		-1.67	0.36	
Race of offender									
Black	0.0326	0.130	1.033	0.03	.148	1.031	-0.292	0.338	0.747
Racial composition of county									
Percent black in county	-0.044	0.134	0.989	0.001	0.023	1.001	-.130	0.052	0.878*
Interaction term	0.019	0.007	1.017*	0.008	0.009	1.008	0.047	0.015	1.048**

Figure 8.1   Interaction of Offender Race and Percent Black in County: Full Sample

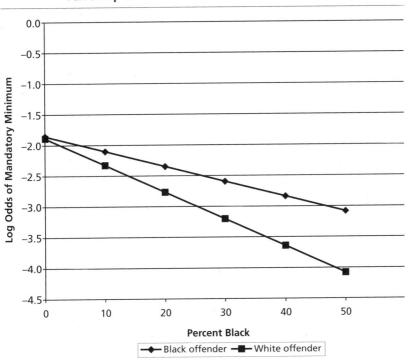

between whites and blacks as percent black in the county increases. Figure 8.2 shows the race–percent black interaction in the three-strikes subsample. Here, again, while the odds of receiving a mandatory minimum decrease for both white and black offenders as percent black in the county increases, the rate of decrease is less for black offenders, creating a similar pattern in which the black versus white difference in mandatory application increases with percent black. Thus, the black versus white gap in mandatory application increases with county percent black, even though race does not have a significant effect itself, and even though both blacks' and whites' odds of receiving mandatory minimums decrease with percent black.

Discussion

Again, we are well aware of the limitations of these data. They lack measures of defendants' socioeconomic status, type of attorney, pretrial release status (bail), the identity or characteristics of victims, measures of evidence strength, and indications of charging decisions and the likelihood of conviction, as these

Figure 8.2   Interaction of Offender Race and Percent Black in County: Three-Strikes Subsample

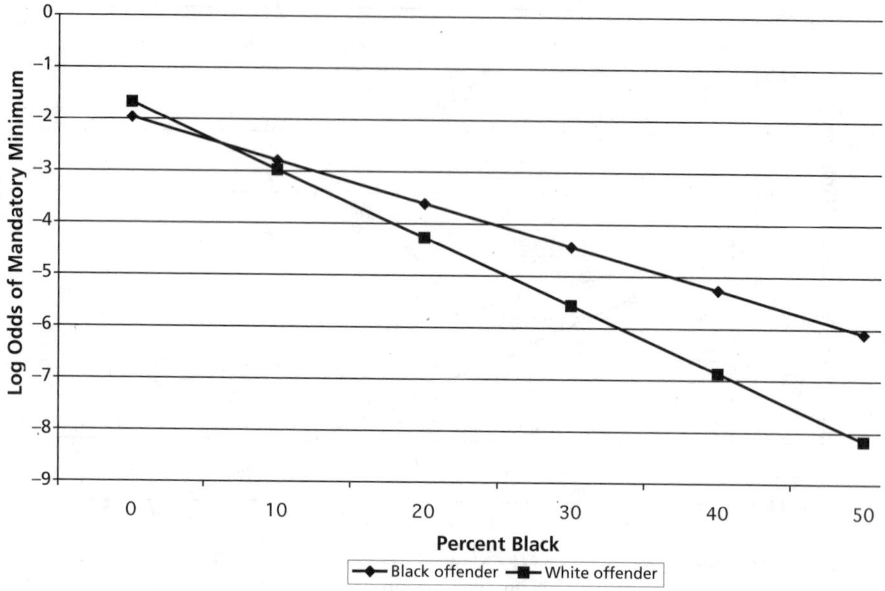

variables are not collected by the PCS. In particular, because we have no data on charging decisions, we cannot determine how often prosecutors reduce a mandatory-eligible charge to a lesser charge. We thus can say nothing about the processes by which prosecutors decide to charge a mandatory-eligible offense in the first place, nor any plea bargaining that may lie behind this decision.

However, while some have noted that mandatory sentences foster charge manipulation (Tonry 1992; Farrell 2003; Bjerk 2005), in states like Pennsylvania the availability to prosecutors of the choice between mandatory minimums and guidelines would seem to render charge bargaining less relevant or necessary. This is because, in contrast to the mandatory sentencing contexts in other states (as described in Bjerk 2005), *prosecutors need not reduce charges* in order to use the mandatory minimums as plea-bargaining leverage. That is, prosecutors can threaten to apply the mandatory, or allow the offender to be sentenced under the (usually lower) guidelines, without altering the charge in any way. In other words, Pennsylvania's system enables *sentence bargaining* between mandatory sentences and guidelines. Thus the lack of data relevant to charge reduction, while not ideal, may not be as serious a limitation to our analysis as it might at first seem.

With these caveats, the key question posed by this chapter is: What affects prosecutorial decisions of whether to apply mandatory minimum sentences?

The answer appears to be rather complicated. The very complexity of our findings, however, supports the usefulness of the focal concerns perspective as an orienting framework for studying prosecutorial discretion. We suggest that prosecutors, like judges, focus on offender blameworthiness, community protection, and practical considerations such as uncertainty reduction, organizational constraints, and the surrounding court community context. The degree to which prosecutors and judges agree or disagree on their view of these focal concerns likely varies according to court community interorganizational relations and politics (for an examination of the latter phenomenon, see Ulmer 1997; Eisenstein, Flemming, and Nardulli 1988). Thus, one important contribution of this analysis is to theoretically extend the focal concerns perspective to encompass prosecutorial discretion. In addition, this analysis makes the kind of contribution to criminal justice theory called for by Tom Bernard and Robin Shepard Engel (2001) by investigating factors that affect the decisions and discretion of one important set of criminal justice actors—prosecutors—and comparing them to findings from studies that focus on judges, another important set of criminal justice actors.

First, legally relevant factors such as offense severity, prior record, and mandatory-eligible offense type strongly influenced whether an offender received a mandatory minimum sentence, but extralegal factors mattered as well. This suggests that prosecutors' decisions about criminal punishment, like judges', are strongly influenced by focal concerns of perceived blameworthiness and protection of the community, as indicated by offense type, severity, and characteristics as well as the prior record of the defendant. We also found modest support for a crime control argument (and also the focal concern of community protection), in that the proportion of courts' caseloads consisting of violent crimes had positive effects on the chances of three-strikes mandatory imposition. However, these legally relevant and crime context factors are not the only determinants of mandatory application.

Not surprisingly, prosecutors applied mandatory minimums substantially less often to those who negotiated guilty pleas in the full sample and in the drug subsample, and substantially less often to those with nonnegotiated guilty pleas in the three-strikes subsample. In all analyses, those convicted by trial were more likely to receive mandatory minimums. This suggests that prosecutors may use the threat of applying a longer mandatory sentence as a key piece of leverage to obtain guilty pleas, and thus more certain convictions, a scenario predicted by Michael Tonry (1992). It also suggests that prosecutors frequently de-mandatorize cases in exchange for plea agreements, in that negotiated plea agreements tend to protect offenders from mandatory minimums.

In terms of focal concerns, plea agreements and trial convictions may signal a variety of different things about defendant blameworthiness and dangerousness, or practical constraints to prosecutors. On the one hand, working with the prosecution to reach a plea agreement, or outright pleading guilty (as in a nonnegotiated or open plea) might indicate remorse (or might also follow from cooperation with law enforcement), which might lower perceived moral blameworthiness. In addition, ethnographic data suggest that pleading guilty and showing remorse are often seen as a first step toward rehabilitation (Ulmer and Kramer 1996). On the other hand, if a defendant makes the entire courtroom workgroup go to trial and then loses, ethnographic data indicate that this often indicates the lack of remorse, and a lack of truthfulness as well, and by implication increased blameworthiness (Ulmer 1997; Flemming, Nardulli, and Eisenstein 1992). These kinds of explanations may lie behind the finding for the three-strikes model, in which nonnegotiated pleas are rewarded with significantly lower odds of mandatory imposition, but the same is not true for negotiated pleas (the effect is in the expected direction but not substantively large or significant). That is, pleading guilty without a bargained agreement may be taken by prosecutors as a signal of remorse in the cases eligible for three-strikes mandatory minimums. By contrast, the lack of a significant effect for negotiated pleas in the three-strikes subsample may indicate that prosecutors are not especially willing to withhold three-strikes mandatory minimums as a plea-agreement concession.

In addition, plea agreements and trials entail a variety of practical constraints and consequences that might influence prosecutors' decisions to apply mandatory penalties. One key practical constraint is, of course, organizational efficiency. Rewarding eligible defendants for pleading guilty by forgoing the imposition of mandatory sentences encourages guilty pleas and moves cases through the system. Second, as Albonetti (1987) argued, plea agreements have an uncertainty-reduction value for prosecutors. They allow prosecutors to avoid the uncertainties of trials and to obtain convictions they might not otherwise obtain (see Kramer and Ulmer 2002, pp. 918–919; see also Smith 1986). Organizational efficiency and uncertainty reduction might be especially pertinent explanations for the significant effects of negotiated pleas on mandatory application in the full sample and especially in the drug subsample. Drug cases are so numerous, and might be comparatively fraught with evidentiary uncertainty (due to vagaries of informant testimony, disputes over drug amounts and purity, search and seizure issues, etc.), that prosecutors might be more willing to de-mandatorize such cases in exchange for relatively fast and certain convictions.

Our findings regarding the relationship between guidelines and mandatory minimums are quite interesting. When prosecutors are faced with a situation in which the mandatory minimum substantially exceeds the guideline minimum, they tend not to apply the former. This suggests the possibility that when prosecutors are faced with mandatory minimums they think are excessive—that is, if the mandatory exceeds the prosecutor's sense of the defendant's blameworthiness or danger to the community—they opt for guideline sentencing. This suggests that the guidelines may provide a fairer result for such offenses. Furthermore, this pattern of opting for guideline sentencing when the mandatory minimum is significantly more severe likely characterizes drug cases much more than three-strikes cases. Prosecutors likely see three-strikes offenders (all of whom are convicted of and have a history of serious personal crimes) as particularly blameworthy or dangerous offenders, and are less willing to forgo substantial mandatory minimum sentences for them.

We found little evidence of a direct effect of being black on receiving the mandatory minimums. However, Hispanics were considerably more likely to receive mandatory minimums across the board. We found that prosecutors apply mandatory minimums against males more than females in all of our models. This finding is consistent with studies in the sentencing literature that show that females are often seen by judges as less blameworthy, less dangerous, and more amenable to rehabilitation, and that they present practical problems (such as the potential impact of a female defendant's imprisonment on her children, if any), and are thus usually sentenced more leniently than men (see Zatz 2000; Demuth and Steffensmeier 2004). If so, this analysis extends that argument to prosecutors as well as judges.

Previous research suggests that judges attribute greater seriousness or risk to certain classes of offenders such as young black males and young Hispanic males. We suggested earlier that this effect may also generalize to prosecutorial discretion. We found partial support for this, with prosecutors being strongly more likely to apply mandatory minimums to young Hispanic males, and moderately more likely to do so to older Hispanic males, in the full sample. Young Hispanic males also seem to be singled out for mandatory application among drug cases. Overall, these patterns at least partially support the contentions of the focal concerns perspective and of the causal attribution and uncertainty avoidance theory that the effect of defendant social statuses on criminal punishment is often situational. That is, the social status characteristics of defendants combine in specific situations of decisionmaking discretion to mobilize attributions about character, dangerousness, rehabilitative potential, or practical consequences, and can do so differently in different types of cases. In the case of mandatory sentences, Hispanic males seem to be particularly targeted, especially young Hispanic males convicted of drug offenses.

We did not find that young black males were particularly disadvantaged in mandatory minimum application. This finding may reflect the fact that previous studies have found that the primary effect of being young, black, and male occurs in the incarceration decision more than in the sentence length decision (see Zatz 2000). Since the mandatory application versus guideline sentencing choice is primarily one involving sentence length, our findings may not be as surprising as they appear. Furthermore, as shown in Chapter 5, the patterns of gender-specific black and Hispanic disparity have changed since the early 1990s (see also Steffensmeier and Demuth 2001).

A key contextual proposition of racial threat theory is that minorities will be subjected to greater social control in contexts where minority populations are larger and seen as more threatening. What we found instead was that in the full sample, whites' likelihood of receiving mandatory sentences decreased to a greater extent than did blacks'. A similar pattern occurred in the three-strikes subsample. Thus, in both cases, the black versus white gap in mandatory application increased with county percent black. That the black versus white gap increased with percent black is consistent with racial threat, but the finding that blacks' odds of receiving mandatory minimums also decline (though not as sharply as whites') with county percent black cannot easily be accounted for by racial threat theory.

Our findings have complex and mixed implications for racial threat theory. First, Hispanics may be replacing African Americans as the minority who mobilize stereotypes of criminal dangerousness or blameworthiness (see also Steffensmeier and Demuth 2000, 2001; Spohn and Holleran 2000). Second, racial threat responses may be gender- and age-specific—that is, focused on particular age and gender groups (in this case, primarily young Hispanic males). And third, the county racial composition may condition the extent and nature of racial advantage or disadvantage in mandatory sentencing in complex ways that cannot be fully explained by racial threat theory.

Beyond the effects that race or ethnicity have or do not have in our models, however, it is crucial to realize that *about 70 percent* of all the mandatory-eligible offenders in our sample were black or Hispanic, especially black (51 percent) (see Table 8.1). These percentages are ridiculously disproportionate to the sizes of these groups in Pennsylvania's population (about 10 percent black, 4 percent Hispanic). These descriptive figures, along with some of the findings from our models, could support an argument that mandatory minimums are a type of what Eduardo Bonilla-Silva (1997) calls "racialized social systems." That is, even though they are racially neutral on paper, mandatory minimums (mainly those involving drugs) disproportionately impact black and Hispanic minorities because they encompass offenses in which they are disproportionately involved (Beckett and Sasson 2000; Tonry 1992).

Finally, our findings regarding the effect of court size on mandatory application were not what we expected. Court size displayed little connection to prosecutors' decisions to apply mandatory minimums. Since judicial sentencing decisions tend to be more lenient in large jurisdictions (Eisenstein, Flemming, and Nardulli 1988; Ulmer 1997; Ulmer and Johnson 2004), this finding suggests that prosecutorial and judicial decisions may differ in relation to court community factors associated with jurisdiction size. This question of how court community size affects prosecutorial discretion is an interesting direction for further research.

Conclusion

Our findings support the long-suspected notion that mandatory minimums are not mandatory at all, but simply substitute prosecutorial discretion for judicial discretion (Tonry 1992). It is well known that over 90 percent of cases in most jurisdictions in the United States are guilty pleas, and that a large portion of these are prosecutor-negotiated plea agreements. Prosecutors have great influence through charging, sentence bargaining, and in the case examined here, the application of mandatory minimums. Our findings suggest that the focal concerns perspective is a useful heuristic for prosecutorial decision criteria regarding sentencing outcomes, just as prior research shows it to be useful for conceptualizing judicial discretion. We argue that legally relevant factors, case-processing concerns (i.e., rewarding guilty pleas), and social statuses (i.e., gender, as well as ethnicity and age) shape prosecutors' perceptions of blameworthiness and community protection, and thus their decisions to apply mandatory minimums. In addition, the social contexts surrounding courts (e.g., violent crime rates, percent black) might shape prosecutors' perceptions of both community protection and practical constraints (e.g., political ramifications of seeking or not seeking mandatory minimums for certain offenders).

We encourage much more research on prosecutorial decisions that directly affect sentencing outcomes. Too often, studies of sentencing discretion, including our own, focus on judges, and leave out prosecutors, who are crucial players in courtroom workgroups. There appear to be an increasing number of legal situations where prosecutors have great or perhaps even complete control over sentencing outcomes (Stith and Cabranes 1998; Hartley, Maddan, and Spohn 2007). For example, motions for "substantial assistance" departures under the US Sentencing Guidelines are controlled by federal prosecutors, as are guideline sentence reductions for defendants' "acceptance of responsibility." In jurisdictions with capital punishment, prosecutors have the discretion to seek the death penalty or not. Future research should examine these kinds of prosecutorial decisions about sentencing as we have examined the application of mandatory minimums.

Judges and prosecutors may or may not use their discretion in drastically different ways. However, prosecutorial and judicial discretion differ drastically in their visibility and formal accountability. The larger legal and sociological questions are: Whose discretion does a society rely on in criminal punishment—the relatively visible and accountable discretion of judges, or the relatively invisible and unaccountable discretion of prosecutors? And what are the consequences of that choice?

Importantly, our findings indicate an important yet complex role of guidelines in the application of mandatory minimums. The guidelines seem to provide a fallback position for prosecutors when mandatory minimums apply. This may reflect the perception that the guidelines offer a fairer penalty in general relative to the focal concerns of prosecutors. This might be particularly true of Pennsylvania's drug guidelines, as these guidelines were developed and revised in the 1990s with broad-based input, including considerable input from the District Attorneys Association (as described in Chapter 3). Further, the guidelines might merely provide a logistical foundation for plea negotiation, such that they provide for a reasonable sentence reduction vis-à-vis the mandatory minimum, and are readily acceptable to the judge, since it means that he or she is not departing from the guidelines. Regardless, the sentencing guidelines play an important role in sentencing even when legislatively-set mandatory minimums apply. The fact that the Pennsylvania Commission on Sentencing set the guidelines independently of the mandatory minimums, though a politically risky position, seems to have resulted in the guidelines serving as a functional and arguably fairer alternative to mandatory sentences.

Notes

1. While mandatory minimums always apply for charges of first- and second-degree murder, the prosecutor must make a motion to apply the mandatory minimum for other cases, including all drug-related mandatory minimums and Pennsylvania's second- and third-strike mandatory provisions. These latter are included in our analyses.

2. Florida statute 775.084 (3)(a)(6) states: "For an offense committed on or after October 1, 1995, if the state attorney pursues a habitual felony offender sanction or a habitual violent felony offender sanction against the defendant *and the court, in a separate proceeding pursuant to this paragraph, determines that the defendant meets the criteria under subsection (1) for imposition of such sanction,* the court must sentence the defendant as a habitual felony offender or a habitual violent felony offender, subject to imprisonment pursuant to this section *unless the court finds that such sentence is not necessary for the protection of the public*" (emphasis added). Thus the habitual offender designations studied by Charles Crawford and colleagues (Crawford, Chiricos, and Kleck 1998; Crawford 2000), while informative, do not isolate prosecutorial discretion the way that the mandatory minimums analyzed here do, because (1) the court (judge), in addition to the prosecutor, determines whether the defendant meets the criteria for its application, and (2) the court can find that the designation is "not necessary" and choose not to apply it.

3. John Wooldredge and Amy Thistlethwaite (2004) draw from focal concerns in their sentencing analyses, but do not explicitly frame their analyses of charging and prosecution decisions around focal concerns.

4. The order of causality for mode of conviction on the imposition of mandatory sentences is debatable. On the one hand, prosecutors might hold out the possibility of not applying the mandatory minimum in exchange for a guilty plea. On the other hand, qualitative research by Jeffery Ulmer (1997) reports that sometimes, if prosecutors pursue the mandatory minimum, defense attorneys feel that they then have nothing to lose by going to trial. If the defendant is convicted after trial, he or she then faces the mandatory minimum. Either way, qualitative evidence suggests that withholding the mandatory minimum is often a strong inducement to plead guilty, whatever the prosecutor's motives.

5. As argued in Chapter 7, this may not be true in nonroutine, sensational cases, which can make court community activities highly visible in large urban areas.

6. The cross-level interaction term represents the effect of being black in a given county with a given percent black population. To properly interpret the cross-level interaction effect, one must consider all three coefficients in the cross-level interaction model (not the direct effects in Table 8.2) simultaneously. For a black offender, this effect is obtained as follows: I_B + (1 × coefficient for black) + (percent black × coefficient for percent black) + (1 × percent black × interaction term), where I_B is the intercept for the model, with white as the reference category. For a white offender, this effect is simply the slope of the coefficient for percent black plus the intercept (I_W) from an identical model, with black as the reference category rather than white (in other words, the effect is obtained by substituting 0 for 1 in the above formula).

9

Can Guidelines Change Sentencing Practices?

THUS FAR WE have reviewed the development and history of the Pennsylvania Commission on Sentencing and examined sentencing outcomes under its guidelines. In this chapter we examine the degree to which Pennsylvania's sentencing guidelines have actually changed certain kinds of sentencing practices. In general terms, this is a case study of the regulatory influence of sentencing commissions, in that we examine how Pennsylvania's courts implemented changes in the state's guidelines. Specifically, the PCS developed and implemented dramatic changes to its sentencing guidelines in 1994, and then modified them slightly in 1997, as described in previous chapters. The first empirical question we ask, therefore, is whether these guideline changes changed courts' sentencing decisions. Second, we ask whether courts appeared to adjust to the changes, suggesting that the changes merely shifted the locus of sentencing authority.

Conflicting perspectives exist on whether guidelines are likely to dramatically change sentencing patterns. One view is the "legalistic" model, which presumes that the activities and decisions of judges, prosecutors, and defense attorneys are primarily determined by the rule of law in their decisionmaking. This presumption is strengthened when considering the policies of sentencing commissions, because legislatures have invested considerable authority in them and their guidelines. For example, legislatures often empower sentencing commissions through broad-based memberships (i.e., often including judges, prosecutors, legislators, scholars, and sometimes others), strong mandates, and enforcement mechanisms designed to overcome resistance to change. In Pennsylvania, the eleven-member commission contains four judges, four legislators, and three gubernatorial appointments, of which one must be a prosecuting attorney, one a defense attorney, and the one a law professor or criminologist (Act 319 of 1978). Based on these legislative ingredients, a legalistic perspective would expect the guidelines emanating from these sentencing commissions to be influential.

James Eisenstein, Roy Flemming, and Peter Nardulli, however, derived two important hypotheses about the impact of criminal justice reforms based on their court community perspective, identified in Chapter 1. First, they concluded from their research that "the more radical a proposed change the less likely is its adoption" (1988, p. 294). Their point is that existing norms and practices in a given court, and the sentencing decisions resulting from following these norms and practices, are the result of "accommodations among competing values and interests that support these values, accommodations that are superimposed on a common basic structure supported by broad consensus" (p. 294). By implication, the more the guidelines depart from traditional practices in the court community—that is, the less they mesh with local views and interests—the less likely the court communities will conform to the guidelines.

A second hypothesis they derived from their multistate study is that reforms from above often are unused. They pointed out that there are reward structures supporting current practices that reflect a "routine that cuts the costs of calculation, reduces uncertainty, and helps produce similar outcomes in equivalent cases" (p. 297). Eisenstein and colleagues did not argue that reforms are powerless to effect change, but that change is filtered through and applied within a local court community, which will view change as potentially disruptive to its current equilibrium.

Jeffery Ulmer (1997) later provided support for this view in the context of the Pennsylvania guidelines as they existed in the late 1980s and early 1990s. Ulmer viewed court communities as social worlds, each with its distinctive social organization and order. Variations in guideline implementation resulted from the guidelines' embeddedness in such local social orders. In some court communities, the guidelines became central to case processing and sentencing, while in others, participants felt free to disregard the guidelines when they conflicted with local norms and court culture. Furthermore, we argued (Ulmer 1997; Ulmer and Kramer 1998) that the guidelines were embraced and followed to the extent that they served the practical interests of court community participants, or provided them with some benefit that they did not have previously.

Furthermore, Eisenstein, Flemming, and Nardulli (1988), Ulmer (1997), and Rodney Engen and Sara Steen (2000) argued that the organizational dynamics of the court community act as a decisionmaking filter for guidelines and other sentencing reforms. In effect, the sentencing commission develops guidelines, promulgates them (submits guidelines for legislative approval and trains judges, prosecutors, probation officers, and other court officials, and monitors application of the guidelines), and then court community participants filter the guidelines through their organizational norms. This is an example of the "transformation of policy intentions" through implementation, as described by sociologists such as Carroll Estes and Beverly Edmonds (1981) and Peter Hall and Patrick McGinty (1997). Relatedly, another observer of guidelines, Joachim Savelsberg, predicts that guidelines will fail to be implemented as intended, because they "have to be implemented through networks of decision makers in complex administrative environments and by actors with internalized substantive rationales" (1992, p. 1361).

Despite the fact that sentencing guidelines have been the most prominent criminal justice reform of the past three decades, there is very little research on the impact *over time* of either the initial guidelines (except see Miethe and Moore 1985; Moore and Miethe, 1986; US Sentencing Commission 1991) or changes in guidelines (except see Engen and Steen 2000). However, Michael Tonry, while acknowledging frequent use of plea bargaining, concluded from his review of the research that "guidelines have altered sentences practices and patterns" (1996, p. 33).

Research on the Impact of Guidelines

Policymakers, particularly legislators, assume that courts will implement sentencing guidelines as intended, despite the research findings cited above. The reality seems to be mixed. For example, Minnesota's initial guidelines attempted to increase the sanctions for violent offenders and reduce them for repeat theft offenders. Research by Terence Miethe and Charles Moore (1985, 1988) and Kay Knapp (1987) found that local courts adapted to the attempt to increase sanctions for violent offenders by using departures to soften the penalties for those offenders. Also, prosecutors responded to attempts to reduce penalties for the repeat theft offenders by prosecuting offenders for separate theft offenses rather than just prosecuting on one offense, or consolidating them so that the prior record score would be higher, thereby raising the guideline sentence recommendation.

Of particular relevance to this chapter is Engen and Steen's research on the impact of guideline changes in the state of Washington on sentencing. Their study was limited to change in Washington's drug guidelines in the period 1986 to 1995. Their research question addressed "whether and how the exercise of discretion by courtroom workgroups affects the relationship between sentencing reforms and sentencing outcomes" (2000, p. 1358). As expected, they found that the guideline changes did in fact alter sentencing practices as intended, but they also found that case-processing factors conditioned the changes. For example, the guidelines increased sentence severity for delivery of narcotics as intended, but the overall impact was greater for offenders who went to trial as compared to those who pled guilty. They also found that, subsequent to the guideline changes, the severity of charges decreased, suggesting prosecutorial manipulation of the guidelines to ameliorate the increased severity of the guidelines and to obtain plea agreements.

Ilene Nagel and Stephen Schulhofer (1992) studied the implementation of the US Sentencing Guidelines for drug offenders, for whom those guidelines (based on congressionally enacted mandatory minimums) raised the recommended sentences considerably over past practice. They interviewed judges,

US attorneys, federal defenders, defense attorneys, and probation officers in several districts and found that prosecutors manipulated guideline factors in one-quarter to one-third of the cases to obtain guilty pleas and to diminish the severity of sentences. Again, this indicates the importance of local sentencing norms that evolve over time, and the propensity for court decisionmakers to "adjust" the guidelines toward greater consistency with past practices, rather than ignoring or openly subverting guidelines. Nagel and Schulhofer found that federal court contexts influenced the degree of guideline circumvention. Guideline compliance was influenced by the interrelationship of the attitudes and activities of the key players—judges, US attorneys, federal defenders, and probation officers. Thus they found that federal court communities had established norms of interaction between the key actors, and a scale of justice as to what was the appropriate penalty. Moreover, they found that the patterns of decisionmaking varied among the districts, resulting in disparate "adjustments" to the guidelines.

However, both of these studies, while revealing some court manipulation of the guidelines, found that the courts generally applied the guidelines as intended. In both Minnesota and the federal courts, guideline systems were designed to severely restrict judicial discretion. However, Pennsylvania's guidelines, while highly *prescriptive,* are relatively low in *presumptiveness,* providing much wider ranges and exhibiting much greater difficulty in overturning departure sentences on appeal.

Prior Studies of the Impact of Pennsylvania's Guidelines

Although there has probably been more research on Pennsylvania sentencing patterns than on any other state, there have been only two studies that examined the impact over time of the sentencing guidelines. John Kramer and Robin Lubitz (1985) examined the impact of the guidelines on both racial disparity and sentencing severity. They concluded that the guidelines had reduced disparity and increased the severity for the four key felony offenses they studied. However, the validity of the findings is limited, because the pre-guideline sample came from only twenty-three of Pennsylvania's sixty-seven counties, and the guideline sentences were for 1983 cases, with some underreporting.

The second study, by Robin Lubitz and Cynthia Kempinen (1987), used data collected by the Administrative Office of Pennsylvania Courts to study changes in charging practices before and after implementation of the guidelines. This study examined the argument that one key mode of adaptation by local courts to guidelines like Pennsylvania's, which are based on the offense of conviction, would be increased charge bargaining to control the offense of conviction and thus the guideline recommendation. Lubitz and Kempinen found that, in fact, after implementation of the guidelines, there was a significant increase in the percentage of convictions in which charges were dropped or reduced. When plotting these changes by quarter, before and after guideline implementation, they found that there was a consistent increase in both of these indicators over the three-year period examined, and the finding was consistent for all categories of crimes and for all types of counties. Interestingly, however, the data indicated that the trend *predated* implementation of the guidelines. While the increase in charge reduction is consistent with an interpretation that the courts adjusted to the guidelines by engaging in more charge bargaining, the fact that the trend predated the guidelines suggests that it was not a reaction to the guidelines but a part of a broader overall change in case processing.

Furthermore, we found (Ulmer 1997; Ulmer and Kramer 1996, 1998; Kramer and Ulmer 2002) that prosecutors and defense attorneys were more likely to make sentence agreements the subject of plea negotiations, *and to use the guidelines to do so,* rather than charge bargaining. We argued that the Pennsylvania guidelines provided a structured "menu" of sentence options to be bargained. We argued, in other words, that the guidelines enhanced sentence bargaining (including bargaining for downward departures) and made it more attractive, rather than fostering an increase in charge bargaining.

Changes to the Pennsylvania Guidelines and Their Impact: Five Questions

In this chapter, we focus on five primary research questions regarding the changes in Pennsylvania's guidelines in the 1990s. First, did the guidelines successfully increase the penalties for serious violent offenders, as intended? Second, did the change in the guidelines to presumptive nonconfinement reduce the use of incarceration for these offenders? Third, did the narrowing of guideline ranges reduce the dispersion of sentences for the less serious offenders? Fourth, did the development of intermediate punishment guidelines for mid-level offenders stimulate the use of such alternatives? Finally, did the intermediate punishment funding provided by the legislature to the Pennsylvania Commission on Crime and Delinquency in the late 1990s stimulate the use of such punishment?

Methodology

We divided PCS data into three time frames, representing sentencing under the 1991 guidelines, 1994 guidelines, and 1997 guidelines. Guideline changes apply to offenses committed after the date of implementation of the change. Consequently, defendants may be sentenced under a particular set of guidelines for several years after changes have been implemented in these guidelines. For example, when we refer to the 1991 guideline sentences, we mean sentences for cases that entered the system prior to the time when the 1994 changes took effect. Because only offenses committed after the date the 1994 guidelines took effect (August 12, 1994) were supposed to be sentenced under the 1994 guidelines, 1991 guideline sentences continued to occur for several years after the 1994 implementation.[1] The same is true for the 1997 guideline changes. Methodologically, this means that we cannot simply compare sentences from year to year, but must compare sentences given under the 1991 guidelines, the 1994 guidelines, and the 1997 guidelines.

In our review in Chapter 3, we alluded to significant changes that the PCS made to the calculation of prior record score. Because our focus was on changes in specific sentencing recommendations, we did not study the impact of the changes in the calculation of PRS. However, to control for any effects of changes in PRS, we mostly focused our analysis on offenders with a PRS of zero because the commission did not make any changes to the treatment of this category. Further, where it was necessary to examine sentences in matrix cells with larger PRS scores, we limited the cells to those with PRSs less than repeat felony offender (RFEL) and repeat violent offender (REVOC) status, because the focus of the commission's changes in PRS was to isolate serious repeat felony offenders and repeat violent offenders. The RFEL and REVOC categories contain relatively few offenders, so by dropping them we do not lose much information, but we largely prevent the guidelines' PRS changes from clouding our comparisons.

Findings: Increased Penalties for Serious Violent Crimes

As previously shown in Table 3.1, the guideline recommendations for key violent felonies were adjusted during each of the three periods addressed in this study. A key focus of the PCS was on raising the sentence recommendations for serious violent crimes. The commission's recommendations were raised in 1994 and again in 1997 for third-degree murder, attempted murder, rape and involuntary deviate sexual intercourse, and robbery (with serious bodily injury). For burglary of an occupied home, the guideline recommendation was not raised in 1994 but was raised in 1997.

Table 9.1 reports the average minimum sentences under the 1991, 1994, and 1997 guidelines for each of these offenses at zero PRS.[2]

For offenses for which the guideline-recommended sentences were increased in both 1994 and 1997 (third-degree murder, attempted murder, and robbery [with serious bodily injury]), we find that actual court sentences did increase. It should be noted that the sentences for third-degree murder and attempted murder increased much more significantly than the twelve-month increases in both 1994 and 1997. The almost fifty-month increase between the 1994 and the 1997 guideline sentence for third-degree murder reflects to a great extent the doubling of the statutory maximum passed in a legislative special session on crime in 1994–1995. The legislature increased the statutory maximum from twenty to forty years, and therefore the courts could sentence

Table 9.1   Average Incarceration Sentences for Serious Violent Crimes Under the Pre-1994, 1994, and 1997 Guidelines

Offense	Pre-1994	1994	1997
Murder	86.3	97.7	136.5
Attempted murder	45.4	93.4	107.9
Aggravated assault	32.3	29.0	28.9
Robbery with SBI	27.8	31.3	34.0
Rape/IDSI	47.0	54.6	52.2

these offenders to minimums of up to twenty years. The maximum of the guideline standard range increased accordingly, from 120 to 240 months. For attempted murder, the average minimum more than doubled, from forty-five months to more than ninety months under the 1994 guidelines, and then increased another fourteen months with the 1997 guidelines. As for third-degree murder, the legislature dramatically increased the maximum sentence for attempted murder from ten years to forty years.[3]

However, for rape and involuntary deviant sexual intercourse, average court sentences increased commensurate with the increase in the guidelines in 1994, but then dropped slightly under the 1997 guidelines. Such a minor drop may reflect some shift in the overall severity of the offenses due to perhaps more prosecutions for rape offenses that might have historically not been prosecuted or charge bargained.

The guideline recommendations for burglary of an occupied home did not change in 1994; however, in 1997 the lowest minimum sentence in the guideline range increased by six months. Table 9.1 indicates, as expected, that average minimum court sentences for burglary of an occupied home did not change noticeably with implementation of the 1994 guidelines, but increased almost four months with the 1997 guidelines, consistent with the increase in the guideline recommendation.

Overall, the data support the conclusion that the guidelines successfully increased court sentences for serious violent offenders overall. Also, the legislative changes in statutory maximums for murder and attempted murder seemed to considerably impact the length of minimum sentences for these offenses. However, as we discussed in Chapter 4, downward departure rates for serious violent offenses were substantial under the 1997 guidelines, especially in a handful of counties.

Impact of Shifts in Guidelines for Less Serious Offenders

The data examining guideline recommendations for less serious offenders are organized around three different types of changes that the PCS made in this area of the matrix, as shown in Table 9.2. The first changes were to the 1/0

Table 9.2   Sentence Guidelines for Less Serious Offenses over Time

Offense Gravity Score	Prior Record Score					
	0	1	2	3	4	5
5						
Pre-1994 Guidelines	0–11.5	3–11.5	5–11.5	8–11.5	18–27	21–30
1994 Guidelines	RS–6	1–6	3–9	6–11.5	9–15	12–18
1997 Guidelines	RS–9	1–12	3–14	6–16	9–16	12–18
4						
Pre-1994 Guidelines	0–11.5	0–11.5	0–11.5	5–11.5	8–11.5	18–27
1994 Guidelines	RS–3	RS–6	RS–9	3–9	6–11.5	9–15
1997 Guidelines	RS–3	RS–9	RS–11.5	3–14	6–16	9–16
3						
Pre-1994 Guidelines	0–6	0–11.5	0–11.5	0–11.5	3–11.5	5–11.5
1994 Guidelines	RS–RIP	RS–3	RS–6	RS–9	3–9	6–11.5
1997 Guidelines	RS–1	RS–6	RS–9	RS–11.5	3–14	6–16
2						
Pre-1994 Guidelines	0–IP	0–3	0–11.5	0–11.5	0–11.5	2–11.5
1994 Guidelines	RS	RS	RS–RIP	RS–3	RS–6	1–6
1997 Guidelines	RS	RS–2	RS–3	RS–4	RS–6	1–9
1						
Pre-1994 Guidelines	0–IP	0–3	0–6	0–6	0–6	0–6
1994 Guidelines	RS	RS	RS–RIP	RS–RIP	RS–3	RS–6
1997 Guidelines	RS	RS–1	RS–2	RS–3	RS–4	RS–6

Notes: RS = restorative sanctions.
RIP = restrictive intermediate punishment.

(OGS/PRS) and 2/0 cells, where the commission established nonincarceration presumptive guidelines in 1991 and maintained that recommendation in 1994 and in 1997. However, there were two differences that occurred when the 1994 guidelines and 1997 guidelines were implemented that did not occur with implementation of the 1991 changes. First, the commission in 1991 merely changed the guideline ranges in cells 1/0 and 2/0 to presumptive nonconfinement, from ranges of zero to six months and zero to twelve months. It did this in response to the legislative mandate to identify offenders appropriate for intermediate punishment under Act 193. But with a comprehensive review of the guidelines already in process, the commission realized that there might be major changes forthcoming. Therefore, it made responsive, but insignificant, changes in 1991. Since the changes were minor, the commission did not engage in a significant training process to implement them; rather, the commission waited for the results of its comprehensive review of guidelines that it had embarked on in 1990. Statewide training and the rationale for the changes accompanied the comprehensive guideline changes submitted to the General Assembly in 1994. This training is an important ingredient, and in some respects any changes in cells 1/0 and 2/0 under the 1994 guidelines are likely the result of this training.

A second change for the less serious offenders occurred in cells 1/1 and 1/2. In 1994 the commission established presumptive nonconfinement guidelines in these cells, whereas the 1991 guidelines provided ranges of zero to three months and zero to six months, respectively. However, as a result of criticism after the 1994 guideline changes that judges' discretion had been overly restricted, the commission revised the standard range in 1997 to again allow for incarceration. Thus, for these two cells, we have a shift from standard-range guidelines that provided judges with the flexibility to incarcerate or not, then to presumptive nonconfinement, and finally a return to the discretion to incarcerate in the standard range in 1997.

Finally, for several cells in the guideline matrix, the commission left to the court the decision of whether to incarcerate or not, but narrowed the guideline range. While this occurred for several cells in the lower part of the matrix, we focus our analysis on cells 3/0, 4/0, and 5/0. These zero prior record score cells provide a good test of the impact of narrowing the ranges, because they contain many cases, and they avoid confounding any shifts in the distribution of offenders between guideline cells caused by changes in the measure of PRS.

To study the impact of these guideline changes, we examine the types of sentences given to determine whether there were shifts paralleling changes in the guidelines. We conduct these analyses for all offenses and then only for theft offenders, to determine whether the changes were maintained for specific offenses.

Changes in Incarceration: Cells 1/0 and 2/0

Table 9.3 presents the data on changes in the types of sentences in terms of incarceration, restrictive intermediate punishment, and probation for each set of guidelines, by all offenses and also by theft offenses only. Interestingly, the likelihood of incarceration dropped dramatically in both of these guideline cells under both guideline revisions. In cell 1/0, incarceration declined from 23.0 percent under the 1991 guidelines to 15.9 percent under the 1994 guidelines, and then continued to decline to 11.8 percent under the 1997 guidelines. For theft offenses the changes were similar. For cell 1/0, incarceration for theft declined from 30.4 percent of all sentences to 14.3 percent, for a proportional decrease of 53.0 percent. For offenders sentenced in cell 2/0, incarceration dropped from 29.8 percent to 17.9 percent, a 39.9 percent decline. For theft offenses in this cell, the decrease was 44 percent, which is moderately higher than the overall decline. The drop in incarceration in cell 2/0 showed a slightly smaller decrease in incarceration than in cell 1/0. This is not surprising in view of the slightly greater seriousness of the offenses in cell 2/0.

An important part of the attempt to decrease the reliance on incarceration was to increase the availability of intermediate punishment programs and

Table 9.3   Type of Sentence by Guideline Cell for All Offenses and for Theft Offenses

OGS/PRS	All Offenses			Theft Offenses		
	1991	1994	1997	1991	1994	1997
1/0						
Incarceration	21.8	15.3	11.8	30.4	21.2	14.3
RIP	2.6	6.5	6.6	2.9	6.7	6.0
Probation	77.6	78.2	81.5	66.7	72.1	79.6
2/0						
Incarceration	29.2	19.6	18.6	30.7	21.4	17.2
RIP	3.2	6.4	5.5	3.1	7.2	5.5
Probation	67.2	74.0	75.9	66.3	71.4	77.3
1/1						
Incarceration	36.1	22.4	23.5	40.0	26.2	24.7
RIP	2.6	6.9	8.2	1.7	7.2	14.5
Probation	61.3	70.7	68.3	58.3	66.5	60.8
1/2						
Incarceration	47.3	25.5	27.0	49.7	29.1	32.9
RIP	2.7	11.8	5.9	2.5	5.6	4.0
Probation	50.0	62.7	67.1	47.7	65.3	63.1
3/0						
Incarceration	33.3	22.7	24.1	33.9	22.6	23.9
RIP	2.8	9.4	8.2	2.7	8.1	6.7
Probation	63.9	67.9	67.7	63.4	69.3	69.4
4/0						
Incarceration	37.4	29.5	33.4	*	*	*
RIP	3.4	7.6	5.4	*	*	*
Probation	59.3	63.0	58.9	*	*	*
5/0						
Incarceration	46.6	42.9	39.9	*	*	*
RIP	2.8	6.3	7.2	*	*	*
Probation	50.5	50.8	53.0	*	*	*

Note: *The PCS reduced the rank of theft offenses such that there were very few under the 1994 and 1997 guidelines at 4/0 and 5/0.

courts' use of these programs. The sentences in Table 9.3 indicate that RIP sentences significantly increased in both cells 1/0 and 2/0. However, the vast majority of the declines in incarceration were the result of increasing use of probation sentences. Thus it would seem that RIP sentences did not effectively widen the net of more severe penalties.

In view of the fact that the 1991 guidelines established nonconfinement as the presumptive sentence in the standard range, the magnitude of these changes is surprising, but strongly supports the importance of PCS implementation sessions held statewide, and the importance of initiatives by the Pennsylvania Commission on Crime and Delinquency to encourage the use of intermediate punishments.

Changes in Incarceration: Cells 1/1, 1/2, and 3/0

The second set of guideline changes are even more dramatic than the changes to cells 1/0 and 2/0, because the shifts went from wide ranges that included confinement, to nonconfinement, and then back, to allow for limited confinement under the 1997 guidelines. For example, in Table 9.2, we find that cell 1/1 went from a range of zero to three months of confinement and then to restorative sanction with the option for one month of confinement instead.

What happened to the use of confinement under these rather convoluted changes in the guidelines? Interestingly, incarceration sentences declined from 36.1 percent to 22.4 percent under the nonconfinement guidelines set in 1994; then, when the commission opened the guideline to allow for one-month confinement, 1997 confinement sentences stabilized, with an increase of less than 1.0 percent. For theft offenders in cell 1/1, we find that incarceration declined from 40.0 percent to 26.2 percent, and then declined another 1.5 percent under the 1997 guidelines. For cell 1/2, we find a similar decline in incarceration, and we find that incarceration increased only slightly under the 1997 guidelines, when judges were again given the option to incarcerate in the standard range. When we examine theft offenses, we find that incarceration declined similarly.

Regarding the use of intermediate punishment, we find several interesting patterns. First, for cell 1/1, we find that these intermediate punishment sentences increased under both the 1994 and the 1997 guidelines. But we find that growth for the use of RIP was particularly pronounced for theft offenders, for whom the proportion who received these sentences rose from 1.7 percent to 7.2 percent under the 1994 guidelines, and then more than doubled, to 14.5 percent, under the 1997 guidelines. On the other hand, for offenders in cell 1/2, the pattern was considerably different. Here, RIP sentences increased for all offenders and for theft offenders under the 1994 guidelines, but dropped under the 1997 guidelines. For all offenses, the drop in RIP sentences was from 11.8 percent to 5.9 percent, with most of this drop coming through increased use of probation sentences. It is not clear why there would be a shift from RIP to probation, but one of the concerns in the use of RIP was to avoid "widening the net" by sentencing people to RIP who would otherwise have received probation. Whatever the reason for the declines in RIP use in cells 1/0 and 1/2, they clearly are not consistent with RIP widening the net by encompassing greater numbers of less serious offenders. Also, funding in 1997 targeted the use of RIP for the more serious Level 3 and Level 4 offenders, and thus may have stimulated a decline in RIP for the less serious offenders in cells 1/1 and 1/2 as a result of devoting RIP resources to more serious offenders.

Cell 3/0 shifted from a standard range of zero to six months of confinement, to a standard-range sentence of nonconfinement, back to a standard-range of restorative sanction with the option for one month of incarceration.

Incarceration declined from 33.4 percent under the 1991 guidelines to 23.9 percent under the 1994 guidelines, and there was effectively no change when incarceration was again provided in the standard range in 1997. Overall this reflects a 28.7 percent decline in incarceration. The findings are similar for theft offenses, which saw an overall incarceration decline of 29.5 percent.

Changes in Incarceration: Cells 4/0 and 5/0

Cells 4/0 and 5/0 were used to test the impact of narrowing the guideline standard ranges. However, insufficient theft offenses in these OGS categories existed to support a separate analysis. To test for the impact of narrowing the ranges, we focused on changes in incarceration sentences, changes in the average incarceration sentence, and changes in the variation in incarceration sentences. Cell 4/0 went from a range of zero to eleven and a half months of incarceration under the 1991 guidelines, to restorative sanction with an option of up to three months of incarceration under both the 1994 and the 1997 guidelines. It is clear that the commission encouraged greater use of nonconfinement sentencing options in these cells. We see in Table 9.3 that incarceration sentences declined from 38.1 percent to 32.5 percent under the 1994 guidelines, and then dropped slightly to 32.1 percent under the 1997 guidelines. This overall decline of 6.0 percent in incarceration sentences represents a 15.7 percent drop. Thus, although the commission was not restricting the confinement decision under the guidelines, the use of incarceration dropped. This probably reflects the impact of training by the PCS and by the Pennsylvania Commission on Crime and Delinquency, which were encouraging greater use of nonincarceration sentences. For cell 5/0, incarceration decreased 14.4 percent, dropping from 46.6 percent to 39.9 percent.

Multivariate Analysis:
Changes in Incarceration in the Lower Guideline Cells

The guidelines seemed to have dramatically changed sentences for the less serious offenders. This is important because it documents the impact of guidelines on sentencing patterns, but we cannot reject the argument that the decline came from shifts in the types of cases falling into these guideline cells. Such a shift might have come from changes in plea negotiations, such that a different category of offenders were falling into these cells under the different guidelines. We do not think this is likely, since we looked at offenders for whom there was very little room to negotiate. Rather, we think two other alternatives are more likely. One possibility is that more serious offenders were negotiating pleas down to the less serious offenses we are studying here. We do not believe this occurred to a great extent, because the guidelines reduced sentencing discretion considerably for these more serious offender cells, and we think that this would have reduced prosecutors' motivation to charge bargain. An alternative explanation is that the declines represent individuals who might have negotiated pleas into these cells in the pre-1994 guideline era, but were unable to get the prosecutor to negotiate pleas down to these less serious cells after the 1994 guideline changes.

Regardless of the reason, it is important to ensure that we are comparing similarly situated offenders. In Table 9.4, we provide three models for offenders in the lower guideline cells, with Model 1 being a simple logistic regression comparing sentences under the 1994 guidelines and sentences under the pre-1994 (1991–1993) guidelines, with sentences under the 1997 guidelines (1997–2000) as a reference category.[4] The data indicate that pre-1994 offenders were almost three times as likely to be incarcerated as the 1997-era offenders, indicating that the changes in the guidelines dramatically reduced incarceration for these offenders. Further, the 1994-era offenders were slightly more likely to be incarcerated than the 1997-era offenders (.05 increase in odds).

In Model 2, we add controls for gender, race, and age. These controls make little difference in the incarceration decisions between the three eras. Model 3 adds urban county location (Pittsburgh, minus Philadelphia; see endnote 5) to the equation, and reveals that each of these factors seems to play an important role in the incarceration decision. However, these factors do not change the risk of incarceration found in Model 1 across the time periods.

Overall, it is clear that the guidelines changed sentencing patterns and diminished incarceration for the least serious offenders. These are offenders for whom most guideline systems do not prescribe sentences, because they involve local resources that are hard to consider in a statewide guideline system. In Pennsylvania, county jails are of course administered and largely funded by individual counties, as are probation systems. This means that from the view of focal concerns, local resources are a particularly important pragmatic issue because of jail costs and resource constraints.

The guideline changes of the 1990s seem to have reduced the use of incarceration and narrowed the dispersion of sentences. PCS-sponsored training of court community personnel in the guideline changes certainly played a significant role in implementing the changes, as we suggested when discussing the dramatic decline in use of incarceration in cells 1/0 and 2/0 in 1994. We can explore this further by examining sentencing changes for mid-level offenders.

Guideline Changes for Mid-Level Offenders: Promoting the Use of RIP

This phase of the analysis is considerably more complex than the previous analyses. First, the guideline reforms in 1994 and 1997 made changes to the OGS categorization of drug amounts for offenses involving delivery, and possession with intent to deliver, as well as to the measure of prior record. These

Table 9.4 Likelihood of Incarceration in Lower Guideline Cells

	Model One			Model Two			Model Three		
	b	Standard Error	Odds	b	Standard Error	Odds	b	Standard Error	Odds
Constant	-2.819	0.028***	0.060	-1.720	0.044***	0.179	-1.585	0.044***	0.205
1991–1993[a]	1.032	0.019***	2.807	1.030	0.019***	2.801	1.028	0.019***	2.795
1994 era[a]	0.041	0.022	1.042	0.048	0.022*	1.049	0.049	0.022*	1.051
OGS	0.316	0.009***	1.372	0.320	0.01***	1.378	0.342	0.01***	1.408
PRS	0.498	0.009***	1.645	0.509	0.01***	1.664	0.530	0.01***	1.698
Gender				-0.452	0.017***	0.636	-0.467	0.017***	0.627
Race				-0.170	0.016***	0.844	0.057	0.017**	1.058
Age at DOS				-0.012	0.001***	0.988	-0.011	0.001***	0.989
Urban							-0.761	0.014**	0.467

Notes: a. 1997–2000 cases are the reference category.
*p < .05; **p < .01; ***p < .001.

changes compromise our ability to ensure that we are comparing similar offenders during the three guideline phases. Second, in 1994 the commission established four levels in the guideline matrix wherein certain purposes of sentencing were set forth. In 1997 the commission expanded the four levels created in the 1994 guidelines to five. Level 3 (demarcated by the shaded area in Figure 3.1) primarily focused restricted intermediate punishment on offenders who historically received county jail sentences. In 1997 the commission created Level 4 to establish restricted intermediate punishment as a guideline option for offenders targeted for state imprisonment in the standard guidelines. The primary focus of these changes was to develop RIP sentences that would involve drug treatment for drug-dependent offenders. Level 5 was for the most serious offenders, for whom state incarceration was the prescribed sentence.

In coding the offenses and the guideline cells for this part of the analysis, we used the 1997 guidelines as the base and then coded the 1994 and 1991 guidelines to be as comparable as possible. We excluded offenders with prior record scores greater than 5 because the changes to the guideline prior record scores in 1994 and 1997 primarily focused on increasing the weighting of serious violent offenses so that they would quickly move such offenders to the newly created RFEL and REVOC categories. We therefore excluded these categories from the analysis to limit the impact of PRS changes on the evaluation.

We have created what we think are comparable groups across the three guideline eras. However, with the numerous changes that the commission made to the OGS categorization of types and amounts of drugs, this was not a simple process. The coding decisions were simplified since we decided that we wanted to focus only on those drug offenses that fell into Level 3 or Level 4 of the 1997 guidelines (the levels explicitly targeted to promote the use of RIP). We decided to use the 1997 guidelines as the base of comparison and then to develop as similar groups as possible in the 1991 and 1994 guidelines. For heroin this meant that we wanted to create drug-amount categories of 10 to less than 50 grams, 1 gram to less than 10 grams, and less than 1 gram. Level 3 and Level 4 cocaine offenses involved possession with the intent to deliver or delivery of drug amounts of less than 2.5 grams, 2.5 to less than 10 grams, and 10 to less than 50 grams. We confronted another problem with attempting to isolate cocaine offenses when we realized that the data would not allow us to distinguish between sentences for cocaine, PCP, and methamphetamine under the 1991 guidelines. Therefore we combined these drugs in our analyses. Traditionally, most of the violations among these offenses involve cocaine, so that we will generally refer to this category as cocaine.

We created drug amount categories for Level 3 and Level 4 offenders by first excluding from the analysis all heroin and cocaine convictions of 50 grams or more. This was done because such convictions result in guideline recommendations to Level 4 in the 1994 guidelines and Level 5 in the 1997 guidelines. These levels call for state imprisonment without the option of exchanging the incarceration for RIP. The rest of the drug-trafficking convictions for these drugs were categorized as Level 3 and Level 4 in the 1997 guidelines. The categories in the 1991 guidelines for heroin were less than 2 grams, 2 to 100 grams, and more than 100 grams. The same amount categories prevailed for cocaine, PCP, and methamphetamine. The challenge we confronted was how to code the categories for less than 2 grams and 2 to 100 grams in the 1991 guidelines into the three categories in the 1994 and 1997 guidelines. We decided to combine the 1997 guidelines' 1 to 10 and 10 to less than 50 grams categories to create a category as equivalent as possible to the 2 to 100 grams category in the 1991 guidelines. We thought this a reasonable categorization because historically, prosecutions are much more frequent in Pennsylvania for smaller drug amounts. That is, convictions and sentences for smaller drug amounts are much more numerous than those for larger amounts. We also assumed that the less than 2 grams category in 1991 was equivalent to the less than 1 gram category in 1994 and 1997.

For the 1994 categories, we had to assume that the best estimate of less than 1 gram of heroin was the 2.5 grams category, so the 2.5 to 50 grams category was the best equivalent to the 1 gram to 50 grams category for heroin. For cocaine, the 1994 and 1997 drug categories were the same. Although these are unfortunate grouping decisions, we felt that these decisions established the most equivalent categories possible given the data.

Level 3 Drug Trafficking Sentences

Table 9.5 reports on heroin offenders at Level 3, or for whom the guideline standard range provides for jail incarceration under the 1997 guidelines. Here we find that in the largest category of heroin amounts (1 gram to less than 50 grams), incarceration rose slightly, from 85.9 percent to 87.5 percent, under the 1994 guidelines, and then dropped back to 81.8 percent under the 1997 guidelines. When we distinguish between counties that received RIP funding from the Pennsylvania Commission on Crime and Delinquency, we find that funding did seem to slightly reduce reliance on incarceration under the 1997 guidelines. Funded counties dropped below an 80 percent incarceration rate, compared to 86 percent for unfunded counties. But overall, incarceration remained the dominant sentence, and neither the guideline changes nor funding made a significant dent in the reliance on incarceration.

However, heroin traffickers in the lowest category (less than 1 gram) show a dramatic decline in incarceration, from 84.0 percent to 55.2 percent, under the 1997 guidelines. While both funded and unfunded counties show declines in incarceration, the decline in funded counties is 38.6 percent, while for unfunded counties it is 25 percent. Changes in both the funded and unfunded counties are very significant. The separation of RIP-funded and RIP-unfunded counties provides some implications about the impact of funding versus the impact of the guidelines without funding. Obviously, both seem to be significant. Also important is the fact that these decreases in incarceration sentences

Table 9.5 Sentences for Level 3 Heroin Offenses over Time

	All Counties			Funded Counties			Unfunded Counties		
	1991	1994	1997	1991	1994	1997	1991	1994	1997
Heroin, 1–50 grams									
Incarceration	85.9	87.5	81.8	84.4	86.0	79.1	88.1	89.3	85.8
RIP	0.6	4.0	4.2	1.0	3.2	5.1	0.0	5.0	2.8
Probation	13.5	8.4	14.0	14.6	10.8	15.8	11.9	5.3	11.3
Heroin, < 1 gram									
Incarceration	84.0	59.8	55.2	78.9	52.0	48.4	93.8	92.8	70.1
RIP	3.0	11.3	20.3	4.0	13.4	25.8	1.0	1.3	14.7
Probation	13.0	29.0	24.5	17.1	34.6	25.8	5.2	6.7	15.3

were accompanied by an increase of 3.0 to 20.3 in RIP sentences. In funded counties, almost 26 percent of offenders were receiving RIP sentences under the 1997 guidelines. This is a tremendous shift from 4 percent under the 1991 guidelines.

We next turn to cocaine offenders at Level 3. Table 9.6 reports our findings for the three categories of drug amounts. For the 10 to less than 50 grams category of cocaine, incarceration dropped from 91.2 percent to 86.5 percent, with most of the drop coming for the 1994 guideline sentences. Incarceration rates were not substantially affected by whether the county was RIP-funded or not. It should be noted that although the drop in incarceration was relatively minor, what drop did occur resulted primarily from the increase in RIP sentences, particularly in the funded counties. It should also be noted that we do not find RIP sentences replacing probation, so that there does not appear to be a "widening of the net" in using RIP sentences for offenders previously given probation.

Next we focus on a comparison of sentences for cocaine trafficking in amounts between 2.5 and 10 grams. For Level 3 offenders, incarceration sentences decreased 5.0 percent under the 1994 guidelines. Then, following RIP funding from the Pennsylvania Commission on Crime and Delinquency for twelve counties, incarceration decreased another 6.0 percent, to a level of 80.5 percent under the 1997 guidelines.[5] The impact of the movement to RIP for these offenders is illustrated by the increase in RIP sentencing in 1994 of 3.6 percent, and then a more dramatic 5.3 percent increase in RIP sentences under 1997 guideline sentences.

Separating out the RIP-funded versus RIP-unfunded counties provides dramatic illustration of the impact of funding. Funded counties increased the percentage of cases that resulted in RIP by 3.8 percent under the 1994 guidelines, but when funding was in place under the 1997 guidelines, another 10.5 percent of offenders received RIP. On the other hand, the counties without funding decreased their reliance on incarceration, and did so partly by increases in RIP sentences and partly by increases in probation sentences. In fact, the unfunded counties showed a very similar increase to the funded counties under the 1994 guidelines, but when funding was disbursed, the unfunded counties showed only a slight increase in RIP sentences under the 1997 guidelines.

There are two observations to keep in mind here. First, the decreases in incarceration appear to be accounted for by increases in the use of RIP. Second, while the guidelines are an important policy-setting vehicle, it is the combined effect of the policy along with the RIP funding stimulus provided by the Pennsylvania Commission on Crime and Delinquency, beginning in 1997, that created the dramatic impact on sentencing.

For trafficking in small amounts of cocaine, less than 2.5 grams, we find that incarceration declined from 79.5 percent under the 1991 guidelines to 72.3 percent under the 1994 guidelines, and then to 71.8 percent under the 1997

Table 9.6 Sentences for Level 3 Cocaine Offenses over Time

	All Counties			Funded Counties			Unfunded Counties		
	1991	1994	1997	1991	1994	1997	1991	1994	1997
Cocaine, 10– < 50 Grams									
Incarceration	91.2	87.1	86.5	90.6	86.5	84.6	92.4	87.5	87.8
RIP	0.9	4.3	5.3	0.9	4.7	6.9	0.9	4.1	4.2
Probation	7.8	8.5	8.1	8.5	8.8	8.5	6.7	8.4	7.9
Cocaine, 2.5–10 grams									
Incarceration	91.5	86.5	80.5	90.9	85.4	76.3	92.3	87.3	83.0
RIP	0.9	4.5	9.8	1.0	4.8	15.3	0.9	4.3	6.5
Probation	7.6	9.0	9.7	8.1	9.9	8.4	6.7	8.4	10.5
Cocaine, < 2.5 grams									
Incarceration	79.5	72.3	71.8	73.8	68.4	61.9	90.2	75.0	75.0
RIP	4.0	8.7	11.8	5.0	8.8	13.2	0.02	8.6	11.4
Probation	16.5	19.0	16.4	21.2	22.8	24.9	7.8	16.4	13.7

guidelines. This represents a 9.6 percent decrease in the use of incarceration for trafficking in cocaine under 2.5 grams. Simultaneously, RIP sentences increased from 4.0 percent to 11.8 percent, with probation sentences staying almost static. Comparing RIP-funded and RIP-unfunded counties, we find that funded counties started with lower levels of incarceration, but that both funded and unfunded counties decreased their use of incarceration for these offenders in a similar manner, and both increased their use of RIP sentences.

Level 4 Drug Trafficking Sentences

For Level 4 cocaine and heroin dealers, we could not identify a good comparison sample for sentences under the 1994 guidelines, so we limited our comparison to sentences under the 1991 guidelines with sentences under the 1997 guidelines. Tables 9.7 and 9.8 report our findings for these offenders, who are targeted for state incarceration under the guidelines but for whom there is the opportunity to provide RIP alternatives.

Table 9.7   Sentences for Level 4 Heroin Offenses over Time

	All Counties		Funded Counties		Unfunded Counties	
	1991	1997	1991	1997	1991	1997
Heroin, 1–50 grams (2–100 grams under 1991 guidelines)						
Incarceration	97.1	91.0	95.7	89.7	100	93.1
RIP	0.0	4.0	—	5.4	0.0	1.7
Probation	2.9	5.0	4.3	4.9	0.0	5.2
Heroin, < 1 gram						
Incarceration	90.4	79.8	88.5	73.6	94.3	88.2
RIP	.8	13.7	.7	20.1	1.1	5.2
Probation	8.8	6.4	10.8	6.3	4.6	6.6

Table 9.8   Sentences for Level 4 Cocaine Offenses over Time

	All Counties		Funded Counties		Unfunded Counties	
	1991	1997	1991	1997	1991	1997
Cocaine, 2.5–50 grams						
Incarceration	96.1	91.4	96.3	90.0	95.6	92.6
RIP	.5	4.8	.5	6.3	.4	3.4
Probation	3.4	3.8	3.2	3.7	4.0	3.9
Cocaine, < 2.5 grams						
Incarceration	92.1	82.4	96.6	75.4	95.6	87.2
RIP	1.9	11.4	2.4	18.8	.6	6.3
Probation	6.0	6.3	6.9	5.8	3.8	6.5

In Table 9.7, where we report changes in use of incarceration for heroin sentences, we find only a small decline in use of incarceration for trafficking in 1 gram to 50 grams, from 97.1 percent to 91.0 percent. Table 9.8 reports Level 4 sentences for cocaine trafficking and reveals that those trafficking in the larger category, 2.5 to 50 grams, showed only a small drop in incarceration, from 96.1 percent to 91.4 percent. RIP sentences did not change substantially, and controlling for county funding shows that while funded counties clearly used RIP sentence more frequently, such sentences are not a major sentencing option. The dominant sentence for those trafficking in 2.5 to 50 grams of heroin is incarceration. Consequently, the provisions created in the 1997 guidelines to allow courts the opportunity to use RIP sentences as alternatives to state imprisonment for mid-level drug traffickers did not substantially divert mid-level heroin offenders from state imprisonment.

Much more dramatic shifts in sentencing for Level 4 offenders occurred for the offenders trafficking in the lowest category of heroin and cocaine. For heroine traffickers (Table 9.7) of less than 1 gram, incarceration sentences declined from 90.4 percent to 79.8 percent. This reduction was accompanied by an increase in RIP sentences from .8 percent to 13.7 percent. For trafficking in small amounts of cocaine (Table 9.8), very similar changes occurred. Incarceration sentences decreased from 92.1 percent to 82.4 percent (10.5 percent overall). Both decreases in incarceration are almost totally explained by increases in RIP sentences, with only minor shifts from probation to RIP sentences. Further, the funded counties had an increase of almost 20 percent in RIP sentences, whereas the unfunded counties showed only a 4.1 percent increase.

Discussion

We started this chapter with the question of whether changes in sentencing guidelines changed sentencing practices. We focused on three types of policy changes: (1) increasing sentence severity for serious violent offenses, (2) narrowing guideline ranges and setting presumptive nonconfinement sentences for the least serious offenders, and (3) establishing structured sentencing alternatives in the form of RIP sentences for mid-level drug offenders. In all three areas we found significant changes, although within each we found important nuances.

Less Serious Offenders

There are two key reasons that we thought guidelines would not have significant impact on sentences for offenders represented in the lowest tier of the sentencing guideline matrix. First, the PCS has historically avoided restrictive guidelines for these offenders, because of the peculiar nuances of local justice resources and the fact that the costs are borne by the county. In many respects, this is an accommodation of local county interests and autonomy. Second, because these offenses often represent the most frequently occurring crimes (such as retail theft, simple possession of small drug amounts, etc.), we expected counties to have developed strong informal "going rates" that would be highly resistant to change. Third, from an enforcement perspective, these less serious offenders receive relatively minor sanctions and therefore the threat of appeal of the sentence is a weak enforcement mechanism.

Despite what we viewed as considerable resistance to change, the findings indicate that, in fact, changes in the guidelines in the 1990s resulted in considerable reduction in the use of incarceration for relatively minor offenders. The guidelines systematically reduced the proportion of offenders who were incarcerated according to the eight cells that in 1994 were changed from allowing incarceration to setting presumptive nonconfinement. Even reversing this change for several cells in 1997 did not return sentencing patterns to their pre-1994 levels. When including basic controls for offense, offender, and county size, the basic findings were maintained.

The first issue is why the guideline changes had such a sizable impact on sentences we viewed as highly resistant to change. We think this resulted from several important processes that the commission engaged in to develop commitment to the guideline changes. First, it conducted a survey of judges, district attorneys, probation officers, and defense attorneys. This was a way to indicate that change was coming, and to ask for these groups' input. Second, the commission expanded the role of judges by augmenting its four-judge membership with what was called a "rural county advisory committee." This was created in response to judicial appointments to the commission who were typically from the metropolitan areas of Pittsburgh and Philadelphia, and in response to complaints from smaller-county judges that their voices were not being heard on the commission. Third, the commission met with the various constituencies to solicit their input. Finally, the commission conducted major training across the state on the guideline changes.

One interesting finding that may give us a hint about why the impact was so significant comes from a particular outcome. Nested in our overall findings was the fact that the setting of presumptive nonconfinement for matrix cells 1/0 and 2/0 in 1991, in response to Act 319 of 1978, had little impact on sentencing practices. The data presented in this chapter indicate that there were relatively high incarceration rates under the 1991-era guidelines, despite the changes in 1991 to set presumptive nonincarceration sentences for these cells. Yet, with basically no change in these cells under the 1994 guidelines, we found major resultant drops in incarceration rates. The only difference between the two time periods was that the commission worked with those in the field in developing commitment to the changes as noted above, and trained the courts in terms of the guideline changes. We suggest that this decrease in incarceration supports the importance of these outreach processes in changing behavior patterns.

Overall Changes

Another indicator of the subtleties of implementing changes in the guidelines was found in the sentencing response of courts to the implementation of RIP sentences. While the guidelines were changed to encourage these sentences in 1994, we found that additional incarceration decreases occurred when funding was made available to counties to expand RIP sentences in 1997. In some cases, it seemed that the funding was the major stimulus for greater use of RIP sentences.

What do these subtleties suggest about the successful implementation of changes in sentencing guidelines? First, they suggest that comprehensive training and communication are important in the implementation process. Second, the interorganizational commitment of agencies in support of the policy change enhances the impact. As described in Chapter 3, the cooperation that was integral to the development and implementation of the changes in the guidelines began in the late 1980s, when the General Assembly developed legislation supporting intermediate punishment (eventually passed in 1990). This provided major credibility and stimulus to the changes. The commission also worked with the District Attorneys Association, the Department of Corrections, and the Pennsylvania Commission on Crime and Delinquency. The eventual funding through the Pennsylvania Commission on Crime and Delinquency was targeted to reduce the state's reliance on incarceration and replace this with a stronger emphasis on effective treatment, particularly drug treatment. The active support of the politically powerful District Attorneys Association was particularly important, since without it, the guideline changes would probably have been impossible.

We also emphasize the courts as a filter for the policy changes. For example, the fact that minimal shifts from incarceration to RIP sentences occurred for mid-level drug traffickers indicates the discretion of local courts in assessing the appropriateness of RIP sentences and targeting those offenders whom they defined as deserving or most amenable to treatment. Clearly, most local courts typically deemed mid-level heroin and cocaine traffickers unsuitable for RIP sentences. In view of the fact that the RIP sentences were targeted at drug-dependent offenders, the data may reflect that these offenders were traffickers, but were not selling drugs as a means to support their use of drugs. The policy-filtering role of local courts was also supported by the shifts in sentencing for the least serious offenders, for whom the courts generally sentenced in conformity with the guidelines, but also used their discretion to depart from them.

These findings suggest that sentencing guidelines can be a means to reduce reliance on incarceration and to shift the use of limited local and state facilities. As we move into the twenty-first century, with prison populations in the United States at all-time highs, Pennsylvania's development and implementation of sentencing policy illustrates how coordinated efforts can change who goes to prison and for how long.

Notes

We acknowledge Carrie Williamson's contribution as coauthor of an earlier version of this chapter.

1. Due to changes in data collection for sentences reported to the commission in 1995, this dataset is not used in this analysis, because it does not contain the detailed information on sentencing normally collected and needed for our analysis.

2. The analysis does not include offenders sentenced under any mandatory minimum provisions, in order to isolate the impact of the guidelines from the application of mandatory minimums.

3. If serious bodily injury does not result from the attempt, solicitation, or conspiracy to commit murder, then the statutory maximum is set at twenty years.

4. For this analysis we omitted Philadelphia County, because many of the less serious offenses falling into these lower guideline cells are sentenced not in common pleas courts as they are in the rest of the state, but in Philadelphia's municipal court, and these courts do not submit guideline sentencing forms to the PCS. Data on less serious offenses from Philadelphia are therefore typically either missing or of questionable validity.

5. Funding was provided to twelve counties in 1997 to support RIP drug treatment sentences.

10

Lessons from Pennsylvania's Struggle for Justice

THE LITERATURE ON sentencing guidelines, and sentencing reform in general, is necessarily a mixture of ideology and empirical evaluation. The Pennsylvania Commission on Sentencing has received mixed evaluations on both scores. As we discussed in Chapter 2, it was criticized early in its history, by Susan Martin (1983), for failing to write guidelines that stayed within prison population constraints, failing to tightly restrict the judiciary, and failing to politically sell the guidelines. Martin's criticisms reflected her judgments about the use of imprisonment, the political environment at the time, and political purposes within which the commission was created and functioned. Such criticisms also reflected differing assessments of the sentencing guideline recommendations, and value of the simple versus complex guidelines. As chronicled in Chapters 2 and 3, the PCS valued relatively simple and "user-friendly" guidelines that explicitly gave courts and localities a meaningful amount of discretion; since then the PCS has evolved the guidelines to embrace somewhat more complexity and more specific sentence recommendations. In part, Martin's criticisms missed some of the political difficulties. It was clear that the Pennsylvania legislature was concerned more about sentence severity (as evidenced by the proposed mandatory minimums at the time) than prison populations or sentencing disparity, as reflected in the commission's mandate and membership.

By contrast, when the US Sentencing Commission released its complex set of guidelines, containing what are widely viewed as excessively harsh penalties and tight appellate constraints on judges, they were harshly criticized. The critical reaction to the US Sentencing Guidelines perhaps chilled and slowed the sentencing guideline movement, because the US guidelines represented a model to which states were highly resistant. Yet the US guidelines illustrate an important reality about structuring sentencing discretion. If the goal is to develop highly presumptive guidelines that severely restrict judicial discretion, then the guidelines must consider as accurately as possible almost all factors that need to be considered at sentencing. As Barry Ruback (1998) pointed out, the federal robbery guidelines result in 18,579,456 possible sentencing combinations. The key point made by Ruback is that they are excessively complex, and that this complexity results in resistance and a lack of understanding.

Pennsylvania's guidelines represent a compromise between the complexity of attempting to delineate and control each important ingredient to be considered at sentencing versus what it viewed as overly simple guideline models developed in Minnesota and Washington early on. In 1994 and 1997, the PCS evolved somewhat more complex guidelines, with presumptive nonconfinement and narrower ranges. Further, the PCS incorporated an exchange model of sanctions such that intermediate sanctions were incorporated into the matrix, and explicitly established that the more restrictive of these intermediate penalties were to be used as an equivalent to incarceration.

Another key evolution of Pennsylvania's guidelines in 1994 and 1997 was the PCS's articulation of explicit sentencing purposes attached to its five guideline levels. In effect, these purposes and levels were the commission's explicit codification of its views about key focal concerns of punishment: moral blameworthiness, community protection, and practical constraints and consequences. The guidelines expressed the commission's view that its guiding principles should vary from restorative sanctions for the least serious offenders to incapacitation and retribution for the most serious offenders. Restrictive intermediate punishment was viewed as a rehabilitative alternative to retributive punishment prescribed under the guidelines, alternatives that would in turn protect the community by hopefully reducing recidivism, and that would address key practical constraints like limited prison and jail capacity. These innovations reflect an important part of the evolution of the PCS in its study and development of guidelines.

So, have the PCS and its guidelines been a "success"? There are numerous possible indicators of the success of sentencing commissions and their guidelines. One underrated measure is *survival*. A sentencing commission potentially faces opposition and hostility from groups such as judges, prosecutors, defense bars, parole boards, corrections departments, critical legislators, and other public interest groups, and also challenges from alternative sentencing structures like mandatory minimums (including three-strikes laws). For a commission to be able to survive all this opposition and then be able to write guidelines and have them adopted is no small achievement. Although there are numerous examples of failed sentencing commissions—such as in Massachusetts, where sentencing guidelines were never adopted; in New York, where the sentencing commission was simply abolished (see Griset 1994, 1995); and in Wisconsin and Tennessee, where sentencing guidelines were adopted but commissions to monitor and revise guidelines were abolished—most sentencing commissions and their guidelines have survived (see Bureau of Justice Assistance 1996). The PCS has succeeded in this sense where others have failed. Still, survival seems too low a threshold to declare the PCS successful.

Another indicator is the ability of the commission to be an *active participant* in sentencing and to be called upon by the legislature, not only through the guideline process but in other ways as well. While we cannot speak to the success of other commissions in this regard, the PCS has seen strong growth in its budget over the past two and a half decades. It has become an important agency in the state (in 1984 it was specifically identified as an "agency of the General Assembly"). Its data and analysis provide important feedback in the consideration of legislation, and often the commission is an important shaper of legislation, such as the intermediate punishment legislation in 1990. As the 1990s offered an opportunity to reverse some of the reliance on incarceration, the PCS played a key role as a vehicle to set standards for the use of intermediate punishment programs, and was instrumental in marshaling funding for those programs. The commission worked with the Department of Corrections, the District Attorneys Association, and the Pennsylvania Commission on Crime and Delinquency to obtain, in 1997, more than $7 million for drug and alcohol treatment as part of its diversion of offenders from county and state incarceration. This support increased to $17.9 million in the 2007–2008 budget. The PCS was called upon to identify individuals eligible for boot camp in its guidelines, and its mandate now also includes the ongoing evaluation of the effectiveness of the boot camp.

As mentioned in Chapter 3, legislation is pending, with broad support, that will give the commission the responsibility to write parole and re-parole guidelines. This bill will also expand the commission's research responsibilities to include collecting and disseminating information regarding effectiveness of parole dispositions. Further, the legislation will provide ex officio positions on the commission for the secretary of corrections and the chair of the Pennsylvania Board of Probation and Parole. One interesting side component of the legislation is a slight move to encourage the consideration of correctional resources in the adoption of parole guidelines. The legislation states that the guidelines shall "provide for prioritization of incarceration, rehabilitation and other criminal justice resources for offenders posing the greatest risk to public safety" (HB 4:4).

The PCS has played a significant role in assessing the impact of potential sentencing legislation, and has used such data repeatedly in its many testimonies before the General Assembly. On the other hand, an indicator of the weakness of the commission vis-à-vis other interests is the passage of mandatory minimums for drug trafficking, gun, and three-strikes" offenses. The commission failed to stave off such legislation. It did, however, work with other agencies and the legislature in narrowing the scope of that legislation (the three-strikes legislation in particular).[1] One interesting side note regarding Pennsylvania's sentencing guidelines is the fact that their development was not guided by mandatory minimums. Whereas the US Sentencing Commission determined that the federal sentencing guidelines needed to be consistent with mandatory minimums, such as those for crack and powder cocaine, the PCS developed its own guidelines independent of and generally more lenient than the mandatory minimums.

Another indicator of success is the ability to adapt to changing conditions and evolve, and to continue to make significant changes in the guidelines that cause important changes in sentencing patterns. On this score, the commission's record has been mixed. As shown in Chapter 9, its 1994 and 1997 guideline changes have been accompanied by significant changes in sentencing patterns, particularly the increased use of intermediate punishment. Furthermore, as shown in Chapter 5, racial and ethnic disparity has been reduced over time, though it still persists. On the other hand, state and county prison populations rose dramatically throughout the 1990s, despite significant diversion of offenders from incarceration to restorative sanction, intermediate punishment, and restrictive intermediate punishment. The guidelines were not able to avoid major overcrowding in Pennsylvania's prisons—such a task was simply beyond their control.

As discussed in Chapter 4, the effectiveness of sentencing guidelines is often measured in terms of the extent of conformity. However, this is an inexact assessment of effectiveness, since prosecutors are able to manipulate the offense of conviction and thus the offense gravity score, the prior record score, or even the application of the deadly weapon enhancement. Furthermore, the guidelines themselves (as well as the mandatory minimums) lend themselves well to sentence bargaining, a point earlier made by Jeffery Ulmer (1997). These realities generally reduce, if not eliminate, the need to depart from the guidelines. Logically, the more the guidelines are "managed" by prosecutors in negotiating pleas, the lower the departures.

So, departures may reflect the inability of the guidelines to control sentencing. On the other hand, departures might also reflect the simple reality that guidelines can't always accurately classify like and unlike offenders and offenses. It is the local court's responsibility to consider the guidelines and then determine the appropriate penalty. As we found in Chapter 4, if relatively broad categories of offense severity and prior record classify dissimilar offenders as similar, then departures are the vehicle for correcting this problem. Of course, such discretion may well reinstate the disparity that the guidelines were intended to reduce or eliminate. And we do find gender and racial/ethnic disparity in the departure decisions.

Earlier literature from the court community perspective (Eisenstein, Flemming, and Nardulli 1988) suggested that, in fact, guidelines were likely to make little difference in sentencing, because the "going rates" that have traditionally evolved in courts will conflict with guidelines, and will remain the local sentencing benchmarks. However, with the passage of time it is likely that the going rates themselves will shift, as they have, with turnover in members of the judiciary and in prosecutors and as guidelines become the going rates (a process described in Ulmer 1997 and Ulmer and Kramer 1998). This is hinted at by the extent of the changes that occurred in sentences before and after the 1994 guideline changes. It is equally clear that there were localities where the judges resisted the guideline changes of the 1990s. Whether this resistance reflects a conflict with past local going rates or just resistance to the particular concept of diverting offenders from state prison to RIP is not clear.

Given the history of Pennsylvania's sentencing guidelines, what empirical and policy lessons can be learned from their impact? The preceding empirical chapters each provided detailed discussions of particular dimensions of guideline sentencing: departures, disparity, local variation, trial penalties and plea rewards, mandatory minimums as an alternative "competitor" sentencing structure to guidelines, and then the impact of guidelines on overall state sentencing patterns. Below, we summarize what seem to be key overarching empirical themes that recur through the analytical chapters.

Empirical Lessons

Six Theoretical Propositions: How Have They Fared?

Our empirical analyses of sentencing under Pennsylvania's guidelines have been guided by an integrated focal concerns and court community perspective, described in Chapter 1 and elaborated in various other chapters. In particular, Chapter 1 laid out six theoretical propositions that together sketch a generic model of sentencing and its embeddedness in local contexts. How have these propositions fared in our analyses?

> *Proposition 1: Sentencing severity and decision criteria (even guideline-based), use of guidelines, and compliance and departure from guidelines are all likely to vary among local court communities.*

This proposition is supported throughout our analyses. We found that departures varied by county (a finding elaborated even further in Johnson 2005). We also found significant between-county variation in sentencing severity along a variety of dimensions (departures, incarceration, type of incarceration, length, imposition of mandatory minimums). Additionally, key predictors, including guideline-based predictors, varied significantly between courts in their effect on various sentencing decisions. We also found that implementation of the RIP initiative varied between counties—with some counties embracing these initiatives more than others.

> *Proposition 2: Sentencing decisions are joint acts (often reflecting the influence of prosecutors and defense attorneys as well as judges) made on*

the basis of decisionmakers' definitions of blameworthiness, community protection needs, and practical constraints and consequences.

Definitive support for this proposition would have to come in the form of qualitative interview and observational data on sentencing decision processes. However, the qualitative data from interviews with judges about their departure decisions in Chapter 4 are consistent with this proposition, as are our quantitative findings. We have also certainly uncovered evidence that sentencing is usually a joint decision, typically involving the heavy influence of prosecutors, as we argued in Chapters 4, 7, and 8 in particular.

Proposition 3: Definitions of blameworthiness and dangerousness are mostly determined by formal legal and policy structures such as guidelines, but are also potentially determined by local decisionmakers' substantively rational interests, attitudes, stereotypes, and biases.

Again, we don't have a great deal of direct qualitative, processual evidence to demonstrate this proposition definitively, but our data are certainly consistent with it. Guideline factors that represent formal rational criteria for sentencing are always the prime determinants of sentencing outcomes. However, organizational and extralegal factors matter as well. That these extra-guideline factors significantly influence sentencing alongside the guideline factors suggests a discretionary process whereby local actors make punishment decisions partly based on guidelines and partly based on their own, or their court community's, locally defined substantively rational criteria. For example, this process potentially allows stereotypes and biases that are linked to particular social statuses to influence the assessment of focal concerns and, in turn, sentencing decisions (see Bridges and Steen 1998; Steen, Engen, and Gainey 2005).

Proposition 4: The influence of defendant social status characteristics (race, ethnicity, gender, age, class, etc.) on sentencing outcomes is likely to be conditional. The influence of status characteristics on sentencing likely depends on a defendant's specific combination of status characteristics.

Evidence for this claim is found in Chapters 4, 5, and 8. Most notably, gender strongly and clearly conditions the role of race and ethnicity. Minority men tend to be treated more harshly, and minority women (as well as white women) more leniently. To a lesser extent, age also contextualizes race/ethnicity effects. Furthermore, the influences of race and ethnicity are sometimes conditional on mode of conviction and vice versa. Finally, race and ethnic effects vary significantly by county, and seem to be linked to court contextual characteristics like size and county minority composition in complex ways. Overall, however, we find substantial support for the notion that the effects of social status characteristics on sentencing outcomes are contingent upon one another, and are also mutually interrelated with mode of conviction and court contexts.

> *Proposition 5: The interpretation and prioritization of the focal concerns is influenced by the local culture, politics, organization, and resources of court communities, controlling for the influence of guidelines. This is especially true of practical constraints and consequences.*

Our several investigations of between-county variation in sentencing strongly suggest support for this proposition, though we cannot provide more direct support without processual data on actual participants' interpretations and interactions. However, three sets of facts suggest that the assessment of focal concerns, and in turn guideline sentencing, is contextually embedded: (1) that sentencing varies so much between counties, (2) that several contextual characteristics we examined produce distinct and meaningful differences in a variety of sentencing outcomes, and (3) that the effects of case- and offender-level predictors vary between counties, sometimes in interaction with contextual features. In particular, practical constraints seem to often loom large in local considerations, specifically caseloads (which exerts direct effects on several sentencing outcomes though not interaction effects with mode of conviction) and jail space.

> *Proposition 6: The less that a guideline system restricts sentencing-stage discretion, the more that local interpretations of focal concerns can influence sentencing, and the greater the potential for disparity.*

As mentioned in Chapter 1, Pennsylvania presents a particularly instructive context in which to study guideline sentencing, because its guidelines throw into bold relief the universal dilemma of sentencing: the dilemma between the goal of uniformity and logically formal-rational rules, and the goal of individualized justice, which necessitates local discretion and substantively rational considerations (see Savelsberg 1992; Ulmer and Kramer 1996). We have argued that the Pennsylvania context is advantageous theoretically in that the tensions and negotiations between logically formal rationality and substantive rationality in sentencing are particularly pronounced.

Pennsylvania chose far less restrictive guidelines than those in the federal model, and arguably those in the Minnesota model. This additionally allowed discretion to tailor individual sentences to specific offenders and situations as local courts and actors see fit also allows greater potential for residual disparity. And in fact, we do find meaningful extralegal disparity of various types. Interestingly, we find that disparity is less under the later, more restrictive 1997 guidelines than under the earlier, less restrictive guidelines of the 1980s and early 1990s. To fully test this sixth proposition, one would need to compare the amounts of extralegal disparity existing under more and less restrictive guideline systems. Future research should undertake this.

Three Empirical Themes

The analyses in Chapters 4–9 present many detailed and complex findings. Yet it seems that three empirical themes have recurred throughout: social status disparity, trial penalties and plea rewards, and local variation. We recommend these themes as issues that the sentencing guideline movement (and sentencing reform more broadly) should wrestle with. One of these themes, disparity, is a long-standing one that has been on the agenda since guidelines were conceived. We believe insufficient attention has been paid to the other two, and suggest that they occupy a more prominent place in discussions about guideline sentencing.

Social status disparity. The problem of unwarranted disparity based on race/ethnicity, gender, age, or socioeconomic status has been one of the key concerns behind the development of sentencing guidelines since their beginnings in the 1970s. Unwarranted racial and ethnic disparity (that is, disparity that remains after legally prescribed factors have been accounted for) is widely seen as especially pernicious. Such disparity cuts to the very heart of US notions of equality before the law.

We have no definitive evidence for this claim, but our impression is that racial and ethnic disparity in sentencing is not a central focus of sentencing policy initiatives and discussions the way it once was. This seems true in Pennsylvania as well. Legislative discussions about sentencing policy and PCS-sponsored research and reports have focused more on issues like the effectiveness of boot camp, the implementation and effectiveness of RIP programs, the desire to increase sentence severity for violent offenses, and the predictive value of prior record. These are all worthwhile and understandable goals, especially given the PCS's need to accommodate changing legislative and gubernatorial agendas. We are not suggesting that Pennsylvania's policymakers are unconcerned about disparity. We do think, however, that findings like those presented in this book warrant renewed focus and discussion of disparity, especially as it involves race and ethnicity.

Disparity remains important because the legitimacy of the criminal justice system is at stake, especially in the eyes of minorities. The perception that criminal justice institutions are biased against certain minority groups erodes those groups' trust in, and increases their alienation from, courts and government. Public surveys show that blacks in particular have consistently less favorable attitudes toward and less confidence in police, courts, and criminal justice in general; these attitudes are partially fed by perceptions of pervasive anti-black bias, particularly against males (Tyler and Huo 2002). Though not to the same extent, Hispanic groups also tend to have more negative views of criminal justice institutions than whites, and perceptions of anti-Hispanic bias are common (Carr, Napolitano, and Keating 2007).

Tom Tyler and Y. J. Huo's research (2002) focuses on how people from a variety of ethnic groups view the law in relation to their personal experiences with the criminal justice system. They find that the degree to which people feel that they (and others) have been treated fairly shapes their acceptance of and trust in the legal process. They show that minority group members (especially African Americans) who feel that they have been treated unfairly are significantly less willing to trust subsequent legal decisions or the motives of criminal justice authorities. Tyler and Huo argue that criminal justice authorities can obtain greater legitimacy and compliance by encouraging judgments that legal procedures are fair and authorities' motives are benevolent. They maintain that treating people with fairness, dignity, and respect heightens both of these judgments.

In this light, the fact that we find various examples of disparity among minority males, even after controlling for the guideline-relevant factors, offense types, and other relevant individual and contextual predictors, seems particularly disconcerting. True, such disparities are often moderate in size, and are secondary to legally relevant factors and mode of conviction, but they are still evident. This raises two questions that we invite readers to answer for themselves (see also Steen, Engen, and Gainey 2005). First, how believable is it that the status-based sentencing differences we presented (with controls) have nothing to do with the status-linked stereotypes about focal concerns? Second, how likely is it that the disparities we have found, even though they are inferior in predictive power to guideline-relevant factors, offense types, and mode of conviction, could be rendered spurious if we had more information about factors such as evidence strength, unmeasured qualitative distinctions between crimes and their circumstances, unmeasured characteristics of prior criminal records, or unmeasured victim characteristics? These are all examples of factors identified in Chapter 4 as underlying many departure decisions for serious violent offenders. Recall, however, that factors such as victim vulnerability and harm, and other circumstantial factors related to legal culpability, are often incorporated into the OGS classification, as are some distinctions about the severity of prior convictions. Obviously, we cannot definitively answer these questions with the data that we have.

We also recognize that the racial and ethnic differences we found could be conflated with socioeconomic status or employment, variables for which we have no data. We would not be surprised if this were the case. However, future research using more extensive offender data than provided by the PCS files will have to answer this question. In general, we agree with Marjorie Zatz (2000) that the role of social class–related variables in producing sentencing disparity is understudied.

We have found that social status disparity is complex and conditional, and that it crops up in various windows of discretion—departures, the prison versus jail distinction, trial penalties, and prosecutors' decisions to apply mandatory minimums. It is also noteworthy that Pennsylvania's guidelines seem to have reduced racial and ethnic disparities, and that the 1997 guidelines were more restrictive than those promulgated in the 1980s. It would be tempting to conclude that more restrictive guidelines might be the answer to the remaining disparities that exist. Yet further restricting discretion does not seem to be the best answer because, as Joachim Savelsberg (1992) and many others have argued, sharply restricting discretion in the name of formal rationality can cause as many problems as it solves. In fact, the single biggest criticism of the US Sentencing Guidelines of the pre-*Booker/Fanfan* era was that they went too far in restricting judicial discretion, and removed a degree of flexibility seen as necessary for avoiding inappropriate sentences in idiosyncratic cases.

Perhaps one solution lies in sentencing guidelines' and sentencing commissions' unique ability to render sentencing disparity visible, a point suggested by Savelsberg (1992). Here we return to our comments above about the centrality of reducing unwarranted disparity to the guidelines' mission. What if sentencing commissions were to periodically publish disparity statistics, or perhaps commission independent researchers to do so? What if sentencing commissions were to take the lead in fostering greater understanding of the complex roles of race, ethnicity, and gender in conditioning disparity as a part of their regular guideline training for judges, and what if such training were extended to prosecutors?[2] What if judges and prosecutors were to be given periodic summaries of their own sentencing and case-processing data, broken down by race, ethnicity, and gender? With the 1998 release of sentencing information by judge, the PCS is now in a position to conduct such an analysis.[3]

These might seem like relatively weak solutions, but recent research in the psychology of racial bias suggests that they might work. Psychologists have found that most people do not think of themselves as racially or ethnically prejudiced, and do not approve of such prejudice. However, an intriguing body of experimental evidence shows that racial stereotypes operate to a great extent at a subconscious level, out of individuals' routine awareness (Harris 2007). People are capable of making decisions and acting on the basis of racial/ethnic stereotypes and biases without intending to do so, and without being aware of it (Devine 2001). However, when people are alerted to the issue of bias (for example, seeing a video or hearing a brief presentation about it), this tends to bring stereotypes and biases into awareness and people (at least those who do not overtly espouse racist beliefs) typically become more careful not to discriminate (Sommers and Ellsworth 2000, 2001). In other words, the very act of making racial bias visible, even in general terms, tends to reduce it in practice. Thus, it is when racial/ethnic bias is hidden and out of awareness that it may seep into sentencing. Making it visible may be a particularly effective, and relatively untried, means of reducing it. In discussing race and policing, David Harris describes the value of research on racial bias this way:

> For the many social scientists and others who study and work with police departments, the utility of research on issues in which race and policing intersect seems obvious. But to police, this research, and the increase in public scrutiny that occasionally comes with it, does not always seem a service to the profession. But the fact is that much of what actually matters in terms of race and the way human beings think is largely hidden in the unconscious. . . . Only making these hidden racial biases salient can help us to combat their influence. Work on racial bias or race and policing helps us to do this, by forcing the institutions of policing to come to grips with these possibilities; the institutions, in turn, can help individual officers to confront these hidden biases as well. (2007, p. 21)

While Harris's comments are directed at bias in policing, we would strongly echo them for courts and sentencing as well. We believe that the same sentiments apply.

Race and ethnicity are unambiguously unwarranted influences on sentencing. Gender is less so. Throughout our analyses, gender is the most consistently influential social status factor. Women are less likely to be incarcerated, especially in state prison, and are more likely to receive shorter sentences. They are more likely to receive downward departures, and less likely to receive upward departures. Furthermore, the influence of gender is relatively uniform across localities. We found no evidence that contextual features condition the effects of gender.

The gender differences in sentencing are strong, consistent, and durable across time, a finding backed by other research as well. For example, Barbara Koons-Witt (2002) and Timothy Griffin and John Wooldredge (2006) found that gender differences persisted both before and after sentencing reforms in Minnesota and Ohio, respectively (see also Curry, Lee, and Rodriguez 2004 for a good review of recent research and theory on gender and sentencing). However, another question to be raised is, are all gender differences in sentencing unwarranted? On the one hand, gender is an ascribed social status that has no inherent connection to "just deserts" or, in our terms, perceived blameworthiness. Advocates of guidelines from early on have included gender among the proscribed influences on sentencing, along with race/ethnicity and social class. On the other hand, criminal justice practitioners often articulate some thought-provoking arguments about why women "score" differently on the focal concerns of sentencing, and claim that these arguments are based on their personal experience with female versus male offenders. For example, based on anecdotal evidence we have gathered over the years through interviewing and observing in court settings (see also Steffensmeier, Kramer, and Streifel 1993), judges, prosecutors, probation officers, and even defense attorneys often argue that women offenders are typically less likely to be violent. They observe that women are often involved in crime (especially drug trafficking) in connection with men (often abusive and coercive men), and tend to play more minor roles in such crime. These factors lower the perceived blameworthiness of many women offenders. They also believe women to be more amenable to rehabilitation and less likely to recidivate. Finally, judges and others often express concern about the "collateral damage" that incarceration (especially lengthy state prison sentences) might have on the children of offenders who are single mothers.

Research and theory on gender and crime also paint different portraits of male versus female crime and criminality (Steffensmeier and Allan 2000). For example, the anecdotal perceptions of court community actors noted above have some basis in reality: (1) most serious and violent crime is committed by men, (2) women typically have restricted criminal opportunities compared to men, (3) women are typically subjected to stronger informal social controls and have stronger conventional social bonds than men (especially young men), (4) women property and drug offenders frequently have male co-offenders and play subordinate roles, and (4) women are typically less likely to recidivate than men (see Steffensmeier and Allan 2000; Giordano, Cernkovich, and Rudolph 2002).

Thus we would encourage more explicit reconsideration of the appropriate and inappropriate relationships between gender and sentencing based on our findings as well as on those of other studies (see Koons-Witt 2002). Ultimately, decisionmakers will assess offenders in terms of focal concerns. Given well-known gender differences in crime and criminality, some of these assessments are likely to vary with gender. What seems more problematic is the use of gender as a stereotypical cue for attributing focal concerns–relevant offender characteristics.

Trial penalties and plea rewards. Our findings regarding trial penalties and their variation have important implications for sentencing guidelines and legal ethics. The US legal system guarantees every criminal defendant the right to a jury trial, yet in all our analyses we find that defendants are substantially penalized if they exercise this right and then lose. Furthermore, our findings seem to point to bona fide trial penalties in the form of additional punishment for trial defendants, and not only differential leniency for those who plead guilty (though that appears to occur as well). In addition, trials are associated with strongly decreased odds of downward departures, and increased odds of upward departures. Furthermore, this jury trial penalty is not evenly assessed, but depends on the seriousness and type of offense, the offender's prior record, several court contextual characteristics, and more troubling for the spirit of the guidelines, sometimes race. Such realities may seem inconsistent with the US notion of "equal justice under law."

Are guilty plea versus trial sentencing differences unwarranted disparity? It seems that US procedural law would frown on the free and unfettered exercise of the right to jury trial, and would encourage sentencing to be based on factors that can be proven at trial, a position strengthened by the recent *Blakely v. Washington* and *United States v. Booker/Fanfan* decisions. An absolutist perspective would regard plea bargaining and plea versus trial sentencing differences as ipso facto unconstitutional, because they might have a chilling effect on exercising the right to trial, and nothing that chills this exercise can be constitutional. From this position, any evidence of "trial penalties"—that is, of those who go to trial receiving longer sentences than those who plead guilty—provides grounds for sharp criticism and redress. By this logic, it follows that it is inappropriate for sentencing guidelines to facilitate or allow such sentence differentials.

However, the US Supreme Court has long upheld the concept of plea bargaining. We can identify a "pragmatic" position, which holds that there are legitimate grounds for differences in the sentences of those who plead guilty versus those who go to trial and lose. These reasons seen as legitimate would include rewarding cooperation with law enforcement, rewarding a defendant's taking responsibility for his or her actions or expressing remorse, and punishing convicted defendants who presented false cases at trial. It can also be argued that rewarding guilty pleas is necessary and rational for courts and prosecutors (Smith 1986). Pragmatists about the right to trial would even object to the term "trial penalty," because in their view, trial defendants are not necessarily penalized illegitimately merely for going to trial. In fact, recall from Chapter 2 that the PCS early on proposed to specify cooperation with law enforcement and other guilty plea–related factors as explicit reasons for mitigating sentences, and some commissioners wanted to go even further in encouraging guilty pleas.

This pragmatic position seems to hold sway in contemporary criminal justice, and current case law as well as the federal sentencing guidelines deem certain reasons for plea versus trial sentencing differences acceptable. For example, the federal guidelines allow a 2–3 offense-level discount for "acceptance of responsibility" and "extraordinary acceptance of responsibility." The federal guidelines also famously allow for downward departures based on "substantial assistance to law enforcement." While in principle neither of these sentencing discounts is inherently connected to pleading guilty, US Sentencing Commission data show that in practice they occur very rarely in connection with trial cases. They function as de facto plea rewards (Ulmer 2005).

These de facto plea rewards in the federal system do imply one conceptual model for structuring plea rewards and trial penalties, and perhaps parsing out warranted and unwarranted plea versus trial disparity. Perhaps sentencing commissions could codify and structure certain sentencing discounts or mitigation factors for particular reasons deemed appropriate, such as concrete, demonstrable statements and acts displaying remorse, offender-initiated efforts at rehabilitation (such as voluntarily participating in drug or alcohol treatment even before sentencing), or offender-initiated restorative efforts to victims. Some would also view assisting law enforcement as a defensible reason for a miti- gated sentence. These efforts would be along the lines of what the initial Penn- sylvania guidelines tried to do.

There might also be aggravating sentencing factors spelled out for things like presenting false or misleading evidence at trial, as with the "obstruction of justice" sentence enhancement in the federal guidelines. On the other hand, many legal ethicists would agree that simply giving defendants more severe punishment because they refused to plea bargain and went to trial and lost, in the spirit of the old courthouse saying "He takes some of my time, I'll take some of his" (Uhlman and Walker 1980), is inappropriate. By specifying ap- propriate and inappropriate grounds for plea versus trial sentencing differ- ences, guidelines might reduce the extent of such blatant trial penalties.

Finally, we believe our trial penalty analyses points the way to an under- researched role of emotion in a vital social institution—courts—and in their punishment decisions. As Lawrence Sherman recently stated, the study of criminal justice should better understand the role of emotion, and "emotional 'hot spots' of criminal justice activity could be mapped and studied, including arrests, high speed chases, *sentencing decisions,* [and] the first day's release from prison" (2003, p. 26, emphasis added). Certainly, many scholars have discussed the role of emotion, especially fear, in communities and collective discourse about crime and punishment (e.g., Reiman 1995). However, very lit- tle explicit attention has been given to the potential role of emotion in actual criminal punishment decisions, such as sentencing.

The focal concerns perspective has not explicitly addressed the role of emotion in sentencing, but such a role is quite compatible with it, and is ar- guably implicit within the notion of focal concerns. That is, types of cases and defendants could mobilize negative emotional responses among sentencing decisionmakers, and this could color the assessment of defendants and appro- priate punishments with relation to focal concerns, especially perceived blameworthiness or perceived dangerousness and community protection. The criminal justice process exemplifies the formalized process of constructing and judging moral character, and constructing and assessing levels of criminal threat to the community. This process requires both the *rational-legal work* of establishing guilt (whether the defendant's actions caused the accused harm to the victim) and the *emotion work* (Hochschild 1979, 1983) of establishing moral blameworthiness (feelings that the offender is morally culpable and de- serves punishment) or dangerousness to the community (fear of the offender).

Those interested in sentencing reform should address such realities, and should have a conversation about whether plea versus trial sentencing dispar- ities are warranted or unwarranted in principle. If they are found to be war- ranted, then care should be taken to prevent trial penalties from becoming win- dows of extralegal disparity.

Local variation. What can or should sentencing guidelines do about it? Our empirical analyses show that local variation clearly permeates most aspects of sentencing. Just as trial penalties are locally variable, so too are the effects of other important variables, such as offense type and severity, prior record, gender, and race and ethnicity. Sociologically, this supports the notion that law and other distal structures are very often mediated by and become embedded in local culture, organizations, and interests (Ulmer 1997; Blumer 1990; Hall and McGinty 1997). This means that what kind of sentence one receives, and why one receives it, in part depend on where one is sentenced. This would seem to undermine the principle of equal justice valued in most modern legal systems.

However, some might argue that principles of democracy, local autonomy, and decentralized government mandate the ability of local jurisdictions to fashion punishments as they see fit, at least within broader legal parameters. Thus it seems that criminal punishment presents a situation in which key principles of US democracy foster unequal treatment before the law.

Local variation, and local court autonomy, always loomed as a large, if not always explicitly stated, concern in the politics of Pennsylvania's guidelines (Martin 1983). Judges and prosecutors in many counties, particularly smaller ones, resisted the notion of statewide uniformity in sentencing. In fact, many argued that the only reason for adopting sentencing guidelines and mandatory minimums in the first place was to address problems with sentencing in Philadelphia. They feared that, for example, sentencing in small, rural, socially conservative counties would be dictated by sentencing norms designed for large, metropolitan counties seen as more tolerant of crime and vice. In fact, as mentioned, the PCS appointed an advisory board of rural county judges in the early 1990s as an attempt to better address these concerns, and to combat the perception that the guidelines were being developed with only Philadelphia and Pittsburgh in mind. The PCS was mindful of the balance between allowing for the autonomy of local courts to sentence in accord with local concerns, norms, and constraints, but also the desire to provide meaningful boundaries on such sentencing autonomy.

Should the court community of Clinton County, a small, rural, low-crime, Republican county, be made to sentence the same way as the court community of Philadelphia, a metropolitan, relatively high-crime, Democratic county, or vice versa? That is a legitimate question for those in the trenches of local courts to ask, and it resists pat answers. Local counties and their courts have different politics, cultures, resource constraints, organizational infrastructures, interorganizational relations, and perceived needs. This reality has been at the heart of the court community perspective since it was articulated by James Eisenstein, Peter Nardulli, and Roy Flemming in the 1980s. It strikes us as a mistake to unthinkingly categorize all local variation in sentencing as unwarranted disparity. Further, with judges and district attorneys placed in office through county-based elections, their commitment to the local political culture is compelling.

Yet here again is the formal versus substantive rationality dilemma. The opportunity to tailor guidelines to or embed them in local "contours of justice" (Eisenstein, Flemming, and Nardulli 1988) is also the opportunity for unwarranted and invidious local differences to creep in. Most would agree that local jail space is a defensible influence on certain sentencing decisions, for example, but what about minority composition? We did not find a great deal of unambiguous support for racial threat arguments about minority composition and sentencing, but allowing latitude for local variation in sentencing does open up this empirical possibility. And what about other factors that we have found to influence sentencing severity or to condition sentencing criteria, such as caseloads, court size, and trial rates? Are these defensible local constraints that should legitimately be allowed to shape local court practices? Or are they factors that should have nothing to do with the ultimately moral decision of what punishment is appropriate for an individual and his or her crime? And how would a sentencing commission go about allowing localities to adapt their sentencing practices to some local considerations, but discourage them from allowing others to influence sentencing? Perhaps as a start, commissions could at least explicitly state their positions about what are and what are not appropriate boundaries for local variation, if any, as a philosophical matter. Ultimately, these are legal and ethical questions that sentencing commissions, other policymakers, and the public must answer. We merely wish to draw attention to them, and to argue that the criminal justice community has not sufficiently grappled with them.

Future research should extend and refine our analysis with more and better measures of organizational and jurisdictional contexts. For example, more direct measures of court organizational culture, such as measures of predominant case processing and sentencing norms from surveys or interviews, would advance our understanding of the role of organizational culture in punishment decisions. Also, future studies should improve on our measure of local political context. Our county percent Republican measure could be replaced by more refined and specific survey measures of local publics' and decisionmakers' attitudes on a variety of criminal justice policy concerns. Furthermore, future studies should attempt to replicate our finding that blacks and Hispanics receive longer sentences in places with larger black and Hispanic populations. Such research should also investigate whether there is a "tipping point" for black and Hispanic populations, at which these contextual features might dampen rather than aggravate racial or ethnic sentencing disparities (a point suggested in Britt 2000, p. 711). In addition, our study was limited to a three-year time period, 1997–1999. Future studies should investigate the kind of historical variation in the effects of defendant social statuses and contextual factors on sentencing noted by Ruth Peterson and John Hagan (1984).

Final Thoughts

The sentencing reform movement was in reality many movements, and Pennsylvania's history as part of this process subjected it to considerable criticism (Martin 1983; Tonry 1996). However, short-term assessments of social movements, such as sentencing reform, may miss important long-term effects. The PCS was established with some difficult hurdles to overcome. The initial conflict between the legislature and the judiciary that spawned mandatory sentencing proposals in the 1970s eventually gave birth to the commission, but with costs. The commission did not have corrections-official representation, nor did it have a mandate to consider correctional capacity. Further, many supporters did not endorse guidelines, as they wanted to either reduce judicial discretion or protect it. Finally, the enforcement of guidelines rests with the appellate courts, and while the Superior Court early on did strongly enforce the guidelines and attempted to build a common law of sentencing, the Supreme Court in *Devers* curtailed that development in 1988.

These hurdles were serious impediments, but what we can learn from the Pennsylvania experience is that information, credibility, and persistence are important factors in an agency creating legitimacy and ultimately having an impact. While having legislative members on the commission might cause some political problems, as politicians might tend to focus on the political liability of their decisions on a sentencing commission, the fact that PCS had legislative members gave it entrée to the legislative process. Importantly, this meant that it had access to proposed legislation *before* it became a public issue. This often enabled the commission to stay ahead of coming developments, and allowed it to deflect or at least blunt the impact of sentencing initiatives that it opposed. A key example of this was the PCS's role in scaling back three-strikes legislation, as described above and in Chapter 3.

Finally and most importantly, the PCS built its credibility on information and science. It developed a monitoring system that made it *the* source of information when sentencing legislation was proposed. This brought commission staff to the forefront of many deliberations regarding sentencing proposals. These data also made for natural linkages with the corrections department, the state criminal justice planning agency, and the governor's policy office. These alliances became central to the evolution of the credibility of the commission as a major criminal justice agency in the state. This is underscored by the linkage of intermediate punishment with the PCS and its guidelines, the PCS's ongoing role in evaluating the state's boot camp, and the current state legislature's consideration of a significant expansion of the commission's mandate and membership. If these changes occur, Pennsylvania's sentencing commission might well have the broadest mandate and scope of influence over criminal punishment of any sentencing commission in the United States.

The guidelines have been in effect for more than two decades. If their role changes as dramatically in the next two decades as it did in the first two, it will be an interesting adventure to observe. The Pennsylvania Commission on Sentencing has persisted in the struggle for justice, and emerged as a predominant presence in Pennsylvania sentencing.

Notes

1. When three-strikes legislation was first proposed in the mid-1990s, the District Attorneys Association asked for help in assessing its impact, because it viewed the legislation as being on a "fast track" to passage. After public hearings and a coordinated effort among the district attorneys, the PCS, and the Department of Corrections, it took two and a half years for the bill to finally pass. In the amendment process, the bill's impact was reduced to the extent that there are now very few offenders sentenced under its provisions.

2. In 2004, at the summer meetings of trial judges, Kramer gave a major presentation on the impact of race and ethnicity on sentencing in Pennsylvania. The president of the Trial Judges Association at that time had adopted the issue of race and sentencing as the major theme of his administration.

3. The data for 2001–2005 are not yet publicly available, but will be in the near future, providing opportunity for such analysis.

Research Methods
Appendix

Chapter 4: Sentencing Serious Violent Offenders

As predictors of guideline departures, we use a combination of legally pre-scribed, case-processing, offender-related, and county contextual factors that have been important explanatory or control variables in prior research (see Zatz 2000; Spohn 2000). The quantitative data presented in this chapter en-compass all of the selected serious violent offenses reported to the PCS for years 1997–1999 and sentenced under the revised 1997 guidelines.

We restricted our selection of serious violent offenses to those identified by the state legislature in Pennsylvania's three-strikes act: third-degree murder and attempted murder, aggravated assault with serious bodily injury or at-tempted serious bodily injury, rape and involuntary deviant sexual intercourse, robbery with serious bodily injury or threatened serious bodily injury, and bur-glary of an occupied home. Although burglary is not usually considered a vi-olent offense, the Pennsylvania legislature and the Pennsylvania Commission on Sentencing defined burglary of an occupied home as a violent crime be-cause of the high potential for violence. Guideline severity rankings of these offenses (inchoate offenses are included) range from 8 to 14. Consistent with previous research, we simultaneously include offense severity and offense type in our models.[1]

Criminal history is measured by prior record score as defined in the 1997 guidelines, the details of which are discussed in Chapter 3. We also control for whether a mandatory minimum was applied. We include the application of mandatory minimums because doing so controls for situations in which judges' discretion to depart below guidelines is restricted by the application of a mandatory minimum by the prosecutor (there is no "safety valve" provision in Pennsylvania law). It is thus possible that application of a mandatory minimum would mandate a sentence in the aggravated range, or even an upward depar-ture. Second, while the minimums in the Pennsylvania sentencing guidelines are commonly less than applicable mandatory minimums, it is theoretically possible in rare cases for the mandatory minimum to be less than the guideline minimum (if, for example, certain guideline enhancements apply, or if the offender is a repeat violent felon). This latter scenario seemed to be an important situation to control for in our analyses. Incidentally, this is why the probability of a downward departure associated with applying a mandatory minimum is not zero in our analyses.

Offender characteristics included in the quantitative analysis are defendant's age, gender, and race and ethnicity (white, black, and Hispanic). The case-processing variable included in our analysis is type of conviction, differentiated as jury trial, bench trial, nonnegotiated plea,[2] and negotiated plea. To examine intercounty variation, we examine dummy variables for court size, and individual county dummy variables. Unfortunately, we lack data on several variables potentially relevant to substantively rational considerations, such as defendants' social class, education, marital status, employment status, pretrial release status, and type of defense counsel (see Zatz 2000). We also note, however, that these are general limitations of many sentencing datasets. Unfortunately, we also lack data on the characteristics of victims (such as race), or of the victim-offender relationship. It is entirely likely that these factors affect downward departures, but we cannot assess their influence.

Interview Data

We initially intended to interview both judges and prosecutors for the sampled cases. However, limited resources required that we choose between, on the one hand, sampling fewer cases and interviewing both the prosecutor and the judge for each case, or on the other hand, sampling more cases and interviewing only the judge. While it is not ideal, we chose the latter strategy for several reasons. First, under Pennsylvania's guidelines, judges retain considerable sentencing discretion and organizational power (Cirillo 1986; Del Sole 1993; Ulmer 1997). Sentencing decisions, especially decisions to depart from the guidelines, are formally the sole responsibility of judges. Judges are also not obligated to accept plea agreements and are not obligated to follow prosecutors' sentencing recommendations (although they usually do). Furthermore, judges are legally obligated to state the reasons for any departure sentence in the case record. Therefore, since we were interested in discovering the reasons and case circumstances surrounding specific departure decisions, we determined that the judge would be the court actor centrally responsible for and knowledgeable about these decisions. This is true even though, as we describe later, judges routinely do accept plea agreements for downward departures. Second, attempting to interview prosecutors would also not have been feasible, because there were often as many different prosecutors as there were cases before a particular judge. For example, three different prosecutors handled four departure cases sentenced by one judge in a large urban county. In addition, we were cautioned by court administrative personnel that attempting to locate the prosecutors would be very time consuming, because some would have moved on to other jobs.

The interviews focused on case circumstances, sentencing decision criteria, reasons for the downward departures, and how the present case contrasted with similar cases that did not result in departures. We identified forty-two judges in ten counties (varying in size from large metropolitan to medium-sized urban to small rural) for our judge sample, and we interviewed thirty-six of these judges (the others were unavailable). This represents 83 percent of the forty-two judges targeted for interviews, and these interviews covered 109 of the 134 cases in our subsample.

In contacting judges for interviews, we began by calling the judge and then, when he or she agreed to be interviewed, we faxed a copy of the name of the defendant and the docket number so that they could check their records in preparation for the interview. In fact, in most interviews, the judges had pulled the files for the cases, and had extensive notes that they had made at sentencing. Although we were concerned that providing the judges the cases ahead of time might give them an opportunity to "create" reasons to rationalize their departures, we saw this as less of a problem than asking judges to try to remember cases that they sentenced many months earlier without preparation.

Chapter 5: Racial, Ethnic, Gender, and Age Disparity

In this chapter, we analyze the dichotomous dependent variables using HLM logistic regression models, and our continuous dependent variable, logged sentence length, using HLM linear and logistic regression. We estimate fixed effects logistic and linear models in HLM, with no county-level predictors, in order to control for between-county variation in the dependent variables, and in predictors' effects. We return to the analysis of between-county variation and various contextual effects, and cross-level interaction effects, in several later chapters.

We checked the robustness of our findings by estimating a variety of model specifications, and a variety of modeling techniques. Since the early 1980s (see Berk 1983; Peterson and Hagan 1984), it has become typical for sentencing length analyses to include a Heckman (or modified Heckman) two-step correction for selection bias stemming from the incarceration decision, a procedure also recommended by Steven Klepper, Daniel Nagin, and Luke-John Tierney (1983). Modeling sentence length among incarcerated offenders resembles an analysis of a truncated sample, and of the potential for selection bias (Winship and Mare 1992). Selection bias is endemic to research on criminal justice decisionmaking (Klepper, Nagin, and Tierney 1983; Zatz and Hagan 1985; Bushway, Johnson, and Slocum 2007), and there is no foolproof, definitive way to deal with it (Stolzenberg and Relles 1997). The Heckman correction itself has been criticized as being very sensitive to violations of its assumptions and to high degrees of correlation between the predictors in the selection equation and those in the selected equation (Winship and Mare 1992; Stolzenberg and Relles 1997; Bushway, Johnson, and Slocum 2007).[3] On the other hand, Ross Stolzenberg and Daniel Relles (1997) argue that (1) empirical results do not support the wholesale abandonment of the Heckman correction, (2) the Heckman correction performs relatively well in cases where the potential for selection bias is severe, and (3) the Heckman correction tends to worsen estimation compared to uncorrected results when the potential for selection bias is slight or moderate. In any case, we assessed the sentence length findings by including and not including a Heckman two-step correction (performed in Stata 9) for selection bias stemming from the incarceration decision. The correction made little substantive difference to the findings of interest here.

Some researchers use tobit analysis to analyze both sentence length and incarceration decisions together, effectively treating them as a single dependent variable of sentencing severity (e.g., Bushway and Piehl 2001; Albonetti 1998). We do not do so here, for three reasons. First, tobit analysis cannot be accommodated in HLM. Second, it is open to debate whether the incarceration and length decisions are made concurrently, as tobit assumes, rather than consecutively. Third, prior research on Pennsylvania sentencing has shown that the incarceration and length decisions differ, sometimes considerably, in the degree to which extralegal variables affect them (e.g., Ulmer 1997; Steffensmeier and Demuth 2001). It is possible to decompose tobit effects into separate components for incarceration and length (see Albonetti 1998, for example), but such a process is computationally cumbersome.

Nonetheless, we replicated the analyses below using tobit regression (in Stata 9) with robust standard errors clustered by county, treating incarceration and length as one overall "sentencing severity" variable (with the nonincarceration cases measured as having zero incarceration length). The results were congruent with what we report in the chapter. The model specifications we report are the ones we view to be the best sets of predictors to include, in order to avoid multicollinearity or problematic variable distributions.

The distribution of sentence length is somewhat skewed, suggesting that it might be appropriate to log this dependent variable. Since sentence length is logged, the antilog of the regression coefficients allows a proportional interpretation. For example, if the antilog of a coefficient for a continuous variable predictor is 1.10, this means that a one-unit increase in this predictor is associated with a 10 percent increase in sentence length. If a dummy variable predictor had the same antilog coefficient, it would mean that membership in this category (e.g., race, trial conviction) is associated with a 10 percent increase in sentence length.

In supplemental analyses for Chapter 5, we also controlled for whether a mandatory minimum sentence was applied. Those results did not differ substantially from the results reported here, and the effects of race, ethnicity, and gender did not differ at all. We chose not to control for whether a mandatory minimum was applied, because it is beyond the scope of this book to differentiate between the effects of mandatory minimum legislation versus court sentencing discretion on racial, ethnic, or gender disparity in sentencing.

Here and in subsequent chapters, we included dummy variables for whether race, ethnicity, gender, and mode of conviction were missing or not in our models. This allowed us to retain in our models cases that were missing data for these variables, and to control for whether these cases were systematically different in their sentencing outcomes (they were not—their effects were not statistically significant). These three dummy variables for missing data are included in the models, but are not shown, for table clarity. As an alternative to this dummy variable procedure, we estimated HLM models without these three missing-data dummy variables, but with HLM 6's full information maximum likelihood estimation (MLE) option.[4] Thus, MLE makes maximal use of the information available in the data. However, the results did not differ meaningfully from those we report here.

Chapter 6: Location Matters: Variation Between Counties

Sentencing can be broken down into a two-stage decisionmaking process (Wheeler, Weisburd, and Bode 1982): (1) the decision about whether or not to incarcerate (and what type of incarceration), and (2) if incarceration is selected, the decision about its length. We did not replicate this chapter's analyses (as opposed to those in Chapter 5 and 7) using tobit regression, because our discussions of county jail space specify relationships between such space and incarceration but not sentence length, requiring us to separately model these two outcomes. Our coding of incarceration, its type, and length (which is logged due to skewness) follows that of previous chapters.

Like in the previous chapter, we also estimated our sentence length models with and without a Heckman selection bias correction factor for the risk of not being selected into the incarcerated population (see Berk 1983; Peterson and Hagan 1984). Because our results do not differ substantially with and without the Heckman correction factor, and because of concerns about this correction introducing more bias rather than reducing it (see our discussion in this appendix material regarding Chapter 5, above), we present the uncorrected results here. Likewise, the coding of our individual-level independent variables also remains the same as in the previous chapter.

Court and County Contextual Measures

The characteristics that we include for Pennsylvania's sixty-seven counties in our analysis are court size, caseload, caseload composition, trial rate, available incarceration capacity of each county, percent black, percent Hispanic, and percent Republican voters. Following Jeffery Ulmer (1997), we trichotomized our measure of court size into large courts, medium courts, and small courts based on both the number of trial judges in the county and the proportion of cases adjudicated in each county. Our measure of court caseload was created by dividing the number of total criminal cases in a county by the number of sentencing judges (this dividend was subsequently divided by 100 for ease of interpretability). It therefore serves as an indicator of the relative caseload of judges in each county. We measured trial rate as the percentage of cases convicted through jury trial in each county. We elected to analyze the effect that jury trial rate exerted at the aggregate level. This was done because prior research suggests that bench trials are used differently across counties, sometimes being akin to nonnegotiated pleas (see Ulmer 1997). We present an extended treatment of the effects of bench and jury trials on sentencing in Chapters 7 and 8, as well as in Chapter 5.

As an indicator of county political context, percent Republican is measured as the percentage of the county population who voted for the Republican candidate in the 2000 presidential election. We also included a relative measure of the available jail space in each county. This variable was calculated as the total number of jail beds in each county divided by the number of cases in that county. The higher the ratio of jail beds to cases, the higher the relative jail capacity. For our racial threat hypotheses, percent black and percent Hispanic represent the percentages of the county population that were identified as black or Hispanic, respectively, in 2000. Finally, we included measures of the amount of crime in the counties, since previous aggregate-level research suggests that these may affect sentencing, and are thus important control variables for our purposes (e.g., Sutton 2000; Britt 2000; Bridges and Crutchfield 1988; Myers and Talarico 1987). The index crime rate measures the overall level of crime in each county. In supplementary models, we included county poverty rates (measured as the percentage of individuals in a given county living below the poverty level) as a contextual predictor of sentencing outcomes. Since it never significantly predicted our outcomes of interest, we omit it from our presentation below. We also tested models examining the county-level unemployment rate to examine additional macroeconomic contextual effects on sentencing outcomes. These results are not reported here because they were generally similar to our poverty findings, and because multicollinearity problems precluded the simultaneous inclusion of both unemployment and poverty in our models.

Hierarchical Modeling

Hierarchical linear modeling is desirable because of the multilevel nested nature of our sentencing data and our research questions. A two-level hierarchical structure characterizes our data, with offenders nested within different county-level courts. HLM techniques provide several advantages over traditional analytical strategies such as ordinary least squares. HLM allows for the partition of variance within and between counties, which allows the researcher to evaluate the amount of variation that exists at each level of analysis. Given that criminal cases are nested within county-level courts, similarities among cases at the county level are likely to occur. Statistically, this means that residual errors tend to be correlated within counties, violating the OLS assumption of independent error terms and risking the misestimation of standard errors. HLM overcomes this difficulty "by incorporating into the statistical model a unique random effect for each organizational [i.e. county level] equation" (Bryk and Raudenbush 1992, p. 84). Moreover, whereas OLS regression inappropriately bases statistical significance for contextual variables on the number of individual cases, HLM adjusts the degrees of freedom to correctly represent the number of level-two units. HLM also allows one to overcome the aggregation bias that can occur when a variable takes on different meanings at different levels of analysis (e.g., the mean rate of trials exerts an effect above and beyond the individual-level trial effect). And finally, HLM allows one to model heterogeneity of regression coefficients. For example, the effect of being a minority offender may vary across counties. HLM allows the researcher to model this variation by estimating a separate set of regression coefficients for each county-level unit. The researcher can then assess the degree of variation that exists among these key individual-level factors (e.g., race, gender, mode of conviction), before attempting to explain this variation using county-level covariates (e.g., court size, caseload pressure, percent minority). Overall, then, HLM allows one to more precisely estimate regression coefficients, while simultaneously modeling separate but interrelated units of analysis—individual case and offender characteristics (i.e., level one) that are nested within (and potentially interact with) particular county-level court contexts (i.e., level two).

In examining both the judicial decision regarding whether or not to incarcerate and also the decision regarding sentence length, we employ hierarchical logistic regression models (for the dichotomous in/out incarceration decision), hierarchical multinomial regression models (for the county jail versus state prison analysis), and hierarchical linear regression models (for the continuous sentence length decision).[5] Models were estimated in HLM 6 (statistical details on statistical estimation procedures for the kinds of hierarchical models we estimate here are found in Raudenbush et al. 2004 and in Ulmer and Johnson 2004).

Here and in later chapters using HLM, we grand mean center our predictors' effects. Grand mean centering risks the introduction of estimation bias in the individual-level effect, because this coefficient is a weighted combination of the between- and within-county effects. While group mean centering provides an unbiased estimator for the individual-level effect (Bryk and Raudenbush

1992, pp. 117–121; Britt 2000), it artificially constrains county-level compositional differences, thereby complicating assessment of sentencing variation across counties. Given the present focus on these county-level differences, we elected to grand mean center our variables. Supplemental analyses demonstrated that this research strategy did not significantly alter our findings or conclusions regarding the impact of any of our individual-level sentencing factors.

Not surprisingly, some of our county-level predictors were correlated with one another. In preliminary models, we investigated the potential effects of multicollinearity in two ways. First, we utilized factor analytic procedures to reduce collinearity among our level-two predictors. Although this is a potentially useful technique, we decided that the resulting sacrifice of theoretical and conceptual clarity was not justified. We therefore elected to retain separate level-two variables in our analyses. To ensure that our findings were not the result of idiosyncratic relationships among our level-two predictors, we examined several reduced models of contextual effects, limiting our predictors to those that were relatively unrelated. Given our investigation of these alternative model specifications, we are confident that our results are robust across model specifications, despite the presence of collinearity among some of our county-level variables. Moreover, the HLM program we utilize gives the user an error warning if severe collinearity is detected. This did not occur in any of our models.

Random Effect Results

The following table shows the results for the random effects for a hierarchical logistic model of overall incarceration (since random effects could not be computed for the multinomial model jail and prison incarceration) and the hierarchical linear model of sentence length presented in Table 6.2. These values are the data on which Figures 6.1 and 6.2 are based.

Variable	Variance Component		Standard Deviation	
OGS	Incarceration: .02	length: .01	Incarceration: .14	length: .08
PRS	Incarceration: .03	length: .005	Incarceration: .17	length: .07
Presumptive disposition	Incarceration: .27	length:	Incarceration: .52	length:
Guideline minimum	Incarceration:	length: .0001	Incarceration:	length: .01
Negotiated plea	Incarceration: .21	length: .03	Incarceration: .46	length: 17
Bench trial	Incarceration: NS	length: .02	Incarceration: NS	length: .16
Jury trial	Incarceration: .18	length: .03	Incarceration: .42	length: .17
Black	Incarceration: .04	length: .0015	Incarceration: .20	length: .04
Hispanic	Incarceration: .09	length: .02	Incarceration: .31	length: .15

Note: NS = not significant.

Chapter 7: Guilty Pleas vs. Trial Convictions: Unwarranted Disparity?

Dependent Variables

As in previous chapters, we logged the sentence length for two reasons. First, the distribution of sentence lengths is quite skewed, and logging the dependent variable is a commonly used technique for addressing this kind of violation of OLS assumptions (Hanushek and Jackson 1977). Second and more important for this chapter's analyses, the offenses in our sample differ in the lengths of sentences that are *possible* for courts to give, since they each have different sentencing guidelines and statutory maximums. This means that the offenses differ in the absolute size of effects that trial conviction could possibly have. In other words, a bigger trial penalty in terms of *absolute size* is possible for third-degree homicide than for robbery, because the statutorily defined maximum sentence (as well as the guideline recommendation) is higher for third-degree homicide. Logging the sentence length (and interpreting the antilog of predictors' coefficients) therefore allows us to examine the proportional rather than absolute differences in sentence lengths associated with our variables of interest, and thus allows us to avoid findings that are merely an artifact of differences between offenses in the sentences that are legally possible.

Independent Variables

We employ several of the same individual- and contextual-level predictors as in previous chapters. The key variable of interest in our analysis is mode of conviction, or whether the defendant was convicted by guilty plea, bench trial (trial by judge), or jury trial. We measure mode of conviction with two dummy variables, coded 1 if the offender was convicted through a bench trial or a jury trial, and coded 0 if the offender pled guilty. Another key variable of interest is court caseload. We measure this as the mean of the annual number of cases processed by a given court from 1997 to 2000. Other contextual variables include court size, county violent crime rates for 1998 (for the analysis of serious violent crimes) and overall crime rates (for the analysis of less serious offenses), percent black, percent Republican, local jail space, and the proportion of cases in a county in which offenders were convicted by jury trial (the jury trial rate). We estimated models by substituting overall trial rates (including bench trials) for jury trial rates. Results were not meaningfully different.

Analytical Techniques

As in Chapter 6, we used hierarchical logistic regression for incarceration decisions, hierarchical multinomial regression for county jail or state prison (versus no incarceration), and hierarchical linear regression for logged sentence length (for similar applications, see Ulmer and Johnson 2004; Wooldredge and

Thistlethwaite 2004; Kautt 2002; Britt 2000). Unless otherwise noted, statistical tests are based on robust standard errors. We did estimate tobit models, which included our level-one predictors (in Stata 9), and the level-one effects in these models did not differ substantially from those we present here. Before estimating our main models, we estimated unconditional models for incarceration and logged length. These showed modest but significant intercounty variation in both dependent variables, indicating that HLM was appropriate.

In addition, we estimated both fixed effect models and random effect models that allowed our key predictors, namely the jury trial effects and hypothesized level-one interactions, to vary randomly between counties. In Chapter 6, we saw that many predictors' effects, including trial, displayed significant random variation between counties. Our random effect models for the serious violent offense models show that trial effects do not display significant random effects. Therefore, we rely on the fixed effect models for our analyses of serious violent offense cases, and display random effects for our analysis of less serious offense cases.

As in previous chapters, we present results from sentence length models uncorrected for selection bias stemming from the incarceration decision. Among the serious violent offenses in particular, only 12 percent of cases did not result in incarceration, and thus the degree of sample truncation is relatively slight. In such a case, selection bias due to the incarceration decision is unlikely to be a serious problem, and the Heckman correction may actually make estimates worse, especially since the predictors of incarceration and length are correlated (Stolzenberg and Relles 1997). However, we duplicated all of the sentence length analyses using the Heckman correction (estimated in Stata 9, with robust standard errors clustered by county) for the likelihood of incarceration, and the results do not differ meaningfully from those we present (for example, among the serious violent offenses, the jury trial effect on logged length in the uncorrected model is .45, and .48 in the corrected model, both significant at p < .0001). We also replicated the findings for the less serious offenses with and without a two-step Heckman correction for selection bias stemming from the incarceration decision, and also with a tobit analysis combining incarceration and nonincarceration sentences. Even though there is greater potential for selection bias because more of the less serious cases receive nonincarceration sentences, neither procedure substantively affects the trial penalty findings we report here, at least for the individual-level effects.

Supplemental Material for Table 7.7

The table below shows cross-tabulations of modes of conviction by offenders' minimum sentences relative to the guideline standard-range minimums, for both incarceration disposition and sentence length.

As mentioned in the chapter, we replicated the analysis in Table 7.7 separately for serious violent offenses and less serious offenses. *Serious violent*

Recommended vs. Actual Sentences by Modes of Conviction, All Offenses (minus missing cases)

	Incarceration Disposition				Sentence Length (nonincarceration cases not included)			
	Below Guideline Minimum	Equal to Guideline Minimum	Above Guideline Minimum	Total	Minimum Below Guideline Minimum	Minimum Equal to Guideline Minimum	Minimum Above Guideline Minimum	Total
Nonnegotiated pleas	2,433 (11%)	16,093 (72%)	3,715 (17%)	22,241	2,372 (22%)	1,398 (13%)	7,184 (66%)	10,954
Negotiated pleas	7,961 (10%)	56,659 (71%)	15,427 (19%)	80,047	6,349 (17%)	4,814 (13%)	26,167 (70%)	37,330
Bench trials	313 (7%)	3,496 (82%)	451 (11%)	4,260	514 (19%)	397 (14%)	1,837 (67%)	2,748
Jury trials	78 (4%)	1,600 (79%)	360 (18%)	2,038	116 (7%)	167 (10%)	1,417 (83%)	1,700
Total	10,785	77,848	19,953	108,586	9,351	6,776	36,605	52,732

offenses: For the odds of receiving nonincarceration when guidelines called for incarceration: bench trial, .48, jury trial, .30; for the odds of receiving incarceration when the guidelines did not call for incarceration: bench trial, .39, jury trial, 3.56. For the odds of receiving a minimum sentence below the standard-range minimum: bench trial, .52, jury trial, .24; for the odds of receiving a minimum sentence above the standard-range minimum: bench trial, 1.19 (not significant), jury trial, 2.24. *Less serious offenses:* For the odds of receiving nonincarceration when guidelines called for incarceration: bench trial, .41, jury trial, .20; for the odds of receiving incarceration when the guidelines did not call for incarceration: bench trial, .66, jury trial, 1.80. For the odds of receiving a minimum sentence below the standard-range minimum: bench trial, .70, jury trial, .26; for the odds of receiving a minimum sentence above the standard-range minimum: bench trial, 1.80, jury trial, 5.20.

Chapter 8: Guidelines and Mandatory Minimums

We coded our dependent variable, mandatory minimum application as 0 if the mandatory was not applied, and 1 if the mandatory was applied. The legally relevant control variables that we include in the analyses are the severity of the current offense, the mandatory-eligible offense type (type of drug offense, or whether the offense was a second- or third-strike violation), and the prior criminality of the offender. Offense severity and prior record are measured the same way as in prior analyses Offense types in our sample include delivery of and possession with intent to deliver marijuana, cocaine, heroin, and other drugs, as well as second- and third-strike violations. We analyze all cases together, and then split the sample into separate subsamples comprising drug-trafficking offenses and third-strike offenses in order to investigate whether distinctive patterns emerge for different types of mandatory-eligible offense groupings.

The amount of drugs involved in drug-trafficking offenses is also a potentially important influence on whether an offender receives a mandatory minimum. Recall from Chapters 2 and 3 that distinctions between drug amounts are captured by and measured in the OGS and presumptive guideline sentence recommendation. We therefore do not include drug amount as a separate variable, since it would be highly collinear with these two other measures. We measure mode of conviction with a set of dummy variables—negotiated guilty plea, nonnegotiated plea, and "other" (i.e., no contest pleas)—with trials serving as the reference category.

We tested two alternative measures of the distance by which the mandatory deviates from the guideline minimum. We subtracted the presumptive guideline minimum from the mandatory sentence for each given offense, and created the following variables: (1) a measure of the size of the difference (in months) for cases when the mandatory exceeded the guideline minimum, and

(2) a measure of the size of the difference when the mandatory was equal to or below the guideline minimum. These variables allow us to capture the length by which the mandatory is either greater than or less than the presumptive guideline minimum, respectively.

As mentioned in Chapter 8, we investigated the effects on mandatory application of the difference in sentence length between the mandatory minimum and the guideline minimum. In preliminary analyses, we first differentiated mandatory distance below versus above the guidelines, because these two factors likely have qualitatively different meaning and different consequences of applying the mandatory for prosecutors. To us, it made little sense to simply construct one continuous variable of "distance of the mandatory from the guideline" (either above or below), because this would have confounded these two very different mandatory-guideline relationships. The variable measuring distance of the mandatory below the guideline recommendation never achieved significance in any of our models (and the situation of the guideline exceeding the mandatory minimum is rare anyway). However, the variable measuring distance above the guideline recommendation is significant in several models, so this is the variable we present in our findings.

As in Chapters 4 and 5, we created dummy variables for our racial/ethnic and gender distinctions, and age was treated as a continuous variable (an age-squared variable was tested and found nonsignificant among this mandatory-eligible subsample of offenders, and therefore not included in these analyses). As in Chapter 5, we later included several dummy variables denoting membership in different age, race/ethnicity, and gender groupings (e.g., young black males, young Hispanic males). For this purpose we divided age as follows: young offenders twenty-five and under versus older offenders twenty-six and over. Young white males served as the reference category for this portion of the analysis. These race/ethnicity, gender, and age categories were added to the models (see Table 8.3) together as a block, in place of the black, Hispanic, and female dummy variables and the continuous age variable (as done by Steffensmeier, Ulmer, and Kramer 1998; Spohn and Holleran 2000; Kramer and Ulmer 2002; and others).

We included county percent black as a direct effect and then in cross-level interaction with defendant race.[6] We also included court size and percent distribution of offense types brought before the court (defined as drug, property, violent, and other offenses from the full PCS dataset for the years included in the analysis) as control variables. Regarding caseload composition, prior research has found that the proportion of violent crime that makes up a court's caseload can influence sentencing practices (Ulmer and Johnson 2004; Johnson 2006, 2005). We therefore controlled for the percentage of court caseloads made up of violent crime. We also explored several other county-level control variables (e.g., violent crime rates, percent drug caseload, percent Republican), but these were highly correlated with court size, violent crime caseload, and percent black.

In our hierarchical models, we tested for variance across counties and found that approximately 6 percent of the variance was accounted for at level two (e.g., between counties). An intraclass correlation coefficient is typically not reported with a dichotomous outcome, since the level-one variance is artificially constrained to be between 0 and 1. Alternate methods of computing the variance are possible using the assumption that the level-one mean equals 0 and the level-one variance equals pi-squared divided by 3. However, there is still much debate regarding meaningfulness of the resulting statistic (Bryk and Raudenbush 2002). Nevertheless, for informative purposes, we chose to simply estimate our unconditional model under this assumption above, which produces variance components that can be used to estimate the proportion of the total variance existing at level two (for an analogous use of this strategy, see Johnson 2006, pp. 279, 281). The variance components are as follows:

	Variance Component	Standard Deviation	df	X^2	P-value
Level 2	.00968	.09837	58	371.01	0.000
Level 1	.14085	.37530			

In addition, we explored the possibility that the slope of each predictor might vary across contexts by allowing the model to assess random effects. This is important because, if an effect does vary across contexts and the model does not account for this, the standard error will be underestimated, thereby affecting tests of significance for that variable. Thus some variables were estimated as random effects, while others were estimated as fixed effects. Effects with significant random variance components were as follows. Full model: negotiated plea, nonnegotiated plea, and race. Drug subsample: negotiated plea, nonnegotiated plea, and heroin. Three-strikes subsample: negotiated plea, third strike.

Also, as with our previous HLM analyses in other chapters, we estimated models of our dichotomous dependent variable using the natural log of the odds as the link function (Bernoulli distribution). We again grand mean centered our level-one predictors, because we were interested in between-county variation rather than in merely controlling for it while looking at individual-level effects.

Notes

1. Rodney Engen and Randy Gainey (2000) argued that models of sentencing under guidelines should include some measure of the guideline presumptive sentence as a control variable. This is unnecessary for the present analysis, since the presumptive sentence is incorporated into our dependent-variable downward departures.

2. These categories are coded by the court and they are assumed to categorize a plea as "nonnegotiated" whenever entered by the defendant with no explicit promises

made by the prosecution (analogous to what John Padgett [1985] called an "implicit" plea).

3. Other methods for dealing with selection bias exist (Winship and Mare 1992), though "none of them work well all the time" (Stolzenberg and Relles 1997, p. 503). Other methods, such as full information maximum likelihood estimation of both the selection equation and the selected equation simultaneously, are also possible, but not in HLM. Also, methods to deal with censoring, such as tobit regression, are not possible in HLM.

4. Restricted maximum likelihood (REML) is the default option for estimating two-level models in HLM 6. For a discussion of the use of restricted maximum likelihood versus full information maximum likelihood procedures, see Bryk and Raudenbush 2002.

5. We conducted deviance statistic tests on level-one coefficients to determine whether random or fixed effects were most appropriate for our data. In each case, the deviance tests were significant, indicating that random coefficients were more appropriate. We therefore specified random level-one coefficients for all variables. However, we also analyzed our models with only the legal (OGS, PRS, and offense type) and extralegal (age, race/ethnicity, gender, and mode of conviction) level-one variables of interest specified as random effects. These latter models increased the number of counties for which unique regression coefficients could be calculated, and they did not change the results in substantively meaningful ways, so we report our findings from these latter analyses.

6. Percent Hispanic did not vary sufficiently across counties to include this variable at the county level. Fifty-eight counties had below 2 percent Hispanic population, and only nine counties had greater than 2 percent Hispanic population.

References

Adams, K., and C. Cutshall. 1987. "Refusing to Prosecute Minor Offenses: The Relative Influence of Legal and Extralegal Factors." *Justice Quarterly* 4:595–609.

Akers, Ronald, and Christine Sellers. 2004. *Criminological Theories.* Los Angeles: Roxbury.

Albonetti, Celesta. 1986. "Criminality, Prosecutorial Screening, and Uncertainty: Toward a Theory of Discretionary Decision Making in Felony Case Processing." *Criminology* 23:623–644.

———. 1987. "Prosecutorial Discretion: The Effects of Uncertainty." *Law and Society Review* 21:291–313.

———. 1991. "An Integration of Theories to Explain Judicial Discretion." *Social Problems* 38:247–266.

———. 1997. "Sentencing Under the Federal Sentencing Guidelines: An Analysis of the Effects of Defendant Characteristics, Guilty Pleas, and Departures on Sentencing Outcomes for Drug Offenses." *Law and Society Review* 31:601–634.

———. 1998. "The Role of Gender and Departures in the Sentencing of Defendants Convicted of a White Collar Offense Under the Federal Sentencing Guidelines." *Sociology of Crime, Law, and Deviance* 1:3–48.

———. 2002. "The Effects of the 'Safety Valve' Amendment on Length of Imprisonment for Cocaine Trafficking/Manufacturing Offenders: Mitigating the Effects of Mandatory Minimum Penalties and Offender's Ethnicity." *Iowa Law Review* 87:401–433.

Albonetti, Celesta, and John Hepburn. 1996. "Prosecutorial Discretion to Defer Criminalization: The Effects of Defendant's Ascribed and Achieved Status Characteristics." *Journal of Quantitative Criminology* 12(1):63–81.

Allen, Francis A. 1964. *The Borderland of Criminal Justice.* Chicago: University of Chicago Press.

Alozie, N. O., and C. W. Johnston. 2000. "Probing the Limits of Female Advantage in Criminal Processing: Pretrial Diversion of Drug Offenders in an Urban County." *Justice System Journal* 21(3):239–259.

American Friends Service Committee. 1971. *Struggle for Justice: A Report on Crime and Punishment in America.* New York: Hill and Wang.

Anglin, M. Douglas, and Yih-Ing Hser. 1990. "Treatment of Drug Abuse." In *Drugs and Crime,* edited by Michael Tonry and James Q. Wilson. Chicago: University of Chicago Press.

251

Auerhahn, Kathleen. 2007. "Just Another Crime: Examining Disparity in Homicide Sentencing." *Sociological Quarterly* 48:277–314.

Austin, Roy, and Kimberly Kempf. 1986. "Older and More Recent Evidence of Racial Discrimination in Sentencing." *Journal of Quantitative Criminology* 2(1):29–48.

Bailey, Walter C. 1966. "Correctional Outcome: An Evaluation of 100 Reports." *Journal of Criminal Law, Criminology, and Police Science.* 57:153–171.

Barkan, Steven, and Steven Cohn. 2005. "Why Whites Favor Spending More Money to Fight Crime: The Role of Racial Prejudice." *Social Problems* 52(2):300–314.

Beckett, Katherine, and Theodore Sasson. 2000. *The Politics of Injustice: Crime and Punishment in America.* Thousand Oaks, CA: Pine Forge.

Beim, Aaron, and Gary Alan Fine. 2007. "The Cultural Frameworks of Prejudice: Reputational Images and the Postwar Disjuncture of Jews and Communism." *Sociological Quarterly* 48:373–398.

Bennett, William J., John DiIulio, and John Walters. 1996. *Body Count.* New York: Simon and Schuster.

Bergstrom, Mark H., and Joseph S. Mistick. 2003. *The Pennsylvania Experience: Public Release of Judge-Specific Sentencing Data.* University Park: Pennsylvania Commission on Sentencing.

Berk, Richard. 1983. "An Introduction to Sample Selection Bias in Sociological Data." *American Sociological Review* 48:386–398.

Bernard, Thomas, and Robin Shepard Engel. 2001. "Conceptualizing Criminal Justice Theory." *Justice Quarterly* 18:1–30.

Bjerk, David. 2005. "Making the Crime Fit the Penalty: The Role of Prosecutorial Discretion Under Mandatory Minimum Sentencing." *Journal of Law and Economics* 48:591–625.

Black, Donald. 1976. *The Behavior of Law.* New York: Academic Press.

Blumer, Herbert. 1955. "Reflections on Theory of Race Relations." In *Race Relations in World Perspective,* edited by A. W. Lind. Honolulu: University of Hawaii Press.

———. 1990. *Industrialization as an Agent of Social Change.* New York: Aldine de Gruyter.

Bobo, Lawrence, and Vincent Hutchings. 1996. "Perceptions of Racial Group Competition: Extending Blumer's Theory of Group Position to a Multiracial Social Context." *American Sociological Review* 61:951–972.

Bonilla-Silva, Eduardo. 1997. "Rethinking Racism: Toward a Structural Interpretation." *American Sociological Review* 62(3):465–480.

Bontrager, Stephanie, William Bales, and Ted Chiricos. 2005. "Race, Ethnicity, Threat, and the Labeling of Convicted Felons." *Criminology* 43(3):589–622.

Brereton, David, and Jonathan Casper. 1982. "Does It Pay to Plead Guilty? Differential Sentencing and the Functioning of Criminal Courts." *Law and Society Review* 16:45–70.

Bridges, George S., and Robert Crutchfield. 1988. "Law, Social Standing, and Racial Disparities in Imprisonment." *Social Forces* 66:699–724.

Bridges, George S., and Sara Steen. 1998. "Racial Disparities in Official Assessments of Juvenile Offenders." *American Sociological Review* 63:554–571.

Britt, Chester. 2000. "Social Context and Racial Disparities in Punishment Decisions." *Justice Quarterly* 17:707–732.

Bryk, Anthony, and Stephen Raudenbush. 1992. *Hierarchical Linear Models: Applications and Data Analysis Methods.* Newbury Park, CA: Sage.

Bryk, Anthony, Stephen Raudenbush, Yuk Fai Cheong, and Richard Congdon. 2004. *HLM6: Hierarchical Linear and Nonlinear Modeling.* Chicago: Scientific Software International.

Bryk, Anthony, Stephen Raudenbush, and Richard Congdon. 1996. *HLM: Hierarchical Linear and Nonlinear Modeling with the HLM/2L and HLM/3L Programs.* Chicago: Scientific Software International.

Bureau of Justice Assistance. 1996. *National Assessment of Structured Sentencing.* Washington, DC: US Department of Justice.

Bushway, Shawn, Brian Johnson, and Lee Ann Slocum. 2007. "Is the Magic Still There? The Relevance of the Heckman Two-Step Correction for Selection Bias in Criminology." *Journal of Quantitative Criminology* 23:151–178.

Bushway, Shawn, and Anne Morrison Piehl. 2001. "Judging Judicial Discretion: Legal Factors and Racial Discrimination in Sentencing." *Law and Society Review* 35:733–764.

Bynum, T. S. 1982. "Prosecutorial Discretion and the Implementation of a Legislative Mandate." In *Implementing Criminal Justice Policies,* edited by M. Morash. Beverly Hills, CA: Sage.

Carr, Patrick, Laura Napolitano, and Jessica Keating. 2007. "We Never Call the Cops and Here Is Why: A Qualitative Examination of Legal Cynicism in Three Philadelphia Neighborhoods." *Criminology* 45:445–480.

Church, Thomas. 1979. "In Defense of Bargain Justice." *Law and Society Review* 13:509–525.

Cirillo, Vincent. 1986. "Windows of Discretion in the Pennsylvania Sentencing Guidelines." *Villanova Law Review* 31:1309–1349.

Cole, George F., and Christopher Smith. 2005. *Criminal Justice in America.* New York: Thomson-Wadsworth.

Crawford, Charles. 2000. "Gender, Race, and Habitual Offender Sentencing in Florida." *Criminology* 38(1):263–280.

Crawford, Charles, Ted Chiricos, and Gary Kleck. 1998. "Race, Racial Threat, and Sentencing of Habitual Offenders." *Criminology* 36(3):481–513.

Curry, Theodore R., Gang Lee, and S. Fernando Rodriguez. 2004. "Does Victim Gender Increase Sentence Severity? Further Explanations of Gender Dynamics and Sentencing Outcomes." *Crime and Delinquency* 50(3):319–343.

Del Sole, Joseph A. 1993. "Appellate Review in a Sentencing Guideline Jurisdiction: The Pennsylvania Experience." *Duquesne Law Review* 31:479–504.

Demuth, Stephen, and Darrell Steffensmeier. 2004. "The Impact of Gender and Race-Ethnicity in the Pretrial Release Process." *Social Problems* 51(2):222–242.

Dershowitz, Allan. 1976. *Fair and Certain Punishment.* New York: McGraw-Hill.

Devine, Patricia G. 2001. "Implicit Prejudice and Stereotyping: How Automatic Are They?" *Journal of Personality and Social Psychology* 81:757–759.

Dixon, Jo. 1995. "The Organizational Context of Criminal Sentencing." *American Journal of Sociology* 100:1157–1198.

Dowd, Don W. 1984. "The Pit and the Pendulum: Correctional Law Reform from the Sixties into the Eighties." *Villanova Law Review* 29(1):1–20.

Eisenberg, Ronald. 1994. "Sentencing Guidelines—1994 Amendments." Memo to Gary Tennis, Chief, Legislative Unit Philadelphia District Attorney's Office.

Eisenstein, James, Roy Flemming, and Peter Nardulli. 1988. *The Contours of Justice: Communities and Their Courts.* Boston: Little, Brown.

Eisenstein, James, and Herbert Jacob. 1977. *Felony Justice: An Organizational Analysis of Criminal Courts.* Boston: Little, Brown.

Engen, Rodney, and Randy Gainey. 2000. "Modeling the Effects of Legally-Relevant and Extra-Legal Factors Under Sentencing Guidelines: The Rules Have Changed." *Criminology* 38:1207–1230.

Engen, Rodney, Randy Gainey, Robert Crutchfield, and Joseph Weis. 2003. "Discretion and Disparity Under Sentencing Guidelines: The Role of Departures and Structured Sentencing Alternatives." *Criminology* 41:99–130.

Engen, Rodney, and Sara Steen. 2000. "The Power to Punish: Discretion and Sentencing Reform in the War on Drugs." *American Journal of Sociology* 105:1357–1395.

Estes, Carroll, and Beverly Edmonds. 1981. "Symbolic Interaction and Social Policy Analysis." *Symbolic Interaction* 4:75–86.

Everett, R. S., and R. A. Wojtkiewicz. 2002. "Difference, Disparity, and Race, Ethnic Bias in Federal Sentencing." *Journal of Quantitative Criminology* 18:189–211.

Ewing, Sally. 1987. "Formal Justice and the Spirit of Capitalism: Max Weber's Sociology of Law." *Law and Society Review* 21:487–512.

Farr, Kathryn A. 1984. "Maintaining Balance Through an Institutionalized Plea Negotiation Process." *Criminology* 22:291–319.

Farrell, Jill. 2003. "Mandatory Minimum Firearm Penalties: A Source of Sentencing Disparity." *Justice Research and Policy* 5(1):95–115.

Fearn, Noelle. 2005. "A Multilevel Analysis of Community Effects on Criminal Sentencing." *Justice Quarterly* 22:452–487.

Feeley, Malcolm. 1979. "Perspectives on Plea Bargaining." *Law and Society Review* 13:199–209.

Ferdinand, Theodore. 1992. *Boston's Lower Criminal Courts, 1814–1850.* Newark: University of Delaware Press.

Fine, Gary Alan. 1984. "Negotiated Orders and Organizational Cultures." *Annual Review of Sociology* 10:239–262.

Fisher, George. 2003. *Plea Bargaining's Triumph.* Stanford: Stanford University Press.

Flemming, Roy B., Peter F. Nardulli, and James Eisenstein. 1992. *The Craft of Justice: Politics and Work in Criminal Court Communities.* Philadelphia: University of Pennsylvania Press.

Frankel, Marvin. 1972. *Criminal Sentences: Law Without Order.* New York: Hill and Wang.

Frase, Richard S. 1993. "Implementing Commission-Based Sentencing Guidelines: The Lessons of the First Ten Years in Minnesota." *Cornell Journal of Law and Public Policy* 2:2279–2337.

Free, Marvin. 2002. "Race and Presentencing Decisions in the United States: A Summary and Critique of the Research." *Criminal Justice Review* 27:203–232.

Frohmann, Lisa. 1991. "Discrediting Victims' Allegations of Sexual Assault: Prosecutorial Accounts of Case Rejections." *Social Problems* 38:213–226.

Garfinkel, Harold. 1956. "Conditions of Successful Status Degradation Ceremonies." *American Journal of Sociology* 61:420–424.

Garland, David. 2001. *Culture of Control: Crime and Social Order in Contemporary Society.* Chicago: University of Chicago Press.

Giordano, Peggy, Stephen Cernkovich, and Jennifer L. Rudolph. 2002. "Gender, Crime, and Desistence: Toward a Theory of Cognitive Transformation." *American Journal of Sociology* 107:990–1064.

Goffman, Erving. 1963. *Stigma: Notes on the Management of Spoiled Identity.* Englewood Cliffs, NJ: Prentice Hall.

Griffin, Timothy, and John Wooldredge. 2006. "Sex-Based Disparities in Felony Dispositions Before and After Sentencing Reform in Ohio." *Criminology* 44:893–924.

Griset, Pamela L. 1994. "Determinate Sentencing and the High Cost of Overblown Rhetoric: The New York Experience." *Crime and Delinquency* 40:532–548.

———. 1995. "Determinate Sentencing and Agenda Building: A Case Study of the Failure of a Reform." *Journal of Criminal Justice* 23:349–362.

Guo, G., and H. Zhao. 2000. "Multilevel Modeling for Binary Data." *Annual Review of Sociology* 26:441–462.

Hagan, John. 1975. The Social and Legal Construction of Criminal Justice: A Study of the Presentence Process." *Social Problems* 22:620–637.

Hagan, John, and Kristen Bumiller. 1983. "Making Sense of Sentencing: Race and Sentencing Outcomes." In *Research on Sentencing: The Search for Reform,* edited by A. Blumstein, J. Cohen, S. Martin, and M. Tonry. Washington, DC: National Academy Press.

Hagedorn, John. 1994. "Homeboys, Dope Fiends, Legits, and New Jacks." *Criminology* 32(2):197–220.

Hall, Peter M. 1997. "Meta-Power, Social Organization, and the Shaping of Social Action." *Symbolic Interaction* 20(4):397–418.

Hall, Peter, and Patrick McGinty. 1997. "Policy as the Transformation of Intentions: Producing Program From Statute." *Sociological Quarterly* 38(3):439–467.

Hanushek, Eric A., and John Jackson. 1977. *Statistical Methods for Social Scientists.* New York: Academic Press.

Harris, David A. 2007. "The Importance of Research on Race and Policing: Making Race Salient to Individuals and Institutions Within Criminal Justice." *Criminology and Public Policy* 6:5–24.

Hartley, Richard, Sean Maddan, and Cassia Spohn. 2007. "Prosecutorial Discretion: An Examination of Substantial Assistance Departures in Crack Cocaine Cases." *Justice Quarterly* 24:382–407.

Hobbs, Jody M. 1996. "Structuring Sentencing Discretion in Pennsylvania: Are Guidelines Still a Viable Option in Light of *Commonwealth v. Devers?" Temple Law Review* 69:936–974.

Hochschild, Arlie Russell. 1979. "Emotion Work, Feeling Rules, and Social Structure." *American Journal of Sociology* 85:551–575.

———. 1983. *The Managed Heart: The Commercialization of Human Feeling.* Berkeley: University of California Press.

Hofer, Paul. 2000. "Federal Sentencing for Violent and Drug Trafficking Crimes Involving Firearms: Recent Changes and Prospects for Improvement." *American Criminal Law Review* 37(4):41–73.

Holleran, David, and Cassia Spohn. 2004. "On the Use of the Total Incarceration Variable in Sentencing Research." *Criminology* 42(1):211–240.

Holmes, Malcolm, Howard Daudistel, and William Taggart. 1992. "Plea Bargaining Policy and State District Court Caseloads: An Interrupted Time Series Analysis." *Law and Society Review* 26:139–159.

Huebner, Beth, and Timothy Bynum. 2006. "An Analysis of Parole Decision Making Using a Sample of Sex Offenders: A Focal Concerns Perspective." *Criminology* 44(4):961–992.

Jacobs, David, Jason Carmichael, and Stephanie Kent. 2005. "Vigilantism, Current Racial Threat, and Death Sentences." *American Sociological Review* 70(4):656–677.

Jacoby, Joan. 1979. "The Charging Policies of Prosecutors." In *The Prosecutor,* edited by W. McDonald. Thousand Oaks, CA: Sage.

Johnson, Brian. 2003. "Racial and Ethnic Disparities in Sentencing Departures Across Modes of Conviction." *Criminology* 41:449–488.

———. 2005. "Contextual Disparities in Guideline Departures: Courtroom Social Contexts, Guideline Compliance, and Extralegal Disparities in Criminal Sentencing." *Criminology* 43(3):761–798.

———. 2006. "The Multilevel Context of Judicial Sentencing: Integrating Judge and County Level Influences." *Criminology* 44(2):259–298.

Kalberg, Stephen. 1980. "Max Weber's Types of Rationality: Cornerstones for the Analysis of Rationalization Processes in History." *American Journal of Sociology* 85:1145–1179.

Kalven, Harry, and Hans Zeisel. 1966. *The American Jury.* Boston: Little, Brown.

Kautt, Paula. 2002. "Location, Location, Location: Interdistrict and Intercircuit Variation in Sentencing Outcomes for Federal Drug-Trafficking Offenses." *Justice Quarterly* 19:633–671.

Kautt, Paula, and Miriam Delone. 2006. "Sentencing Outcomes Under Competing but Coexisting Sentencing Interventions: Untying the Gordian Knot." *Criminal Justice Review* 31(2):105–131.

Kautt, Paula, and Cassia Spohn. 2002. "Cracking Down on Black Drug Offenders? Testing for Interactions Among Offenders' Race, Drug Type, and Sentencing Strategy in Federal Drug Sentences." *Justice Quarterly* 19(1):1–35.

King, Nancy, David Soule, Sara Steen, and Robert Weidner. 2005. "When Process Affects Punishment: Differences in Sentences After Guilty Plea, Bench Trial, and Jury Trial in Five Guideline States." *Columbia Law Review* 105:960–1009.

Kingsnorth, Rodney F., and Randall C. MacIntosh. 2004. "Domestic Violence: Predictors of Victim Support for Official Action." *Justice Quarterly* 21(2):301–328.

Kingsnorth, Rodney, Randall MacIntosh, and Sandra Sutherland. 2002. "Criminal Charge or Probation Violation? Prosecutorial Discretion and Implications for Research in Criminal Court Processing." *Criminology* 40(3):553–579.

Klepper, Steven, Daniel Nagin, and Luke-John Tierney. 1983. "Discrimination in the Criminal Justice System: A Critical Appraisal of the Literature." In *Research on Sentencing: The Search for Reform,* edited by Alfred Blumstein, Jacqueline Cohen, Susan E. Martin, and Michael H. Tonry. Washington, DC: National Academy Press.

Knapp, Kay. 1987. "Implementation of the Minnesota Guidelines: Can the Innovative Spirit be Preserved?" In *The Sentencing Commission and its Guidelines,* edited by Andrew von Hirsch, Kay Knapp, and Michael Tonry. Boston: Northeastern University Press.

Koons-Witt, Barbara. 2002. "The Effect of Gender on the Decision to Incarcerate Before and After the Introduction of Sentencing Guidelines." *Criminology* 40:297–328.

Kramer, John H., and Robin Lubitz. 1985. "Pennsylvania's Sentencing Reform: The Impact of Commission-Established Guidelines." *Crime and Delinquency* 31(4):481–500.

Kramer, John H., Robin Lubitz, and Cynthia Kempinen. 1989. "Sentencing Guidelines: A Quantitative Comparison of Sentencing Policy in Minnesota, Pennsylvania, and Washington." *Justice Quarterly* 6(4):565–587.

Kramer, John H., and Anthony Scirica. 1986. "Complex Policy Choices: The Pennsylvania Commission on Sentencing." *Federal Probation* 50:15–23.

Kramer, John H., and Darrell Steffensmeier. 1993. "Race and Imprisonment Decisions." *Sociological Quarterly* 34:357–376.

Kramer, John H., and Jeffery Ulmer. 1996. "Sentencing Disparity and Departures from Guidelines." *Justice Quarterly* 13:401–425.

———. 2002. "Downward Departures for Serious Violent Offenders: Local Court 'Corrections' to Pennsylvania's Sentencing Guidelines." *Criminology* 40: 897–931.

Kress, Jack M. 1980. *Prescription for Justice: The Theory and Practice of Sentencing Guidelines.* Cambridge, MA: Ballinger Publishing.

Kurlychek, Megan, and Brian Johnson. 2004. "The Juvenile Penalty: A Comparison of Juvenile and Young Adult Sentencing Outcomes in Criminal Court." *Criminology* 42:485–515.

LaFree, Gary. 1985. "Adversarial and Nonadversarial Justice: A Comparison of Guilty Pleas and Trials." *Criminology* 23:289–312.

Levin, Martin. 1977. *Urban Politics and the Criminal Courts.* Chicago: University of Chicago Press.

Liska, Allen E. 1990. "The Significance of Aggregate Dependent Variables and Contextual Independent Variables for Linking Macro and Micro Theories." *Social Psychological Quarterly* 53:292–301.

Liska, Allen, J. J. Lawrence, and Michael Benson. 1981. "Perspectives on the Legal Order: The Capacity for Social Control." *American Journal of Sociology* 87:412–426.

Loftin, Colin, Milton Heumann, and David McDowall. 1983. "Mandatory Sentencing and Firearms Violence: Evaluating an Alternative to Gun Control." *Law and Society Review* 17:287–318.

Loseke, Donileen. 1993. "Constructing Conditions, People, Morality, and Emotion: Expanding the Agenda of Constructionism." In *Constructionist Controversies: Issues in Social Problems Theory,* edited by Gale Miller and James Holstein. New York: Aldine de Gruyter.

Lubitz, Robin, and Cynthia Kempinen. 1987. "The Impact of Pennsylvania's Sentencing Guidelines: An Analysis of System Adjustments to Sentencing Reform." Report to the Pennsylvania Commission on Sentencing and the Pennsylvania Commission on Crime and Delinquency. Harrisburg: Commonwealth of Pennsylvania.

Maines, David. 2001. *The Faultline of Consciousness: A View of Interactionism in Sociology.* New York: Aldine de Gruyter.

March, James, and Herbert Simon. 1958. *Organizations.* New York: Wiley.

Marsh, Robert M. 2000. "Weber's Misunderstanding of Chinese Law." *American Journal of Sociology* 106:281–302.

Martin, Susan. 1983. "The Politics of Sentencing Reform: Sentencing Guidelines in Pennsylvania and Minnesota. In *Research on Sentencing: The Search for Reform,* edited by A. Blumstein, J. Cohen, S. Martin, and M. Tonry. Washington, DC: National Academy Press.

Martinson, Robert. 1974. "What Works? Questions and Answers About Prison Reform." *The Public Interest* 35:22–54.

Mather, Lynn. 1973. "Some Determinants of the Method of Case Disposition: Decision-Making by Public Defenders in Los Angeles." *Law and Society Review* 7:187–216.

———. 1979. "Comments on the History of Plea Bargaining." *Law and Society Review* 13:281–285.

McClea, Sam. 1976. *Staff Report on the Use and Impact of Mandatory Sentencing in Pennsylvania.* Harrisburg, PA: House Judiciary Committee.

Mears, Daniel P. 1998. "The Sociology of Sentencing: Reconceptualizing Decision-making Processes and Outcomes." *Law and Society Review* 32:667–724.

Mears, Daniel P., and Samuel H. Field. 2000. "Theorizing Sanctioning in a Criminalized Juvenile Court." *Criminology* 38:983–1020.

Meeker, James, and Henry Pontell. 1985. "Court Caseloads, Plea Bargains, and Criminal Sanctions: The Effects of Section 17 P.C. in California." *Criminology* 23:119–143.

Miethe, Terence. 1987. "Charging and Plea Bargaining Practices Under Determinate Sentencing: An Investigation of the Hydraulic Displacement of Discretion." *Journal of Criminal Law and Criminology* 78(1):155–176.

Miethe, Terence, and Charles Moore. 1985. "Socioeconomic Disparities Under Determinate Sentencing Systems: A Comparison of Preguideline and Postguideline Practices in Minnesota." *Criminology* 23:337–363.

———. 1988. "Officials' Reactions to Sentencing Guidelines." *Journal of Research in Crime and Delinquency* 25:170–187.

Miller, JoAnn Langley, and John Sloan. 1994. "A Study of Criminal Justice Discretion." *Journal of Criminal Justice* 22(2):107–123.

Moore, Charles, and Terence Miethe. 1986. "Regulated and Non-Regulated Sentencing Practices Under Minnesota Felony Sentencing Guidelines." *Law and Society Review* 20:253–265.

Mustard, David. 2001. "Racial, Ethnic, and Gender Disparities in Sentencing: Evidence from the US Federal Courts." *Journal of Law and Economics* 44:285–314.

Myers, Martha, and Susette Talarico. 1987. *The Social Contexts of Criminal Sentencing.* New York: Springer-Verlag.

Nagel, Ilene H., and Stephen J. Schulhofer. 1992. "A Tale of Three Cities: An Empirical Study of Charging and Bargaining Practices Under the Federal Sentencing Guidelines." *Southern California Law Review* 66:501–566.

Nardulli, Peter F., James Eisenstein, and Roy B. Flemming. 1988. *The Tenor of Justice: Criminal Courts and the Guilty Plea Process.* Urbana: University of Illinois Press.

Nelson, James F. 1992. "Hidden Disparities in Case Processing: New York State, 1985–1986." *Journal of Criminal Justice* 20:181–200.

O'Donnell, Pierce, Michael Churgin, and Dennis Curtis. 1977. *Toward a Just and Effective Sentencing System: Agenda for Legislative Reform.* New York: Praeger.

Ouchi, William G., and Alan L. Wilkins. 1985. "Organizational Culture." *Annual Review of Sociology* 11:457–483.

Packer, Herbert L. 1968. *The Limits of the Criminal Sanction.* Stanford: Stanford University Press.

Padgett, John F. 1985. "The Emergent Organization of Plea Bargaining." *American Journal of Sociology* 90:753–800.

Parent, Dale F. 1988. *Structuring Criminal Sentences: The Evolution of Minnesota's Sentencing Guidelines.* Stoneham, MA: Butterworth Legal.

Paternoster, Raymond, Robert Brame, Paul Mazzerole, and Alex Piquero. 1998. "Using the Correct Statistical Test for the Equality of Regression Coefficients." *Criminology* 36:859–866.

Pennsylvania Commission on Sentencing. 1997. *Sentencing Guideline Implementation Manual,* 5th Edition. State College: Pennsylvania Commission on Sentencing.

Peterson, Ruth D., and John Hagan. 1984. "Changing Conceptions of Race: Towards an Account of Anomalous Findings of Sentencing Research." *American Sociological Review* 49:56–70.

Raudenbush, Stephen, Anthony Bryk, Yuk Fai Cheong, and Richard Congdon. 2004. *HLM 6: Hierarchical Linear and Non-Linear Modeling.* Lincolnwood, IL: Scientific Software International.

Reiman, Jeffrey. 1995. *The Rich Get Richer and the Poor Get Prison.* Boston: Allyn and Bacon.

Reitz, Kevin. 1997. "Sentencing Guideline Systems and Sentence Appeals: A Comparison of Federal and State Experiences." *Northwestern University Law Review* 91:1441–1506.

Revelant, Angelica L. 2005–2006. "Indeterminate Immunity: A Review of the Pennsylvania Sentencing Guidelines." *Penn State Law Review* 187.

Rhodes, William. 1979. "Plea Bargaining: Its Effect on Sentencing and Convictions in the District of Columbia." *Journal of Criminal Law and Criminology* 70:360–375.

Robinson, James, and Gerald Smith. 1971. "The Effectiveness of Correctional Programs." *Crime and Delinquency* 17:67–80.

Rose, Dina, and Todd Clear. 1998. "Incarceration, Social Capital, and Crime: Implications for Social Disorganization." *Criminology* 36(3):441–481.

Rosett, Arthur, and Donald Cressey. 1976. *Justice by Consent: Plea Bargaining in the American Courthouse.* Philadelphia: Lippincott.

Ruback, R. Barry. 1998. Warranted and Unwarranted Complexity in the Federal Sentencing Guidelines." *Law and Policy* 20:357–382.

Sampson, Robert J., and Janet L. Lauritsen. 1997. "Racial and Ethnic Disparities in Crime and Criminal Justice in the United States." In *Ethnicity, Crime, and Immigration: Comparative and Cross-National Perspectives,* vol. 21, edited by M. Tonry. Chicago: University of Chicago Press.

Savelsberg, Joachim. 1992. "Law That Does Not Fit Society: Sentencing Guidelines as a Neoclassical Reaction to the Dilemmas of Substantivized Law." *American Journal of Sociology* 97:1346–1381.

Schmidt, Janell, and Ellen Hochstedler Steury. 1989. "Prosecutorial Discretion in Filing Charges in Domestic Violence Cases." *Criminology* 27(3):487–509.

Sherman, Lawrence. 2003. "Reason for Emotion: Reinventing Justice with Theories, Innovations, and Research." *Criminology* 41:1–38.

Silver, Eric. 2000. "Actuarial Risk Assessment: Reflections on an Emerging Social Scientific Tool." *Critical Criminology* 9:123–143.

Singer, Richard. 1978. "In Favor of Presumptive Sentences Set by a Sentencing Commission." *Crime and Delinquency* 24:401–427.

Smith, Brent, and Kelly Damphousse. 1998. "Terrorism, Politics, and Punishment: A Test of Structural-Contextual Theory and the 'Liberation Hypothesis.'" *Criminology* 36:67–92.

Smith, Douglas A. 1986. "The Plea Bargaining Controversy." *Journal of Criminal Law and Criminology* 77:949–968.

Sommers, Samuel R., and Phoebe Ellsworth. 2000. "Race in the Courtroom: Perceptions of Guilt and Dispositional Attributions." *Personality and Social Psychology Bulletin* 26:1367–1379.

———. 2001. "White Juror Bias: An Investigation of Prejudice Against Black Defendants in the American Courtroom." *Psychology, Public Policy, and Law* 7:201–229.

Spears, J., and Cassia Spohn. 1997. "The Effect of Evidence Factors and Victim Characteristics on Prosecutors' Charging Decisions." *Justice Quarterly* 16:559–578.

Spohn, Cassia. 1990. "Decision Making in Sexual Assault Cases: Do Black and Female Judges Make a Difference?" *Women and Criminal Justice* 2:83–105.

———. 2000. "Thirty Years of Sentencing Reform: The Quest for a Racially Neutral Sentencing Process." *Criminal Justice: The National Institute of Justice Journal* 3:427–501.

———. 2002. *How Do Judges Decide? The Quest for Fairness and Justice in Punishment.* Thousand Oaks, CA: Sage.

Spohn, Cassia, Dawn Beicher, and Erika Davis-Frenzel. 2001. "Prosecutorial Justifications for Sexual Assault Case Rejection: Guarding the 'Gateway to Justice.'" *Social Problems* 48:206–235.

Spohn, Cassia, and Jerry Cederblom. 1991. "Race and Disparities in Sentencing: A Test of the Liberation Hypothesis." *Justice Quarterly* 8:305–327.

Spohn, Cassia, and Miriam DeLone. 2000. "When Does Race Matter? An Analysis of the Conditions Under Which Race Affects Sentence Severity." *Sociology of Crime, Law, and Deviance* 2:3–37.

Spohn, Cassia, John Gruhl, and Susan Welch. 1982. "The Effect of Race on Sentencing: A Reexamination of an Unsettled Question." *Law and Society Review* 16:71–88.

Spohn, Cassia, and David Holleran. 2000. "The Imprisonment Penalty Paid by Young Unemployed Black and Hispanic Male Offenders." *Criminology* 38:281–306.

———. 2001. "Prosecuting Sexual Assault: A Comparison of Charging Decisions in Sexual Assault Cases Involving Strangers, Acquaintances, and Intimate Partners." *Justice Quarterly* 18(3):651–688.

Stanko, Elizabeth A. 1981–1982. "The Impact of Victim Assessment on Prosecutors' Screening Decisions: The Case of the New Your County District Attorney's Office." *Law and Society Review* 16(2):225–239.

Steen, Sara, Rodney Engen, and Randy Gainey. 2005. "Images of Danger and Culpability: Racial Stereotyping, Case Processing, and Criminal Sentencing." *Criminology* 43:435–468.

Steffensmeier, Darrell. 1980. "Assessing the Impact of the Women's Movement on Sex-Based Differences in the Handling of Adult Criminal Defendants." *Crime and Delinquency* 26:344–357.

Steffensmeier, Darrell, and Emilie Allan. 2000. "Looking for Patterns: Gender, Age, and Crime." In *Criminology,* edited by J. Sheley. Belmont, CA: Wadsworth.

Steffensmeier, Darrell, and Stephen Demuth. 2000. "Ethnicity and Sentencing Outcomes in US Federal Courts: Who Is Punished More Harshly?" *American Sociological Review* 65:705–729.

———. 2001. "Ethnicity and Judges' Sentencing Decisions: Hispanic-Black-White Comparisons." *Criminology* 39:145–178.

Steffensmeier, Darrell, and Chris Hebert. 1999. "Women and Men Policymakers: Does the Judge's Gender Affect the Sentencing of Criminal Defendants?" *Social Forces* 77:1163–1196.

Steffensmeier, Darrell, John H. Kramer, and Cathy Streifel. 1993. "Gender and Imprisonment Decisions." *Criminology* 31:411–446.

Steffensmeier, Darrell, John H. Kramer, and Jeffery Ulmer. 1995. "Age Differences in Sentencing." *Justice Quarterly* 12:701–719.

Steffensmeier, Darrell, Jeffery T. Ulmer, and John Kramer. 1998. "The Interaction of Race, Gender, and Age in Criminal Sentencing: The Punishment Cost of Being Young, Black, and Male." *Criminology* 36:763–798.

Stith, Kate, and Jose A. Cabranes. 1998. *Fear of Judging: Sentencing Guidelines in the Federal Courts.* Chicago: University of Chicago Press.

Stolzenberg, Ross, and Daniel Relles. 1997. "Tools for Intuition About Sample Selection Bias and Its Correction." *American Sociological Review* 62:494–507.

Strauss, Anselm. 1987. *Qualitative Analysis for Social Scientists.* New York: Cambridge University Press.

Sudnow, David. 1965. "Normal Crimes: Sociological Features of the Penal Code." *Social Problems* 12(4):255–264.

Sutton, John. 2000. "Imprisonment and Social Classification in Five Common Law Democracies, 1955–1985." *American Journal of Sociology* 106:350–386.

Tamilia, Patrick R., and John J. Hare. 2000. *Keystone of Justice: The Pennsylvania Superior Court.* Harrisburg: Commonwealth of Pennsylvania.

Taylor, Marylee. 1998. "How White Attitudes Vary with the Racial Composition of Local Populations: Numbers Count." *American Sociological Review* 63:512–536.

Tonry, Michael. 1987. "Sentencing Guidelines and Their Effects." In *The Sentencing Commission and Its Guidelines,* edited by Andrew von Hirsch, Kay A. Knapp, and Michael Tonry. Boston: Northeastern University Press.

————. 1992. "Mandatory Penalties." In *Crime and Justice: A Review of Research,* vol. 16, edited by Michael Tonry. Chicago: University of Chicago Press.

————. 1996. *Sentencing Matters.* New York: Oxford University Press.

Tonry, Michael, and Richard Frase (eds.). 2001. *Sentencing and Sanctioning in Western Countries.* New York: Oxford University Press.

Twentieth Century Fund. 1976. *Fair and Certain Punishment.* New York: McGraw-Hill.

Tyler, Tom R., and Y. J. Huo. 2002. *Trust in the Law: Encouraging Public Cooperation with the Police and Courts.* New York: Russell-Sage.

Uhlman, Thomas, and N. Darlene Walker. 1979. "A Plea Is No Bargain: The Impact of Case Disposition on Sentence." *Social Science Quarterly* 60:218–234.

————. 1980. "'He Takes Some of My Time, I Take Some of His': An Analysis of Judicial Sentencing Patterns in Jury Cases." *Law and Society Review* 14:323–341.

Ulmer, Jeffery T. 1997. *Social Worlds of Sentencing: Court Communities Under Sentencing Guidelines.* Albany: State University of New York Press.

————. 2000. "The Rules Have Changed, So Proceed With Caution: A Comment on Engen and Gainey's Method for Modeling Sentencing Outcomes Under Guidelines." *Criminology* 38:1231–1244.

————. 2005. "The Localized Uses of Federal Sentencing Guidelines in Four US District Courts: Evidence of Processual Order." *Symbolic Interaction* 28:255–279.

Ulmer, Jeffery T., and Mindy Bradley. 2006. "Variation in Trial Penalties Among Serious Violent Offenders." *Criminology* 44(3):631–670.

Ulmer, Jeffery, and Brian D. Johnson. 2004. "Sentencing in Context: A Multilevel Analysis." *Criminology* 42(1):137–177.

Ulmer, Jeffery T., and John Kramer. 1996. "Court Communities Under Sentencing Guidelines: Dilemmas of Formal Rationality and Sentencing Disparity." *Criminology* 3:306–332.

————. 1998. "The Use and Transformation of Formal Decision-Making Criteria: Sentencing Guidelines, Organizational Contexts, and Case Processing Strategies." *Social Problems* 45:248–267.

Ulmer, Jeffery T., Megan Kurlychek, and John Kramer. 2007. "Prosecutorial Discretion and the Imposition of Mandatory Minimums." *Journal of Research in Crime and Delinquency* 44(4):427–458.

Ulmer, Jeffery, and Christine van Asten. 2004. "Restrictive Intermediate Punishments and Recidivism in Pennsylvania." *Federal Sentencing Reporter* 16(3):182–187.

US Sentencing Commission. 1991. *The Federal Sentencing Guidelines: A Report on the Operation of the Guidelines System and Short-Term Impacts on Disparity in Sentencing, Use of Incarceration, and Prosecutorial Discretion and Plea Bargaining.* Washington, DC: US Sentencing Commission.

————. 1998. *United States Sentencing Commission: Guidelines Manual.* Washington, DC.

————. 2001. *Office of Policy Analysis Variable Codebook.* Washington, DC.

Vogel, Mary Elizabeth. 1999. "The Social Origins of Plea Bargaining: Conflict and the Law in the Process of State Formation, 1830–1860." *Law and Society Review* 33:216–246.

von Hirsch, Andrew. 1976. *Doing Justice: The Choice of Punishments.* New York: Hill and Wang.

von Hirsch, Andrew, Kay A. Knapp, and Michael Tonry. 1987. *The Sentencing Commission and Its Guidelines.* Boston, MA: Northeastern University Press.

Walker, Samuel. 1993. *Taming the System: The Control of Discretion in Criminal Justice.* New York: Oxford University Press.

Washington Sentencing Guidelines Commission. 1999. *Washington Sentencing Guidelines Implementation Manual.* Olympia.

Weidner, Robert, Richard Frase, and Jennifer Schultz. 2005. "The Impact of Contextual Factors on the Decision to Imprison in Large Urban Jurisdictions: A Multilevel Analysis." *Crime and Delinquency* 51(3):400–424.

Wheeler, Stanton, David Weisburd, and Nancy Bode. 1982. "Sentencing the White Collar Offender: Rhetoric and Reality." *American Sociological Review* 47:641–659.

Wilkins, Leslie T., Jack M. Kress, Don M. Gottfredson, Joseph C. Calpin, and Arthur M. Gelman. 1978. *Sentencing Guidelines: Structuring Judicial Discretion.* Washington, DC: National Institute of Law Enforcement and Criminal Justice.

Wilson, James Q. 1983. *Thinking About Crime.* New York: Basic.

Winship, Christopher, and Robert Mare. 1992. "Models for Sample Selection Bias." *Annual Review of Sociology* 18:327–350.

Wooldredge, John. 1989. "An Aggregate Level Examination of the Caseload Pressure Hypothesis." *Journal of Quantitative Criminology* 5:259–270.

Wooldredge, John, and Amy Thistlethwaite. 2004. "Bilevel Disparities in Court Dispositions for Intimate Assault." *Criminology* 42(2):417–456.

Zatz, Marjorie. 1984. "Race, Ethnicity, and Determinate Sentencing: A New Dimension to an Old Controversy." *Criminology* 22:147–171.

———. 2000. "The Convergence of Race, Ethnicity, Gender, and Class on Court Decisionmaking: Looking Toward the 21st Century." *Criminal Justice: The National Institute of Justice Journal* 3:503–552.

Zatz, Marjorie, and John Hagan. 1985. "Crime, Time, and Punishment: An Exploration of Selection Bias in Sentencing Research." *Journal of Quantitative Criminology* 1:103–126.

Index

About the Book

SENTENCING GUIDELINES, ADOPTED by many states in recent decades, are intended to eliminate the impact of bias based on factors ranging from a criminal's ethnicity or gender to the county in which he or she was convicted. But have these guidelines achieved their goal of "fair punishment"? And how do the concerns of local courts shape sentencing under guidelines? In this comprehensive examination of the development, reform, and application of sentencing guidelines in one of the first states to employ them, John Kramer and Jeffery Ulmer offer a nuanced analysis of the complexities involved in administering justice.

John H. Kramer is professor of sociology and crime, law, and justice at Pennsylvania State University. Formerly, he was executive director of the Pennsylvania Commission on Sentencing, and he served as staff director of the US Sentencing Commission from 1996 to 1998. **Jeffery T. Ulmer** is associate professor of sociology and crime, law, and justice at Pennsylvania State University. He is author of *Social Worlds of Sentencing* and coauthor (with Darrell J. Steffensmeier) of *Confessions of a Dying Thief.*